The Law Lab Book

Case Studies for Legal Learning

First Edition

Jennifer N. Pahre
University of Illinois at Urbana-Champaign

cognella®
SAN DIEGO

Bassim Hamadeh, CEO and Publisher
Angela Schultz, Senior Field Acquisitions Editor
Michelle Piehl, Senior Project Editor
Jordan Krikorian, Editorial Assistant
Susana Christie, Senior Developmental Editor
Alia Bales, Production Editor
Emely Villavicencio, Senior Graphic Designer
Trey Soto, Licensing Specialist
Natalie Piccotti, Director of Marketing
Kassie Graves, Senior Vice President, Editorial
Jamie Giganti, Director of Academic Publishing

Cover image: Copyright © 2018 iStockphoto LP/BCFC.

Printed in the United States of America.

cognella® | ACADEMIC PUBLISHING
3970 Sorrento Valley Blvd., Ste. 500, San Diego, CA 92121

For Bob—

I am delighted to return the honor.

Brief Contents

Detailed Contents

Acknowledgments

MANY PEOPLE PLAYED A ROLE IN THE CREATION OF THIS BOOK.

I must start by thanking my husband, who read every word, and let me bend his ear during many dinners to discuss the framing of key chapters and the content of the Law Labs. Bob, your knowledge and insight upgraded everything about this book.

My sons, Jay and Eric, continue to support and inspire. Thank you for indulging in my ruminations about potential Law Labs, and for cheering me on when I felt soggy about the work.

My education was firmly supported by my late parents, James and Joan Noe. They taught me that studying history is important, and that the law is inherently interesting. Since before I married their son, Richard and Janice Pahre have been steadfast supporters of my professional and personal goals, and I have learned much through many years of conversations with Jeff and Pat Pahre.

I was fortunate in the course of my legal careeer to work with many fine attorneys. Their inspiring examples helped me better understand the profession's underlying ethos of service. Their number is too great to list here individually, but I must particularly thank Minnesota attorney John Anderson, Illinois attorney Nathaniel Schmitz, and my former law partner, Champaign Circuit Court Judge Sam Limentato. I greatly enjoyed working with you.

Without the kind encouragement of my friends and colleagues at the University of Illinois College of Law, this book would certainly not have been written. Vik Amar, Lesley Wexler, Eric Johnson, and Kelly Salefski supported the creation of my Law Lab class. Jennifer Robbennholt encouraged me to move from concept to book and offered guidance on how to achieve the transformation. In an impactful three-minute conversation, Verity Winship and Kenworthey Bilz suggested that I retain research assistants—without whose support my sanity would have fled many moons ago. Heidi Hurd offered me a helping hand at an important time, Margaret Wright offered many valuable comments, and Virginia Vermillion (with whom I practiced law decades ago) first suggested that I consider academia. I am grateful to all of you.

Of course, this book was written for students, and without their probing questions and determined desire to learn, it would not exist. In particular, I wish to thank Nicholas Hall for the "Law Lab" appellation, which perfectly captured the concept.

Cognella editors Michelle Piehl, Susana Christie, and Alia Bales have given me excellent guidance over the course of this project, and made the writing process much easier. I also gratefully acknowledge the four anonymous peer referees for many valuable insights and suggestions.

Finally, I must thank my research assistants, aka "The Team." Sana Rizvi, Cara Shanahan, and Joe Lehman, I sincerely appreciate your hard work and unflagging enthusiasm.

Even with all this help, I fear that errors lurk within. They are my sole responsibility.

Introduction

THERE ARE MANY JOBS IN THE LEGAL PROFESSION, JUST AS THERE ARE MANY AREAS OF LAW IN which legal professionals work. One attorney may practice transactional business law, creating new corporate enterprises and protecting the rights and economic vitality of existing businesses. Another attorney may choose to practice family law, focusing on adoptions, divorces, and estate planning. A third attorney may focus on criminal law, starting their career as a prosecutor. Perhaps the prosecutor will later become a judge, guiding cases through the trial process.

Although the same credentials are required for all these jobs, they are quite different. The transactional attorney will work diligently with corporate officers and managers to draft complex agreements at the conclusion of careful negotiations, paying attention to minute details that can matter greatly. The family law attorney will spend many hours meeting with clients, some of whom are in crisis, and will use the justice system to resolve personal situations that may be emotionally challenging for their clients. The prosecutor will spend long days reviewing reports about crimes, deciding which matters to prosecute and which to negotiate. She will present cases in court, hoping to persuade jurors to convict. But if that same prosecutor is elevated to the bench and becomes a judge, she must serve as a neutral arbiter of the rule of law, upholding due process and the other constitutional guarantees that promote just outcomes.

These are only a few examples of the many different jobs in the law. The field of law is so broad that law schools undertake to teach students about career options, along with legal ethics, practical skills, and the substance of the law.

American law schools spend three years teaching full-time future practitioners about legal ethics and the substance of the law. Among other subjects, law students take courses in constitutional law, torts, contracts, real property, criminal law, and civil and criminal procedure. Then, depending upon which areas of law interest them, students will take electives that deepen their knowledge in their chosen future practice areas. All this instruction, including skills classes, ethics courses, and experiential learning, trains future lawyers to assist their clients competently, meaningfully, and ethically.

Most undergraduates interested in the law would like to understand some of the doctrinal law that is delivered in law school. While a nuanced understanding of any legal subject cannot be achieved without years of study, students can perceive the basic contours of some areas of the law in less time. This book provides some of that knowledge.

In addition, most students who are interested in the law would like to know how it operates in different fields and venues. They would like to know what different legal professionals do, how they do it, and what is important for their work. A few students may find internships that can help them understand more about the law and jobs in the legal profession, but these can be difficult to secure. With some advanced work, however, we can begin to explore the different things lawyers and judges do, as well as different areas of law. This is the function of the Law Labs.

Role of the Law Labs

The Law Labs present fictional legal scenarios for you to resolve, working with others in a group setting. Each Law Lab is different: one week, your group will be lawmakers, tasked with drafting a particular set of rules, and another week you will work as governmental attorneys, completing a critical assignment. In some Law Labs you are state court judges, and in several Law Labs (particularly in the early weeks), you will serve as United States Supreme Court justices, applying key provisions of the Constitution to cases before the Court. The Law Labs present hypotheticals in different contexts so that you can better understand the law, and also begin to think about how legal professionals work with it.

Each Law Lab comes at the end of the chapter that gives a brief overview of the substance of a particular area of law. In fact, each Law Lab requires you to learn some of the doctrinal law that is relevant to that Law Lab. The early chapters also review some pertinent history to aid in understanding key developments of the law. These overviews provide enough depth so that the Law Lab can be meaningfully worked through.

In order to complete each Law Lab, you will first review the substance of the law in each chapter. You will then read and consider the chapter's Law Lab, focusing on the facts and legal rules that apply to it. After that, you will engage with other members of your group to resolve the Law Lab. In many cases, the Law Lab will include a key legal test that you must apply or several questions that you must answer. Sometimes, there are multiple issues that you will need to address. Often, the Law Lab will have no single or simple right answer. Accordingly, you will learn about some of the complexities in that area of substantive law, and how they affect legal decision-making.

At the beginning of the Law Lab, two members of your group will be assigned jobs. One person will be appointed to serve as the discussion leader, and one person will be the official scribe. When you are chosen to be the discussion leader, one of your tasks will be to make sure everyone has a chance to give an opinion. Every person in the group should offer an opinion as to how they think the Law Lab should be resolved, because sharing opinions is an effective way to develop a deeper understanding of what is important about the issues in the Law Lab. Then, the entire group should discuss these opinions and ideas, and work toward a resolution. At some point, the discussion leader will call for a vote. This can occur several times, but a final vote should be taken near the end of the Law Lab.

The scribe will prepare a summary of the final vote. At the end of the Law Lab, after going over the vote and comments with the discussion leader, the scribe will send the teacher a summary of three things: 1) the names of the people who were present, 2) how the group as a whole resolved the Law Lab, and 3) how each person voted.

Some Law Labs may present scenarios that generate strong opinions. You should think about what is meaningful about the facts and the law in the Law Lab, and *why* these things are significant to you. You will need to defend your beliefs thoughtfully, and listen as your colleagues defend theirs. You should also assess the concerns and thoughts that your peers share. During this process, you will learn what assumptions are behind your beliefs and the beliefs of your colleagues, and you will test the quality of those assumptions. You will learn what is important about the scenario, why it matters, and how it should affect the resolution of the Law Lab.

As you work through the scenarios, also reflect on the role each Law Lab asked you to fulfill. Did you like the scenario where you were a neutral arbiter of justice? Or did you prefer the Law Lab where you were a prosecutor, deciding which crimes a defendant should be charged with? Did you most enjoy the collaborative Law Labs, where you worked together to create a useful legal contract or important legislation? Your best chance for a rewarding legal career will be found where your own talents and preferences are mapped into your legal work. Some people are natural advocates, drawn to the excitement and challenges of an active courtroom practice. Others enjoy delving into the intricacies of legal doctrine, and excel at writing briefs arguing for a particular outcome. Still others want to guide decision-makers in high-stakes situations, using the tools of the law.

As you go through the Law Labs, think about the work that best suits your talents and preferences. You will find a rewarding legal career where your talents and preferences meet the needs of the profession.

CHAPTER 1

The Roots of the Rule of Law

Wherever law ends, tyranny begins.
—John Locke, *Two Treatises of Government, 1689,*
Book II, Section 202 of Chap. XVIII, "Of Tyranny"

Introduction

For over four millennia, **laws** have regulated human conduct. Laws are binding decrees that say what conduct is proscribed or permitted, establish the penalties for noncompliance, and set forth the processes to be used to accomplish certain civil, commercial, and personal endeavors. In every society, laws define what is right and what is wrong, announce what shall be done, and declare what must not be done. The concept of **justice** has always been linked to laws.

Yet, despite the existence of codes of laws, in every age, the powerful have worked to subjugate or eliminate the disadvantaged or unpopular. Collectively, the North American slave trade and the actions of Hitler, Stalin, and Mao caused the deaths of tens of millions of people. The laws in effect at the time in the United States, Germany, the USSR, and China did not impede enslavement or genocide.

Mere legislative enactments cannot guarantee justice. Laws may be equitable or unjust, and the processes they establish may be careful or casual. Further, the enforcement of laws and the use of legal processes may be methodical and appropriate or irrational and unfair.

The **rule of law** contemplates something more. The rule of law describes a robust system of equitable **substantive laws** supported by fair, well-administered **procedural laws** that drive just outcomes. Defining the rule of law in a few words is difficult, but it certainly requires that laws be publicly debated, collectively agreed upon and enacted, and uniformly administered. Further, it demands that all persons have the same rights and receive the same benefits under those laws: no special classes or persons are exempt, and neutral tribunals preside over all proceedings. The rule of law requires just laws that are transparently written and fairly and uniformly administered.[1]

Our understanding of the rule of law evolved over the past millennia. This chapter surveys some of the notable historic codes of law, starting with the earliest codes from ancient civilizations. These early codes were enacted chiefly to support the rule of those in power. However, through long years of conquest, conflict, and accord, concepts of justice and fairness became more clearly defined. Painful struggles heralded the emergence of fresh ideas and the recognition of new types of rights. We began to require our leaders to recognize our right to live without fear of harm, no matter our social status. We began to demand that our governments protect our liberty interests as well as our lives. We asked for fair laws, sustained using proper procedures. We came to believe that if we have a just and well-administered legal code that supports fair play and equality, then our liberty, our property, our lives, and our well-being will be better preserved.

Further, protected by a robust rule of law, we can freely express our opinions, participate in civic matters, and pursue our interests in safety. We can share ideas about government, justice, peace, and prosperity and remain protected from the arbitrary whims of the cruel and powerful. One important role of the law is to encourage such discussions, so that we can develop new ways to "promote the general Welfare and secure the Blessings of Liberty," key goals set forth in the Preamble of the United States Constitution, America's founding document.

THE RULE OF LAW KEY TERMS

The following key terms are defined in this chapter. They are also defined in the Glossary.

Abuse of Power	Homicide	Precedents
Circumstantial Evidence	Justice	Presumption of Innocence
Code of Hammurabi	Law of the Twelve Tables	Procedural Law
Code of Justinian	Laws	Right of Appeal
Code of Ur-Nammu	Legal Redress	Rule of Law
Code of Urukagina	Lex Talionis	Ruling on the Merits
Civil Rights	Mosaic Law	Solonian Constitution
Draco's Code	Murder	Substantive Law
Due Process	Opportunity to Present	Suffrage
Exercise of Discretion	Evidence	Vigilante Justice
Ex Post Facto Laws	Perjury	

---

1 A leading jurist in the United Kingdom offers this definition: "All persons and authorities within the state ... should be bound by and entitled to the benefit of laws publicly made, taking effect in the future, and publicly administered by the courts." *See* Tom Bingham, *The Rule of Law* (2010). This citation, and those that follow in the footnotes, are in the Bluebook format used by legal professionals. See *The Bluebook: A Uniform System of Citation* (21st ed., 2020).

Historic Codes of Law

Legal systems developed hand-in-hand with civilizations. Early humans lived in tribes that had no formal systems of law. To maintain power, leaders relied upon physical force and control of resources. With the emergence of agriculture, tribes became territory-based communities with established customs that governed their commercial and personal dealings. These unwritten customs became the earliest laws.

As communities grew in size, trade increased, and so did the scope of human conflict. The early kings fought and amassed power, asserting claims of divine authority. They secured influential allies, suppressed dissent, and exploited the less powerful. Discrete classes formed, and the poor and enslaved were made to serve the rich and influential.

Over the past three millennia, however, communities found that absolute authority was fraught with dangerous temptations. The masses demanded legal safeguards against oppression and arbitrary despotism. Gradually, the unchecked authority of kings and the ruling classes waned, and more democratic ideas about governance took shape.

This chapter samples some of the historic legal codes for insight into what was important in early societies. We will also consider early milestones in Western law that contributed to the modern rule of law in the United States. The development of Western law was not linear: like flowers, legal concepts sprouted here and there, died off, and returned in clusters in different times and places. It was the work of later jurists to gather those concepts, consider them, and enshrine them in legal codes.

FIGURE 1.1 Wild columbine flower

The Ancient Legal Codes

The first written laws were inscribed in cuneiform script upon clay tablets and came from ancient societies in Mesopotamia. The kings whose names they bear created them to gain prestige, to promote wealth-making commerce, to buttress slaveholding and gender roles, and to reduce the discord caused by private retribution. To these kings, a successful society required the support of the law for these purposes. Although remote in time, these early laws contain concepts that we recognize as important today.

Cuneiformists: Limited By Language

The Code of Urukagina is the earliest known legal code. Other codes may exist but remain unexcavated. It is also possible that earlier codes have been unearthed but not yet translated. Due to the small number of cuneiformists, only about 10 percent of all currently known ancient legal texts have been translated. Happily, a machine translator has been created, and in the next few decades, it could begin to decipher the untranslated texts that remain, including 69,000 ancient Mesopotamian administrative records. Unfortunately, machine translators can only learn from previously deciphered texts. Without more translators, important documents may never be translated, and their insights forever lost.

FIGURE 1.2 Fragment of the Code of Urukagina

The very earliest legal code that we know about is the **Code of Urukagina**, which dates from about 2300 BC. No copies have been unearthed, but its contents have been gleaned from other ancient documents that reference it. Urukagina was the king of two neighboring Mesopotamian city-states, Lagash and Girsu, located in modern Iraq. Claiming divine authority, he overthrew his predecessor, Lugalanda, whose reign was notable for corruption and oppression of the poor. In contrast, Urukagina's code contains provisions designed to limit the **abuse of power**. For example, the code preserves the right of a poor man to decline to sell to a man of higher status and decrees that the rich must pay in silver when buying from the poor. The code also protects the property of the poor, outlawing the theft of produce from subsistence gardens. Notably, it includes the Sumerian word *ama-gi*, which means "freedom" or "exemption from obligations," the earliest known usage of this concept.

The first legal code that has survived, albeit incompletely, is the **Code of Ur-Nammu**, dating from about 2100 BC. Ur-Nammu was the founder of the Third Dynasty of Ur, also located in modern Iraq. Following a prologue that implores key deities to support the laudable kingship of Ur-Nammu, the code delivers a series of laws. They are styled in the "x crime yields y punishment" format:

FIGURE 1.3 Fragment of the Code of Ur-Nammu

If a man commits a murder, that man must be killed.

If a man knocks out the eye of another man, he shall weigh out ½ a mina of silver.

The laws concerning crimes against women are framed as violations of the rights of the men to whom the women were deemed to belong:[2]

FIGURE 1.4   Roman slaves in collars

If a man assaults the virgin slave of another man, he must pay that man five shekels of silver.

If a man accuses the wife of another man of adultery, and the river ordeal[3] proves her innocent, then the man must pay one-third a mina of silver.

The code affirms distinctions between classes, and slaves should remember their station:

If a man's slave-woman compares herself to her mistress, and speaks insolently to her, her mouth shall be scoured with one quart of salt.

Importantly, the code contains a rule against **perjury**:

If a man appears as a witness, and was shown to be untruthful, he must pay fifteen shekels of silver.

The code of Ur-Nammu requires criminal offenders to be tried and punished by the government, a notable effort to end **vigilante justice** and suppress blood feuds.

In about 1750 BC, 350 years after the Code of Ur-Nammu, the important **Code of Hammurabi** appeared. King Hammurabi was ambitious and ultimately brought much of Mesopotamia under his rule. He claimed to have received his code from Shamash, the Babylonian god of justice. The code was written in Akkadian, the common language of Babylonia, and inscribed on tall monuments called stelae that were placed in public locations for viewing. The code contains 282 laws, likely a collection of legal precedents established during Hammurabi's rule. Almost half of these concern contract dealings, and

---

2   *See* Elizabeth Meier Tetlow, *Women, Crime and Punishment in Ancient Law and Society*, 14 (2014).

3   This likely involved being submerged in or being required to cross a particular river. If you survived, you were innocent. *See* P. Kyle McCarter, "The River Ordeal in Israelite Literature," 66 *Harv. Theo. Rev.*, 403 (1973).

Hammurabi's Code

In 1901, archaeologists dug up what looked like a giant stone pillar. Etched on the flat side were the words:

> Anu and Bel called by name me, Hammurabi, the exalted prince, who feared God, to bring about the rule of righteousness in the land, to destroy the wicked and the evil-doers; so that the strong should not harm the weak; so that I should rule over the black-headed people like Shamash, and enlighten the land, to further the well-being of mankind …

While Hammurabi thought himself to be a great vanquisher of evil and the protector of the weak, his laws continued some unfortunate traditions. One such tradition required defendants to jump into one of the two rivers in Mesopotamia to prove the truth of their utterances. If they survived, they were telling the truth. If not, then they had received their just punishment.

FIGURE 1.5 Hammurabi's law preserved

one-third addresses issues in family law (such as paternity, inheritance, and divorce). The remainder relates to crimes, punishment, and governance.

The criminal provisions in the Code of Hammurabi differ from preceding codes. Instead of requiring payments to victims of crimes, this code lists specific physical punishments for perpetrators. Some of the penalties follow the doctrine of **lex talionis**, retaliative punishments that mirror offenses (such as an eye for an eye and a tooth for a tooth).

As with the other ancient codes, criminal punishments in the Code of Hammurabi depend upon the social status of the accuser and the accused. If a person of the upper class breaks a commoner's bone, he must pay one pound of silver. However, if a person strikes someone of a higher class, then the penalty is sixty lashes with an ox-whip.[4]

The code establishes, for the first time, the **presumption of innocence**, and it also suggests some procedural safeguards to support fair outcomes, such as the **opportunity to present evidence**[5] during trials.

About a millennium later, to the west of Babylonia, the ancient Israelites were developing their own legal code. **Mosaic Law**, or the Law of Moses, is recorded in the first five books of the Hebrew Bible.[6] Most modern scholars believe that the content was organized and edited over a long period of time, perhaps from the tenth to the fifth century BC.[7] Mosaic Law offers a comprehensive collection of rules meant to regulate and improve the lives of the ancient

---

4   *See* H. Dieter Viel, *The New Complete Code of Hammurabi* (2012).

5   *See* Ann Wolbert Burgess et al., *Victimology: Theories and Applications* 103 (2009).

6   These books are known in Hebrew as Bereshit (Genesis), Shemot (Exodus), Vayicra (Leviticus), Bamidbar (Numbers), and Devarim (Deuteronomy). The Torah can refer to these five books (collectively known as the Chameesha Choomshey Torah) to commandments found in books in the Hebrew Bible, or more broadly, to the oral tradition of laws.

7   In the State of Israel, most educators hold the secularist position that the Torah is the product of the national life of ancient Israel. *See* "Judaism: The Written Law—Torah," Jewish Virtual Library, jewishvirtuallibrary.org/the-written-law-torah (last visited June 17, 2020). The precise process by which the Torah was composed is the subject of vigorous debate.

Israelites. Transgressions were seen as offenses against God, which is not surprising: ancient Israel was a theocracy, rather than a monarchy.

The Law of Moses includes the Ten Commandments, a criminal code, social laws (addressing inheritance, marriage, divorce, and property), food laws (governing what may be eaten and how to cook and store food), purity laws, laws governing feast days and the preparation of sacrifices and offerings, and instructions for the priesthood and the management of sacred objects, such as the Ark of the Covenant and the Tabernacle. In the Talmud, the central text of rabbinical Judaism, there are 613 commandments, which include both prohibited and obligatory acts.

Murder and kidnapping are prohibited.[8] Fornication and rape are crimes with harsh penalties (usually stoning). On some occasions, the code authorizes payment to the fathers of women who are wronged. For example, a man who assaults a woman alone in a field must marry her and pay her father a dowry of fifty shekels of silver.[9]

The code forbids the theft of money and the withholding of wages. You must not fail to pay a debt, and you must return an item that someone entrusted to you. You may neither overcharge nor underpay, and you must not insult or harm others with words.[10]

FIGURE 1.6 The Ark of the Covenant

---

8   From Ex. 21:13–14. These are the 482nd and 473rd commandments as listed by Moses ben Maimon (1135–1204), also known as Maimonides, from his *Mishneh Torah*. Maimonides was a Sephardic Jewish philosopher who became one of the most influential Torah scholars of the Middle Ages. All commandments in the Torah here carry the Maimonides numbering as typically presented.

9   *See* Deut. 22:13–29 and commandments 132–135.

10   Lev. 19:11, commandment 467; Lev. 19:13, commandment 475; Lev. 19:11, commandment 211; Lev. 25:14, commandment 500; Lev. 25:17, commandment 501.

The Mosaic Code recognizes the necessity of **legal redress** for acts that cause harm and requires judges to apply the law against the one who assaults another or damages another's property.[11] As part of that redress, judges must determine the correct amount of damages for an injury inflicted by a goring ox, by an animal that eats someone's crops, and for injury caused by fire.[12]

The Mosaic Code is also concerned with **due process**. Judges must be familiar with judicial procedure. Witnesses are required to appear and testify and must not testify falsely.[13] Uncorroborated testimony should not be considered, and perjurers should be punished.[14] Judges may only hear testimony if both sides are present and can refuse to hear testimony from relatives of litigants.[15] Murderers are not to be put to death before trial, and the death penalty is not to be imposed based solely upon **circumstantial evidence**.[16]

The manner of the judicial **exercise of discretion** is also important. Judges must not accept bribes, and should be courageous, unaffected by threats. They must decide cases fairly, and may not seek to lighten or increase established penalties.[17] In particular:

> A judge must not have mercy on the poor man at trial.

> A judge must not respect the great man at trial.[18]

Further, the poor and disadvantaged must also be treated fairly:

> A judge must not pervert a case involving a convert or orphan.[19]

These ancient codes show that early societies were concerned about identifying wrongs and establishing penalties for those wrongs. Leaders recognized the power that came with the development and enforcement of just laws: they would gain the confidence of the masses, who would believe that their interests would be protected. By binding all members of society to a single set of substantive and procedural rules, the less advantaged were better protected from the influential or powerful.

Of course, slavery and discrimination continued throughout the early world. The powerful and well-connected exercised influence and amassed more wealth, and the poor and marginalized suffered in silence, fearing deadly reprisals. Despite developments in laws and legal thinking, the rule of law had not come to fruition.

---

11 Ex. 21:18, commandment 481.
12 Ex. 21:28, commandment 463; Ex. 22:4, commandment 464; Ex. 22:5, commandment 466.
13 Deut. 1:17, commandment 541; Lev. 5:1, commandment 570; Ex. 20:14, commandment 576.
14 Deut. 19:15, commandment 573; Deut. 19:19, commandment 577.
15 Ex. 23:1, commandment 566; Deut. 24:16, commandment 575.
16 Num. 35:12, commandment 486; Ex. 23:7, commandment 555.
17 Ex. 23:8, commandment 565; Deut. 1:17, commandment 564; Lev. 19:15, commandment 561 and 563; Deut. 25:2-3, commandments 553 & 554.
18 Lev. 19:15, commandment 558; Lev. 19:15, commandment 559.
19 Deut. 24:17, commandment 562.

Early Greek and Roman Law

While the Mosaic Code guided the lives of the early Israelites, the Greek city-state of Athens had developed a tradition of oral law. As the laws were not fixed in writing, Athenian aristocrats easily manipulated them to gain advantage and exploit other members of society. Left without a way to obtain justice, families resorted to murders and feuding. In an effort to manage growing conflict, after 900 years of the oral code, the governing families of Athens authorized Draco, a Greek noble, to prepare a legal text that would become the first Athenian constitution. **Draco's Code**, or the Draconian Constitution of 620 BC, was the result.

The code includes provisions governing voting, the organization of government, and punishments for crimes. Significantly, it distinguishes between **murder** (intentional killing) and **homicide** (unintentional killing) and requires cases to be tried by governmental agents. Notably, the code dictates the death penalty for most offenses, including the theft of a cabbage, and calls for enslavement for unpaid debt.

The harsh nature of the code and its provisions regarding debt management led to grave difficulties. Poor farmers and laborers could not repay loans from the wealthy and were forced into slavery. Further, commoners were denied all participation in the political process. Clashes between the aristocracy and the masses increased in frequency and intensity. When insurrection threatened, the Athenians elected Solon, a popular military leader, to be chief magistrate of Athens. The Athenians instructed him to write a reformed constitution that would calm the conflict and improve the plight of commoners and the poor.

The resulting **Solonian Constitution** canceled all debts, freeing those who had been enslaved due to money owed. The new constitution also made it illegal to secure a debt through human bondage. In addition, by establishing wealth rather than birth as the requirement for holding political office, the constitution permitted more people to play a role in government. While the reforms did away with Draco's Code, Solon retained Draco's distinction between intentional and unintentional killing, which we continue to recognize. Solon also implemented two significant changes to procedural law: first, any Athenian could bring suit (not just the party that was most directly injured), and second, there was a **right of appeal** of magistrates' verdicts to a court of citizens.

Solon's constitution was not uniformly popular. The aristocracy had hoped for small and symbolic changes, and the masses had wanted sweeping land redistribution and social reform. Nonetheless, the Athenians agreed to be bound by it. The constitution and the revisions that followed served as the foundation for

FIGURE 1.7   The Roman Forum

Knowledge Is Power

For much of Rome's history, its law was held exclusively by the powerful and those privileged enough to be taught the oral Roman legal code. The Twelve Tables marked a turning point for this tradition. Created in response to pressure from the masses, the laws of the Twelve Tables were publicly displayed, so that they could be read by every literate person in Roman society.

The publication of laws is a critical component of the rule of law. If a legal code is publicized, citizens can work together to address abuses of power that arise from laws which are facially preferential or discriminatory.

FIGURE 1.8   The Twelve Tables of Rome

Athenian law for nearly a thousand years, until the sixth century AD.

Meanwhile, across the Ionian Sea, Rome was also enduring unrest. In 509 BC, the last of the Roman kings was overthrown and the Roman Republic founded. Under the new Republic, the upper-class patrician magistrates managed daily governance, and upper-class patrician priests interpreted the law.[20] Accordingly, the masses were excluded from all aspects of the government and its operation. The **Law of the Twelve Tables**, from about 450 BC, was an effort to resolve the resulting class struggle.

The Twelve Tables establish and describe the rights of all Roman citizens. While the complete content of the Twelve Tables has been lost, excerpts and quotations from other sources tell us that they include procedural law and well as substantive law, and provide social protection and some **civil rights** for all members of society.[21]

The Twelve Tables include laws governing trial practice. There must be a trial before anyone is executed. If there is a civil dispute, and the parties resolve it themselves, the magistrate will announce the resolution. If not:

> [T]he parties shall state their case before the assembly in the meeting place or before the magistrate in the marketplace before noon. Both parties being present shall plead the case throughout together.[22]

It is important to appear on time:

---

20   The *patricians* comprised the upper class in Roman society and were the aristocrats who originally ruled ancient Rome. The *plebians* were the common citizens.

21   *See* Gary Forsyth, *A Critical History of Early Rome: From Prehistory to the First Punic War* (1ˢᵗ ed., 2005).

22   All references to the content of the Twelve Tables are derived from the Avalon Project of Yale Law School's Lillian Goldman Law Library. *See* "The Twelve Tables," The Avalon Project, Yale Law School, https://avalon.law.yale.edu/ancient/twelve_tables.asp. (last visited Jun. 17, 2020).

If one of the parties does not appear the magistrate shall adjudge the case, after noon, in favor of the one present.

The loser in a court case must pay the assessed judgment within thirty days. Otherwise, the winning party may bring the debtor back to court, and unless payment is then immediately made, the winning party has the right to bind the debtor with weights of no less than fifteen pounds. If the failure to pay continues, the debtor is to be brought to the praetor for three successive market days, and on the third day the debtor will be executed or sold as a slave.

Roman society was utterly patriarchal. The Twelve Tables requires women, no matter their age, to be subject to guardianship "because of their levity of mind." Further, children with birth defects must be killed by their fathers "immediately."

Interestingly, the Twelve Tables declares that citizens have the right to say what is lawful:

Whatever the people ordain last shall be legally valid.

The Twelve Tables were publicly displayed, and students of the law studied them. They served Rome for over nine hundred years until the key reform, the **Code of Justinian** (which later became known as the *Corpus Juris Civilis*), was implemented around 529 AD.

By the sixth century AD, the Roman Empire had grown to encompass the Western Empire and the Eastern (Byzantine) Empire. Emperor Justinian I wished to create a unifying body of law that would add to his fame and broadly express Roman legal tradition and culture. He commissioned jurists to gather, assess, and refine the existing law.

As initially published, the code consisted of three parts, written in Latin: 1) the Codex, stating the laws of the Roman Empire; 2) the Digesta, a summarization of key writings on law and justice, including interpretations of the law that had the force of law; and 3) the Institutiones, which summarized the Digesta, and was intended to be a textbook for students of law. A fourth section, the Novellae, consisting of laws passed after 532 AD, was included later. The Codex, Digesta, Institutiones, and Novellae were the only references that could be cited in Roman courts of law.

The initial Codex (the Codex Vetus) promptly proved to be outdated and cumbersome, and a new Codex was published to replace it.[23] The new version, which runs to one million words, broadly regulates life and society in the Roman Empire. It is highly theistic: the first book concerns ecclesiastical law, and it opens with a provision requiring all persons within the empire to adhere to a particular type of Christianity (Chalcedonian,[24] as opposed to other early religious sects). Other provisions designate Christianity as the state religion, deny citizenship to non-Christians, and make pagan practices punishable by execution.

---

23 Called the *Codex Repetitae Praelectionis*, this new version is what is meant by "Codex" in today's scholarly communities.
24 Chalcedonian Christians adopted the Christian theology from the Council of Chalcedon (451 AD) that the divine and human are conjoined in the one person of Jesus of Nazareth.

A World of Legal Traditions

The law of the United States flows from the Western legal tradition explored in this chapter. In other parts of the world, other legal traditions developed.

Around 620 AD, early Muslim communities emerged in Mecca and Medina, located in modern Saudi Arabia. They were guided by the revelations of the Prophet Muhammad and followed the standards of conduct set forth in the Quran. Islamic law, or the Sharia, supports Muslims as they express their religious convictions in this world and reach for the world to come. The Sharia includes not only legal prohibitions, but also ethical edicts that instruct individuals about what they are morally required to do.

Ancient India maintained an independent and distinct Hindu legal tradition. It focused on promoting *dharma*, a combination of duty and righteousness. Its codes governed not only a person's obligations to society, but also most aspects of daily life, including appropriate dress and purification rituals. The Indian justice system had a hierarchy of courts, rising from village councils to the King's Court.

Kǒng Fūzǐ (or Confucius) was a Chinese teacher and philosopher who lived from 551 to 479 BC. Confucius emphasized the cultivation of virtue and the importance of key personal relationships as the foundations for society. However, he also noted that society requires laws, as some people will not feel bound to follow moral rules. Confucianism rose to influence the legal systems and cultures of China, Japan, and Korea. Confucius left behind a collection of sayings, including, "Study the past if you would define the future."

The extent to which these ancient legal traditions influence today's laws varies by nation and by topic.

The Codex includes the inevitable listing of crimes and punishments, reviews the duties of officials, sets rules concerning taxation, government, the military, and lists the obligations of civil service personnel. It also addresses family law matters, such as marriage, divorce, and inheritance, as well as commercial matters, such as contracts and the purchase and sale of property.

Unsurprisingly, the Codex preserves the distinction between the free and the enslaved. Fathers are given absolute authority over their children, including initially the power of life and death. In addition, the elder father in the male line has the exclusive right to own property, such that all purchases by his children become his. Nonetheless, there are rules protecting the rights of women under certain circumstances. For example, there are provisions designed to protect women from exploitation (including being forced into prostitution), and rapists are punished severely. Married women have certain rights, including the right to be consulted before their husbands assume major debt.

There are also rules governing formal procedural law. These establish protocols for the development of legal issues in a case and for the presentation of evidence. A **ruling on the merits** may occur only at the end of the trial process.

While the Codex sets forth the governing laws, the Digesta includes a comprehensive collection of legal writings that counsel may rely upon as **precedents**. Although there are flaws in its organization,[25] the Digesta's contribution to the *Corpus Juris Civilis* is critical.

All in all, Justinian's *Corpus Juris Civilis*—Codex, Digesta, Institutiones (and Novellae)—remains a remarkable achievement: a complete legal code, an extensive reference guide, and a detailed legal textbook. The *Corpus Juris Civilis* captured an important body of law for later jurists and

---

25   Scholars note that the Digesta's flaws include the "appalling arrangement" of its organization. *See* Alan Watson, "The Importance of 'Nutshells,'" 42 *Am. J. Comp. L.* 2 (1994). *See also* Fritz Schultz, *History of Roman Legal Science* 150–52 (1967).

legislatures to contemplate and set forth a system for the resolution of legal problems. It unquestionably influenced the development of the Western legal codes.

And yet, by modern standards, the *Corpus Juris Civilis* fails as a rule of law. Certainly, it extensively regulated the commercial, civic, and personal lives of Roman citizens, providing them with a single set of substantive and procedural rules that were to be equitably applied. However, the *Corpus Juris Civilis* was a product of its time in history: it criminalized certain religious exercises, did not provide equal rights for minorities and women, and supported slavery.

Although Roman law endured in the East until Constantinople fell to the Ottoman Empire in 1453, by the sixth century AD, the Roman Empire had declined in Europe. In its wake, feudal systems arose, and Europe reverted to customary law and royal decrees. A remnant of the Justinian Code endured in the form of the Canon Law of the Roman Catholic Church, and as Western societies emerged from the dark ages, there was renewed interest in the *Corpus Juris Civilis*. Scholars debated existing texts, and major new portions were discovered that sparked further discussion.[26]

When the authors of the United States Declaration of Independence determined to break away from the most powerful empire in the world, they looked to history to see how it could best be done. They considered the framework of the new government, and the way authority should be managed. They had studied the classics, and in their revolutionary moment, they reached for the examples of Greece and Rome.[27] The notion of learned senators to help guide the ship of state comes from Roman law,[28] and the Founders adopted the Roman Republic's division of power as a key safeguard against oppression.[29] But the Founders distilled from Roman law something more than ideas about the potential architecture of a new government: they captured the spirit of republican civic responsibility. As James Madison said:

> It is evident that no other form would be reconcilable with the genius of the people of America; with the fundamental principles of the Revolution; or with the honorable determination which animates every votary of freedom, to rest all our political experiments on the capacity of mankind for self-government.[30]

The Founders knew that prior republics had failed due to factionalism and internal dissent. To prevent this, they considered, debated, and incorporated new concepts into the formative documents of the new nation. But the core notion of civic responsibility came from Roman law. While the

---

26   In 1135, a copy of the Digesta, which had been lost to western Europe, was discovered in Amalfi, Italy. This furthered the interests of scholars in the legal schools of Germany, Italy, and France, who studied the Codex, Digesta, the Institutiones, and the Novellae, seeking to harmonize the rules. They wrote in the margins or between the lines of the texts, expanding and explaining ideas in "glosses." They became known as the Glossators.

27   John and Abigail Adams were separated for long periods of time during the nation's formative days and wrote many letters to each other. At John's instigation, Abigail signed some of her letters to him as "Portia." Portia was the wife of Brutus, who overthrew the Roman emperor (and dictator) Julius Caesar.

28   *See* Caroline Winterer, *The Culture of Classism: Ancient Greece and Rome in American Intellectual Life, 1780–1910* (2002).

29   *See* R.A. Ames and H.C. Montgomery, "The *Influence of Rome on the American Constitution*," 30 *The Classical Journal* 19–27 (1934).

30   The Federalist No. 39 (James Madison).

The Napoleonic Code and the Civil Law Tradition

In 1799, sixteen years after the American Revolutionary War, Napoleon Bonaparte seized political power in France in a coup d'état. As the new emperor, he determined to codify all the civil and criminal laws of France, using the old Code of Justinian as his inspiration. The Napoleonic Code was drafted by commission and became effective in 1804.

Napoleon's code diverges from Roman law: it is secular and rational, written in clear language in the vernacular. Further, it relies upon the primacy of legislative enactments rather than upon juries or judicial discretion. The notion was that judges should simply apply the laws with minimal interpretation, and therefore achieve broad uniformity in outcomes. The Napoleonic Code protects key gains achieved through the French Revolution by guaranteeing **suffrage**, property rights, and religious freedom for all male citizens. It also confirms the traditional authority of the father over the wife and children in the family unit, and supports enslavement in the French colonial territories (but not in France itself).

The code contains rules designed to support due process. Laws must be duly enacted and officially published, and secret laws and **ex post facto laws** are prohibited.

In addition to influencing the development of the western European legal systems, the Napoleonic Code found its way to the state of Louisiana. Following sharp conflict, Spain ceded the area to France, which sold it in 1802 to the United States. Louisiana's state law thus includes civil law elements.

FIGURE 1.9 The Napoleonic Code

obligation to set aside the plowshare and take up the sword is referenced in the Old Testament,[31] the Roman idea of civic virtue is more nuanced: citizens should understand and respect the law, strive for moral excellence, and be prepared to fulfill their obligations to the nation—even if that means going to war.[32] These ideas sustained the emerging nation as it fought for independence and moved toward a new model of governance.

Conclusion and Introduction to the Law Lab

Since the times of the early Mesopotamian kings, legal codes have established what may be done and what may not be done. They have described the rights people may exercise, the actions that will be punished, and the protocols that regulate commerce, governments, communities, family life, and dispute resolution.

One enduring function of the law has been to establish a process through which injured persons may obtain redress. In every era, lawmakers have crafted regulations to guide the work of jurors, judges, and advocates in dispute resolution. They have prepared laws establishing the process by which cases should be presented and adjudicated. Today, such a process is included in the legal code of every developed nation. It has been an important part of our American legal tradition, although there have been lamentably uneven outcomes in various times and places.

This week, for your first Law Lab, you will step into this lawmaking tradition. You will develop a set of rules that will be used to guide the work of jurors in a trial. A citizen in our town of Liberty Springs has been injured in an accident and

---

31   *See Isaiah* 2:4 (King James); *Joel* 3:10 (King James); and *Micah* 4:3 (King James).

32   *See* William Young, "Civic Virtue and Western Civilization," *Nat'l Ass'n of Scholars Blog* (Dec. 01, 2011), https://www.nas.org/blogs/article/civic_virtue_and_western_civilization.

seeks compensation for her injuries. The Law Lab outlines the facts of the case and then asks for your guidance on the key rules that will direct the jurors' efforts.

Think about the historic legal codes you have reviewed and what they require of those who help resolve cases. What guidance will permit a jury to properly review and assess a case? What attributes—such as impartiality, fairness, and diligence—are important? What rules will make the process fair to both sides? You must answer the question posed to all lawmakers, ancient and modern: what rules will best produce fair and equitable outcomes? In this time and place, what laws will best serve the interests of justice?

Lawmaking Law Lab

INTRODUCTION

The rule of law requires that legal disputes be resolved fairly. This is important not only for the litigants in a particular case, but for the peace and stability of society. The public should have confidence in the legal system and in the legal professionals who administer it. They should believe that if they come to court, their cases will be properly administered and adjudicated. The public must not think that private retribution is necessary or appropriate.

The section that follows describes a serious accident and the conflict that resulted from it. Dispute resolution has failed to resolve the controversy, and the parties are now in court. In this Law Lab, you are lawmakers. After you read about the accident, you will be asked to prepare the rules that will guide the work of the jurors who will decide the case. With your guidance, the case can be resolved in a way that supports the interests of justice.

Factual Background

The Parties

This dispute involves two people, Mara Smith and Blaine Holder. Both are residents of the town of Liberty Springs, named for its notable thermal springs. Liberty Springs is located in the state of Franklin, a new addition to the United States of America.

Mara is the plaintiff, the person who filed the lawsuit. Before the accident, Mara was an active and healthy thirty-two-year-old woman, working as a teacher. Mara lives with her sister Livia on a parcel of land on the outskirts of town. Mara and Livia keep an herb garden and a small herd of dairy goats. They often sell herbs and homemade cheeses.

Blaine is the defendant, the person whom Mara sued. Blaine is a farmer who lives outside town with his wife and three young children. He grows mainly wheat on his acreage, but he also has plots for vegetables (including squash and melons) and a few fruit trees. Blaine often brings his vegetables and fruits to Liberty Springs on summer market days. He displays his produce in a large red cart.

The Accident

Mara and her sister Livia enjoy shopping at markets, particularly outdoor markets that feature fresh farm produce. Their favorite market is the farmer's market in Liberty Springs, located on a hillside overlooking the town square.

On the day of the accident, Mara and Livia went together to the farmer's market, hoping to purchase fresh apples and pears. Blaine had brought his red cart to town on that day, and parked it in his usual space on the hillside. It was filled with melons that he hoped to sell.

FIGURE 1.10   Produce market

While Mara and Livia were visiting their usual provider of fresh apples, Blaine's cart came loose from its hillside placement and rolled downhill toward Mara and Livia. The cart gathered speed as it came down the hill, and when it approached Mara and Livia it was rolling fast. At the last moment, Livia was able to get out of the way, but the cart struck Mara on her right side. Mara sustained serious injuries, including a concussion, three broken ribs, and a fracture of her right arm at the elbow joint. She also received face and neck lacerations that have left disfiguring scars.

Blaine asserts that he is not responsible for the accident. He states that he properly braced the cart when he parked it in the morning, as he does whenever he brings the cart to the market. He claims that someone must have removed the heavy wooden block that he routinely used to keep the cart from moving. Blaine has witnesses that are prepared to testify on his behalf.

Mara, too, has witnesses. One witness will offer testimony that Blaine appeared distracted when he was setting up his cart on the day of the accident. Another will testify that, after the accident, the wooden block Blaine used to brace his cart was found on the ground some distance from where the cart had been parked.

The case will be heard before a judge, with a jury deciding whose story is right. The jury will determine if Blaine is responsible for Mara's injuries.

Drafting Rules for the Jury

Laypersons have long been involved in dispute resolution. In earlier times, neighbors gathered and passed judgment based upon what they knew about the facts and the people involved in a case. Today, juries are randomly drawn from the wider population. Modern juries in the United States serve a critical function: they decide the truth of the matters presented in a legal case. Jurors assess the evidence at trial and determine whose story is right. They decide who should prevail in the court case before them.

Juries receive their guidance from the judge presiding over the case. Judges usually give juries instructions twice. First, jurors receive instructions before the trial begins. These opening instructions explain how the trial process works and guide the jury's analysis of the case. Among other things, the opening instructions tell jurors what they may consider and what they should not consider as evidence in the dispute.

Second, jurors receive closing instructions at the end of trial proceedings. The closing instructions guide their deliberations and tell the jurors how to work together to reach a verdict. These instructions often include a verdict form that the jury will complete and present at the end of their deliberations.

You will now develop rules to govern the jury's work in the case. You will draft both the opening instructions and the closing instructions. As you think about what is important, you may wish to review some of the legal codes noted in the chapter. Certainly, prior lawmakers considered juror neutrality and a careful assessment of truthfulness to be critical. In addition, the administration of justice requires the use of proper process. Thus, jurors should reach their decision only after all the evidence has been presented and evaluated.

Make sure that your designated scribe writes down the rules you ultimately select. Unwritten rules are easily subject to drift and misinterpretation, and we want our jury instructions to be firmly settled.

Drafting Opening Instructions

First, think about the rules that the judge should give to the jury before the trial begins. What guidance should the jurors follow as they hear the statements of the advocates and the testimony of the parties and witnesses?

You may wish to consider the duties of the jurors. Again, it is the job of jurors to find the facts and truth from the evidence presented. Jurors should follow the law, whether they agree with it or not. As the case is presented, they should strive to avoid personal likes, opinions, and prejudices. You may wish to think about the possible role of outside opinions and information sources and also about the sharing of information with those not involved in the case. Should jurors be allowed to discuss the case with their friends and family? Should there be admonishments about things the jurors should not do? How can you encourage the jurors to remain impartial and consider all the evidence? Finally, should the jurors swear an oath in connection with their work before the evidence is presented? If so, what should that oath say?

Drafting Closing Instructions

Next, think about the rules that will best guide the jurors as they deliberate. What rules will best support the jurors' assigned work of fact-finding as they deliberate and make their determinations?

The jurors need to know what they will be doing when they deliberate. They should understand that they are to discuss the case among themselves and share their opinions about the evidence and witnesses. Perhaps they should be reminded of their duty to be fair and neutral. Perhaps they should receive instructions on their decorum and the need for civility. There should be instructions about the selection of a foreperson, and how that selection process might be navigated.

The jurors will require an explanation about the standard that they must apply to the evidence that they view (this is called the burden of proof). What does it mean if they think that one side's version of events is more plausible than the other side's? Does that mean that they should find in favor of that side? Should they only find in favor of one side if they strongly believe that side's version, or should they find in favor if they simply think it is slightly more likely to be true?

Should the jurors' verdict be unanimous? If so, what should they do if they cannot reach an agreement? If jurors have questions about the case or about their work, what steps should they take?

Finally, would a verdict form be helpful? If so, what should it say?

Once you have prepared your rules for the jury, read through them as if you were jurors. Would the guidance you have provided enable you to properly work toward a fair assessment of the evidence in this case?

Conclusion

As fact-finders in legal disputes, jurors shoulder an awesome and historic responsibility. In deciding the outcome of legal disputes, they support law and order in society, performing work that is critical to the interests of justice. In American courts, agents of government and citizens walk hand-in-hand to support the rule of law.

The trial court, the litigants, and the jurors look forward to receiving your guidance. Please reach out if you have any questions about your work in connection with this Law Lab.

CHAPTER 2

The Common Law and Our Federal Republic

The glory of justice and the majesty of law are created not just by the Constitution—nor by the courts—nor by the officers of law—nor by the lawyers—but by the men and women who constitute our society—who are the protectors of the law as they are themselves protected by the law.

—Attorney General Robert F. Kennedy, address for the Law Day Ceremonies of the Virginia State Bar, given in Roanoke, Virginia, May 1, 1962

Introduction

When crafting the documents that would create the United States, the fifty-five Framers[1] considered historic legal documents and codes of law. The first chapter surveyed some of those historic legal codes, noting the emergence of concepts that became important to the modern rule of law. The Framers also pondered the inequities suffered under the reigns of the kings and emperors and examined the works of commentators and philosophers on justice and governance. Finally, they considered the **common law** of England, an important body of law derived from judicial decisions. The common law became the foundation for the operation of the legal system in the United States.

As we noted in Chapter 1, the Framers understood the importance of **separation of powers**, which ensures that no single person or entity can exert too much control over governmental operations. Accordingly, they created separate branches of government to fulfill administrative, lawmaking, and adjudicative functions, and embedded checks on the authority of those branches. In addition, the Framers adopted a **federal system** rather than a **unitary system** of government. In federal systems, political authority is divided between a national government and subnational units of government (the state governments). The federal government is given the authority to handle matters best managed at the national level. These matters include the regulation of interstate commerce, foreign relations (including war), and the conduct of trade with other nations. Some operations are jointly shared with the states, and the remainder fall entirely within the states' ambit (such as education and local policing). In the United States, Tribal governments operate as other, self-governing sovereigns.[2]

---

1. The fifty-five Framers were those appointed to be delegates to the 1787 Constitutional Convention and who helped draft the Constitution. They are distinguished from the Signers, who executed it.
2. Tribal nations are described as "domestic dependent nations" by the federal government. The governments of the 574 Native American Tribes recognized by the United States operate apart from federal and state governments: each is a separate sovereign nation. Tribal governments provide emergency services, operate court systems, and undertake health care, education, and other governmental endeavors.

As a result of the Framers' decisions, the federal government, the governments of the states, and the governments of the Tribes all have their own political bodies and taxation rights. They also have their own courts and their own prosecutors who pursue those who violate their laws. Further, as sovereigns, they are also largely immune from suit, much like the old English kings.

In this chapter, we consider how our federal system of divided governance can pose challenges to the rule of law in the United States. To do this, we must first delve into the history of the common law. The common law broadly governed the lives of the colonists under British rule and became the foundation for the legal codes and rule of law in the United States. The common law gave the Framers a variety of key legal concepts, including the venerated prohibition against **double jeopardy**, which means a person cannot be tried twice for the same crime. From the common law the United States also inherited the doctrine of **sovereign immunity**, which prohibits suit against the federal government, state governments, and Tribes without their consent.

After exploring the history of the common law, in this chapter's Law Lab, you will serve as Supreme Court justices. You will consider whether the doctrine of sovereign immunity should apply to a federally recognized Tribal nation that has been sued in state court. The Pokagon Band of the Potawatomi has objected to state court jurisdiction in a lawsuit filed against it. You must decide if the common law doctrine of sovereign immunity should support its position.

COMMON LAW KEY TERMS

The following key terms are defined in this chapter. They are also defined in the Glossary.

Adversarial System	**Divine Right**	**Legal Precedent**	**Sovereign Immunity**
Case Law	**Double Jeopardy**	**Legal Reasoning**	***Stare Decisis***
Common Law	**Equitable Remedies**	**Magna Carta**	**Trial by Ordeal**
Court of the Star Chamber	**Federal System**	**Prerogative Courts**	**Unitary System**
	Feudal System	**Separation of Powers**	**Writ**

The Common Law Tradition in the United States

The common law tradition began in North America with the arrival of the first colonists from England. In 1607, the London Company founded the first permanent English settlement in Jamestown, Virginia. The London Company was created by royal charter to support settlement in North America. Other charters followed, and each gave the chartered company an exclusive geographic area to explore and settle.

The first enslaved persons arrived in North America in 1619, most likely from the Kingdom of Ndongo, now in Angola.[3] By the start of the eighteenth century, there were around 250,000 enslaved Africans and free Europeans living in the colonies. There were also millions of Native Americans living throughout North America.

Each colony had its own distinct legal culture. The plantation owners of Virginia developed a harsh code to maximize human labor and profits from tobacco. The Puritans of Massachusetts sought to preserve religious values in their farming communities. Settlers in Rhode Island embraced religious freedom and the separation of church and state. However, Imperial Britain wished to impose the broad sweep of English law on its colonies across the Atlantic. British-appointed governors designated sheriffs to run jails, choose jurors, and generally administer justice, and the common law of England was their guide.

After declaring independence from England, the former colonies enacted "reception statutes" that endorsed and adopted the common law. Through this process, the United States inherited the **adversarial system**, where contending advocates argue for their clients' interests at trial. From the common law, the American legal system also gained the distinction between criminal and civil law. Perhaps most significantly, the common law provided the critical principle of ***stare decisis*** (using **legal precedent** to decide cases), supporting predictability and consistency in the law. The common law is deeply embedded in the American legal system. Without its common law features, the modern legal landscape in the United States would be unrecognizable.

English Feudalism and the Beginnings of the Common Law

The common law did not spring forth, fully developed, to serve the people who needed it. Instead, like other legal codes, it evolved with the people whose lives it administered.[4]

Before the Norman invasion of the 11th century, a scattered collection of local customs and rules governed the lives of the Anglo-Saxons living in England. Kings relied upon councils to assist with matters of state, and key men in local communities pronounced the law and presided over folk courts.[5] The folk courts gathered local people in juries to decide disputes, issued **writs** to compel people to attend, and relied upon **trial by ordeal** to determine who was telling the truth.

In 1066, William of Normandy crossed the English Channel and conquered the Anglo-Saxons. William then allocated land to his faithful barons and knights, and they began to administer their holdings.[6] In an agricultural society, wealth chiefly comes from the ownership of land, and William's new lords sought to enlarge

---

3   They were captured and left Africa on the vessel *San Juan Bautista*. During the Atlantic crossing, about 150 of the 350 originally put aboard died. The *San Juan Bautista* was taken by privateers, and the surviving captive Africans were transported to Virginia and sold. *See* Lisa Rein, "Mystery of Virginia's First Slaves Is Unlocked 400 Years Later," *African Diaspora Archaeology Newsletter* 9, no. 3, Sept. 2006.

4   The history of the common law, its legal institutions, and its important commentators is greatly abbreviated here. *See* John Langbein, Renee Lettow Lerner, and Bruce P. Smith, *History of the Common Law: The Development of Anglo-American Legal Institutions* (2009).

5   John P. Dawson, *A History of Lay Judges* n. 5 (1960).

6   William ordered a national survey of the lands and people and created a valuation for these that recorded land rights. He wanted to know what resources he had at his disposal. His survey became known as the Domesday Book. It has been cited frequently in the courts as evidence of rights, as recently as the 1961 case *Earl Ivey v. Martin*, 1 Q.B. 232.

their original grants.[7] To affirm his authority and regularize land rights, William imposed a **feudal system**. Complex rules determined the conditions under which the land was to be valued, held, and worked. Feudal customs contemplated reciprocal obligations of support between crown and vassals: each had duties to the other as part of the feudal contract. The king owned all the land, and ruled by **divine right**. As the king's rule had been granted by God, his word was, supposedly, absolute. The vassal barons, sworn to fealty, held their lands under the king. They were obligated to provide military support in quantities that depended upon the size of the territory they had been given. In exchange, the king was to keep the land secure from enemies. Finally, following the tradition of ancient rulers, it was the king's duty to dispense justice.

When they conquered England, William and his Normans brought their own customary law. This was largely administered by clergymen trained in historical Roman law (and later also trained in the canon law of the Roman Catholic Church, the *Corpus Juris Canonici*). The Church operated separate ecclesiastical courts that addressed sacramental matters, including marriages, annulments, legitimacy, wills, and inheritances. In addition, the Church had jurisdiction over all matters touching on vows and heresy.

The unrest and inequality that typically accompanies the rule of foreign conquerors led to the creation of a new, centralized Norman government.[8] However, the customary law of the Norman people did not entirely obliterate that of the Anglo-Saxons: instead, a new collection of rules emerged, based partly on local customs and partly on Norman ideas of governance and justice.

Given the importance of land rights, disputes in the early courts were often related to land ownership and occupancy. The earliest English laws developed to address these disputes, and in the twelfth century, Norman statesmen standardized the rules governing land use and property succession. Further, they began to build and implement a code of law that would uniformly apply to all areas of the kingdom. The Norman court assumed broad judicial powers: royal judges rode circuits, touring the country and deciding cases. Critically, their determinations were largely based upon a central set of rules rather than upon varying local customs. One such rule prohibited the retrial of a defendant for the same offense.[9] Over time, the law became standardized into a consolidated code. The early common law began to take shape, with a unified set of rules to guide the resolution of cases.

The Magna Carta and the Supremacy of the Law

In 1215, England was ruled by King John, a great-great grandson of William the Conqueror. John fought Philip II of France for control of Normandy, and repeatedly pressed his barons for resources for his campaigns. In addition, he used the legal system to maximize revenue, demanding bribes to guarantee

---

7   Robin Fleming, *Kings and Lords in Conquest England* 211 (1991).
8   One law in effect testifies to this unrest. When a man was found dead, he was presumed to be Norman. If the relatives of the deceased could not successfully establish a "presentment of Englishry," then the community had to pay a substantial fine. No payment was required for the death of an English person. Frederick Coyne Hamil, "Presentment of Englishry and the Murder Fine," 12 *Speculum: J. of Mediaeval Studies* 285 (1937).
9   The old pleas of *autrefois convict* (formerly convicted) and *autrefois acquit* (formerly acquitted) were both defenses to prosecution. Akhil Reed Amar, "Double Jeopardy Law Made Simple," 106 *Yale L. J.* 1814 (1997).

outcomes in critical cases. When the king's costly military campaigns failed, the barons revolted. The king had disavowed the feudal contract by treating his vassal lords unjustly, and his failures in war had squandered their resources. The barons renounced their feudal ties, and led by Robert Fitzwalter, they captured London.

The great legal contract **Magna Carta**[10] resulted from an effort to resolve the dispute and restore peace. The purpose of its provisions was to limit the rights of the king over the barons. However, its content encompassed broader ideas. Clauses 39 and 40 are the most famous:

> (39.) No free man[11] shall be seized and imprisoned, dispossessed, outlawed, exiled, or ruined in any way, nor in any way proceeded against, except by the lawful judgment of his peers and the law of the land.

> (40.) To no one will we sell, to no one will we deny or delay right or justice.

Clause 45 requires the appointment of learned and reliable officials:

> (45.) We will appoint as justices, constables, sheriffs, and other officials, only men that know the law of the realm and are minded to keep it well.[12]

The legal protections included in the Magna Carta were remarkable: a prohibition against wrongful imprisonment, open access to courts, and a commitment to apply the law to every free person. However, its undergirding premise was revolutionary: the authority of the king could be confined by a legal document, and therefore he—like all other persons—was subject to the law. The law bound even the king.

The Magna Carta did not resolve the tensions between the king and the barons.[13] However, its symbolic legacy grew, and its contents were revised and renewed by successive monarchs. For example, Edward I, grandson of King John, confirmed it by declaring:

> Know ye ... that the Great Charter of Liberties ... shall be kept in every point without breach.... [and] sent under our seal to our justices ... and to all sheriffs of shires, and to all our other officers, and to all our cities throughout the realm ... [and it will be published and] observed in all points, and that our justices, sheriffs, mayors, and other officials who ... have to administer the

---

10   Magna Carta means "the great charter" in Latin, an appellation that distinguishes it from other charters.
11   Free men of the time included knights, barons, and free peasants (as opposed to the unfree peasants, called villeins). A free person was permitted to travel and was not required to work his lord's land.
12   Courts continue to reference these provisions. For example, In *Gordon v. Justice Court*, 12 Cal.3d 323 (1974), the California Supreme Court cited this clause as requiring a competent judge to preside over a criminal trial where the sentence could include incarceration. *Gordon*, 12 Cal.3d at 326.
13   Pope Innocent III declared it void within months, and the First Barons' War (supported by Louis, king of France) followed. When John died of dysentery in 1216, the Barons sought peace.

FIGURE 2.1 Magna Carta

law of the land, shall allow the said charters in pleas before them and judgments in all their points ... the Great Charter of Liberties [shall be adopted] as common law ... for the relief of our people. [Emphasis added.]

Edward I followed the ancient tradition of publishing his legal code for the people to see. Accordingly, the provisions of the Magna Carta became part of the common law of the United Kingdom. Much later, the essence of clauses 39 and 40 appeared in the Fifth and Fourteenth Amendments of the United States Constitution, which declare that the federal and state governments shall not deprive a person of "life, liberty or property without due process of law."[14]

Legal Reasoning and Legal Precedent in the Common Law

As English law became more cohesive and widely administered, scholars reached for a way to memorialize it. In 1235, Henry de Bracton published a guide to law and procedure, *De legibus et consuetudinibus Angliae* (On the Laws and Customs of England). It provided a systemic explanation of the law for practitioners

---

14   *See* John P. Kaminski and Richard B. Bernstein, *The Bill of Rights*, in *Roots of the Republic: American Founding Documents Interpreted* 423 (Stephen L. Schechter, ed., 1990). *See also Magna Carta Commemoration Essays*, Henry Elliott Malden, M.A. Ed., for the Royal Historical Society, 1917.

and judges.[15] Critically, Bracton included examples of how judges had applied the law in prior court cases. He added comments about those cases and about the judges who decided them. This work, accordingly, introduced lawyers to the concept of **legal reasoning** and **case law** and foreshadowed important later publications of annual reports and digests of legal cases.[16]

By the middle of the thirteenth century, the English legal system had grown, and a collection of centralized royal courts applied the common law. Different courts handled different types of cases. The King's Bench handled disputes between the king and subjects; the Court of Common Pleas adjudicated disputes between subjects; and the Court of Exchequer collected royal revenue and taxes. The Chancery, an administrative office headed by the chancellor of England, prepared all the documents needed to commence litigation in all the courts. To start a case, a specific type of claim (such as trespass) had to be stated, and litigants had to pay a fee. The responding party had the opportunity to file a reply, and then the case was heard. This process marked the creation of a uniform scheme to regulate written court pleadings.

When Edward I assumed the crown in 1272, he launched an inquest to hear complaints about abuses of power by royal administrators. He reformed the law and streamlined its administration. He also convened parliamentary sessions to update and capture the common law, creating the first written code of English statutory law.

The reign of Edward I also saw substantial changes to the legal profession. Universities did not teach the substance of the common law or the operation of the English legal system. They instead taught Roman law and canon law. Perceiving the need for formal legal education, a group of lay legal professionals established a place for such instruction in London. Students of the law lived in four residence halls near the courts: Gray's Inn, Lincoln's Inn, Inner Temple, and Middle Temple.

FIGURE 2.2 Middle Temple

Law students watched court proceedings, listened to talks given by senior barristers, discussed hypothetical cases, and read Bracton. By the end of the fifteenth century, students deemed worthy to join the legal profession as *barristers* were called to the bar by the administrators of the four Inns of Court.[17] The

---

15   Henry de Bracton was a priest and jurist who worked as a justice for King Henry II. Some quantity of the text was likely composed by William of Raleigh, a justice in Devon, and passed to Bracton. The content was influenced by the Institutiones of the Justinian Code. Notably, Bracton states that the king must be subject to the law, as the law makes the king: "there is no king (*rex*) where will (*voluntas*) rules rather than law (*lex*)." *The Cambridge History of Medieval Political Thought C.350–1450*, James Henderson Burns, Ed., Cambridge University Press 429 (1988).

16   Today, the opinions of federal trial judges, federal appellate justices, and state court appellate justices are gathered and published in volumes of legal reporters. These legal opinions are of critical importance to practitioners. Before the development of modern digital technologies, long rows of legal reporters graced the libraries of courthouses, law firms, corporations, and law schools throughout the nation.

17   The Inns of Court are still the professional associations that supervise and discipline trial lawyers in England and Wales. All barristers must belong to one of them. Like many other important institutions, they have an unfortunate history of exclusion and discrimination. England's first African barrister was Christian Frederick Cole, who was also the first Black graduate of the University of Oxford. He was admitted to the Inner Temple in 1883. The first woman to be admitted to an Inn of Court was Helena Normanton. The Middle Temple

Inns of Chancery supported legal education for students who did not wish to practice in court. Those students became known as *solicitors*.[18]

Students of the law soon found Bracton's work to be outdated. They made and circulated notes of legal arguments to capture newer practices. These notes began to be formally collated and published and came to be called Year Books. Judges and barristers referred to the reported cases in the Year Books when similar cases came along, further bolstering the key role of legal precedent in the common law. Not only was there a written legal code, but now there was a body of case law explaining how it should be applied.

The Star Chamber and the Reaffirmation of the Rule of Law

By the middle of the thirteenth century, trial by ordeal had been abolished,[19] and the use of torture in legal proceedings had come into question. In the fourteenth century, the common law courts began to refuse to authorize torture as a means of obtaining evidence. Judges felt that torture generated unreliable information, degraded those associated with it, and that persons who had not been convicted of a crime should not have to endure it. By the sixteenth century, common law courts uniformly rejected torture as a means of obtaining testimonial information.[20]

However, the English legal system faced serious operational challenges. Two rival branches of the house of Plantagenet, the houses of Lancaster (represented by a red rose) and of York (represented by a white rose), fought battles for thirty years across the countryside. The War of the Roses resulted in a general breakdown of the English justice system. It ended in 1485 when the Lancastrian Henry VII defeated King Richard II at the Battle of Bosworth Field and seized the crown. Henry VII then prudently married Elizabeth of York, uniting the claimants and founding the Tudor dynasty.

Henry VII needed to restore royal authority and calm tensions. He sent justices of the peace across the land to fortify support for the common law. In addition, to demonstrate the scope of his authority and increase the influence of the law, he created a new collection of courts. These came to be called **prerogative courts** due to their origins in royal privilege. One such court was the Court of Poor Men's Causes, created to address small civil claims filed by poorer people. It was a popular court, because the costs to start and pursue an action were much lower than in other courts.

---

admitted her in 1919 after passage of the Sex Disqualification (Removal) Act, which provided that gender should not automatically disqualify someone from a civil or judicial post.

18   The distinction continues. Today, barristers may advocate for their clients in all English courts. Solicitors may appear in some lower courts, but their practice usually consists of advising clients and drafting legal documents.

19   Ordeals continued to be used into the seventeenth century in cases involving suspected sorcery (witch hunts). *See* Robert Bartlett, *Trial by Fire and Water* (1986).

20   *See* Tom Bingham, *The Rule of Law* 15 (2010). When the Privy Council of King Charles I wanted to use torture to question the murderer of the Duke of Buckingham in 1628, the presiding judges declared its use to be contrary to the law. *See* David Jardine, *A Reading on the Use of Torture in the Criminal Law of England* 10–2 (1837).

The **Court of the Star Chamber** was at the other end of the spectrum of prerogative courts. It was originally established to enforce laws against influential people whom common law judges might hesitate to punish. It was run by a collection of the king's counselors and common law judges, who viewed their authority as flowing from the king's personal sovereign power.

As their authority came directly from the king, the Star Chamber judges believed they were not required to follow the substantive or procedural rules of the common law. They met in secret, acted upon any information received, and could impose any punishment (except execution). Most of the time, the outcome of a Star Chamber case was a fine or a term of imprisonment, but punishments could include whipping, branding, or mutilation.

At the start of the reign of King Henry VIII (son of Henry VII) in 1509, the Court of the Star Chamber was well regarded. The court performed important work and was the first legal body to recognize the subtler crimes of criminal attempt, conspiracy, and libel. But when Cardinal Thomas Wolsey and Archbishop Thomas Cranmer assumed its leadership, it became a political tool to punish those who opposed the policies of the king.

FIGURE 2.3 Private judicial examination in the Star Chamber

Critics of the Court of the Star Chamber included Sir Edward Coke, a distinguished barrister and a judge. When serving as chief justice, he publicly rejected the king's right to exercise broad prerogative powers and create legislation by proclamation. Rather, Coke believed in the even-handed application of the common law. He prepared eleven volumes of commentary on the common law and included a copy of the record of proceedings for each important case. His work comprised the only formal collection of case law at the time and was the main source for citations used by practitioners for many years.[21]

By the time Charles I became king in 1625, the Court of the Star Chamber was firmly associated with the abuse of power. Charles found it a ready tool for his purposes. As Parliament would not approve taxation measures to finance his war against Spain, Charles imposed a forced tax: his subjects would pay,

---

21   Sir Edward Coke published four volumes on the substance of English law: *The Institutes of the Lawes of England*. These covered real property, medieval statutory law, criminal law, and the jurisdiction of the English courts.

or they would be imprisoned. Parliament rebelled, finding that this law violated the spirit of the Magna Carta. Under the direction of Sir Edward Coke, Parliament prepared the historic Petition of Right of 1628 that demanded the king's recognition of four principles: 1) no taxation without Parliamentary consent; 2) no imprisonment without just cause; 3) no quartering of the king's soldiers in private homes; and 4) no martial law in peacetime.

Although Charles I agreed to accept the terms of the Petition of Right, he thereafter ignored its requirements. It remains in force, however, and its influence descends to the Third, Fifth, Sixth, and Seventh Amendments to the United States Constitution.

Rather than continuing to deal with the demands of a hostile Parliament, Charles I used the Court of the Star Chamber during the eleven years of his personal rule (when he claimed, as king by divine right, he need not consult with Parliament). In 1641, when the disagreements between the king and Parliament escalated to civil war, the Court of the Star Chamber ceased operations. Following bloody conflicts, the king's supporters were defeated, and Charles I was tried for high crimes. Despite his protests that no court could adjudicate a case against a king,[22] he was sentenced to death and executed. The struggles between the English Stuart monarchs and Parliament finally ended when James II, the last Stuart monarch in the direct male line, was deposed in 1688 in the Glorious Revolution.[23] The 1689 Bill of Rights that followed terminated the crown's prerogative practices of interfering with the courts and suspending the law without the consent of Parliament. The monarchy was now subject to the will of Parliament, and the people were theoretically free from arbitrary governmental practices. The English legal system was maturing to become a rule of law.

The Creation of the Court of Equity

Through war and peace, the common law persisted, increasing in scope and complexity through centuries of judicial decisions. The English law courts had become quite different from the civil law courts of Europe, which declined to apply the doctrine of *stare decisis*.[24] However, the increasing cohesiveness of the common law left little room for judicial flexibility. Outside of the prerogative courts, relief in civil cases was limited to the payment of money damages or the recovery of land or property. Sometimes, these awards were insufficient to provide an injured party with just redress.

There was one additional option for the litigant who believed justice had not been served in their case: they had the right to petition the king for extraordinary relief. The office of the lord chancellor, the highest-ranking among the English officers of state, reviewed these claims. Over time, the chancellor's

---

22 He said: "A king cannot be tried by any superior jurisdiction on earth." Whitelocke Bulstrode, *Memorials of the English Affairs* 502 (1853).

23 It was also called the Bloodless Revolution. The Catholic James II was replaced by his Protestant daughter, Mary II, and her husband, William III, the prince of Orange.

24 For example, in France, each case is decided on an individual basis, referencing applicable statutes and the judge's interpretation of those statutes. Further, judges take the lead in preparing a case for court, and juries are not used except in a *court d'assises* (Assize Court) that hears felony cases. James W. Garner, "Criminal Procedure in France," 25 *Yale L. J.* 262 (1916).

jurisdiction developed into a separate Court of Chancery that addressed cases where strict application of the common law led to hardship or unfairness.

In order to achieve just outcomes, the Court of Chancery created a supplemental collection of new remedies and forms of relief. Over time, as the decisions of the Court of Chancery were reported and studied, these became the modern collection of **equitable remedies**.[25]

Litigants who went to the Court of Chancery appreciated the broader set of available remedies. They also found that the court was more efficient and less expensive than the regular common law courts. Predictably, the Court of Chancery expanded rapidly, gaining prestige and revenue.

The common law judges objected to the loss of cases and, more particularly, to the loss of income that resulted. Finally, a royal decree declared that the Chancery could only accept a case if an award of damages from a common law court would not provide an adequate remedy.

The equitable remedies offered by the Court of Chancery endured and became part of the law of the land. They remain today as a special collection of remedies in American and English law that are only accessible to certain litigants who cannot be restored to justice through an award of money damages. Judges who preside over American courts of equity have more flexibility to provide suitable remedies than judges who preside over common law courts. This flexibility descends directly from jurisdiction enjoyed by the old chancellors of England.

---

25 The two main early remedies in the Court of Chancery were *injunction* and *specific performance*. An injunction is an order that requires someone to stop (or start) doing something. Specific performance is an order requiring someone to fulfill their obligations under a contract. These remedies were not available in common law courts.

Oliver Wendell Holmes Jr.

Associate Justice, United States Supreme Court (1902–1932)

Acting Chief Justice, United States Supreme Court (January 1930-February 1930)

Prior to his elevation to the US Supreme Court, Justice Holmes sat on the Supreme Judicial Court of Massachusetts as both an associate and chief justice. He authored *The Common Law*, a compendium of lectures he delivered on the Anglo-American common law, ranging from torts and crimes to contracts and property.

FIGURE 2.4   Justice Oliver Wendell Holmes Jr.

Once on the Supreme Court, Justice Holmes rejected legal formalism, which requires judges to apply the law without addressing public policy or social interests.

(continued)

Justice Holmes stressed that the Constitution is an experiment, and that the states should be permitted to operate as they see fit within its guidelines. While some of his free speech opinions have been (at least partially) overturned since his tenure on the Court, and his support of eugenics has been widely condemned, Justice Holmes nevertheless left a profound mark upon United States law.

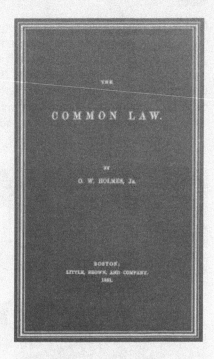

FIGURE 2.5   Holmes's *The Common Law*

FIGURE 2.6   Engraving of the Court of Chancery

Conclusion and Introduction of Law Lab

The common law of England became the foundation for state and federal legal codes in the United States. The common law stands as a body of judge-made and judicially interpreted rules that are separate from statutory and regulatory rules. Many of its principles guided the Framers as they constructed the documents that created the nation. From the common law, we gained the use of legal precedent, which gives the law stability and predictability. The common law also provided the concept of due process, the right to challenge the lawfulness of a sentence of imprisonment, and the prohibition against double jeopardy. Among other rights, they appear in the United States Constitution and in the constitutions of all the states.

In addition, the common law gave us the doctrine of sovereign immunity, the idea that the Crown (or government) could not be required to appear in court without its consent. Rooted in the supposedly divine rule of kings, the doctrine became part of the common law and traveled to America with the colonists. In its modern iteration, it permits the federal government, the states, and the Tribes to stand aloof from judicial process. Thus, in the United States, the federal government, the states, and the Tribes may decide if, where, and how they may be sued. The locations and qualities of their chosen venues may not ideally align with the interests of the litigants who wish to file suit.

The operation of the common law in the United States is not seamless. Its principles came from England's historic unitary system of government. Sometimes, applying common law precepts to our federal system can present challenges. One challenge arises simply because we have a federal system, where state, national, and Tribal governments are all separate sovereigns. While in many places each sovereign's authority is entirely distinct, in some areas, authority overlaps. For example, some crimes can result in violations of state law, federal law, and also Tribal law.

In this week's Law Lab, you are members of the Supreme Court of the United States, an exalted (if remote) descendant of the old common law courts of England. You preside over a collection of state, federal, and Tribal courts associated with separate sovereigns. You have agreed to review a case involving a federally recognized Tribe that has been sued in state court. The person who filed suit contends that the Tribe breached a contract and wants the state court to adjudicate the case. However, the Tribe has not consented to appear in state court. It operates its own Tribal court and maintains that this case belongs in that court.

Your law clerks have prepared a memorandum about the case, and it is provided on the next pages. There are several sections. First, the memorandum describes the facts leading up to the case in the Factual Background section. In the Procedural Posture section, the memorandum tells what has happened in the case so far. The Issue section describes the key questions for the Court, and the applicable legal precedent follows in the next sections. Finally, the memorandum describes the arguments made in legal briefs filed by the litigating parties and by other entities that are interested in the outcome of the case.

Review all this information, think about the parties' positions, and decide which arguments matter the most. Consider the scope of and reasons for sovereign immunity and the rights of those who seek justice. Debate your position and make your ruling. What you determine will become precedent across the land, guiding the operation of the justice systems of the nation.

Sir William Blackstone

Sir William Blackstone was an English jurist and politician. He was born in 1723 to a middle-class family in London. He studied law in the Middle Temple of the Inns of Court, and was admitted to the bar in 1746. Initially an indifferent advocate, he was drawn into the administration of Oxford University, where he flourished.

In 1753, Blackstone began lecturing on English law at Oxford. This marked the first occasion where lectures on English law had been given at an English university. His initial treatise, *An Analysis of the Laws of England*, was a summary of his lectures for his students' use. The book sold out, and Blackstone's quality was recognized. He was endowed as Oxford's inaugural Vinerian Professor of English Law.

Blackstone's second treatise, *A Discourse on the Study of Law*, ensured his fame, and he was elected a member of Parliament. But these successes merely preceded his crowning achievement: his four-volume *Commentaries on the Laws of England*, which remained in production for over 150 years.

The *Commentaries* provide a graceful and coherent overview of English law. Some of the Framers consulted its volumes, and the *Commentaries* became the chief source of knowledge of the common law in the United States after the Revolutionary War. Both Supreme Court Chief Justice John Marshall and President Abraham Lincoln read and relied upon the *Commentaries* to support their legal arguments.

Despite the passage of years, the *Commentaries* are still cited in Supreme Court decisions and referred to in law school texts. It was Blackstone who first said, "It is better that ten guilty persons escape than that one innocent suffer." This maxim, called "Blackstone's Ratio," continues to be discussed in American law schools today.

FIGURE 2.7 Statue of William Blackstone outside the E. Barrett Prettman Federal Courthouse

Supreme Court Justice Law Lab

MEMORANDUM

To: The Honorable Chief Justice and Associate Justices of the United States Supreme Court

From: The Law Clerks of the Supreme Court

Re: *Ruisseau v. Pokagon Band of Potawatomi Tribe*, On Review Following Grant of Petition for Certiorari

Your Honors:

Please allow this summary to assist you as you prepare for deliberations in the above-referenced matter. The footnotes contain references to the supporting documents, should you care to review them.

Factual Background[1]

The Potawatomi Tribe

The Potawatomi are Native American peoples of the Great Lakes and Midwestern regions of the United States. Historically, they were farmers and hunters. They grew staple crops, fished for trout and salmon, hunted deer and elk, and tapped maple trees for syrup. Along with the Ojibwe and Odawa nations, they were members of the Council of the Three Fires, a long-standing alliance of culturally related peoples. Pushed to the west by settler encroachment, the Potawatomi were compelled to cede their lands by the United States' Indian Removal Act, which directed that all American Indians be relocated to areas west of the Mississippi River. The 1833 Treaty of Chicago set forth the conditions of the removal of the Potawatomi, and in 1837 most of the

---

1   The historic details about the Pokagon Band are accurate, if abbreviated. The dispute, like those described in the other Law Labs, is entirely fictitious.

Potawatomi completed a devastating journey called the Trail of Death that led them to Nebraska, Kansas, and Oklahoma. A few bands remained behind, some in hiding.

One small Potawatomi band demonstrated an attachment to Catholicism, and was allowed by treaty to remain in its homeland. Leopold Pokagon was a key leader of this group, and its descendants became the Pokagon Band of the Potawatomi Indians. They moved to Silver Creek Township, near Dowagiac, Michigan, and following painful legal maneuvers, gained the right to remain. After many years of work, in 1994 the Pokagon Band of Potawatomi achieved federal recognition as a sovereign Tribal nation. This Tribe is now one of twelve federally recognized Tribes in Michigan and one of 574 such Tribes in the United States. The Tribe operates three casinos, including the Four Winds Casino Resort in New Buffalo, Michigan.

The Contract Dispute

The construction and maintenance of the band's casinos and other properties have been profitable for local vendors. The Pokagon Band asserts that it has worked with many vendors in Indiana and in Michigan and has given those vendors hundreds of millions of dollars. Its casinos have made the Tribe an important community employer.

Using some of the revenue raised by its casinos, the Pokagon Band has recently begun to further develop its property in Dowagiac, Michigan. It has constructed a new health clinic, a cultural center, and new residences for some Tribal members. It has also become interested in restoring the Dowagiac River where it abuts Tribal lands. In the early 1900s, the river was dredged and straightened and lost its natural flood plains. The planned restoration will restore hydrological function and dramatically increase river habitat, benefiting many wetland and aquatic species.

As part of the restoration project, the Pokagon Band entered into a contract with a hydrologist, Dr. Aristo Ruisseau, to perform tasks related to a site study. The work was to be done by a certain date, specified in a written contract. Payment was to be made upon completion of the work. The contract was silent as to any dispute resolution procedures.

According to representatives of the Pokagon Band, Dr. Ruisseau did not complete the work specified in the contract. The Tribe asserts that the work was essentially abandoned by Dr. Ruisseau not long after it was begun.

Dr. Ruisseau, however, asserts that he required additional information and special permits from the Tribe to fulfill his contractual obligations. He claims that the Tribe did not provide the information or the permits. He alleges that the Tribe's failure to do these things breached the contract.

Procedural Posture

Dr. Ruisseau filed a lawsuit seeking money damages for breach of contract in Cass County Circuit Court, a Michigan state court in the county where the Tribe's main offices are located. Dr. Ruisseau argued that his case should be heard in Michigan state court. In response, the Pokagon Band filed a motion to dismiss his lawsuit. The Tribe claimed that, as a sovereign Tribal nation, it is not required to respond to cases filed against it in any state court unless it consents to do so, and it has not consented to do so. The Pokagon Band operates a Tribal court, and contract claims against the Tribe may be heard in that court.

Following precedent set by this Court, the Cass County Court agreed with the Pokagon Band and consequently dismissed Dr. Ruisseau's state court case. Dr. Ruisseau appealed the dismissal of his case to the Michigan Court of Appeals. The Court of Appeals affirmed the propriety of the dismissal. Dr. Ruisseau fared no better before the Michigan Supreme Court, which also confirmed that the Pokagon Band was not required to appear in state court. Dr. Ruisseau then filed a Petition for Certiorari,[2] which this Court granted.

Issue: Sovereign Immunity of Tribal Nations in Contract Cases

This Court must decide, in the context of a contract dispute, if the sovereign immunity of the Pokagon Band of the Potawatomi protects the Tribe from suit in state court. The Court must consider whether its 1998 decision in *Kiowa Tribe of Oklahoma v. Manufacturing Technologies, Inc.*, 523 U.S. 751 (1998), should continue to stand as binding precedent.[3]

American Law on Sovereign Immunity

State and Federal Sovereign Immunity

Historically, sovereign immunity referred to the notion that the king could not be sued without his consent. The power of government rested with the sovereign, and no person had the right to challenge the king's authority. Sovereign immunity meant that the king could not be held accountable in courts of law for any wrongdoing.

In the United States, although the government rests with the people, a remnant of the doctrine of sovereign immunity remains. Recent court cases confirm that the federal government "is immune from suit unless it has waived its immunity," and waivers of sovereign immunity "are to be construed narrowly."[4]

Some scholars argue that the doctrine has no place in the United States, as it permits a common law doctrine to supersede the Constitution, which declares itself (along with laws and treaties) to be "the Supreme law of the Land."[5] In addition, sovereign immunity could permit the avoidance of federal and state accountability for misdeeds, which is inconsistent with the ends of justice.[6] However, there are practical reasons to perpetuate the doctrine. Sovereign immunity gives governments the space to consider meaningful policy changes that are widely supported, rather than hastily implementing policies in response to actual or threatened individual lawsuits. In addition, sovereign immunity protects

---

2   A Petition for Certiorari is a request that the Supreme Court accept a case for review. The Supreme Court is under no obligation to grant a Petition for Certiorari.

3   Citations to United States court cases follow a standard format. Each citation begins with the names of the parties, then identifies the legal reporter (the book of court opinions) where the opinion may be found. The reporter's name is abbreviated to a standard format. The volume number of the reporter appears before the abbreviation, and the page number of the case listed after the abbreviation. Finally, the citation notes the year that the opinion was issued. Thus, the citation *Kiowa Tribe of Oklahoma v. Manufacturing Technologies, Inc.*, 523 U.S. 751 (1998), tells the reader that the case is located in volume 523 of the U.S. Reports at page number 751, and that the Court's opinion was issued in 1998. *See The Bluebook: A Uniform System of Citation* (21st ed., 2020).

4   *Price v. United States*, 69 F. 3d 46 at 49 (5th Cir. 1995).

5   U.S. Const. art. VI.

6   *See* Erwin Chemerinsky, "Against Sovereign Immunity," 53 *Stanford Law Review* 1201–1224 (2001).

governments, their personnel, and their financial resources from the burden and expense of potentially voluminous and meritless litigation.

This Court has confirmed that, in addition to the federal government, the states possess sovereign immunity and may not be sued in their own courts without their consent. Further, the states generally may not be sued in federal court unless they agree to appear.[7]

Both federal and state governments have chosen to waive sovereign immunity to some extent. They have created special courts where injured persons may present some types of claims. In addition, the Federal Tort Claims Act permits suits against the federal government for certain types of harm caused by federal employees, and the Tucker Act waives immunity for claims that arise out of certain federal contracts. Further, there is no federal sovereign immunity in refund cases filed by taxpayers, and Congress enacted legislation waiving federal immunity for patent infringement claims. There are, however, limitations in the scope of relief available and in the places where lawsuits may be filed.

The Immunity of Tribal Nations

Since the Cherokee Cases of the early 1830s, Tribal nations have had the status of "domestic dependent nations" under federal law.[8] This means that federally recognized Native American Tribes have the right to make their own civil and criminal laws and to have Tribal courts adjudicate disputes under their laws. It also means that the Tribes generally enjoy sovereign immunity in federal, state, or Tribal court. This Court has recently affirmed the rights of the Tribes granted through historic treaties with the United States.[9]

A Tribe's immunity from suit exists unless it is withdrawn by treaty or congressional act.[10] In addition, like the states and the federal government, a Tribe may consent to be sued, and it may also agree to appear in a particular court.

The Key Precedent: 1998 Kiowa Tribe Case

A contract dispute involving the Kiowa Tribe of Oklahoma yielded the key ruling that applies to the current case involving the Pokagon Band. The Kiowa Tribe's industrial development commission agreed to buy stock from Manufacturing Technologies, Inc., for the sum of $285,000. The contract signed by the parties stated that "nothing ... subjects or limits the sovereign rights of the Kiowa Tribe of Oklahoma." When the Tribe defaulted, Manufacturing Technologies sued for damages in Oklahoma state court. It argued that Tribal immunity should be confined to legal transactions made on reservations and to Tribal governmental activities. The trial court disagreed and dismissed the case, finding that the sovereign immunity of the Kiowa Tribe precluded the state court suit, even though the contract was signed off Tribal lands.

---

7   *Hans v. Louisiana*, 134 U.S. 1 (1890).
8   The Marshall Trilogy of Cherokee Cases defines the rights of Indian Tribes under federal law and the relationship between the Tribes and the federal government. They are *Johnson v. M'Intosh*, 21 U.S. 543 (1823), *Cherokee Nation v. Georgia*, 30 U.S. 1 (1831), and *Worcester v. Georgia*, 31 U.S. 515 (1832).
9   *McGirt v. Oklahoma*, 591 U.S.___ (2020).
10 *Iron Crow v. Oglala Sioux Tribe*, 231 F.2nd 89 (8th Cir. 1956).

Leopold Pokagon and the Pokagon Band

Leopold Pokagon was the spokesperson for the Pokagon Band, the name given to four villages of Catholic Potawatomi. He was born around 1775, and some details of his life are known only through the Pokagon Band's oral histories.

Pokagon became a Tribal leader around 1826. His most pressing concern was Indian removal, the United States governmental policy of forced relocation of Native Americans from their Tribal lands. Pokagon knew connections with politically important organizations such as the Catholic Church could prove vital. He arranged to be baptized, along with his wife and a large number of Tribal members, and accepted the residency of a mission priest. Pokagon emphasized his followers' conversion during negotiations of the 1933 Treaty of Chicago, securing his followers' right to remain. Then, he used money paid under the treaty to purchase lands for his people, taking title in the same way as neighboring private landowners.

Despite these measures, the United States government's military attempted to remove the Pokagon Band. In the last year of his life, Pokagon traveled to Detroit and convinced Michigan Supreme Court Associate Justice Epaphroditus Ransom to write an order halting the military's actions. This effort permitted the Pokagon Band to stay on their lands.

The name "Pokagon" (poké-igan) means "the rib" or "a shield" in Potawatomi. The Pokagon Band maintains that, just as a rib protects the heart, Leopold Pokagon protected his people.

Leopold Pokagon

FIGURE 2.8 Leopold Pokagon

The case was appealed and rose to this Court. Justice Anthony Kennedy wrote the majority opinion, which affirmed that the sovereign immunity enjoyed by Indian Tribes extends to civil suits on contracts, whether those are made on or off the reservation, and whether they concern governmental or commercial activities. Justice John Paul Stevens wrote a dissenting opinion, arguing that a state should be able to regulate Tribal dealings that take place off Tribal lands.

Briefs

In addition to the briefs filed by the parties, the United States attorney general's office filed an *amicus curiae* brief.[11] This submission argues that the doctrine of Tribal sovereign immunity is firmly fixed in American jurisprudence and should not be modified. Other Tribal nations have also filed briefs in support of the Pokagon Band. The briefs submitted by the Tribal nations argue that their right of sovereignty must be fully preserved to ensure their right to self-government. An inherent quality of Tribal self-governance is the ability to decide when and where a Tribe may be subjected to litigation, and removing that power would reduce the Tribes' status to that of subject nations. In addition, revoking Tribal sovereign immunity would require Tribes to shoulder additional burdens and expenses that they cannot afford financially. Further, the Pokagon Band has agreed that this case may be litigated in its Tribal Court, and so Dr. Ruisseau's dispute will be adjudicated. The record on appeal does not contain any facts indicating that any ruling issued by the Pokagon Band would be unjust.

The Small Business Association of Michigan has filed an *amicus curiae* brief supporting Dr. Ruisseau's position. The briefs filed by and for Dr. Ruisseau argue that, without recourse to state courts, contracts with Tribes in Michigan may become difficult to enforce. While the Pokagon Band's internal Tribal Court may competently serve the interests

---

11   *Amicus curiae* is Latin for "friend of the court." Amicus briefs are filed by those who are not parties to a case, but who have an interest in its outcome.

of Tribal members, it does not have the same experience with complex contract matters as the state court. Further, the Tribe cannot reasonably be expected to assume an impartial posture with respect to litigation that involves a Tribal contract. As a citizen of the State of Michigan, Dr. Ruisseau should be allowed to access the expertise and neutrality of state court. Perpetuating the sovereign immunity of Tribal courts will leave Michigan businesses without an appropriate legal remedy in Michigan courts and could result in Dr. Ruisseau suffering a substantial and uncompensated financial loss. The likely downstream result would be a reduction in opportunities for the Tribes to engage in commerce and sign contracts with non-Tribal businesses. This outcome, the briefs argue, would be unfortunate for the Tribes as well as for outside businesses.

Conclusion

With the history of sovereign immunity and the arguments of the parties firmly in mind, this Court must debate the merits of the positions of the parties in this matter. The Court must decide whether to maintain the legal precedent of Tribal sovereign immunity established by the 1998 *Kiowa Tribe* case or overturn that precedent and establish another rule. If sovereign immunity is maintained, this case will be adjudicated in the Pokagon Band's Tribal Court. If this Court finds that sovereign immunity should not apply, then the case will remain in Michigan state court.

Here are questions to guide the Court's analysis:

What are the reasons to support continuing sovereign immunity for the Pokagon Band? Does this Court find that those reasons have merit? Which reasons resonate the most strongly?

What are the reasons supporting Dr. Ruisseau's claim that sovereign immunity should not apply to his dispute? Do those reasons have merit? If so, which seem most important?

Consider the key arguments from both sides, and weigh and discuss their relative merits. Which side has the more compelling position, and why? Once the Court has discussed this case, its members will vote on which party should prevail. In deciding this case, this Court will also determine whether the precedent in the *Kiowa Tribe* case should stand. The findings of this Court will become binding precedent throughout the nation.

Following your discussion, the Court's scribe will prepare the opinion as to which side should prevail. The scribe will also identify which justices supported the majority view, and which (if any) dissented.

We hope that this memorandum assists the Court in this matter. Please let us know if we can provide any additional information to assist with deliberations or the preparation of the opinion. As always, your law clerks are eager to be helpful.

CREDITS
Fig. 2.1: Source: https://commons.wikimedia.org/wiki/File:Magna_Carta_%28British_Library_Cotton_MS_Augustus_II.106%29.jpg.
Fig. 2.2: Source: https://commons.wikimedia.org/wiki/File:Middle_Temple_by_Thomas_Shepherd_c.1830.jpg.
Fig. 2.3: Source: https://commons.wikimedia.org/wiki/File:Viviana_examined_by_the_Earl_of_Salisbury,_and_the_Privy_Council_in_the_Star_Chamber.png.
Fig. 2.4: Source: https://commons.wikimedia.org/wiki/File:Justice_Oliver_Wendell_Holmes_standing.jpg.
Fig. 2.5: Source: https://commons.wikimedia.org/wiki/File:The%2BCommon%2BLaw_Cover.JPG.
Fig. 2.6: Source: https://commons.wikimedia.org/wiki/File:Court_of_Chancery_edited.jpg.
Fig. 2.7: Source: https://www.gsa.gov/cdnstatic/Blackstone2.jpg.
Fig. 2.8: Source: https://commons.wikimedia.org/wiki/File:Leopold_Pokagon.jpg.

CHAPTER 3

The Composition of the United States Constitution

A free government is a complicated piece of machinery, the nice and exact adjustment of whose springs, wheels, and weights, is not yet well comprehended by the artists of the age, and still less by the people.
—John Adams to Thomas Jefferson, May 19, 1821

Introduction

The United States Constitution is the nation's founding document, and its terms have guided its operation for over two centuries. The Constitution defines the three branches of government, details the powers of each branch, and establishes the checks and balances that support their proper function. It also secures the liberty and due process rights of the nation's citizens, ensuring that those rights endure.

The Constitution begins with the Preamble, which sets forth its purposes:

> We the people of the United States, in Order to form a more perfect Union, establish Justice, ensure domestic tranquility, provide for the common defense, promote the general Welfare, and secure the Blessings of Liberty to ourselves and our Posterity, do ordain and establish this Constitution for the United States of America.

The Preamble identifies the charterers of the Constitution as the people of the United States, and declares that the Constitution was created to benefit them in a variety of ways. One of those ways is to "establish Justice," a theme that resonates from the earliest codes promoted by the ancient kings. In the United States, however, it is the people who are in charge of this effort.

Designing the nation's government was not a simple task. The Framers had to determine the structure and obligations of each of the branches of the federal government, while considering the rights of the states and of the people. Many provisions of the Constitution were vigorously

FIGURE 3.1 Preamble of the United States Constitution

debated, and its ultimate language was the result of political compromises. Some of those compromises had serious downstream consequences.

In this chapter, we explore the substance of the document that the Framers wrote. We also consider some of the challenges they encountered, including the correct boundaries of governmental authority and the proper division of powers among different branches of government. Finally, in this week's Law Lab, you will address a case involving the scope of powers of the executive branch. As Supreme Court justices, you will decide whether the president's use of powers in a particular setting is consistent with the provisions of the United States Constitution.

UNITED STATES CONSTITUTION KEY TERMS

The following key terms are defined in this chapter. They are also defined in the Glossary.

Advice and Consent Clause	Full Faith and Credit Clause	Privileges and Immunities
Appointments Clause	General Welfare Clause	Clause
Bicameral	Impeachment	Reception Clause
Bills of Attainder	Implied Powers	Recommendations Clause
Case or Controversy Clause	Incorporation of the Bill of	Reserved Powers
Commerce Clause	Rights	State of the Union Clause
Connecticut Compromise	Legal Pragmatism	Strict Construction
Domestic Emoluments Clause	Living Constitution	Supremacy Clause
Enumerated Powers	Necessary and Proper Clause	Take Care Clause
Executive Order	Originalism	Textualism
Extradition	Power of Judicial Review	Three-Fifths Compromise
Foreign Emoluments Clause	Presidential Emergency Powers	Treason
Fugitive	Presidential Veto Power	

The Creation of the United States Constitution

FIGURE 3.2   The Assembly Room of Assembly Hall in Philadelphia, Pennsylvania, site of the 1787 Constitutional Convention

During the summer of 1787, fifty-five Framers came as delegates to Philadelphia, Pennsylvania, for the Constitutional Convention. They came to revise the 1777 Articles of Confederation and Perpetual Union, which had been drawn up to recognize the United States as a new nation. The Articles had served an important purpose: without formal recognition, it would have been difficult for the United States to gain foreign allies and negotiate treaties and trade contracts.

However, it soon became apparent that simply revising the Articles of Confederation was not appropriate. The Articles emphasized state sovereignty and independence and did not permit the national government to operate effectively. For example, under the Articles, the national government did not have the power of taxation and could not coordinate matters of commerce and transportation. This meant that Congress could not compel the states to support the Revolutionary War effort. As a result, George Washington's Continental Army had grave difficulties obtaining critical supplies. In addition, the national government had been unable to respond during Shays' Rebellion, a significant uprising in Massachusetts in 1786. With these experiences in mind, the Framers decided to abandon the Articles and create a new model for the nation's government. They then began to debate the structure and features of that new government.

Baron de Montesquieu and the Separation of Powers

Baron de Montesquieu was a French political philosopher whose contributions to political theory profoundly impacted the composition of the United States Constitution. In the span of his lifetime (1689–1755), Montesquieu witnessed transformative political events that inspired him to consider preventative measures against governmental abuses of power.

Montesquieu's early works, including his 1721 novel *Persian Letters*, established him as one of the great Enlightenment thinkers. Most scholars consider his masterpiece to be his 1748 treatise, *The Spirit of the Laws*. This treatise is widely credited with introducing the theory of separation of powers, now a key feature of constitutions around the world. In *The Spirit of the Laws*, Montesquieu defines three forms of governmental power—legislative, executive, and judicial—and argues that each should be confined to different governing bodies. In theory, this separation of powers would prevent a national government from maintaining the kind of oppressive, absolute power that Montesquieu termed "despotism." This concept was a powerful influence on the Framers, particularly James Madison, who relied on Montesquieu's philosophy in defining separate and balanced roles for each of the three branches of America's national government.

FIGURE 3.3 Charles-Louis de Secondat, Baron de La Brède et de Montesquieu

Key components of the debate included ways to confine the power of the federal government, protect state independence, and promote individual rights. The Framers considered their experiences as crown subjects, thought about the common law, and pondered the key provisions of the Magna Carta. They had before them the examples of the state constitutions and the writings of jurists and philosophers, including William Blackstone, Edward Coke, John Locke, and Montesquieu. With these in mind, the Framers set out to create a document that would balance the requirements of federal authority with state independence and the promise of individual liberty. Concerned about overreach, they separated the power of the federal government into legislative, executive, and judicial branches and included checks and balances that would protect each branch from undue control by another.

Several issues quickly came to the fore. A major issue involved the institution of slavery. Delegates from Northern states argued that slavery was morally repugnant and should not be tolerated in the new nation. In response, Southern delegates announced that they would abandon the convention unless slavery and the slave trade were perpetuated.

In addition, delegates argued about how to properly derive the number of each state's representatives for the new federal legislature. After some discussion, the Connecticut delegation came up with the **Connecticut Compromise,**[1] which would divide the national legislature into two chambers, making it **bicameral**. There remained the question of how to arrange representation in the two chambers. The Northern states sought to tie the number of representatives to the free population in each state, while the Southern states wanted to include enslaved persons in the count in order to enlarge Southern influence.

Finally, delegate James Wilson proposed what became known as the **Three-Fifths Compromise**. Three-Fifths

---

1   The Connecticut Compromise is also known as the Great Compromise of 1787, or the Sherman Compromise (after Connecticut delegate Roger Sherman, who proposed a bicameral legislature).

of a state's enslaved population would be included along with all its free population for apportionment purposes in the House of Representatives. Accordingly, representation would be tied to population in the House of Representatives. Representation would, however, be weighted equally among the states in the Senate. Thus, each state—no matter its size—would have two senators, but the number of representatives would vary according to a state's population.[2]

Having resolved the key issues about the representation in the federal government, the delegates began to craft the provisions of the new Constitution.

The Structure of the United States Constitution

As originally enacted, the main text of the Constitution consists of seven Articles. The first three Articles focus on the powers and operation of the three branches of government: legislative, executive, and judicial. The next three Articles deal with federalism, describing the relationships of the states with the federal government and the rights and responsibilities of the state governments. Finally, the last Article addresses the process of ratification. The main provisions of the Constitution are reviewed here, and the entire text is included in Appendix A.

Article I: The Powers of Congress

Article I of the Constitution vests all the national legislative powers in Congress, which consists of a Senate and a House of Representatives. The key compromises noted above appear in this Article, which stipulates that each state is to have just two senators, but representation in the House of Representative is to be based upon the population of free and enslaved persons (with three-fifths of the enslaved population included). Senators serve for six-year terms, while Members of the House serve two-year terms. Under Section 3 of Article 8, the House of Representatives has the power to bring Articles of **impeachment** against officials who have committed misconduct while in office. However, impeachment cases must be tried by the Senate.

Section 7 of Article I describes how legislation is to be enacted. Bills may originate in either chamber, except revenue bills, which must originate in the House of Representatives. When passed by both chambers, a bill goes to the president for his signature. If the president signs it, the bill becomes a law. If the president vetoes a bill, it will still become a law if two-thirds of both the House and the Senate vote to override the veto.

Article I Section 8 of the Constitution sets forth the **enumerated powers** of Congress. This Section includes the **General Welfare Clause**, which gives Congress the right to levy taxes, to pay debts,

---

2   The Thirteenth Amendment was passed in 1865. It outlawed slavery, nullifying the Three-Fifths Compromise.

Checks and Balances in the Operation of the Government

In addition to a division of power between the legislative, executive, and judicial branches of government, a system of checks and balances ensures that each branch has the ability to check the powers granted to the other two branches.

The legislative branch's lawmaking function is constrained by the president's ability to veto laws and the judicial branch's power to declare laws unconstitutional. In turn, Congress can override a presidential veto with a two-thirds vote in both the House and the Senate. It may also attempt to overturn Supreme Court decisions by passing amendments to the Constitution.

The executive branch's enforcement powers are constrained by the power of Congress to create agencies. In addition, the judicial branch has the ability to declare presidential actions unconstitutional. The president serves as commander in chief of the military, but Congress appropriates military funds and must vote on declarations of war. Congress further constrains the president by controlling the budget, confirming (or rejecting) the president's selections for federal positions, and bringing impeachment hearings when necessary.

The judicial branch, comprised of the Supreme Court and other federal courts, interprets laws and presidential actions to ensure that neither the legislative nor executive branches are acting in violation of the Constitution. This power is balanced by the president's ability to nominate federal judges and the legislative branch's power to both confirm these appointments and impeach errant judges.

and to provide for the "common defense and general Welfare" of the United States. Section 8 gives Congress the authority to borrow money; to pay the nation's debts; to establish laws governing bankruptcy and naturalization; to give inventors and authors rights to their intellectual property; to create a postal system; and to declare war and to provide for the nation's military. Section 8 also contains the important **Commerce Clause**, which bestows upon Congress the right to "regulate Commerce with foreign Nations, and among the several States, and with the Indian Tribes." In a line of cases culminating in *Wickard v. Filburn*, 317 U.S. 111 (1942), the United States Supreme Court confirmed that this clause is to be broadly interpreted, so that Congress has the power to regulate all matters that touch upon interstate commerce.[3]

Article I Section 8 also gives Congress the authority "To make all Laws which shall be necessary and proper for carrying into Execution" the powers of national government. This clause, the **Necessary and Proper Clause**, gives Congress the **implied powers** to act on the nation's behalf. This power was judicially confirmed by the Supreme Court in *McCulloch v. Maryland*, 17 U.S. 316 (1819), when the Court found that Congress had the power to incorporate a bank to serve the national government's interests, and the State of Maryland could not interfere with its operations.

Accordingly, the Constitution gives Congress a defined set of enumerated powers, as well as implied powers that are not defined but are required for Congress to do its work. All remaining powers rest with the states.[4] Thus, the states are said to have all **reserved powers**.

---

3   *Wickard* and other decisions of the New Deal era gave Congress broad legislative power under the Commerce Clause. It was not until 50 years later, in *United States v. Lopez*, 514 U.S. 549 (1995), that the Supreme Court ruled that a federal law was invalid as exceeding the authority of Congress under the Commerce Clause.

4   The Tenth Amendment made this explicit.

While Article I Section 8 describes the scope of congressional powers, Section 9 describes the limits of those powers. The writ of habeas corpus "shall not be suspended, unless when in Cases of Rebellion or Invasion the public Safety may require it." Congress may not pass *ex post facto* laws, which make acts illegal only after they were done. In addition, Section 9 prohibits Congress from passing **bills of attainder**, which use legislation to punish people who have not been formally tried. Finally, this section also includes the **Foreign Emoluments Clause**, an anti-corruption provision declaring that persons holding federal office may not accept remuneration or other benefits from foreign powers.

In establishing the powers of the federal government's legislative branch, the Framers tried to delineate grants of authority that would not be subject to misinterpretation. However, despite their efforts, vigorous debates continued. One continuing disagreement concerned the proper scope of national authority versus states' rights. On the point of slavery, this debate would later escalate and result in the Civil War.

Article II: The President and the Powers of the Executive Branch

Having addressed the legislative branch of the federal government in Article I, Article II focuses on the executive branch.

Article II Section 1 confers federal executive power on the president, who is to hold office for a term of four years. It also sets forth the qualifications that must be met for a person to be president. A president must be a natural-born citizen, at least thirty-five years of age, and must have lived in the United States for at least fourteen years.[5] The vice president shall act as president if the president resigns or cannot serve due to death or disability. Section 1 also includes the presidential oath of office and the **Domestic Emoluments Clause**, which prevents the president from receiving any remuneration other than his salary from the federal government or any state government.

The specific powers of the president are detailed in Article II Section 2. The president serves as the commander in chief of the armed forces and has the authority to negotiate treaties (which must be ratified with a two-thirds vote of the Senate). The president also may grant pardons for federal crimes.

Critically, through the **Appointments Clause**, the president has the right to appoint all members of the federal judiciary and the cabinet officers, subject only to the consent of two-thirds of the Senate, as per the **Advice and Consent Clause**.

Article II Section 3 lists the responsibilities of the office of the president. Under the **State of the Union Clause**, the president must give Congress periodic assessments of the nation's status so that Congress can properly address matters of national importance. Under the **Recommendations Clause**, the president has the duty to recommend such measures as are "necessary and expedient" for congressional

---

5   The Fourteenth Amendment adds the limitation that anyone who swore an oath to uphold the Constitution and later rebelled against the United States is not eligible for office. However, this disqualification may be lifted by a two-thirds vote of each house of Congress. In addition, the Twenty-Second Amendment prohibits anyone from serving more than two terms as president.

Presidential Pardons

In Federalist Number 74, Alexander Hamilton explained that the power to pardon in the United States Constitution was designed to be a check on the criminal justice system. It was to be exercised where a conviction was incorrect or a sentence too severe, or when the national interest requires it. A president who wishes to issue a full pardon can do so before, during, or after a federal offense is committed. Alternatively, a president can issue a reprieve, lessening the severity of a sentence or a conviction.

Interestingly, a presidential pardon may be rejected by the recipient. President Andrew Jackson pardoned George Wilson, who had been convicted of robbing the United States mails and whose partner had just been hanged. For unexplained reasons, Wilson refused the pardon, and the Supreme Court ruled that it had no power to impose it. The Court said, "A pardon is a deed ... [and] delivery is essential, and delivery is not complete

FIGURE 3.4 President Ford's pardon of former president Richard M. Nixon

consideration. The **Reception Clause** requires the president to receive all ambassadors from foreign nations. This clause has been interpreted to give the president the power to craft foreign policy and recognize foreign governments.

The president has the obligation to "take care that the laws be faithfully executed" under the **Take Care Clause**. As noted by the Supreme Court in *Printz v. United States*, 521 U.S. 898 (1997), "The Constitution does not leave to speculation who is to administer the laws enacted by Congress ..." The president accomplishes this task "personally and through officers whom he appoints ..." Further, the president may not decline to enforce laws that are constitutional; he can only use the **Presidential Veto Power** given to him in Article I Section 7. Thus, a president's refusal to follow the law is unconstitutional, as well as a violation of the rule of law.

Article III: *The Judiciary*

After addressing the legislative and executive branches in Articles I and II, the Constitution turns to the courts in Article III. Interestingly, Article III's short sections do not describe the powers and prerogatives of the Supreme Court and do not explain how the federal judiciary is to be organized. This left Congress with the task of setting up the nation's federal court system and gave the Supreme Court the opportunity to develop a strong role in national governance.

Article III Section 1 states that the federal judicial branch is to consist of the Supreme Court and any lower courts that Congress creates. The precise number of judges for the Supreme Court is not set. Federal judges are to "hold their Offices during good behavior," which has been interpreted to mean that they are appointed for life or until they resign, retire, or are impeached.

The types of cases that federal courts may adjudicate are set forth in Article III Section 2. Federal courts must hear cases arising under the provisions of the United States Constitution and under United States laws (including treaties). Federal courts also hear cases involving ambassadors

(continued)

and public ministers, citizens of foreign nations, and citizens of different states. However, the courts may only decide matters that involve "actual cases and controversies." The **Case or Controversy Clause** ensures that the courts do not issue advisory opinions, unlike the highest courts in some other countries. Article III Section 2 also requires all federal criminal cases to be tried by juries.

Article III Section 3 defines **treason** as "levying War" against the United States or supporting the government's enemies. Treason must be proven by the court testimony of multiple witnesses, and punishment may not extend to the heirs of a convicted traitor. This last clause responds to the fact that descendants of an English traitor were considered "tainted" by their ancestor's treason and often lost their own titles or land.

Today, a key feature of the courts is the **power of judicial review**, which is the right to find legislative, executive, or administrative actions to be unconstitutional. The nation's courts acquired that power through the opinion of Chief Justice John Marshall in *Marbury v. Madison*, 5 U.S. 137 (1803). In that case, the Supreme Court ruled that it has the exclusive authority to determine whether or not a law is constitutional. This gave the nation's courts the ability to invalidate actions taken by members of the nation's executive and legislative branches. While not granted in Article III, this power has become firmly rooted in American law. It is undisputed that today's courts have the power to find presidential actions, as well as laws, to be unconstitutional.

Article IV: The States and the Citizens

Having dealt with Congress, the presidency, and the courts, in Article IV the Constitution addresses the relationships among the states and between the states and the federal government.

Article IV opens with two key clauses. The first is the **Full Faith and Credit Clause**, which binds states to recognize public acts, records, and court proceedings from other states. Thus, a marriage or trial judgment in one

without acceptance. It may then be rejected by the person to whom it is tendered ..." *United States v. Wilson*, 32 U.S. 150 (1833). Thus, Wilson's conviction remained in place. Wilson served a ten-year sentence and then accepted a pardon from President Martin Van Buren.[6]

The only president to receive a pardon is Richard Nixon, who was granted full clemency by his successor, President Gerald Ford, for any crimes he committed against the United States while holding office. Ford's administration deemed the pardon necessary to save the nation from the prospect of trying a former president.

---

6   Untitled Note, *The National Gazette* (Philadelphia, Pennsylvania) Jan. 14, 1841, at 2.

John Marshall

Chief Justice, United States Supreme Court (1801–1853)

John Marshall was born in a log cabin on the Virginia frontier in 1755. He rose to become the longest-serving chief justice, clocking in at thirty-four years. Chief Justice Marshall took an institution that the Framers left weak and turned it into an organization powerful enough to regulate overreach in both the legislative and executive branches.

Chief Justice Marshall's most critical and lasting contribution was his opinion in *Marbury v. Madison*, 5 U.S. 137 (1803), where the Supreme Court established that "it is emphatically the province of the judiciary to say what the law is." This opinion created the power of judicial review, establishing that the rulings of the Supreme Court are binding upon the other branches of government.

FIGURE 3.5   Chief Justice John Marshall

state must be recognized by another state. The second clause is the **Privileges and Immunities Clause**, which ensures that a state may not favor its own citizens over those of other states. These two clauses remain important measures to reduce confusion and conflict among the states.

Article IV also addresses the management of **fugitives**, persons who have fled lawful confinement. Article IV Clause 2 requires that fugitives be returned to the states from which they fled, a process known as **extradition**. Article IV Clause 3, the Fugitive Slave Clause, says that "No Person held to Service or Labour in one State ... escaping into another, shall ... be discharged from such Service or Labour" but must be returned "to whom such Service or Labour may be due." This clause was added to ensure that fugitive enslaved persons would be restored to those who claimed to own them. [7]

Article IV Section 3 governs the admission of new states to the nation and also gives Congress the power to manage territories owned by the United States. Article IV Section 4 guarantees the states "a Republican Form of Government," although it does not explain what this means.[8] This section also compels the national government to protect the states from invasion and requires the federal government to assist the states upon their request in the event of insurrection.

Article V: The Procedures for Amending the Constitution

Article V governs the process of amending the Constitution. It sets forth two methods. First, amendments may be proposed by a two-thirds vote of both the Senate and House

---

7   Passage of the Thirteenth Amendment, which abolished slavery, effectively mooted this provision.
8   The Supreme Court has said the question of whether a state government meets this definition is a political question that Congress must address. *See Luther v. Borden*, 48 U.S. 1 (1849).

of Representatives. Alternatively, if the legislatures of two-thirds of the states request an amendment, Congress can call a convention of the states to address the amendment.

There are also two methods for ratification. Congress can simply send a proposed amendment to the state legislatures for ratification, or Congress can call a state ratification convention. Under either method, ratification requires three-fourths of the state legislatures.

These separate methods reflect the preferences of two groups who attended the Constitutional Convention. One group thought that the national legislature should not be involved in the amendment process. The other thought that all amendment proposals should originate in the national legislature, but be ratified by the states. Certainly, the Framers did not want the Constitution to be either too amenable to amendment or so difficult to modify that its faults could not be cured.

Article VI: The Supremacy Clause and Congressional Oaths

Article VI of the Constitution contains the **Supremacy Clause**, which declares that the laws of the United States (including treaties) are the "supreme Law of the Land." The Supremacy Clause confirms that valid federal laws bind the states, no matter what a state law or state constitution may say.

In addition, Article VI requires judges, executive office holders, and federal and state legislators to swear that they will support the Constitution before they assume office. The precise form of the oath is not given. However, Congress may not require that a religious test be imposed as a precondition to holding federal office. Accordingly, while an oath may include words such as "so help me God," the person swearing the oath could choose to omit those words.

The Fugitive Slave Acts

The Fugitive Slave Act of 1793 expressly overruled any state laws that proposed to offer sanctuary and made it a federal crime to assist an escaped enslaved person. However, the free states continued in their efforts to undermine the institution of slavery.

In response, Congress enacted the Fugitive Slave Act of 1850, which required the cooperation of citizens of free states in capturing and returning enslaved persons. It was called the "Bloodhound Bill" because dogs were often used to track those fleeing from enslavement. The Fugitive Slave Act of 1850 was perhaps the most hated federal law in the nation's history. It was largely unenforceable in the Northern states, and only 330 escaped fugitives were returned to captivity between 1850–1860.

In 1862, Congress enacted legislation that prevented the Union Army from returning fugitives to their enslavers. The 1865 ratification of the Thirteenth Amendment, which abolished slavery, entirely nullified the Fugitive Slave Act. Nonetheless, in 1964, Congress took the symbolic step of repealing it.

THE FUGITIVE SLAVE LAW....HAMLET IN CHAINS.

FIGURE 3.6 James Hamlet, first person returned to slavery under the Fugitive Slave Act of 1850

The Federal Oath of Office

The form of the current federal Oath of Office is as follows:

> I (name) do solemnly swear (or affirm) that I will support and defend the Constitution of the United States against all enemies, foreign and domestic; that I will bear true faith and allegiance to the same; that I take this obligation freely, without any mental reservation or purpose of evasion; and that I will well and faithfully discharge the duties of the office on which I am about to enter (so help me God).

Article VII: The Ratification Process

The last Article of the Constitution states that the "Ratification of the Conventions of nine States, shall be sufficient for the Establishment of this Constitution between the States so Ratifying the Same." This short sentence represents the culmination of eight days of debate about how ratification should occur.

Ratification conventions were conducted in all thirteen states. On December 7, 1787, Delaware became the first state to ratify the Constitution, and on June 21, 1787, New Hampshire became the important ninth state. Rhode Island, which had boycotted the Constitutional Convention, initially rejected ratification. Threatened with being considered a foreign government, Rhode Island became the final state to ratify the Constitution on May 29, 1790.[9]

The Bill of Rights

Although the Preamble to the Constitution says it was created to "secure the Blessings of Liberty," its seven Articles say very little about individual rights. In fact, most of the Framers thought that a national government of limited powers would not pose a threat to individual liberty, particularly as state bills of rights remained in effect. However, three delegates refused to sign the Constitution because it did not include a bill of rights.[10] Further, there were widespread objections to the limited guarantees of rights that it did include. When Massachusetts convened a convention to ratify the Constitution, the debate about the inclusion of a bill of rights escalated to a fist fight, and tensions calmed only when Samuel

---

9   The dates of ratification for each state are as follows: Delaware, December 7, 1787; Pennsylvania, December 12, 1787; New Jersey, December 18, 1787; Georgia, January 2, 1788; Connecticut, January 9, 1788; Massachusetts, February 6, 1788; Maryland, April 28, 1788; South Carolina, May 23, 1788; New Hampshire, June 21, 1788; Virginia, June 25, 1788; New York, July 26, 1788; North Carolina, November 21, 1789; and Rhode Island, May 29, 1790.

10   They were George Mason and Edmund Randolph of Virginia and Elbridge Gerry of Massachusetts. Mason was the principal author of the Virginia Declaration of Rights, which heavily influenced the United States Bill of Rights. Many enslaved individuals lived on Mason's plantation, and biographers have struggled to harmonize his views on personal liberty with his views on slavery. Mason once stated: "[I]t is far from being a desirable property. But it will involve us in great difficulties and infelicity to be now deprived of them." John Kaminski, *A Necessary Evil? Slavery and the Debate Over the Constitution* 59 (1995).

Adams and John Hancock agreed that amendments should be proposed.[11] Further, influential Thomas Jefferson was determined to obtain more protection for individual liberties.[12] As a result, when the First United States Congress convened, it immediately began work on a bill of rights.

James Madison was the principal drafter of the Constitution's Bill of Rights. Among other influences, he drew from Virginia's Declaration of Rights, the Magna Carta, and the English Bill of Rights. The new Bill of Rights, consisting of the first ten amendments to the Constitution, became the law of the land on December 15, 1791.

Introduction to the Bill of Rights

An overview of the key components of the Bill of Rights follows. In the coming chapters, we explore some of its most important provisions in depth. Before we begin the overview, however, we must note three things.

First, the Bill of Rights was written to protect the people from overreach by the national government. Its provisions were only made applicable to the states over time, through a process called **incorporation**. Incorporation began when the Supreme Court said that the states, as well as the federal government, must protect the citizens' right of free speech in *Gitlow v. New York*, 268 U.S. 652 (1925). In the decades following *Gitlow*, the Supreme Court issued a series of opinions that steadily incorporated most of the key provisions of the Bill of Rights, requiring the states as well as the national government to honor their terms.

Second, as with the language in the Articles of the Constitution, the meaning of some important terms in the Bill of Rights remains subject to debate. For example, what are "cruel and unusual punishments?" What is required by "due process of law?" What executive actions fall within the scope of presidential authority? The courts of the nation are tasked with answering these questions when they escalate to legal conflicts. Their answers have shifted over time, along with changes in perspective, understanding, and methods of constitutional interpretation.

Finally, while the Bill of Rights provides a broad guarantee of civil liberties, the rights it lists are not absolute. Depending upon the context, a declared right may be firmly limited, and courts have found such limitations to be constitutional. Moreover, some rights may conflict with other rights. For example, although you have the right to free speech, you do not have the right to publish statements that harm the privacy rights of others. Since the Bill of Rights was drafted, there have been vigorous debates about appropriate scope of the rights and liberty interests set forth in the Constitution.

---

11   The fight was between Massachusetts delegates Francis Dana and Elbridge Gerry.
12   Jefferson was in Paris at the time of the Constitutional Convention, serving as minister to France.

Philosophies About Interpretation of the United States Constitution

There are competing philosophies about how judges should interpret the words in the United States Constitution.

Strict Construction calls for enforcing the text of the Constitution as written. **Textualism** and **Originalism** are variations of strict construction. Textualism maintains that if the original words are clear, then no further analysis is necessary, and the intention of the drafters does not matter. Originalism holds that the provisions of the Constitution should be given their "original" meaning. Judges should review the historical context of the key phrases and determine what they meant at the time they were enacted. Justice Hugo Black often applied a strict construction theory to his interpretation of the Constitution, and Justice Antonin Scalia was an originalist.

Opponents of strict construction note that the Constitution's original terms cannot always be appropriately applied to situations that were beyond the experiences of the Framers. Proponents of the philosophy of the **Living Constitution** believe that the Framers crafted the document to have an "open texture" and be subject to interpretation. Judges who apply this philosophy consider not only the words of the Constitution, but also other writings that are relevant, and then apply the intentions of the Framers to modern contexts. They seek to follow "the spirit of the law" rather than "the letter of the law." Justice Stephen Breyer believes in the living Constitution.

The doctrine of **Legal Pragmatism** is another non-originalist view. Those who are in this school apply legal precedent and look to the social and economic consequences that flow from different interpretations of the words in the Constitution. Richard Posner, an American jurist and leading figure in the field of law and economics, is a legal pragmatist.

Overview of the Bill of Rights

The Bill of Rights begins with the First Amendment, which guarantees the freedoms of religion, speech, and the press. It also ensures the right of peaceful assembly and the right to petition the government for redress. It accomplishes all these things in one remarkable sentence:

> Congress shall make no law respecting an establishment of religion, or prohibiting the free exercise thereof; or abridging the freedom of speech, or of the press; or the right of the people peaceably to assemble, and to petition the Government for a redress of grievances.

The First Amendment passed the House of Representatives and the Senate with very little debate.

The Second Amendment concerns the right to bear arms. Interestingly, the states ratified slightly different versions, with varying comma placement and capitalization. The final, handwritten original passed by Congress is the version ratified by Delaware and used by the Supreme Court:[13]

> A well regulated Militia, being necessary to the security of a free State, the right of the people to keep and bear Arms, shall not be infringed.

---

13   In *District of Columbia v. Heller*, 554 U.S. 570 (2008).

This Amendment should be viewed in its historical context. There were a variety of reasons that it was considered important.

First, members of the First Congress were concerned that giving the federal government control over state militia groups would lead to erosion of those groups. Without state forces to balance the federal army and navy, the federal government might feel empowered to encroach on the rights of the states. It was thought that confirming the right to bear arms would make this less likely.

In addition, in the slave states, state militias often policed enslaved persons. Only white men could serve in state militias, and confirming the right of militias to arm ensured their continuing control over enslaved persons.[14] Certainly, the Southern states did not want Black persons to have access to weapons; they greatly feared rebellion, such as the widely publicized bloody insurrection against French colonial rule that resulted in independence in Haiti.[15]

Over time, two models emerged in court opinions to interpret the Second Amendment. The first is the "individual rights" model, which holds that individuals have the right to bear arms. The second is the "collective rights" model, which ties the right to membership in a militia or law enforcement agency. The Supreme Court adopted the "individual rights" model in the key Second Amendment cases *District of Columbia v. Heller*, 554 U.S. 70 (2008) and *McDonald v. Chicago*, 561 U.S. 742 (2010). In *McDonald*, the Supreme Court held that the Second Amendment grants individuals the right to keep and bear arms and is enforceable against the states. The Court also said that the right may be subject to reasonable limitations.

The Third Amendment forbids the peacetime practice of housing soldiers in private homes without the owner's consent.

---

14   *See* Carl T. Bogus, "The Hidden History of the Second Amendment," 31 *UC Davis Law Rev.*, 309, 311 (1998).

15   This revolution was marked by extreme violence, fueled by long years of oppression. The Haitian revolution greatly alarmed slave owners in the United States.

The Haitian Revolution

Before gaining its independence, Haiti was a French colony called St. Domingue. Through African slave labor, St. Domingue maintained successful sugar and coffee industries and a strong trade relationship with American merchants. In 1791, thousands of slaves organized and successfully executed a bloody mass rebellion under the leadership of former slave Toussaint Louverture. In 1804, this revolution created the independent republic of Haiti, the first nation in history to permanently ban slavery from the first day of its existence.

Slaveholders in the United States were greatly concerned that the Haitian revolution would inspire a similar revolt among enslaved persons living on their lands. These fears were exacerbated by the brutal nature of the revolution.

The two rival political parties—Democratic Republicans and Federalists—agreed that the Haitian revolution could threaten American slavery, although the issue of Haiti's independence remained at the center of partisan debate. During the presidency of John Adams, who was strongly opposed to slavery, the United States sent aid to Louverture and his forces. This aid was rescinded by the subsequent Jefferson administration in favor of an isolationist policy to stop the spread of antislavery sentiment. Notably, the federal government did not formally acknowledge Haiti as an independent nation until 1862, after the Southern states had seceded.

FIGURE 3.7 General Toussaint Louverture, commander of the Haitian revolution

This amendment was a direct response to the British Parliament's Quartering Acts that allowed the British Army to house soldiers in private residences during the years before the Revolutionary War. Although no Supreme Court case has relied upon the Third Amendment as the primary foundation for its opinion, it has been referenced as supporting an implicit constitutional right to privacy.[16]

The important Fourth, Fifth, and Sixth Amendments are tied to the details of criminal procedure. The Fourth Amendment protects the people from unreasonable searches and seizures and establishes the requirements for the issuance of warrants. Its provisions have been shaped by the nation's courts, which have addressed 1) the types of governmental activities that rise to the level of a "search" or "seizure"; 2) the showing required to obtain a warrant; and 3) the consequences of violating the amendment's provisions.

The Fifth and Sixth Amendments contain additional provisions that relate to criminal cases, including the prohibition against double jeopardy, the right to refuse to testify, the right to trial by an impartial jury, and the right to call and confront witnesses. The Fifth Amendment also includes the critical Due Process Clause. The notion of due process is central to the rule of law, and is of such profound significance that it is explored at length in its own chapter. In addition, we will revisit the Fourth, Fifth, and Sixth Amendments in the criminal procedure chapter.

The Seventh Amendment provides that federal civil cases must tried before a jury if they would have received a jury trial under the English common law. This amendment has been interpreted to guarantee that trials must have juries of a certain size (at least six people). It also preserves jury verdicts from being arbitrarily overturned. While the Seventh Amendment has never been formally incorporated, all the states have provisions for civil jury trials in their constitutions.

The Eighth Amendment simply states, "Excessive bail shall not be required, nor excessive fines imposed, nor cruel and unusual punishments inflicted." This amendment's prohibition against cruel and unusual punishments has long been a source of intense controversy and has generated a collection of Supreme Court opinions. In addition to outlawing torture and gruesome methods of punishment, it also protects against punishments that are not proportionate to the crime committed. We revisit the Eighth Amendment in a later chapter on Crime and Punishment.

Finally, the Ninth and Tenth Amendments address the rights retained by the states and the people. The Ninth Amendment declares that "the enumeration in the Constitution of certain rights, shall not be construed to deny or disparage others retained by the people." This phrase has been subject to differing interpretations. Some scholars opine that the Ninth Amendment grounds the Constitution in a universe of natural rights: "we are born with more rights than any constitution could ever list or specify."[17] Others maintain that the Ninth Amendment is simply a guide on how to read the Constitution.[18]

The Tenth Amendment declares that the federal government only has those powers that the Constitution has delegated to it; all other powers "are reserved to the States respectively, or to the people." This amendment

---

16   Along with other amendments, it was referenced in the majority opinion in *Griswold v. Connecticut*, 381 U.S. 479 (1965), which confirmed the right of married couples to purchase and use contraceptives.

17   Brian Doherty, *Radicals for Capitalism: A Freewheeling History of the Modern Libertarian Movement* (2007).

18   *See* Laurence H. Tribe, *American Constitutional Law* (2nd ed., 1998).

is now interpreted as confirming the division of power between the states and the federal government. The federal government cannot require the states to pass particular types of legislation or enforce federal law. It can, however, provide funding or other incentives to encourage state cooperation.

Since 1789, a total of twenty-seven amendments have been added to the Constitution. These include the Sixteenth Amendment, which permitted Congress to impose an income tax; the Nineteenth, which granted suffrage to women; and the Twenty-Sixth, which gave all citizens at least eighteen years of age the right to vote.

Conclusion and Introduction to Law Lab

The United States Constitution is both the oldest and the shortest written constitution of any major nation. The provisions it contains have guided the country through over two centuries of war and peace, through times of great fiscal challenge and strong economic growth, and through periods of grave domestic and international crisis. Its enduring value may be tied to the governmental framework it created, the liberties it guarantees, and what it omits as well as what it includes.

The Constitution has permitted the nation to develop in ways that the Framers could not have imagined. Certainly, the federal government of today is very different from the federal government of 1789. One major change concerns the executive branch, which has expanded greatly since the nation's first presidency. George Washington had only four cabinet officers: the secretaries of State, Treasury, War, and the attorney general. Today, there are 15 cabinet officers, all supervising administrative units comprised of a large number of federal agencies.

The historic growth of the executive branch reflects not only that presidents have consistently reached for more power, but also that society has increased in size and complexity. Greater commerce demanded more regulations, along with the administrative support to enforce those laws. We now have agencies that make sure that the planes we fly in are safe, that the food we eat is not tainted, that our waterways are not polluted, that our medicines are effective, and that our banks are secure. We have agencies that explore outer space and maintain our critical interstate infrastructure. Today, the president oversees a broad collection of federal agencies that perform a wide variety of important tasks.

To address the evolving needs of the nation, Congress has passed legislation that gives the president considerably more powers than the Constitution expressly describes. Among other powers, Congress has given the president the authority to declare national emergencies and to invoke emergency powers to appropriately respond to them. In 1917, President Woodrow used his **presidential emergency powers** to declare the first national emergency. Over the past century, presidents have declared dozens of national emergencies, including measures to combat communism, cybercrime, foreign weapons proliferation, and disease.

This week's Law Lab touches on the scope of the emergency authority held by the executive branch. The president has issued an **executive order**, a directive that affects the operation of the federal government. Its constitutionality has been challenged by an organization affected by its provisions. In this Law Lab, you are again a United States Supreme Court justice, and you must decide whether the executive order accords with the Constitution's provisions concerning the scope of presidential power. As with legislation and other governmental actions, the constitutionality of executive orders is subject to judicial review. A finding that it is constitutional means that the actions it outlines can proceed. A finding that it is unconstitutional will render it void.

Note that this Law Lab is complex. It involves an executive order, federal legislation, and presidential emergency powers. Read the summary memorandum in the Law Lab, consider the facts, and revisit the grants of power provided in the Constitution. Review the legal authority provided, and then debate and decide the case. Your decision will determine whether the president can proceed with an agenda that many consider to be vitally important.

Supreme Court Justice Law Lab

MEMORANDUM

To: The Honorable Chief Justice & Associate Justices of the Supreme Court of the United States

From: Law Clerks of the Supreme Court

Re: *The Independent Petroleum Association of America v. Jacqueline Grant, United States Secretary of Energy*, On Review

Your Honors:

Please allow this summary memorandum to assist you as you consider the merits of the appeal in the above-referenced matter. Your Honors must determine whether the President's use of Executive Order (EO) 15013 conforms with the United States Constitution.

Briefly, independent oil and gas producers in the United States challenge the use of presidential emergency powers to support EO 15013. This EO seeks to address climate change by requiring independent oil and gas producers to submit reports explaining how they plan to reduce emissions over time. Without submitting these reports, the independent oil and gas producers cannot obtain permits to operate their businesses.

After noting the views of the scientific community concerning climate change, this memorandum reviews some prior uses of presidential emergency powers and the federal statutes that apply in this particular case. It then reviews the key provisions of EO 15013, the arguments of the parties, and describes what occurred in the case before it came to the Supreme Court.

Factual Background

Climate Change and the Fossil Fuel Industry

One of the greatest current challenges facing the United States (and other nations of the world) is climate change. Scientists have observed, over the last decades, a notable global warming trend, which has been firmly linked to human activities.[1] In particular, the burning of fossil fuels has increased the concentration of greenhouse gases in the atmosphere, causing a rise in average temperatures. Climate change poses threats to human health beyond the risks to life and property posed by increased heat and extreme weather. The melting of polar ice sheets and glaciers increases the likelihood of coastal flooding and

FIGURE 3.8   Fossil fuel refinery

---

1   The Intergovernmental Panel on Climate Change is a group of 1,300 independent scientific experts from around the world. Under the auspices of the United Nations, the panel concluded in its Fifth Assessment Report that there is more than a 95 percent probability that human activities have caused the warming of the planet. Atmospheric carbon dioxide levels have risen from 280 parts per million to 414 parts per million over the last 150 years.

erosion and raises the specter of drought in communities that rely upon snowpacks for drinking water. In addition, climate change affects ecosystems. The oceans are becoming more acidic, affecting marine life. Climate change also alters the home ranges of various species.[2]

Many nations are now considering ways to combat climate change. The United Nations Energy Commission[3] has been exploring the topic of achieving net-zero emissions by 2050. The Commission's First Report provides policy recommendations and lists steps that that fossil fuel companies must take in order to meet the urgent global warming limits outlined by the Paris Agreement, the key treaty on climate change. These steps include reducing emissions over time. Major members of private industry, including the five largest oil producers, have all agreed to reduce their emissions to some extent.[4]

In the United States, individual states have enacted legislation designed to reduce the use of fossil fuels. Illinois, Michigan, Minnesota, Wisconsin, Kansas, and Iowa signed a regional agreement to reduce greenhouse gas emission and combat climate change.[5] California's Global Warming Solutions Act of 2006 sets an absolute statewide limit on greenhouse gas emissions.

At the federal level, some efforts have been proceeding using the Clean Air Act and Clean Water Act. However, this legislation is not an ideal tool for this purpose. Many experts argue that avoiding the worst consequences of climate change will require a market-based approach to reduce carbon emissions. This approach could include a carbon tax or other carbon-pricing options to regulate emissions. Fearing political consequences, however, the United States Congress has been reluctant to adopt such an approach.

Presidential Emergency Powers

The Constitution of the United States does not expressly provide the president with emergency powers. It does vest executive powers in the president, and, in Article II, demands that the president "take Care that the Laws be faithfully executed." Laws can bestow additional powers upon the president, and often with the support of federal legislation, presidents have asserted the power to declare national emergencies. Congress has given over 130 distinct statutory powers to the president that may be used in the event of a national emergency. Most of these do not require a supporting declaration from Congress. These statutory emergency powers address a broad range of topics, including land management, public health, and the use of federal employees and military personnel. They give the president a long list of available actions, including the use of force, the requisition of private property, and the shuttering of radio stations. Over the past decades, dozens of emergencies have been declared and have not officially lapsed.[6]

---

2   A collection of agencies throughout the world are working to address climate change. These include, in the United States, the Center for Climate and Energy Solutions, a bipartisan and independent organization. The facts noted here are from its website: https://www.c2es .org/content/climate-impacts/.

3   This particular agency is fictitious.

4   They are the United States producers Exxon and Chevron; British Petroleum (BP); the French producer Total; and Shell, an Anglo-Dutch firm headquartered in the Netherlands.

5   The agreement is called the Midwestern Greenhouse Gas Reduction Accord. In addition to the states listed, the agreement was signed by the Canadian Province of Manitoba.

6   Congress tried to fix this problem by passing the National Emergencies Act in 1976, which places disclosure and reporting obligations on the president if he wishes to issue an emergency declaration. The act also requires Congress to address pending declared emergencies

Presidents have sometimes used emergency powers to take actions that we now recognize as unconstitutional. President Franklin D. Roosevelt used his emergency powers when he issued an executive order requiring the removal of all Japanese Americans from coastal areas to internment camps during the Second World War. This Court, in *Korematsu v. United States*, 323 U.S. 214 (1944), found that the executive order was not an abuse of the president's powers. In *Trump v. Hawaii*, 585 U.S. (2018), however, this Court repudiated the *Korematsu* decision, although the Court's majority supported the president's executive order restricting immigration.

One Supreme Court case, *Youngstown Sheet & Tube Company v. Sawyer*, 343 U.S. 579 (1952), provides helpful guidance on how to think about the scope of presidential authority. This case reversed President Harry S. Truman's use of emergency powers to take over operations of the nation's privately owned steel mills during the Korean War. This Court found that neither the president's powers as commander in chief nor any claimed emergency powers permitted him to seize private property without supporting congressional legislation.

In a concurring opinion in *Youngstown Sheet & Tube Company*, Justice Jackson divided presidential authority into three distinct categories. First, there are cases where the president is acting with congressional authority. Here, the president's authority is at its strongest, bolstered by congressional approval. Second, there are situations where Congress is silent on the subject. The president's authority is not as strong here because he is stepping forward on his own. Third, there are cases where the president's actions go directly against congressional authority. Here, the president's authority is at its weakest because he is acting against the will of Congress.

The Clean Air Act

In light of the urgency of the climate change crisis and the lack of a comprehensive congressional response, the executive branch of the federal government began to explore other ways to address climate change. After consultation, the president determined that climate change constitutes a national emergency and that the Clean Air Act gives the federal government the authority to address it.

The United States' Clean Air Act is administered by the Environmental Protection Agency in coordination with state, local, and Tribal governments. The act limits national air pollution, establishing how much ground-level ozone, lead, and other compounds are permitted in outdoor air. The act is detailed and comprehensive. Its provisions identify what volume of toxic air pollutants factories can emit and creates a program to phase out compounds that harm the ozone layer. The act also establishes rules to limit pollutants from vehicle engines, mandating continuing reductions in emissions.

Amendments have sought to continue to improve air quality while adding new policy tools. Importantly, the Clean Air Act created an operating permit program for large businesses. Under Title V, businesses must

---

every six months. The legislation failed to do the job, and dozens of federal statutes continue to provide special powers to the president when he declares a national emergency.

have plans in place to minimize air pollution. Further, they must share those plans with the government to obtain permits to operate.[7]

Relying upon these provisions of the Clean Air Act, White House staff prepared a new executive order, EO 15013. It is titled "Addressing the Climate Crisis Through Mandatory Oil Producer Planning," and it affects all oil and gas producers in the United States. It requires oil and gas producers to submit plans explaining how they will reduce emissions to meet the minimum criteria outlined in the United Nations Energy Commission's First Report. Unless they do so, the producers will not be able to obtain operating permits.

Here is an excerpt of EO 15013:

Addressing the Climate Crisis Through Mandatory Oil Producer Planning

By the authority vested in me as President of the United States, by the Constitution and the laws of the United States of America, it is hereby ordered as follows:

Section 1. Policy. The intensifying impacts of climate change present a climate crisis with health, public safety, and economic risks to all Americans. Scientific communities in the United States and abroad warn that the use of fossil fuels has created a global warming phenomenon that is already affecting human populations throughout the world. Climate-related changes will amplify existing risks in society that endanger lives, ecosystems, and our economy ...

Section 2. Mission. We have a narrow moment to pursue action at home and abroad in order to avoid the most catastrophic impacts of the climate crisis. Domestic action must go hand in hand with United States international leadership, aimed at significantly enhancing global action. It is the policy of my Administration to organize and deploy the full capacity of its agencies to combat the climate crisis ...

Section 3. National Emergency. For the reasons stated in Sections 1 and 2, I find that the climate crisis presents a threat to the health and safety of the American public and constitutes a National Emergency.

Section 4. Planning. In order to address this National Emergency, my Administration will advance plans to address climate change. In particular, by and through this Executive

---

7   The Environmental Protection Agency's dedicated website about the Title V Operating Permits is found here: https://www.epa.gov/title-v-operating-permits.

Order, each producer of oil and gas, as defined in this Executive Order, must, within twelve (12) months of its signing, provide to the Environmental Protection Agency Office of Enforcement and Compliance Assurance, a plan illustrating how they will meet the emissions reduction criteria outlined in the United World Energy Agency's First Report. Operating permits will only be issued to those producers who provide such plans ...

Procedural Posture

Representatives of the major oil and gas producers have agreed to provide the requested plans. However, there are about 9,000 independent oil and gas producers in the United States. They produce up to 83 percent of the nation's oil and 90 percent of its natural gas, and they do not wish to abide by the executive order. The Independent Petroleum Association of America (IPPA) serves as their chief voice in government.[8]

On their behalf, IPPA filed suit in federal court, naming as defendant the United States secretary of energy Jacqueline Grant. In its lawsuit, IPPA argues that the president's executive order exceeds the scope of authority legitimately provided by Congress and is therefore unconstitutional. In particular, IPPA maintains that the president's use of the Clean Air Act as the foundation for emergency powers is inappropriate. IPPA notes that the Clean Air Act was passed to address air pollution, not climate change, and it does not mention emergency powers. IPPA also notes that Congress has declined to pass legislation to accomplish what Executive Order 15013 mandates.

In response, the federal government argued that Congress has, by statute, given the president broad emergency powers. Further, this Court previously determined that the Environmental Protection Agency has the authority to regulate greenhouse gas emissions if they endanger public health,[9] and the president's executive order finds that such emissions do endanger public health. The federal government also argues that climate change is easily as serious and wide ranging an emergency as the recent pandemic, which was also the subject of an emergency declaration and presidential action.[10]

The federal trial court determined that EO 15013 was a constitutional exercise of emergency powers under the Clean Air Act. However, the United States Court of Appeals for the District of Columbia Circuit reversed, finding that the provisions in the Clean Air Act did not give the president the emergency authority required to issue the executive order. The United States government appealed, and this Court has now accepted review.

---

8   Section 614A(D) of the United States Internal Revenue Code defines an independent producer as a producer that does not sell more than $5 million in yearly retail sales of oil or gas, or who does not refine more than 75,000 barrels per day of crude oil in a given year.

9   *See Utility Air Regulatory Group v. Environmental Protection Agency*, 573 U.S. 302 (2014).

10   *See* Proclamation 9994, "Declaring a National Emergency Concerning the Novel Coronavirus Disease (COVID-19) Outbreak," found at 85 FR 15337.

Issue: The Use of Presidential Emergency Powers and Executive Orders

This Court must decide whether the president's use of emergency powers to require oil and gas producers to submit plans to address climate change exceeds the scope of executive authority under the United States Constitution. There are several parts to this question.

First, does the president have the authority to declare that climate change is a national emergency? What is the foundation for this authority?

Second, does the president have a constitutional basis to issue the executive order requiring oil and gas producers to submit plans to reduce emissions? Congress has declined to pass legislation directly addressing the reduction in emissions of oil and gas producers. How much does this matter?

Finally, does the Clean Air Act factor into this analysis? If so, how?

If this Court agrees with the federal government, then EO 15013 will remain in effect, and the oil and gas producers will have to comply with its provisions. If not, then the executive order will be rendered void, and the producers will not be required to prepare and report their plans to reduce emissions.

Conclusion

The Court's law clerks remain available to answer any questions that might assist Your Honors in resolving this matter. We look forward to receiving the Court's opinion in this important case.

CHAPTER 4

Freedom of Speech, the Bedrock Right

Truth is powerful, and it prevails.
—Sojourner Truth

Introduction

In the first three chapters of this book, we reviewed ancient legal codes, the history of the common law, and the creation and content of the United States Constitution. In the coming chapters, we will delve into specific provisions in the Bill of Rights. We will consider its provisions on religious freedom, equal protection, and due process. However, before we review those, we must look at freedom of speech, the bedrock right.

The First Amendment of the Bill of Rights expressly affirms the freedoms of speech, religion, press, and assembly. It says:

> Congress shall make no law respecting an establishment of religion, or prohibiting the free exercise thereof; or abridging the freedom of speech, or of the press; or the right of the people peaceably to assemble, and to petition the Government for a redress of grievances.

All First Amendment protections are critical. However, freedom of speech is of vital importance. Without the ability to discuss the important issues of the day, a democratic society cannot properly function. Through dialogue, we can develop ideas about how to improve our lives and the lives of others. We can debate the merits of these ideas and decide which to adopt and which to reject. We can jointly consider the outcomes of our chosen actions and amend future proposals based upon what we learn. By gathering in support of ideas, we can demonstrate that we are invested in those ideas and would like to see them adopted. And we can do these things, even when they involve criticizing the government, without fear of reprisal.

As we noted in the prior chapter, the First Amendment imposed limitations only on the power of the national government. It did not protect the people from abuses of state governmental agencies and officers. In 1868, however, the Fourteenth Amendment was ratified, which prohibits the states from taking "life, liberty or property without due process of law." Over time, the Supreme Court determined that the Fourteenth Amendment incorporates First Amendment rights and makes them applicable to all units of government, state as well as federal. Further, the rights in the First Amendment apply to the actions of all governmental operations, including public employers, courts, legislatures, and executive officials.

Despite the expansive language in the First Amendment's free speech clause, the Supreme Court has ruled that state and federal governments may indeed limit certain types of speech.

Although content restrictions are

FIGURE 4.1   United States Supreme Court

disfavored (particularly for political or religious speech), other restrictions (such as time and place) are not uncommon. Certain forms of speech (like false advertising) that have the potential to cause serious harm are regulated for the public good. In addition, there is no constitutional protection for libel or slander (untrue speech that harms others) or obscene content that lacks serious literary, artistic, political, or scientific value.[1]

The Supreme Court's political free speech cases all wrestle with a collection of important questions. Should the regulation of speech be permitted? What factors determine if particular content falls into

---

[1]   The first key case on the regulation of obscene content was *Roth v. United States*, 354 U.S. 476 (1957), where the Supreme Court found that obscenity was not "within the area of constitutionally protected speech or press." *Roth*, 354 U.S. at 485. The test was "whether to the average person, applying contemporary community standards, the dominant theme of the material taken as a whole appeals to prurient interest." This definition was amended, and in *Miller v. California*, 413 U.S. 15 (1973), the Supreme Court adopted a three-part test. Generally, a state may regulate if the work appeals to prurient interest, offensively describes sexual content, and lacks "serious literary, artistic, political or scientific value." *Miller*, 413 U.S. at 23.

a protected category? How do we make sure we are suppressing only the content that the government may properly regulate?

In this chapter, we first explore key Supreme Court free speech cases that touch on **sedition**, which seeks to incite rebellion against the government. We then review **symbolic speech**, which communicates without spoken words. Finally, we review the free speech rights enjoyed by children, who will grow up to become participants in the democratic process.

FREE SPEECH KEY TERMS

The following key terms are defined in this chapter. They are also defined in the Glossary.

Legal Pragmatism	**Originalism**	**Strict Construction**	**Textualism**
Living Constitution	**Sedition**	**Symbolic Speech**	

Seditious Speech and the First Amendment

Sedition presents an interesting challenge to a democratic nation with a legal tradition of free speech. While the Bill of Rights unquestionably guarantees free speech, seditious speech that gains a popular following can become a threat to a democracy. Accordingly, there is tension between the desire to support free speech and the need to continue governmental operations.

The events that occurred in the United States Capitol on January 6, 2021, provide a troubling example of the seditious use of misinformation. On that date, members of Congress assembled to count the Electoral College ballots following the 2020 presidential election. Joseph Biden had defeated incumbent Donald Trump, and the formal counting of the ballots would confirm Biden as the incoming president.

However, President Trump and his supporters refused to accept that Biden had won the election, asserting that Biden's victory was the result of widespread election fraud. At President Trump's invitation, his supporters gathered near the Capitol at noon for a "Save America" rally that promised to "be wild!" During his speech at the rally, President Trump amplified his claims of fraud and told his followers to "stop the steal" and "fight like hell." He invited them to walk to the Capitol to "give our Republicans … the kind of pride and boldness that they need to take back our country." His followers moved to the Capitol, breached police barriers, assaulted Capitol police officers, and forcibly entered the building.[2]

---

2   The full text of President Trump's speech may be read here: https://www.npr.org/2021/02/10/966396848/read-trumps-jan-6-speech-a-key-part-of-impeachment-trial.

FIGURE 4.2 The storming of the United States Capitol

Five people died as the result of the attack, and more than 100 sustained serious injury. Senate Majority Leader Mitch McConnell (R-KY) characterized the storming of the Capitol as a failed insurrection.[3]

While there is great value in a vigorous debate about the merits of differing political philosophies, false speech that incites dangerous unlawful action should not be protected by the First Amendment. The challenge is in assessing the nature and truthfulness of the speech and the threat it presents.

CRITICAL THINKING As you read each case, consider whether you agree with its ruling. Each Supreme Court decision became binding precedent on every court in the nation. Do you agree with the Court's decision? If so, do you approve of the reason(s) provided by the Court? If you disagree, where do you think the Court made the mistake? Finally, what precedent would you have created to provide the lower courts with guidance in this most critical area of law?

---

3   *See* Patricia Zengerle, Jonathan Landay, and David Morgan, "Under Heavy Guard, Congress Back to Work After Trump Supporters Storm U.S. Capitol," Reuters (Jan. 6, 2021), https://www.reuters.com/article/usa-election-int/under-heavy-guard-congress-back-to-work-after-trump-supporters-storm-u-s-capitol-idUSKBN29B2RJ.

Charles Schenck and the Clear and Present Danger Test

The first key case on seditious speech is *Schenck v. United States*, 249 U.S. 47 (1919). It arose from the political environment surrounding the First World War.

President Woodrow Wilson gave a State of the Union address on December 7, 1915. This was during the time of the First Red Scare, and there was widespread fear that anarchism and bolshevism would spread throughout the world.[4] President Wilson's speech asked Congress to craft a particular type of legislation "to save the honor and self-respect of the nation" from those who have "poured the poison of disloyalty into the very arteries of national life" and "sought to ... debase our politics to the uses of foreign intrigue ..." He described the persons engaging in these actions as "citizens ... born under other flags but welcomed under our generous naturalization laws to the full freedom and opportunity of America" and urged Congress to "enact such laws at the earliest possible moment" because "[t]hey have formed plots to destroy property [and] they have entered into conspiracies against the neutrality of the Government."[5]

Congress was listening, and when the United States entered the war, it passed the Espionage Act of 1917. The act makes it a crime to "interfere with the operation or success of the military or naval forces of the United States ... or willfully obstruct the recruiting or enlistment service of the United States, to the injury of the service or of the United States."[6]

At the time, Charles Schenck was the general secretary of the United States Socialist Party. Schenck was responsible for printing and distributing 15,000 leaflets that advocated opposition to the draft. These leaflets contained statements such as "Do not submit to intimidation" and "Assert your rights."

The police found Schenck and his leaflets during a search of the Socialist Party headquarters. He was arrested and tried. In his defense, Schenck argued that the Espionage Act unconstitutionally violated his First Amendment right of free speech. Nonetheless, he was convicted of violating the act and sentenced to six months in prison.

Schenck appealed his conviction to the Supreme Court, and it agreed to hear his case. In an opinion written by Justice Oliver Wendell Holmes, the Supreme Court unanimously held that Schenck's criminal conviction was constitutional. He could be found guilty of violating the Espionage Act for his leaflet work, because the First Amendment does not protect speech encouraging wartime avoidance of the draft. The opinion states:

> When a nation is at war many things that might be said in time of peace are such a hindrance to its effort that their utterance will not be endured so long as men fight, and that no Court could regard them as protected by any constitutional right.[7]

---

4   The First Red Scare had its genesis in the distrust of radicals due to the Russian Bolshevik revolution. The Bolsheviks, founded by Vladimir Lenin and Alexander Bogdanov, were a far-left faction of Marxism. They took power in Russia in 1917. US citizens were concerned that the revolution would spread to the United States and lead to the confiscation of private property and the repression of religion.

5   The full speech may be found here: https://www.presidency.ucsb.edu/documents/third-annual-message-19.

6   *See* Espionage Act of June 15, 1917, c 30, Section 3, 40 Stat. 217, 219.

7   *Schenck v. United States*, 249 U.S. at 52.

To decide when speech would be regulated, the Court devised the "clear and present danger" test:

> The question in every case is whether the words used are used in such circumstances and are of such a nature as to create a clear and present danger that they will bring about the substantive evils that Congress has a right to prevent.

CRITICAL THINKING   The *Schenck* opinion left many questions in its wake. How "clear and present" must a threat be to permit suppression of speech? In this case, although the leaflets encouraged men to refuse to participate in the draft, there was no evidence that the leaflets stopped anyone from registering for the draft. Should this have mattered, and why or why not? If such evidence should have been required, what evidence would have been needed to meet the clear and present danger test?

Benjamin Gitlow and the Dangerous Tendency Doctrine

A few years later, in *Gitlow v. New York*, 268 U.S. 652 (1925), the clear and present danger test was replaced by an even broader test.

Benjamin Gitlow lived in New York and belonged to the Communist Party. Along with others, he published *The Revolutionary Age*, a radical newspaper. The paper carried a piece called "The Left Wing Manifesto," which advocated the violent overthrow of the federal government. After its publication, in November of 1919, Gitlow and several of his Communist Party colleagues were arrested by police officers in New York City. New York contended that the publication violated a state statute concerning criminal anarchy. The statute's material provisions stated:

FIGURE 4.3   Benjamin Gitlow

> Advocacy of criminal anarchy. Any person who:

> 1. By word of mouth or writing advocates, advises or teaches the duty, necessity or propriety of overthrowing or overturning organized government by force or violence, or by assassination of the executive head or of any of the executive officials of government, or by any unlawful means; or,

> 2. Prints, publishes, edits, issues or knowingly circulates, sells, distributes or publicly displays any book, paper, document, or written or printed matter in any form, containing or

advocating, advising or teaching the doctrine that organized government should be over-thrown by force, violence or any unlawful means ...

Is guilty of a felony and punishable by imprisonment or fine, or both.[8]

At trial, Gitlow's attorney argued that New York's law was unconstitutionally overbroad, as it criminalized speech that was protected under the First Amendment. Further, the attorney pointed out that the manifesto presented no clear and present danger to the operation of the government. Its publication and distribution had incited no violent action. In fact, there "was no evidence of any effect ..."[9]

Nonetheless, Gitlow was convicted. The Supreme Court found that the statute did not penalize publications of discussions, but prohibited language advocating the overthrow of the government by unlawful means. This, the Court said, may be regulated without violating the First Amendment:

[New York] cannot reasonably be required to defer the adoption of measures for its own peace and safety until the revolutionary utterances lead to actual disturbances of the public or imminent and immediate danger of its own destruction; but it may, in the exercise of its judgment, suppress the threatened danger in its incipiency.[10]

Further, the Court stepped away from the clear and present danger test and instead adopted a broader "bad (or dangerous) tendency test":[11]

The general provisions of the statute may be constitutionally applied to the specific utter-ance of the defendant if its natural tendency and probable effect was [sic] to bring about the substantive evil which the legislative body might prevent.[12]

Although the Court adopted the broader test to permit more regulation of speech, it also determined that the right of free speech is a fundamental personal right that must be uniformly protected. Accordingly, through the Due Process Clause of the Fourteenth Amendment, it applies to state governments as well as to the federal government. Gitlow had lost his case, but the people had gained more support for the First Amendment.

Justice Oliver Wendell Holmes penned an eloquent dissent. He argued that abandoning the clear and present danger test was a mistake. He said:

---

8   *See* New York Penal Law, §§ 160, 161.
9   *Gitlow*, 268 U.S. at 656.
10 *Gitlow*, 268 U.S. at 669.
11 The marketplace of ideas appears to shrink during time of war, when courts are less tolerant of dissenting views. *See* Helen Knowles and Steven Lichtman, *Judging Free Speech: First Amendment Jurisprudence of the US* 11 (2016).
12 *Gitlow*, 268 U.S. at 671.

[T]here was no present danger of an attempt to overthrow the government by force on the part of the admittedly small minority who shared the defendant's views. ... Every idea is an incitement. It offers itself for belief and if believed it is acted on unless some other belief outweighs it or some failure of energy stifles the movement at its birth. ... If the publication of this document had been laid as an attempt to induce an uprising against government at once and not at some indefinite time in the future it would have presented a different question. ... But the indictment alleges the publication and nothing more.[13]

CRITICAL THINKING   The *Gitlow* ruling permitted the regulation of speech that potentially advocated violence. What do you think of this opinion's focus on the fact that the speech encouraged illegal action? Do the circumstances and context of the speech matter?

Clarence Brandenburg and Imminent Lawless Action

In subsequent cases, the Supreme Court reverted to a variation of the clear and present danger test to determine the scope of permitted speech.[14] And then, in *Brandenburg v. Ohio*, 395 U.S. 444 (1969), the Supreme Court changed its methodology entirely and established the test still in use today.

Clarence Brandenburg was a leader of the Ku Klux Klan, a white supremacist hate group with a violent history.[15] He gave a speech at a Klan rally in Ohio that celebrated the growing number of Klan members and stated that "if our President, our Congress, our Supreme Court, continues to suppress the white, Caucasian race, it's possible that there might have to be some revengence [sic] taken." The speech was filmed by news media that had been invited to attend. After viewing the televised statement, the Ohio police arrested Brandenburg for violating the Ohio Criminal Syndicalism statute. The statute criminalized advocating "the duty, necessity, or propriety of crime, sabotage, violence or unlawful methods of terrorism as a means of accomplishing industrial or political reform."[16] Brandenburg was fined $1,000 and sentenced to time in prison.

Brandenburg appealed his conviction to the Supreme Court, and it reversed his conviction. A majority of the Court determined that the government's punishment of the abstract advocacy of force violated the First Amendment and found that the Ohio Criminal Syndicalism Statute was unconstitutional. Merely "advocating" violence to effect political and economic change cannot be punished.

---

13   *Gitlow*, 268 U.S. at 673.
14   *See Dennis v. United States*, 341 U.S. 494 (1951) and *Yates v. United States*, 354 U.S. 298 (1957).
15   It is commonly called the KKK. The group targets African Americans, Jews, immigrants, members of the LGBT community, and (in the past) Catholics. It dates back to the Reconstruction period (following the Civil War), and its members have sought to suppress the rights of members of targeted groups through assassination and intimidation.
16   Ohio Rev. Code Ann. Section 2923.13.

FIGURE 4.4 Burning of a cross by the Ku Klux Klan

The Court announced a new two-prong "imminent lawless action" test: advocacy of force or criminal activity may not be suppressed "except where such advocacy is directed to inciting or producing imminent lawless action and is likely to incite or produce such action."[17] This focus on imminence of action brought back the time element of the clear and present danger test, but made it more rigorous.

Brandenburg v. Ohio resolved the long debate about how far the government could go to regulate speech that seeks to incite others to lawless action. The case remains binding precedent, and the test it created has been used in subsequent cases.

CRITICAL THINKING Do you agree with the decision in *Brandenburg* defining the scope of protected seditious speech? Is there any room for improvement? If you were a Supreme Court justice, what precedent would you create?

17   *Brandenburg*, 395 U.S. at 447–48.

Symbolic Speech

Schenck v. United States, Gitlow v. New York, and *Brandenburg v. Ohio* involved spoken or written words used to communicate seditious political content. Often, however, messages are conveyed using symbolic speech. Symbolic speech consists of communication that does not use spoken, written, or signed words. Examples include wearing arm bands and burning or defacing items and symbols relating to the government. The Supreme Court's opinions on the scope of protection afforded symbolic speech demonstrate its evolving understanding of the contours of the First Amendment.

David O'Brien and the Draft Card

On March 31, 1966, David Paul O'Brien (and three others) burned their draft cards in front of a courthouse in South Boston. They were promptly attacked by a crowd of people, and an FBI agent helped O'Brien escape to the safety of the courthouse. There, O'Brien freely confirmed that he had burned his draft card because of his beliefs, knowing that this action violated federal law. He was charged with violating the Universal Military Training and Service Act, which states: any person "who forges, alters, knowingly destroys, knowingly mutilates, or in any manner changes any such certificate"[18] violates the law.

O'Brien argued that the statute's words "knowingly destroys, knowingly mutilates," which had been recently added by amendment, were unconstitutional. He contended that the words served no legitimate legislative purpose and were included only to abridge free speech. He also contended that his act of burning his registration card was protected "symbolic speech" within the First Amendment, as he completed this act in demonstration of the war and the draft.

FIGURE 4.5 Burning draft cards

The federal trial court held that the statute did not violate the First Amendment, and that it resulted from a reasonable exercise of the power of Congress to establish federal armed forces. However, the Court of Appeals for the First Circuit found that the statute was unconstitutional, as it served to abridge free speech. The United States government filed a petition for certiorari, which the United States Supreme Court granted.

Supreme Court Justice Earl Warren drafted the Court's opinion in *United States v. O'Brien*, 391 U.S. 367 (1968). The Court said that while the communicative element in O'Brien's conduct certainly brought the First Amendment into play, it did not necessarily follow that burning the draft card was a protected activity. Congress has sweeping power to raise armies and to make laws to support that effort. Draft cards

---

18   *See* 50 U.S.C. Section 462(b). This wording remains in the statute.

serve several useful purposes, and their destruction or mutilation can create problems: "the continuing availability to each registrant of his Selective Service certificates substantially furthers the smooth and proper function of the system that Congress established to raise armies."[19]

The Supreme Court established a four-part test to determine whether a particular regulation of symbolic speech was permitted under the First Amendment. First, the regulation must be within the constitutional power of the government to enact. Second, it must further an important or substantial governmental interest. Third, that governmental interest must be unrelated to the suppression of free speech. And fourth, the restriction on speech must be no greater than required to further the substantial governmental interest.

The Court found that the government met the test:

> [W]e find that, because of the Government's substantial interest in assuring the continuing availability of issued Selective Service certificates, because amended § 462(b) is an appropriately narrow means of protecting this interest and condemns only the independent noncommunicative impact of conduct within its reach, and because the noncommunicative impact of O'Brien's act of burning his registration certificate frustrated the Government's interest, a sufficient governmental interest has been shown to justify O'Brien's conviction.[20]

CRITICAL THINKING   Do you agree with the Court's decision in *United States v. O'Brien*? If so, do you approve of the four-part test provided by the Court? Do you agree with the Court that "assuring the continuing availability of issued Selective Service certificates" was a "substantial government interest" that requires an exception to the First Amendment? If you disagree, where do you think the Court made the mistake? What precedent would you have created in this case?

Paul Cohen and the Offensive Shirt

On April 26, 1968, Paul Cohen was called to the Los Angeles Superior Court to testify as a witness in a pending case. His attire for his visit to court included a jacket with the words "Fuck the Draft. Stop the War." Cohen later explained that he wore the jacket to protest the Vietnam War.

He removed his jacket before entering the courtroom, but put it back on in the courthouse corridor. A bailiff saw Cohen in the jacket, and arrested him for violating Section 415 of the California Penal Code, which prohibits "maliciously and willfully disturb[ing] the peace or quiet of any

---

19   *O'Brien*, 391 U.S. at 381.
20   *O'Brien*, 391 U.S. at 382.

neighborhood or person [by] tumultuous or offensive conduct." He was convicted and sentenced to thirty days in jail.

Cohen appealed his conviction to the United States Supreme Court, which granted certiorari.

Justice John Marshall Harlan wrote the decision for the sharply split majority in *Cohen v. California*, 403 U.S. 15 (1971). As Cohen's conviction was based solely upon speech rather than conduct, he could only be criminally punished if the words on the jacket were not protected by the First Amendment. Acknowledging that the word *fuck* may well have been offensive, the Court noted that it was not directed at any single person and was not supposed to insult any person, but was rather an expression of Cohen's political views. "Absent a more particularized and compelling reason for its actions, the State may not, consistently with the First and Fourteenth Amendments, make the simple public display here involved of this single four-letter expletive a criminal offense."[21]

CRITICAL THINKING   What do you think of the Court's ruling in *Cohen v. California*? Did it matter that the jacket was worn only outside the courtroom? What messages would have been beyond First Amendment protection, as defined by this ruling?

"Joey" Johnson and the Burning Flag

Gregory Lee "Joey" Johnson was a member of the Revolutionary Communist Youth Brigade. During the 1984 Republican National Convention, he took part in a demonstration against the administration. Participants marched through the streets of Dallas, Texas, carried signs, and also engaged in vandalism. Someone handed Johnson an American flag, and he set it on fire. While the flag burned, the demonstrators shouted protest slogans.

Johnson was charged with violating a Texas statute that prohibits desecration of venerated objects. He appealed his conviction, and the case rose to the Supreme Court.

In *Texas v. Johnson*, 491 U.S 397 (1989), the Court first acknowledged that conduct (in addition to speech) may be "sufficiently imbued with elements of communication to fall within the scope of the First and Fourteenth Amendments."[22] Certainly, not every action taken with a flag is expressive, but in this case, the flag burning occurred as Ronald Reagan was being nominated as president. This rendered the flag burning a communicative action in a way that implicated the First Amendment. The Court found that Johnson's flag burning "constituted expressive conduct, permitting him to invoke the First Amendment."[23] While some conduct would not possess sufficient communicative elements to bring the

---

21   *Cohen*, 403 U.S. at 26.
22   *Texas v. Johnson*, 491 U.S. at 404, citing *Spence v. Washington*, 418 U.S. 405, 409 (1974).
23   *Texas v. Johnson*, 491 U.S. at 403.

FIGURE 4.6 Burning an American flag

First Amendment into play, here there was an intent to convey a particularized message, and there was a great likelihood that the message would be understood by those who viewed it.[24]

In response, Texas claimed that it had an interest in preventing breaches of the peace and that this interest justified Johnson's conviction. The Court noted, however, the flag burning did not lead to any disturbance of the peace. The only evidence of disturbance was the testimony of several persons who had been offended seeing the American flag burn in this way. Accordingly, the interest of Texas in maintaining order was not implicated. And the state's argument that it has the right to preserve the flag's symbolic role did not permit it to "prohibit expression simply because it disagrees with its message."[25]

CRITICAL THINKING   Can you think of expressive conduct that would not be permitted under the test announced in *Texas v. Johnson*? What communicative elements could be problematic?

Children and Free Speech

The Supreme Court has said that children do not "shed their constitutional rights to freedom of speech or expression at the schoolhouse gate."[26] They, too, are entitled to some degree of First Amendment protections.

24   *Texas v. Johnson*, 491 U.S. at 404.
25   *Texas v. Johnson*, 491 U.S. at 416.
26   *Tinker v. Des Moines*, 393 U.S. 503, 506 (1969).

William J. Brennan Jr.

Associate Justice, United States Supreme Court (1956–1990)

Nominated by Republican President Dwight D. Eisenhower, William J. Brennan Jr. made a name for himself as one of the most influential members of the Supreme Court's liberal wing.

He authored the majority opinion in *Roth v. United States*, 354 U.S. 476 (1957), which held that the First Amendment did not protect obscenity. Outside the context of obscenity, however, Justice Brennan was a champion defender of free speech. He wrote the majority opinions in the important cases *Texas v. Johnson*, 491 U.S. 397 (1989), *Tinker v. Des Moines*, 393 U.S. 503 (1969), and *New York Times Co. v. Sullivan,* 376 U.S. 254 (1964).

He believed that the most important opinion he ever authored was *Goldberg v. Kelly*, 397 U.S. 254 (1970), in which the Court determined that welfare benefits could not be terminated without first providing the recipient with a hearing.

FIGURE 4.7 Justice William Brennan Jr.

It is important for the success of our democracy that First Amendment protections exist for school-aged children:

> The classroom is peculiarly the "marketplace of ideas." The Nation's future depends upon leaders trained through wide exposure to that robust exchange of ideas which discovers truth "out of a multitude of tongues, [rather] than through any kind of authoritative selection."[27]

Students should assess and exchange ideas, as this is important for growth:

> [P]eople are unlikely to become well-functioning, independent minded adults and responsible citizens if they are raised in an intellectual bubble.[28]

However, the Supreme Court has acknowledged two important facts: first, children must be protected from some types of content, as they are not yet adults; and second, the educational mission of schools must proceed. Schools have an obligation to teach students a particular curriculum. While some distractions will naturally occur, they cannot repeatedly derail critical instruction.

Accordingly, the important cases concerning free speech for students in schools wrestle with the fact that schools must educate, and that some content that would be permissible in an adult environment might not be appropriate for an underage audience. As always, the question is where and how to draw the line.

---

27   *Keyishian v. Board of Regents*, 385 U.S. 589, 603 (1967).
28   *American Amusement Machine Association v. Kendrick*, 244 F.3d 572, 577 (7th Cir. 2010).

FIGURE 4.8 Tinker protest armbands

The Tinkers and Protest Armbands

We begin our discussion of children and free speech with *Tinker v. Des Moines*, 393 U.S. 503 (1969).

In December 1965, fifteen-year-old John Tinker, John's sister Mary Beth, and their friend Christopher Eckhardt decided to wear black armbands featuring peace symbols to their Des Moines schools. They did this in protest of the Vietnam War and to support the Christmas truce called for by Senator Robert Kennedy. When the school board learned of their plans, it passed a regulation banning the wearing of armbands to school. Students who violated the regulation would be suspended and allowed to return to school after agreeing to leave their armbands at home.

Mary Beth Tinker and Christopher Eckhardt knowingly chose to violate this policy, and the next school day John Tinker joined in. All were suspended from school until after January 1, 1966, when their protest had been scheduled to end.

The Iowa Civil Liberties Union heard about the protest and agreed to help the families with the lawsuit. Eventually, the case came to the Supreme Court, and it was argued before the Court on November 12, 1968.

In a split opinion, the Court found that the First Amendment applies to public schools, and so school administrators must demonstrate constitutionally valid reasons for any specific regulation of speech at school. The Court further determined that the school board's regulation of the children's speech was based upon the wish to avoid any controversy resulting from their expression of opposition to the Vietnam War. However, there was no evidence that instruction was affected by the armbands. Without any such evidence, the Court found that the activity represented constitutionally protected symbolic speech.

Justices Hugo Black and John Marshall Harlan dissented. Justice Black argued that the Tinkers' behavior was disruptive. He said:

[I]f the time has come when pupils of state-supported schools can defy and flout orders of school officials to keep their minds on their own schoolwork, it is the beginning of a new revolutionary era of permissiveness in this country fostered by the judiciary.[29]

Tinker remains a viable and frequently cited Supreme Court precedent, though subsequent Court decisions have refined the scope of children's free speech rights in different contexts.

CRITICAL THINKING   Do you agree with the Court's opinion in *Tinker v. Des Moines*? If you were a Supreme Court justice, what types of expressive speech would you permit at school? If you would suppress disruptive speech, what evidence would you require?

The Students and the School Newspaper

The final case in this chapter is *Hazelwood School District v. Kuhlmeier*, 484 U.S. 260 (1988). This case concerns the scope of schools' editorial control of school-sponsored student newspapers.

Hazelwood East High School is located in St. Louis, Missouri. Students in its Advanced Journalism class wrote articles for the *Spectrum*, a school-sponsored and school-funded newspaper. Robert Reynolds was the principal of the high school. He received the page proofs for each Spectrum issue before publication to decide if they should be approved.

When he received the page proofs for the issue that was to be published in May of 1983, Reynolds pulled two articles that he felt were inappropriate. One article described the experiences of three students who had been pregnant during the school year. The other explored the impact of divorce on a sampling of students attending school. Reynolds had concerns about contextual identification, even though false names were used for the pregnancy piece, and felt that the content of the article might not be appropriate for the younger students. With respect to the second piece, he was concerned that the parents of the divorced students had not consented to the release of personal information about their lives. As the publication deadline was within two days, Reynold permitted the issue to proceed without those two articles.

The students did not like the censorship. They filed an action in federal court, alleging that their First Amendment rights had been violated. They lost at the trial court but won on appeal, and the School District appealed to the Supreme Court.

Quoting *Tinker*, the Supreme Court noted that students do indeed retain some First Amendment rights. However, the rights of students are not as broad as those of adults. Schools need not "tolerate speech that is inconsistent with its basic educational mission."[30] They may set high standards for student

---

29   *Tinker v. Des Moines*, 393 U.S. at 518.
30   *Hazelwood School District v. Kuhlmeier*, 484 U.S. at 266, citing *Bethel School District No. 403 v. Fraser*, 478 U.S. 675, 685 (1986).

speech in school-sponsored papers and refuse to sponsor speech that is "inconsistent with the shared values of a civilized social order."[31] In short, educators could manage the content, as long as their actions were reasonably related to legitimate pedagogical concerns. Finally, the Court found that the principal's conduct met that standard.

Conclusion and Introduction of Law Lab

You have now reviewed a collection of First Amendment Supreme Court cases involving sedition, symbolic speech, and children in public schools.

The Supreme Court has deployed a variety of tests to assess the scope of free speech protection in these cases. In the sedition cases, these tests evolved from the early clear and present danger test, to the dangerous tendencies test, to the imminent lawless action test still in use today. With respect to symbolic speech, the Supreme Court has considered a variety of factors, including the type and scope of interest that the state is protecting, and the nature of the impact of the symbolic speech. In the cases involving students in public schools, the Court has tried to navigate the interests of the state in educating without disruption, the rights of the children under the First Amendment, and the need of the school administration to ensure that content does not run afoul of legitimate social concerns.

In this week's Law Lab, you are again Supreme Court justices. You will need to resolve a brand-new case concerning the scope of the First Amendment's free speech protection in the public-school context. You will need to consider the rights of the students, the interests of the State of Franklin, and the legitimate concerns of the Homewood High School District. The precedent you establish will guide the operations of all the public schools in the nation.

---

31   *Hazelwood*, 484 U.S. at 260, citing *Fraser*, 478 U.S. at 683.

Supreme Court Justice Law Lab

MEMORANDUM

To: The Honorable Chief Justice & Associate Justices of the United States Supreme Court

From: The Law Clerks of the Supreme Court

Re: *Washington and Schultz v. Homewood High*, On Review Following Grant of Petition for Certiorari

Your Honors:

Please allow this summary to assist you as you prepare for deliberations in the above-referenced matter. This case concerns a public-school dress code and the free-speech rights of schoolchildren. The children argue that their right under the First Amendment to publicly express their views about a local development project should take precedence over the school district's dress code. The school district disagrees, noting that the dress code supports an important state purpose.

Factual Background

City of Liberty Springs's School District 99 serves over 400,000 children, and is the largest school district in the State of Franklin. District 99 has faced continuing challenges with overcrowding and a severe achievement gap between students from more affluent and less affluent homes. A substantial number of students enrolled in District 99 come from low-income or single-parent homes. A few years ago, District 99's administration determined to adopt a dress code for all middle and high school students. This is a growing national trend. There are reliable social science studies indicating that adopting dress codes serves the important state interest of improving student performance.

As of September 2016, students attending all District 99 high schools were required to "wear collared shirts (polo shirts or collared button-down shirts), unadorned, in white or light blue," and khaki pants or skirts. Sweaters, coats, and jackets in navy blue were also allowed for chilly weather. Gym-appropriate clothing was also allowed, but only for gym class.

During the prior academic year, Maisie Washington and David Schultz were juniors at Homewood High School, in District 99. They were troubled by news reports describing the environmental impact of a potential new development project. A commercial developer had presented a proposal to establish a new shopping district near Liberty Springs' thermal features. Some people in the community, including Maisie and David, thought that the area around the thermal features should be preserved from development and left in a natural state for the enjoyment of the public. They also worried about the impact of the construction equipment and additional traffic on the thermal springs. During the last week of school before the winter break, both Maisie and David appeared at school wearing white polo shirts with the words "#**Save Our City's Springs!**" written in ink, in large letters, across the back. In addition, the students had attached three-inch plastic buttons on the fronts of their polo shirts. The buttons said, "**SOS = Save Our Springs!**"

At the trial of this matter, there was testimony that at the beginning of the school day, other students approached Maisie and David in the school's main hallway and talked with them. The ensuing discussions

FIGURE 4.9   A thermal feature in Liberty Springs

were lively, and some were quite loud. After a few minutes' delay, all students entered their classrooms to start the school day.

However, when Maisie and David entered their classrooms for their first classes, they were asked to remove the plastic buttons and put sweaters over their shirts. They refused to comply and were suspended until they agreed to appear in the correct uniform. In order to further their education, after two days' suspension, Maisie and David did comply with the dress code. Then, with the assistance of their parents and attorneys from the American Civil Liberties Union, they filed a lawsuit against District 99, claiming that its actions violated their First Amendment right to freedom of speech.

Procedural Posture

District 99 hired counsel to defend the suit brought by Maisie and David and their parents. The District succeeded at the trial court. The jury found that the State of Franklin had a compelling state interest in regulating student attire, and that the students' free speech rights had not been unreasonably infringed. Maisie and David then appealed. The Court of Appeals reversed the trial court's ruling, finding in favor of the students. District 99 then appealed to the Franklin Supreme Court, which again reversed, finding in favor of District 99. Thereafter, Maisie and David petitioned this Court for review, and the Court accepted the case.

Issue: First Amendment Right of Free Speech in High School

The key issue is: does District 99's enforcement of its dress code and its suspension of Maisie Washington and David Schultz violate the Free Speech Clause of the First Amendment of the United States Constitution?

Homewood High is a public high school, not a private school. Therefore, it is bound to follow the law as set forth in the Constitution of the United States and also the Constitution of the State of Franklin, as interpreted by the Supreme Court and state courts of Franklin.

The parties in this case have agreed that this Court should ignore the Constitution of the State of Franklin and focus only on the United States Constitution and Bill of Rights.

Relevant Authority and Considerations

The key case on this subject is *Tinker v. Des Moines*, 393 U.S. 503 (1969), one of this Court's prior opinions.

In *Tinker*, several students wore armbands to school to protest the Vietnam War. The district's School Board passed a resolution proscribing the wearing of armbands, and the students were suspended. This Court found that the suspension was unconstitutional:

> [I]f a regulation were adopted by school officials forbidding discussion of the Vietnam conflict, or the expression by any student of opposition to it anywhere on school property except as part of a prescribed classroom exercise, it would be obvious that the regulation would violate the constitutional rights of students, at least if it could not be justified by a showing that the students' activities would materially and substantially disrupt the work and discipline of the school. ... In the circumstances of the present case, the prohibition of the silent,

passive "witness of the armbands," as one of the children called it, is no less offensive to the Constitution's guarantees. ... As we have discussed, the record does not demonstrate any facts which might reasonably have led school authorities to forecast substantial disruption of or material interference with school activities, and no disturbances or disorders on the school premises in fact occurred. ... In the circumstances, our Constitution does not permit officials of the State to deny their form of expression.[1]

Other relevant cases include *Gilman v. School Board for Holmes County*, 567 F. Supp. 2d (2008), and *Isaacs v. Board of Education of Howard County*, 40 F. Supp 2d 335 (D. Md 1995). In *Gilman*, a trial court in the Northern District of Florida found that the First Amendment supports a student's right to show support for a gay fellow student by wearing a rainbow belt and a T-shirt declaring, "I support gays." The judge determined that the speech had been unlawfully banned due to the personal views of the school's principal, and that the messaging had not caused material disruption in the school. In *Isaacs*, a federal trial judge in the District of Maryland ruled that a student did not have the right to wear a multicolored headwrap to school to celebrate her African American and Jamaican cultural heritage in violation of the school's dress code. The judge distinguished *Tinker*, noting that political speech has special status under the First Amendment.

In addition, a federal trial considered the scope of free speech in schools in *Castorina v. Madison County School Board*, 246 F.3d 536 (6th Cir. 2001). In this case, the United States Court of Appeals for the Sixth Circuit found that, based upon *Tinker* and other Supreme Court rulings, the Madison County School Board could not ban Confederate flag T-shirts while other racial and political symbols (like the "X" symbol associated with Malcolm X) were permitted.

Most recently, in *Mahanoy Area School District v. B.L.*, 594 U.S . ___ (2021), this Court considered the ability of public schools to regulate speech that was made off campus. Brandi Levy attended Mahanoy Area High School, located in Mahanoy City, Pennsylvania. Disappointed that she was not chosen for the school's varsity cheerleading squad, she sent a profane message to a circle of friends via Snapchat. The message featured a picture of Brandi and another student, both posed with raised middle fingers, and included the text "fuck school fuck softball fuck cheer fuck everything." The post was brought to the attention of the administration, and Brandi was informed that she was suspended from cheerleading for one year. Brandi had violated the school's cheerleading code of conduct, which forbade the use of profanity, and required squad members to act with respect toward the school and its personnel.

This Court determined that the school district had indeed violated Brandi's First Amendment rights by suspending her from cheerleading because of her Snapchat post. There was no evidence that the post disrupted student education, and other elements of the case also inclined toward supporting Brandi's First Amendment rights. The Court stated, "America's public schools are the nurseries of democracy," and schools have "an interest in protecting a student's unpopular expression."

---

1   *Tinker*, 393 U.S. at 514.

It should be noted that none of the school districts in the cases mentioned above contended with the same stated governmental interest as is before the Court here. District 99 has determined that wearing uniforms will advance the important state interest of helping to close the educational gap between minority pupils and other students in the district. District 99 argues that it is not discriminating: it has prohibited the display of all symbols on all clothing.

District 99 also introduced evidence about public spaces in its schools dedicated to student views. Each school has a large bulletin board placed in the school cafeteria, where students' comments and essays about their political and social thoughts may be displayed. School administrators receive and review proposed content and post those items that they feel adhere to school guidelines. Maisie and David testified at trial that they did not use the bulletin board for their message, as they said most students at their school ignored it.

Finally, District 99 filed a document collecting the findings of studies concerning the effect of a school uniform policy. These studies show improvement of student outcomes.[2]

Conclusion

We hope that this memorandum has assisted with the Court's preparation in this matter. Please let us know if we can provide any additional information to assist with deliberations. As always, your law clerks are eager to be helpful and look forward to the Court's decision.

---

2   *Cf.* One study was conducted in Sparks Middle School in Nevada. One year after the uniform policy was implemented, school police data showed a 63 percent drop in police log reports, decreases in gang activity, student fighting, graffiti, battery, and property damage. Claudene Wharton, "College of Education Researchers Conduct Study on Impacts of School Uniforms," UNR.edu (Apr. 23, 2013).

CHAPTER 5

Religious Freedom

Leave the matter of religion to the family altar, the church, and the private school, supported entirely by private contributions. Keep the church and state forever separate.

—Ulysses S. Grant, 30 September 1875, speech before the Society of the Army of Tennessee, Des Moines, Iowa

Introduction

In the first chapter, we observed that early societies had no separate religious and political institutions. The rulers of ancient states were also the chief clerics, and the people worshipped as commanded. Wherever you lived, you were a practitioner of that community's religion, on pain of banishment or death.

In contrast, today's United States is marked by religious diversity. Americans hold a wide variety of faiths,[1] and to many, religious practice is important. Religion runs to the core of our personal identity, touching on beliefs about our origins, nature, obligations, and destiny. Matters concerning religious practices bring forth a strong response, and cases that address religious freedom hold a special place in American law.

Two core concepts undergird the freedom of religion in the United States. The first is separation of religion from government. We abandoned the old paradigm of a state religion in favor of a new model. In the new model, religious organizations operate independently, and the government does not favor or disfavor any particular sect or creed.

The second core concept is the right to worship. People must be allowed to practice the religion of their choice, or none at all. A government that does not favor any religion could still discourage all religious practices. Accordingly, in addition to the separation of religion from governmental operations, the people must have legal support for their right to worship.

---

1   As of 2016, the largest denominations were Protestantism (48.9%); Catholicism (23.0%); Judaism (2.1%); Mormonism (1.8%); and Islam (.8%). *See* Frank Newport, *Five Key Findings on Religion in the U.S.*, Gallup (Dec. 23, 2016), https://news.gallup.com/poll/200186/five-key-findings-religion.aspx.

These two concepts are enshrined in the First Amendment. This chapter explores the historical foundation of the First Amendment's religious freedom clauses. It then reviews key Supreme Court cases that protect religious freedom, and the tests that the Court has devised to determine if religious freedom has been unconstitutionally impaired. In reading these cases, you will develop the background needed to complete this chapter's Law Lab, which concerns the public display of a troubling religious artifact.

RELIGIOUS FREEDOM KEY TERMS

The following key terms are defined in this chapter. They are also defined in the Glossary.

Establishment Clause	**High-Wall Theory of**	***Lemon* Test**	**Secular Regulation Rule**
Free Exercise Clause	**Separation**	**Non-preferentialism**	***Sherbert* Test**

The Development of Religious Freedom

The existence of religious diversity precedes the demand for religious freedom. If everyone holds the same belief and worships in the same way, there is little incentive to press for the freedom to observe the faith of your choice.

The Code of Justinian required all persons living in the Roman Empire to practice the Christian faith. The Romans believed that a single state religion was necessary to unify the people and support

FIGURE 5.1 The Last Prayer

the government. As the Roman Empire declined in the west, the Catholic Church rose to fill the void, becoming a seat of temporal power as well as the source of religious authority. The clergy expanded and grew in importance, and for much of the last two thousand years, Catholicism was the official religion of all the European nations.

The transition from a single religion of state to the multiplicity in evidence today was a long and bloody process. Martyrs died because they would not follow governmental religious edicts, and kings and queens were excommunicated because they would not bend the knee to religious leaders.

Our enjoyment of religious freedom owes much to those who gave much for the privilege of practicing their faith.

The Fracturing of Christianity

The expansion of feudalism in Europe led to increased prominence for secular rulers. By the time William the Conqueror invaded England in 1066, European rulers controlled substantial lands and resources. The rise of kings and feudalism did not result in religious diversity. However, as nationalism grew and education centers flourished, conflicts developed between the clergy, the crown, and the citizenry. Grievances mounted, and critics of the Catholic Church openly decried the intemperance and casual religious practices of some of the clergy. The Church lost status in England when the papal seat moved to Avignon in France in 1309, and the effort to restore it to Rome led to schism, division, and further reduction in prestige.

Many criticized the Church's failings, and eventually Martin Luther's[2] work produced a widespread "Reformation" in 1521.

The Reformation fractured Christianity, forging four major religious movements: Lutheranism, Calvinism, Anabaptism, and Anglicanism. The British adopted some of those diverse practices, with downstream consequences for those who later came to live in North America.

FIGURE 5.2 Martin Luther

---

2   Martin Luther decried the clergy's practice of selling indulgences (reductions in punishment for sin). By maintaining that the doctrine of indulgences was theologically wrong, Luther challenged the authority of the pope.

The Rise of Religious Diversity in Medieval England

Henry VIII, the English king notorious for collecting (and beheading) wives, played an interesting part in the rise of religious diversity in England.

FIGURE 5.3 Execution of Anne Boleyn (wife of Henry VIII)

Under the rule of Henry VII, England was a firmly Catholic nation. When Henry VIII assumed the throne in 1509, he initially followed in his father's footsteps, defending the Catholic Church against Protestants. However, Henry VIII's first marriage to Catherine of Aragon did not produce the desired male heir. When the pope refused to annul the marriage, Henry VIII married Anne Boleyn anyway, and established himself as the head of a new Church of England.[3] The Catholic Church, reduced in prestige and power, could not offer meaningful opposition. Henry VIII dissolved the monastcries, appropriated their property and income, and reformed existing Catholic practices in England.[4] Although Pope Paul III excommunicated him, there was no military response, and Henry VIII reigned until he died of old age in 1547.

During this time, most people continued to believe that an official state religion was necessary to maintain political order. Accordingly, English kings and queens implemented practices designed to ensure loyalty to the crown of England. The next fifty years of English history illustrate the tribulations that can flow from the formal linkage of religion and government.

---

3   British monarchs remain the titular head of the Church of England and may not be Roman Catholics. This requirement is codified in the Act of Settlement of 1701.

4   *See* B.W. Bernard, "The Making of Religious Policy 1533–1546: Henry VIII and the Search for the Middle Way" (1998).

When Henry VIII's son, Edward VI, came to the throne, his Protestant advisers encouraged sharp reforms that would eradicate Roman Catholic practices.[5] However, upon Edward's death in 1533, his Catholic half-sister Mary was crowned queen. Mary I aggressively reversed the changes her father and brother had made. In the course of her efforts, over 280 Protestant religious dissenters were burned at the stake, earning her the nickname "Bloody Mary." Mary died in 1558 and was succeeded by her Protestant half-sister, Elizabeth I, who reversed the reestablishment of Roman Catholicism.[6]

One outcome of England's religious turbulence was the rise of the Puritans, members of a reform movement that sought to "purify" the Church of England from Roman Catholic practices. The Puritans frequently clashed with the English crown over the lack of deeper reform. Their desire to live in a society that supported their religious beliefs laid the foundation for the religious and social order in New England and became part of the story of religious diversity in America.

FIGURE 5.4   Queen Mary I

Colonial America and Religious Diversity

Weary of enduring religious persecution, a small group of Separatist Puritans left England, arriving in Plymouth, Massachusetts, in 1620. A larger group of Independent Puritans of more liberal views arrived ten years later and established another settlement in Massachusetts.[7] From 1620 to 1640, about 20,000 Puritans came to New England. Like later settlers, they took up residence in lands inhabited by indigenous peoples of different Tribal nations.[8]

Those early settlements then expanded into new colonies, largely driven by religious preferences. Puritans who believed the Massachusetts settlements were not liberal enough built colonies in

---

5   Among other things, Edward ordered all altars replaced with simple tables; announced that priests could marry; abolished the Mass; and dissolved the Chantries (religious communities focusing on prayers for the dead), seizing their assets for the crown.

6   Elizabeth issued the Religious Settlement of 1559 in an effort to conclude the English Reformation and the turmoil it caused. It confirmed the independence of the Church of England, gave prominence to the Book of Common Prayer (from the reign of Edward I), and included some doctrinal changes appealing to both Lutherans and Catholics. These measures did not entirely resolve religious problems in England. *See* Arthur Geoffrey Dickens, *The English Reformation* (1967).

7   The Separatists left the Anglican Church. The Independents sought to reform the Anglican Church while remaining within it. The Separatists established the Plymouth Bay Colony. The Independents founded the Massachusetts Bay Colony. The Independents rose to prominence in New England.

8   At the time of the arrival of the first colonists, the land that became Massachusetts was inhabited by the Wampanoag, Massachusetts, Nauset, Nipmuc, and Mohican peoples who spoke the Algonquian language. Elizabeth Prine Pauls, "Northeast Indians," Encyclopaedia Britannica, https://www.britannica.com/topic/Northeast-Indian.

Connecticut.[9] Puritans who believed that the Massachusetts groups were too strict moved on to Rhode Island,[10] a colony that became notable for accepting Jews and permitting free religious liberty.[11] Religious diversity—and the disagreements resulting from that diversity—became a feature of American society.

In 1632, the English crown gave the land that would become the Colony of Maryland to Cecil Calvert, the second son of Lord Baltimore.[12] Notwithstanding that he was a Catholic, Calvert hoped to ensure religious tolerance in the territory. He drafted the Maryland Toleration Act, which provided for the free exercise of religion. This act was repealed, and still later, again reenacted.

After Charles II ascended to the throne of England in 1660, he organized the settlement in New Hampshire as a crown colony.[13] He also gained control of the Dutch trading colony of New Amsterdam, and deeded it to his brother James, the Duke of York. Renamed New York in the Duke's honor, the colony grew to become a formidable political force, comprised of French Protestants (Huguenots), Quakers, Puritans, Jews, and Anglicans.[14] The English also gained control of the nearby Province of New Jersey and joined the settlements of East Jersey and West Jersey into a single crown colony.[15]

The English took control of colonial Pennsylvania[16] and founded its capital in 1682. William Penn, a Quaker, modeled the colony on religious tolerance. Penn also received the deed for the "Lower Counties on the Delaware," a land of Quakers and Protestants.[17]

Charles II also hoped to create English colonies in the territory between the established colony of Virginia[18] and Spanish Florida. He encouraged plantation owners to come to the New World from Barbados, an English

---

9   These were founded by Congregationalist Thomas Hooker in 1636. At the time, among others, the Quinnipiac, Mohegan, Pequot, and Munsee Native American Tribes lived in the area. *See Native Americans*, Connecticut History, https://connecticuthistory.org/topics-page/native-americans/.

10 Indigenous people living in the land that became Rhode Island included members of the Narragansett, Niantic, and Wampanoag Tribes. *See* "Native Americans," Rhode Island Dept. of State, https://www.sos.ri.gov/divisions/civics-and-education/for-educators/themed-collections/native-americans.

11 Rhode Island was founded by Baptist Roger Williams. He reasoned that, as faith is the free gift of the Holy Spirit, it cannot be forced upon a person, and consequently strict separation of church and state is required.

12 The indigenous Tribes of this land included the Shawnee and Ohio Valley Tribes, the Susquehannock, the Lenape, the Tutelo, the Saponi, the Nanticoke, and the Powhatan. *People, Tribes and Bands*, Maryland Government https://msa.maryland.gov/msa/mdmanual/01glance/native/html/01native.html.

13 The indigenous Tribes in this area were the Abenaki and Pennacook. "Native American Heritage," New Hampshire Government https://www.nh.gov/folklife/learning-center/traditions/native-american.htm.

14 Many different Native American Tribes lived in the land that became the state of New York. They included the Mohawk, the Mohican, the Abenaki, the Laurentians, the Oneida, the Onandaga, the Cayuga, the Seneca, the Erie, the Delaware, the Poospatuck, and the Mohegan. "New York's Native American History," Smithsonian Mag., https://www.smithsonianmag.com/videos/category/history/new-yorks-native-american-history/.

15 The Native American Tribes living in the land that became New Jersey included the Lenni Lenape (Delaware) people. "History—Native Americans," *New Jersey Almanac*, https://www.newjerseyalmanac.com/native-americans.html.

16 The area was home to the Lenape, Susquehannock, Iroquois, Erie, Shawnee, and other native Tribes. Michael Goode, "Native American-Pennsylvania Relations, 1681–1753," *The Encyclopedia of Greater Philadelphia*, https://philadelphiaencyclopedia.org/archive/native-american-pennsylvania-relations-1681-1753/.

17 The indigenous peoples in this area were the Shawnee and Ohio Valley Tribes, the Iroquois, the Erie, the Lenape Delaware, the Munsee Delaware, and the Susquehannock. *Id.*

18 Virginia became a tobacco plantation colony. The primary cultivators of the crop were enslaved persons from West Africa. The indigenous persons living in the area at the time of colonization included members of the Cherokee, Yuchi, Catawba, Powhatan, Tutelo, and Saponi Tribes. *See* "Virginia's Early Relations with Native Americans," Library of Congress, http://www.loc.gov/teachers/classroommaterials/presentationsandactivities/presentations/timeline/colonial/indians/.

sugar colony supported by enslaved people. They established a colony in the southern part of what is now South Carolina[19] and called it Charles Town.[20] Another group created a second settlement to the north.[21] Due to political disagreements, the colonies of North Carolina and South Carolina were formally given separate status in 1729.

Finally, in 1732, King George II granted Englishman James Oglethorpe a charter to establish the Georgia colony.[22] In 1755, Georgia became a crown colony with freedom to worship for everyone "except papists."[23]

As the result of the influx of these people with diverse backgrounds, each colony developed its own religious character and its own views on religious tolerance. From the Puritans in Massachusetts and Connecticut to the Quakers, Catholics, Baptists, Lutherans, and Jews that scattered across the Middle and Southern Colonies, colonial America was uniquely diverse.[24]

This diversity did not lead to religious sufferance. The Congregationalist Church was officially established in Massachusetts, New Hampshire, and Connecticut. In Pennsylvania and Delaware, all Christian sects were treated fairly equally, but Catholics encountered discrimination, and in at least five colonies, the Church of England was politically dominant, although other religions were tolerated.[25]

Notwithstanding their differing histories and religious views, the colonies were able to work together to achieve independence from England. Their successful break from Great Britain marked the first successful decolonization in the New World.

The First Amendment Religious Freedom Clauses

The delegates that gathered in Philadelphia for the Constitutional Convention of 1787 represented a wide range of religious denominations. Twenty-eight were Anglicans, seven were Congregationalists, and eight were Presbyterians. In addition, there were two Lutherans, two Methodists, two Calvinists, and two others unaffiliated with any particular religion.[26]

---

19   Many of the early settlers came from Barbados, where slavery was well established. In the 1700s, the Carolinas enacted slave laws based upon the brutal codes used in Barbados. Black persons could be legally bought and sold as property and killed if they attempted to run away. The enslaved Africans brought their indigenous religions with them. The most prominent of these was Bakongo. The Gullah culture of South Carolina and Georgia traces back to enslaved persons from West Africa.

20   The land that became South Carolina included the Cherokee, Creek, Cusabo, Catawba, and Siouan Tribes. Stanley South, "The Unabridged Version of Tribes of the Carolina Lowland," Univ. of S. Carolina Scholarly Commons (1972), http://scholarcommons.sc.edu/archanth_books/16?utm_source=scholarcommons.sc.edu%2Farchanth_books%2F16&utm_medium=PDF&utm_campaign=PDFCoverPages.

21   The Native American Tribes in the land that became North Carolina included the Cherokee, the Creek, the Tutelo, the Tuscarora, the Catawba, the Croatan, and the Carolina Siouan. "North Carolina American Indian History Timeline," North Carolina Museum of History, https://www.ncmuseumofhistory.org/american-indian/handouts/timeline.

22   Slavery was originally prohibited by law in the colony, but the restriction was lifted in 1749. Manilio Graziano, *In Rome We Trust: The Rise of Catholics in American Political Life* 30 (2017).

23   The indigenous people in the land that became Georgia included members of the Cherokee, the Creek, the Hitchiti, the Oconee, the Miccosukee, the Timucua, the Apala, and the Yamasee Tribes. *See* "Anatomy of a Land Grab," Georgia Public Broadcasting, https://www.gpb.org/georgiastories/stories/thirst_for_new_land.

24   In addition, enslaved African Americans continued to honor their spiritual worldviews, and some African religions took root in the New World. Muslim Africans were scattered through the slave colonies. *See* Albert J. Raboteau, *Slave Religion: The Invisible Institution in the Antebellum South* (2004).

25   *See* Sanford Cobb, *The Rise of Religious Liberty in America*, 437–38 (1902).

26   *See* Frank Lambert, *The Founding Fathers and the Place of Religion in America* (2003).

James Madison composed the first draft of the Bill of Rights during the First United States Congress, which met from 1789 to 1791 during the presidency of George Washington. The congressmen easily agreed that religious freedom should be ensured at the federal level. Early Americans identified with the religious (and other) preferences of their resident states and did not want the federal government to intrude. Further, they recognized that religion was a divisive issue. Any chance of continuing unification would end if any religious group's interests were violated.[27] The text went through a series of amendments and revisions until the final language was adopted.[28]

The First Amendment opens with two short and simple clauses that guarantee religious freedom:

> Congress shall make no law respecting an establishment of religion, or prohibiting the free exercise thereof.

The first clause is the **Establishment Clause**. This clause expressly forbids lawmaking that supports the establishment of religion. The second clause is the **Free Exercise Clause**, which ensures citizens' right to worship (or not worship) as they choose. These clauses work from the top down, requiring the government to remain disengaged on religious matters, and also from the bottom up, protecting the individual's rights to practice their religion as they choose. The government may not act to promote religion, and the people are free to choose how to worship.

There are a great many Free Exercise and Establishment Clause cases, and we cannot comprehensively treat them here.[29] We can, however, sample a selection of Supreme Court religious freedom cases. We will begin with the Free Exercise Clause cases.

Applying the Free Exercise Clause

Despite the broad phrasing of the two religious freedom clauses, the protection of religious practices is not absolute. As Thomas Jefferson said, "The acts of the body, unlike the operations of the mind, are subject to the coercion of the laws."[30] The government is permitted to regulate conduct, and it is inevitable that some regulations will intrude upon religion practices.

Each one of the cases discussed below features a governmental intrusion upon the exercise of religion. The question for the Supreme Court in these cases is not simply whether a person's ability to practice their religion has been impaired. The Court must decide *whether the impairment is permissible.*

---

27   Ellis M. West, *The Religion Clauses of the First Amendment* 65 (2011).
28   Scholars and jurists use the Framers' edits and revisions to assess the scope of the religious freedom clauses in a variety of contexts. For example, the Framers rejected the narrow prohibition against the establishing of "one religious sect" or "articles of faith" in favor of the broader language. Justice David Souter argued that this means the Framers wanted a high wall of separation between church and state. John A. Fliter, "Keeping the Faith: Justice David Souter and the First Amendment Religion Clauses," 40 *J. of Church and St.* 387, 400 (1998).
29   Free Exercise Clause and Establishment Clause cases have received an abundance of scholarly attention. One comprehensive review is provided by Douglas Laycock in his five-volume set, *Religious Liberty*, published by Eerdmans (2018).
30   Thomas Jefferson, Virginia Statute for Establishing Religious Freedom, introduced 1779, adopted 1786.

The Early Bigamy Cases and the Secular Regulation Rule

Early cases involved federal laws that criminalized bigamy.

Reynolds v. United States, 98 U.S. 145 (1898), concerned the 1862 Morrill Anti-Bigamy Act. This act banned bigamy in federal territories.[31] It was written to address the plural marriage practices of the Church of Jesus Christ of Latter-day Saints (LDS) in Utah Territory.

George Reynolds lived in Utah Territory. He was the secretary to Brigham Young, the second president of the LDS Church. Reynolds offered to serve as a test subject for the federal law, and so he married a second wife before a group of witnesses. He was charged, convicted, fined $500, and sentenced to two years of hard labor. The Utah Territorial Supreme Court upheld the sentence, and Reynolds appealed to the United States Supreme Court.

Reynolds presented a Free Exercise argument to the Supreme Court: his religion required him to marry multiple times, and the Free Exercise Clause ensured his right to practice his religion. Accordingly, any law that prohibited plural marriage was unconstitutional.

The Court did not agree. It found that the convention of single marriage had endured in the common law since the times of King James I and that polygamy was "odious among the northern and western nations of Europe ..."[32] Doctrines of religious belief cannot become superior to the law of the land, as that would "permit every citizen to become a law unto himself."[33] The Court affirmed the conviction: bigamy was illegal, and arguing that your religion supported it would not make it legal.

A second and rather different bigamy case, *Davis v. Beason*, 133 U.S. 33 (1890), arose as the result of the passage of the Edmunds Act in 1882. The Edmunds Act made polygamy a felony, but it went further: it required voters to swear that they were not bigamists or polygamists.[34] In addition, an Idaho statute[35] required voters to swear that they are "not a bigamist or polygamist; [or] a member of any order ... which teaches ... bigamy or polygamy ..."

Samuel Davis (and others) took the required oath. They were members of the Church of Jesus Christ of Latter-Day Saints. There was no evidence that Davis was married, but because of his church membership,

---

31   It provides: "Every person having a husband or wife living, who marries another, whether married or single, in a Territory, or other place over which the United States has exclusive jurisdiction, is guilty of bigamy, and shall be punished by a fine of not more than $500, and by imprisonment for a term of not more than five years." Morrill Anti-Bigamy Act, ch. 125, § 1, 12 Stat. 501 (1862) (codified at Rev. Star. § 5352).

32   *Reynolds*, 98 U.S. at 165.

33   *Reynolds*, 98 U.S. at 167.

34   Edmunds Act, 22 Stat. 30b (1882).

35   Section 504 Rev. Stats. Idaho.

he was convicted of swearing falsely. He appealed his conviction, claiming that requiring him to swear the oath violated the Free Exercise Clause of the Constitution.

The Supreme Court agreed that "legislation for the establishment of religion is forbidden." However, "it does not follow that everything which may be so called can be tolerated."[36] The federal legislature was permitted to establish voter qualifications that would secure obedience to its laws, and Idaho's law was similarly not "open to any constitutional or legal objection" as it "simply excludes from the privilege of voting ... those who have been convicted of certain offenses."[37]

This case became one of the foundational opinions of the **secular regulation rule**, one method of testing laws for compliance with the Free Exercise Clause. The secular regulation rule maintains that *if a law does not have a religious purpose—if it does not seek to affect religious practices—then it is constitutional.* Secular regulations that do not seek to burden religious practices do not violate the Free Exercise Clause.

The rule seems quite simple and evenhanded. However, like many such rules, its application was harsh in unanticipated ways. As we will see, later cases sought to balance claims of conscience against secular regulations.

The School Free Exercise Clause Cases and the *Sherbert* Substantial Burden Test

When the Supreme Court determined in *Cantwell v. Connecticut*, 310 U.S. 296 (1940), that the Free Exercise Clause applied to the states as well as the federal government, cases filed against states began to rise to the Supreme Court. Many involved Jehovah's Witnesses and prayers or flag salutes in public schools. We next review two flag salute cases and one public school attendance case.

The Gobitis Children and the American Flag

Minersville School District v. Gobitis, 310 U.S. 586 (1940), involved Lillian and Billy Gobitis, Jehovah's Witnesses who lived in Minersville, Pennsylvania. For deeply held religious reasons, Jehovah's Witnesses do not salute the flag.[38] A Pennsylvania regulation required public school students to salute the American flag on pain of expulsion. The Gobitis children refused to salute the flag, endured hazing, and were then expelled. A majority of the Supreme Court applied the secular regulation rule and found that the students' expulsion was not unconstitutional. In a ruling with ancient echoes, the Court found that the states were free to enact laws supporting a sense of national unity. As long as these laws were not passed for the

---

36   *Davis*, 133 U.S. at 345.
37   *Davis*, 133 U.S. at 347.
38   According to the Watchtower, their website, Jehovah's Witnesses believe that bowing down to a flag or saluting it is a religious act that ascribes salvation not to God, but to the state or to its leaders. *See* Appendix, *Flag Salute*, Watchtower, https://wol.jw.org/en/wol/d/r1/lp-e/1101983034.

FIGURE 5.5   American flag

purpose of violating religious views, they were not unconstitutional, and personal religious convictions would not permit disobedience to them.[39]

Justice Harlan Stone filed a memorable dissent. He argued that the Constitution's guarantee of liberty "is the freedom of the individual from compulsion as to what he shall think and he shall say."[40] Requiring the children to salute the flag violated the premise behind the First Amendment, that "freedom of mind and spirit must be preserved …"[41]

The Barnett Children and the American Flag

Emboldened by the *Gobitis* decision, the legislature in West Virginia amended its education statutes to require courses in civics, history, and in the federal and West Virginia constitutions. In addition, the West Virginia Board of Education passed a resolution directing all teachers and pupils to conduct a flag salute. Any refusal to do so would be regarded as an act of insubordination. A student's failure to salute the flag would result in expulsion, with readmission denied until compliance was achieved.

Marie and Gathie Barnett were sisters attending elementary school in West Virginia and were Jehovah's Witnesses. They declined to participate in the flag salute and were expelled from school as a

---

39   Tragically, this ruling led to a surge of violence against Jehovah's Witnesses. A mob of over two thousand people burned the Kingdom Hall in Kennebunkport, Maine, on June 9, 1940, and five Witnesses were badly beaten in Rawlins, Wyoming, on June 18. *See* Shawn Francis Peters, *Judging Jehovah's Witnesses: Religious Persecution and the Dawn of Rights Revolution* 84 (2000).

40   *Gobitis*, 310 U.S. at 604.

41   *Gobitis*, 310 U.S. at 606.

result. The Barnetts filed suit, asking that the court issue an order ceasing enforcement of the mandatory flag salute regulations.

The case reached the Supreme Court. In *West Virginia State Board of Education v. Barnette*,[42] 319 U.S. 624 (1943), the Court reversed its holding in *Gobitis*, finding that it was unconstitutional for public schools to compel students to salute the flag. Justice Harlan Stone's concept of freedom from compulsion, expressed in his dissent in *Gobitis*, won the day. The majority opinion declared, "If there is any fixed star in our constitutional constellation, it is that no official, high or petty, can prescribe what shall be orthodox in politics, nationalism, religion, or other matters of opinion or force citizens to confess by word or act their faith therein." It was unconstitutional to repress religious rights for the sake of creating unity.

As Free Exercise Clause cases continued to present themselves, the Supreme Court developed a more nuanced methodology for deciding them. To determine if the Free Exercise Clause had been violated, the Supreme Court deployed what became known as the **Sherbert test.** This test was developed in the Supreme Court case *Sherbert v. Vernor*, 374 U.S. 398 (1963), involving a Seventh-day Adventist who was denied unemployment benefits because she would not work on Saturdays. The Court found that the denial of benefits was unconstitutional, as the state's restrictions on Ms. Sherbert's eligibility for unemployment compensation imposed a heavy burden on the exercise of her faith, and no compelling state interest justified the burden.

The *Sherbert* test has two main parts, and each main part has two subparts. The first main part focuses on the person's religious practices. Here, the court must determine: 1) whether the person has a claim involving a sincere religious belief; and 2) whether the government action substantially burdens the person's ability to act on that belief.

If both elements of the first part are established, then the second main part comes into play. Here, it is up to the government to prove: 1) that it is acting in furtherance of a "compelling state interest"; and 2) that it has pursued that interest in the manner least burdensome to religion. Any law that "unduly burdens the practice of religion" without a balancing compelling state interest would be unconstitutional, even if it were neutral to religion.

The Amish Children and High School Education

A new context for the Free Exercise Clause and *Sherbert* test arose in *Wisconsin v. Yoder*, 406 U.S. 205 (1972). Students from three different Amish families stopped going to high school at the end of the eighth grade due to their families' religious beliefs. Their parents were charged with violating Wisconsin's compulsory attendance laws, which provide that children must attend school until the age of sixteen. With support from William Lindholm, a Lutheran minister, the case ascended to the Supreme Court.

Applying the first main part of the *Sherbert* test, the Court found that the Amish way of life involves deeply held religious convictions. The requirement to attend school beyond the age of sixteen threatens those convictions.

---

42   The family's last name was misspelled by a court clerk as *Barnette*, and the error perpetuated through the court system.

With respect to the second main part, the government's burden of proof, the Court noted that only governmental "interests of the highest order and not otherwise served can overbalance legitimate claims to the free exercise of religion." While some education is needed to prepare citizens to participate in our political system, the government had not shown the additional year or so of formal high school was necessary to serve that interest. Thus, the Amish children could stop attending school at age sixteen.

The Court's application of the *Sherbert* test in *Wisconsin v. Yoder* confirmed the importance of considering the burden on religious practices imposed by a law that was not enacted to have any effect on religion. The Court had moved away from the secular regulation rule that a law could not be challenged as long as it had been enacted with solely secular intent.

Beginning in the 1980s, however, the Supreme Court began to move back toward the earlier position. In *Employment Division v. Smith*, 499 U.S. 872 (1990), a majority of the Court held that laws of general application did not require individualized considerations under the First Amendment. Instead, litigants should seek changes in the offensive state laws by petitioning their legislatures. In response, the Religious Freedom Restoration Act was enacted at the federal level and with similar laws enacted by twenty-one states.[43] These carve out exemptions based upon religion from certain regulations. These statutes have become the basis for newer legal challenges to laws that affect religious practices.

CRITICAL THINKING   Do you think that people should be able to challenge laws of general application on religious grounds? If so, what test would you require litigants to meet?

Applying the Establishment Clause

We now leave the Free Exercise Clause, which supports religious practices, and turn to the Establishment Clause, which bars state support for religion. Under the provisions of the Establishment Clause, the government may not pass legislation to promote theocracy: "Congress shall make no law regarding the establishment of religion ..." This clause was designed to work from the top down, ensuring that the government does not support religious practices.

The Supreme Court made the Establishment Clause applicable to the states in 1947 in *Everson v. Board of Education*, 330 U.S. 1 (1947). Prior to *Everson*, states could legally establish or support religious practices. Or, even if their Constitutions condemned the creation of a state religion (which most of them did), they could still do workarounds. For example, North Carolina's original constitution refused to sanction a state religion. But it also provided that "no person who shall deny the being of God, or the truth of the Protestant religion, or the divine authority of either the Old or New Testaments" would be eligible for "holding any office" (Art. 32).[44]

---

43   42 U.S.C. Section 2000bb-2000bb-4.
44   In *Torcaso v. Watkins*, 367 U.S. 488 (1961), the Supreme Court expressly rendered this type of provision unconstitutional. The case involved a Maryland requirement that a candidate for public office must declare a belief in God.

Once the Establishment Clause was made applicable to the states, the Supreme Court's task was to assess how far the states could go when their regulations or other actions would affect religious practices. Different approaches arose to answer that question.

One prominent theoretical paradigm to the separation of church and state is **non-preferentialism**. This theory maintains that the First Amendment forbids the favoring of a particular religion, and so the government may not take action that benefits one church group over another. However, the First Amendment would not preclude evenhanded public aid to religious groups.

The second theory is the **high-wall theory of separation** of government and religion. Under this paradigm, there must be no support of any religion in any way by the government. The Establishment Clause entirely precludes governmental involvement in religion.

There are a great many Establishment Clause cases. Some address the scope of permitted funding for institutions that are, to a greater or lesser degree, affiliated with religions. Some consider whether any government funds can go to parents who wish to send their children to religious schools instead of to public schools. We will first review Establishment Clause cases that concern prayer in public schools.

CRITICAL THINKING   As you review the Establishment Clause cases noted below, consider whether you agree or disagree with each opinion. Has the state gone too far? Why or why not?

The Establishment Clause and the Purpose and Primary Effect Test

In the 1950s, the New York Board of Regents crafted a voluntary, nondenominational prayer that students could recite at the beginning of the school day. It said, "Almighty God, we acknowledge our dependence upon Thee, and we beg Thy blessings upon us, our parents, our teachers and our Country." The families of a group of students in New Hyde Park from the Herricks Union Free School District found that the prayer contradicted their religious beliefs. Supported by a collection of groups opposed to school prayer, they filed suit, claiming that the prayer violated the Establishment Clause.

The case, *Engel v. Vitale*, 379 U.S. 421 (1962), generated controversy as it rose to the Supreme Court. Due to the fact that the prayer was voluntary, the government argued that it could not offend the Establishment Clause. The New York Court of Appeals agreed, upholding its constitutionality. When the case reached the Supreme Court, the governments of 22 states filed *amicus curiae*[45] briefs urging the Court to affirm the appellate opinion in favor of the prayer.

Justice Hugo Black wrote the majority opinion in *Engel v. Vitale*. The Court found that even though the prayer did not align with any particular established religion, it promoted religious practices, and that was sufficient to violate the First Amendment. The fact that the prayer was voluntary would not save it. The Bill of Rights was created "to forbid the sort of governmental activity which New York has

---

45   They were filed by the Attorneys General of Arizona, Arkansas, Connecticut, Florida, Georgia, Idaho, Indiana, Kansas, Louisiana, Maryland, Mississippi, Nevada, New Hampshire, New Jersey, New Mexico, North Dakota, Pennsylvania, Rhode Island, South Carolina, South Dakota, Texas, and West Virginia.

attempted here."[46] Further, the Framers were aware "that governments of the past had shackled men's tongues to make them speak only the religious thoughts that government wanted them to speak and to pray only to the God that government wanted them to pray to."[47]

The decision was not popular with the American public. Different states persisted in drafting laws adding prayers and Bible readings to elementary school programs. Some of these regulations were unchallenged. But a Pennsylvania Bible reading law was challenged in the 1963 case *School District of Abington Township v. Schempp*, 374 U.S. 203 (1963).

The Pennsylvania law required "[a]t least ten verses from the Holy Bible [be] read … at the opening of each public school on each school day." Edward Schempp, a Unitarian, claimed that the statute violated his family's First Amendment rights and filed suit. The case was consolidated with a similar action filed by Madalyn Murray O'Hair, the founder of the group American Atheists.

The trial court ruled in favor of the plaintiffs, finding that the government intended to introduce a religious ceremony into the public schools, and this violated the Establishment Clause. The State of Pennsylvania appealed, and the case ended up before the Supreme Court.

The Court created a test to determine if a statute violates the Establishment Clause. The test blends components of the secular regulation rule with an assessment of the burden imposed upon religious practices. The test inquires as to the <u>purpose</u> and <u>primary effect</u> of the legislation. If either is to advance (or inhibit) religion, then the statute "exceeds the scope of legislative power" and the enactment is unconstitutional. The majority opinion, written by Justice Thomas Clark, left no room for doubt as to the unconstitutionality of Pennsylvania's statute. Pennsylvania had unconstitutionally enacted a law that requires students to participate in a religious exercise. "We repeat: neither a State nor the Federal Government can constitutionally force a person 'to profess a belief or disbelief in any religion.'…"[48] The statute was thus rendered void by opinion of the Court.

Holiday Display Cases and the Lemon Test

A group of Establishment Clause cases concern holiday displays. Reindeer, trees, menorahs, crèches, and other artifacts have frequently been brought to public spaces during a season of special significance for many religious groups. The cases assess whether and how such displays intrude upon the First Amendment. We will review two of them, as this chapter's Law Lab involves such a display.

The 1984 case *Lynch v. Donnelly*, 465 U.S. 668 (1984), concerned the yearly seasonal display that the city of Pawtucket, Rhode Island, installed in a private park located near a shopping district. The display included a variety of objects, including a Santa Claus house, reindeer pulling Santa's sleigh, figures of carolers, a Christmas tree, cutout animal figures, and a large banner with the words "Seasons Greetings." Also included was a nativity crèche, with the infant Jesus, Mary, and Joseph.

Some residents of Pawtucket and Rhode Island members of the ACLU filed an action in federal court. They argued that including the nativity scene in the holiday display violated the Establishment Clause. The federal court agreed that the government had impermissibly promulgated religious beliefs, affiliating

---

46   *Engel v. Vitale*, 379 U.S. at 435.

47   *Id.*

48   *Schempp*, 374 U.S. 220, citing the concurring opinion of Justice Black in *Torcaso v. Watkins*, 367 U.S. 488, 495 (1961).

the city with the Christian beliefs represented by the crèche. The First Circuit Court of Appeals affirmed, and the case was appealed to the Supreme Court.

In a divided opinion, the Supreme Court reversed, finding that the display did not violate the Establishment Clause. The Supreme Court applied the three-prong **_Lemon_ test** it had created in an earlier case.[49] Under this test, 1) the governmental action (or statute) must have a secular legislative purpose; 2) its principal or primary effect must be one that neither advances nor inhibits religion; and 3) it must not foster "an excessive governmental entanglement" with religion.[50] This test combines the secular regulation rule and burden on religion component from the *Sherbert* test and adds a new component for excessive governmental entanglement. If the law or governmental action violates any of these three principles, it must be struck down.

The Court found that the display had a secular purpose: the celebration of the holiday and depiction of the holiday's origin. This, the Court said, did not unconstitutionally endorse a religion. Further, the trial court's finding that the crèche created divisiveness along religious lines was not sufficient to invalidate governmental conduct, as there was no evidence of impermissible entanglement with religion. Finally, the Court declared: "If the presence of the crèche in this display violates the Establishment Clause, a host of other forms of taking official note of Christmas, and of our religious heritage, are equally offensive to the Constitution."[51] The Court's opinion was sharply split: Justices Brennan, Marshall, Blackmun, and Stevens dissented, arguing that the case did not pass the *Lemon* test.

The last case in this chapter is *County of Allegheny v. ACLU*, 492 U.S. 573 (1989). This case involves a display of 1) a Christmas nativity crèche with a banner saying "Gloria in Excelsis Deo";[52] and 2) a large Hanukkah menorah displayed near a tall Christmas tree.

Since 1981, the Holy Name Society of Pittsburgh had placed a nativity scene with a crèche on the grand staircase of the Allegheny County Courthouse. A menorah, owned by Chabad House, Pittsburgh's Lubavitch Center, was placed by the city near the City-County Building each year with a sign that contained the mayor's name and the phrase "Salute to Liberty."

The Greater Pittsburgh Chapter of the ACLU and a collection of local residents sued the city and county, asserting that the display of the nativity scene in the courthouse and the menorah near the government building violated the Establishment Clause. They lost at the trial court but won on appeal, and the city, county, and Chabad all filed petitions for certiorari.

In a complex opinion, a majority of the Court determined that the nativity scene violated the Establishment Clause, but the menorah did not. The manner of the display was the critical factor: the nativity scene and banner alone, with nothing near it to detract from its religious message, indicated that the county was not just celebrating Christmas as a national holiday, but that it was "endorsing a patently Christian message: Glory to God for the birth of Jesus Christ."[53] This messaging violated the Establishment Clause.

---

49   *Lemon v. Kurtzman*, 403 U.S. 602 (1971). In this case, the Court determined that a Rhode Island law that permitted the state to pay some of the salaries of some parochial teachers was unconstitutional.

50   *Lemon v. Kurtzman*, 403 U.S. at 612–613.

51   *Lynch v. Donnelly*, 465 U.S. at 686.

52   Latin for "Glory to God in the Highest."

53   *ACLU*, 492 U.S. at 601.

However, the menorah was a different matter. As it was displayed near a Christmas tree, adjacent to a sign with the mayor's name and text declaring the city's "salute to liberty," this display was not an endorsement of religious faith. It was, rather, "simply a recognition of cultural diversity."[54] Thus, its presence did not violate the Establishment Clause.

CRITICAL THINKING   In your opinion, did the crèche in *Lynch v. Donnelly* pass the *Lemon* test? If not, do you believe that other religions should have been represented alongside the crèche? Or should religious symbols receive no public recognition at all? Is the *Lemon* test adequate? Does it contain any omissions or oversights?

As you review the two previous cases, consider the role of context in these decisions. Do you think that context can separate a crèche from its inherent symbolism? In what context—considering factors such as location, artistic value, or diversity in representation—could a religious symbol convincingly display a secular message?

Conclusion and Introduction of Law Lab

The Supreme Court has addressed many religious freedom cases during its tenure. It has created a collection of evolving tests to determine whether there has been a violation of the Free Exercise Clause or the Establishment Clause. The tests have considered whether the governmental action or regulation had a secular purpose, whether and how much it affects religious practice, and the degree of connection between the government and religious groups that it caused.

In this week's Law Lab, you will decide a case touching on the right of an exceptional church to display a symbol of its faith. Based upon the cases reviewed above, should the government be permitted to place a removable cover over a holiday display that frightens young children? Consider the different tests that the Court has used and what factors from those tests might be important in this scenario.

---

54   *ACLU*, 492 U.S. at 619.

Sandra Day O'Connor

Associate Justice, United States Supreme Court (1981–2006)

When Sandra Day O'Connor graduated from Stanford Law School in 1952, she sent out job applications to a collection of law firms in San Francisco and Los Angeles. The only offer she received in response was for a legal secretary position. Undaunted, she became a deputy county attorney in San Mateo, California.

Her career progressed, and she eventually gained a position on the Arizona Court of Appeals. When Ronald Reagan nominated her for a position on the Supreme Court in 1981, she secured her place in history as its first female justice.

Her contribution, however, did not end with providing gender diversity to the highest court in the land. Justice O'Connor made a significant impact on Establishment and Free Exercise Clause jurisprudence. In *Lemon v. Kurtzman*, 403 U.S. 602 (1971), the Supreme Court adopted a three-prong test to determine whether governmental action violated the Establishment Clause. This test—the *Lemon* test—became a lightning rod for caustic attacks stemming from its lack of clarity. In *Lynch v. Donnelly*, 465 U.S. 668 (1984), Justice O'Connor suggested the Court adopt a different test to assess violations of the Establishment Clause. Her proposal was the no-endorsement test, which asks if the government's actions communicate either endorsement or disapproval of religion. Although the Court declined to adopt it then, two decades later, in *McCreary County, Kentucky v. ACLU*, 545 U.S. 844 (2005), the Supreme Court incorporated it into the *Lemon* test.

FIGURE 5.6 Justice Sandra Day O'Connor

Supreme Court Justice Law Lab

MEMORANDUM

To: The Honorable Chief Justice and Associate Justices of the United States Supreme Court

From: Supreme Court Law Clerks

Re: *Religious Order of the Human Condition vs. Franklin*, On Application for Petition for Certiorari

Your Honors:

Please allow this summary to assist you as you consider what action(s) should be taken in response to the Petition for Certiorari filed in the above-referenced matter.

The Court should note that, unlike earlier cases, the Petition in this case has not yet been granted. Accordingly, this Court must first determine whether it should be granted. If the Court decides to grant the Petition for Certiorari, it must then decide whether the actions of the government violated the Establishment Clause of the United States Constitution's First Amendment.

Factual Background

During the 2016 holiday season, the Religious Order of the Human Condition[1] installed a statue called *Fleshly Farce* under the dome of the Liberty Springs Capitol Building, not far from a Christmas tree and other items highlighting the seasonal traditions of a variety of religions. The Order's sculpture featured a distorted and frightening face. On its base was a plaque stating, "Fleshly Farce: Accept Your Gifts." Next to this sculpture was a placard which read:

---

1   For purposes of this Law Lab, let us agree that this religious group has been in existence since 2010. It claims to have about 200 adherents in Franklin, with other followers in other states. Its doctrine is focused on nihilism—the belief that life is meaningless.

The State of Franklin is required by the First Amendment of the United States Constitution to allow temporary, public displays in the State Capitol so long as these displays are not paid for by taxpayer dollars. Because the first floor of the Capitol Rotunda is a public place, state officials cannot legally censor the content of speech or displays. The United States Supreme Court has held that public officials may legally impose reasonable time, place and manner restrictions regarding displays and speeches, but no regulation can be based on the content of the speech.

FIGURE 5.7 *Fleshly Farce*

Schoolchildren often visit the Franklin Capitol on field trips, particularly in December, when the holiday displays are up. Three years ago, a group of young schoolchildren from public schools visited the Capitol Building. This group included kindergartners (aged between four and six). They moved through the displays without difficulty until they saw *Fleshly Farce*. This display frightened some of the younger children. In response, the curators of the Capitol Building displays placed a white square of cloth over the sculpture, blocking it from casual viewing. Visitors to the Capitol then had the option of lifting the cloth to view the statue. However, this arrangement meant that the statue was not immediately visible, as were the other structures.

Procedural Posture

The Religious Order of the Human Condition learned that a cloth had been placed over its display, preventing it from being viewed in the same way as the other holiday installations. The Order filed a Petition for Writ of Mandate against the Franklin Secretary of State (which maintains and curates the display) in federal court, claiming a violation of the Establishment Clause. This Petition demanded that the State of Franklin remove the cloth from the display.

The District Court of Franklin denied the petition, finding that the placement of the cloth was a reasonable accommodation of the needs of the public and the desires of the Order. The Order appealed.

The Ninth Circuit affirmed the District Court's ruling, and the Order filed a Petition for Certiorari with the United States Supreme Court. This Petition has not yet been granted by this Court.

Issue: Viewing Restrictions on Religious Displays

Does the State of Franklin's placement of a cloth over the Religious Order of the Human Condition's statue violate the Establishment Clause of the First Amendment, where the sculpture is on public display, in a location frequented by schoolchildren, and some of the visiting children were frightened by it?

Relevant Authority

The First Amendment of the United States Constitution states: "Congress shall make no law respecting an establishment of religion, or prohibiting the free exercise thereof. ..." This clause has been interpreted to require the national and state governments to treat all religions equally, preferring none.

Determining the constitutionality of religious holiday displays requires an analysis that is largely based upon facts. The slightest change in facts can entirely change whether or not a holiday display is constitutional.

In *Lynch v. Donnelly*, 465 U.S. 668 (1984), the Court held that a city-sponsored crèche in a public park did not violate the Establishment Clause because the display included other "secular" symbols, such as a teddy bear, a dancing elephant, a Christmas tree, and a Santa Claus house. In *Allegheny v. ACLU*, 492 U.S. 572 (1989), the Court found that a Nativity scene in a county courthouse accompanied by a banner that read "Gloria in Excelsis Deo" ("Glory to God in the Highest") was unconstitutional because it was "indisputably religious" rather than secular in nature. It also found that a menorah next to a Christmas tree was not of impermissible religious character.

Of special interest is the 1995 case *Capitol Square Review & Advisory Board v. Pinette*, 515 U.S. 753 (1995), where this Court held that a private group of individuals (in this case the Ku Klux Klan) could erect a cross in the Ohio statehouse plaza during the holiday season. The Court relied on the fact that the KKK had requested permission to display the cross in the same manner as any other private group, and that the public park had often been open to the public for various religious activities. Finally, the Court noted that the KKK expressly disclaimed any government endorsement of the cross with written language on the cross.

Displays of the Ten Commandments on government property occasioned two decisions in 2005. This Court determined that one type of display violated the Establishment Clause, and one did not. Again, context and imputed purpose made the difference. In *McCreary County v. ACLU of Kentucky*, 545 U.S. 844 (2005), this Court struck down displays of the Ten Commandments in Kentucky county courthouses but held that a display on the grounds of the Texas State Capitol was permissible in *Van Orden v. Perry*, 545 U.S. 688 (2005). The impermissible displays "stood alone, not part of an arguably secular display," and their history revealed "a predominantly religious purpose."

The question here, however, is more than simply whether a particular religious display must be added to a collection of such holiday displays in a State Capitol building. The question is whether that display, because of qualities it possesses, may be curtained from casual viewing. This Court has permitted the imposition of time, place, and manner restrictions on the exercise of First Amendment Rights, but this particular question has not previously arisen.

Review of Options for the Supreme Court

In light of the new Court membership, you have also asked us to review the options that this Court may exercise in response to a Petition for Certiorari.

The Court may accept review, and decide the case on the merits. Or, the Court may decline review, which it does in response to most of the petitions it receives. The Court can also grant review, vacate the lower court's decision, and send the case back to the lower court without hearing argument or generating an opinion. When it does this, the Court usually gives some direction to the lower court and may ask it to reconsider in light of another decision or legal authority.

This Court can also simply send the case back to the lower court for further action. This option is usually chosen when the Court does not necessarily want the lower court's order to be nullified, but wants that court to do a particular thing—such as look at newly enacted statutes or consider some aspect of the law that could affect the case outcome.

The Court can also issue a summary reversal, which just overturns the opinion below without briefing or oral argument.

Finally, the Court can decide to set the case aside and review it at a later time.

Conclusion

Again, this Court must first decide whether to accept review in this matter. If the Court determines to accept review at this time, it must then decide whether the State of Franklin's placement of a cloth over the Religious Order of the Human Condition's statue violates the Establishment Clause of the First Amendment.

Your law clerks offer their services to respond to any questions this Court may have. We look forward to the Court's opinion in this important matter.

CHAPTER 6

Equal Protection of the Law

Every individual of the community at large has an equal right to the protection of government.

—Alexander Hamilton, Remarks on the Equality of Representation of the States in Congress, Constitutional Convention, Philadelphia, June 29, 1787

Introduction

As we noted in Chapter 2, the Constitution of the United States was written, in part, to "establish Justice … [for] ourselves and our Posterity …" One of its Framers, Alexander Hamilton, is quoted above. He declares that the government must support the rights of all individuals on an equal basis. The government should engage in neither favoritism nor oppression, but extend the same legal protections to all.

Although the Constitution declares that it exists to support justice and its creators spoke earnestly about equality, its provisions were not meant to apply to everyone. The full collection of rights enjoyed by European American men were not extended to women, who could not vote. These rights were also generally withheld from the indigenous people living in North America at the time of the nation's founding. Most profoundly, these rights were entirely denied to enslaved people.[1] Every enslaved person—man, woman, and child—was bound by law to serve the will of another, no matter how difficult, dangerous, or demeaning.

We now recognize that the state-sanctioned denial of liberty and self-determination based upon race, gender, or national origin is a grievous violation of the rule of law. It is contrary to the notion of **equal protection of the law**, which requires that the government extend the same privileges, rights, and protections to all. This idea traces back to the early legal codes. In Chapter 1, we noted that the Mosaic code requires judges to stand neutral, giving neither extra deference to the rich nor special mercy to the poor.

---

1   Article I, Section 9, Clause 1 of the Constitution prohibited Congress from imposing any law banning slavery until at least 1808. This provision was a political compromise. Ten states had already outlawed the importation of enslaved persons, but three states (Georgia and North and South Carolina) demanded that it continue. Although it did not end the institution of slavery, Thomas Jefferson signed a bill in 1807 that abolished the slave trade, effective 1808.

In the United States, as in other nations, the idea of equal protection evolved over time. As we observed in the last chapter, in addition to the injustice endured by enslaved and indigenous persons, members of disfavored religious organizations were legally prevented from holding office. Ethnic and religious minorities were persecuted with minimal governmental response. Legislation, such as the Chinese Exclusion Act of 1882, targeted ethnic or racial groups for unfavorable treatment.[2] In addition, members of the LGBTQ community were subject to violence and dismissal from their jobs based upon their sexual orientation, and were denied the benefits that come from government-recognized marriage. All these types of discrimination have now been found to contravene the principle of equal protection.

This chapter briefly explores the historical underpinnings of the Fourteenth Amendment's Equal Protection Clause and the important federal civil rights acts that support it. The chapter then turns to the key race discrimination cases and those that address discrimination based upon gender identity and sexual orientation. Finally, in this chapter's Law Lab, you will adjudicate a case involving two conflicting important rights: 1) an individual's exercise of religious freedom; and 2) a young couple's right to equal protection of the law.

EQUAL PROTECTION KEY TERMS

The following key terms are defined in this chapter. They are also defined in the Glossary.

Equal Protection of the Law
Jim Crow Laws
Separate but Equal

Slavery and the Civil War

The story of equal protection in the United States is entangled with the institution of slavery.[3] Enslaved persons were brought to the early settlements before the nation's founding. By the time the slave trade was formally abolished in 1808, half a million enslaved persons had been transported to North America.[4] When the Declaration of Independence was signed, most of the enslaved were living in the Southern states, mainly working on plantations.

---

2   *See* 22 Stat. 58, Chap. 126 (1882). This law prohibited the immigration of Chinese laborers. It was repealed in 1943.
3   Enslaved persons have been a part of many societies, dating back to the early Mesopotamian civilizations. The early Codes of Ur-Nammu and Hammurabi had laws concerning slavery. Although slavery now has been abolished by law in all countries, practices akin to it perpetuate. For example, debt bondage still occurs in some countries, and in the United States, penal prisoners may be compelled to work without wages in some states.
4   *See* Herbert S. Klein, *The Atlantic Slave Trade* (1999).

Slavery was always illegal in Pennsylvania, Massachusetts, New Hampshire, Connecticut, and Rhode Island.[5] By 1800, New York and Vermont had outlawed slavery, and New Jersey did so in 1804. Illinois, Indiana, and Ohio had all joined the nation as free states by 1818. Accordingly, in 1820, there were eleven free states in the North and eleven slave states in the South.

When Missouri asked to be admitted to the Union as a new slave state, a heated debate resulted. Northerners argued that the institution of slavery should be entirely abolished, but Southerners maintained that each state should have the right to make its own decision about slavery. The Missouri Compromise of 1820 was the result.

The Missouri Compromise had two components. First, in exchange for the admission of Missouri to the United States as a slave state, the northern territory of Maine would be admitted as a free state, guaranteeing equal congressional representation between the North and the South. Second, slavery would be banned throughout the remaining Louisiana Purchase territory, north of latitude line 36° 30'.

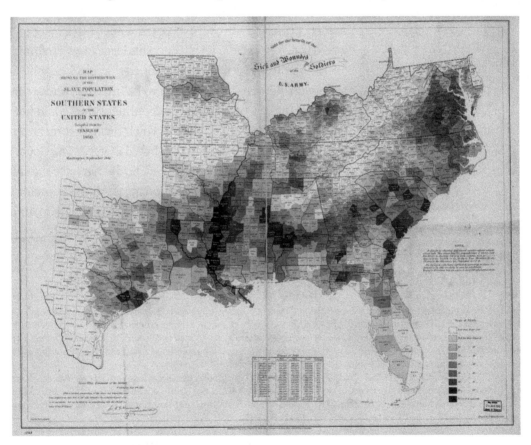

FIGURE 6.1   Map of number of slaves by county from 1860 census

5   Rhode Island's Brown University is one of the nine colonial colleges chartered before the Revolutionary War. It was named for the Brown family, who secured its endowment. The senior Nicholas Brown was a merchant, civil leader, and slave trader. *See* Charles Rappleye, *Sons of Providence: The Brown Brothers, the Slave Trade, and the American Revolution* (2006).

Although slavery would continue in the states that already had it, there was still the question of what happened to enslaved persons who were taken to free states.[6]

Dred Scott was such a person. He was a Black man living in Missouri. In 1836, his enslaver, an army officer, took him to territory that had been designated as "free" under the Missouri Compromise, and then brought him back to Missouri.

In 1846, Dred Scott attempted to purchase freedom for himself and his family. His attempt was rebuffed. He then filed suit, claiming that when he had been taken to a territory that prohibited slavery,

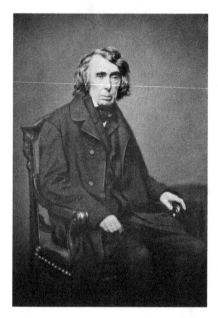

FIGURE 6.2 Chief Justice Roger B. Taney

he had become free by operation of law. The case had a complicated procedural history, but with the continuing support of abolitionist legal advisers, Scott persisted, and his case made its way to the Supreme Court.

The resulting 1857 Supreme Court decision *Dred Scott v. Sandford, 60 U.S. 393 (1857)* is regarded as one of its very worst and has been fiercely criticized for over 150 years.[7] Chief Justice Roger Taney wrote the opinion, and its effect on his legacy was profound.[8]

In *Dred Scott*, the Court determined that Black people "are not included, and were not intended to be included, under the word 'citizens' in the Constitution." Accordingly, they could not claim any "of the rights and privileges which that instrument provides for and secures to citizens of the United States."[9] The Court found that as Dred Scott was not a citizen, he did not have the status to pursue his lawsuit. Finally, for good measure, the Supreme Court struck down the Missouri Compromise as an unlawful limitation on the institution of slavery.[10]

6   Recall that the Fugitive Slave Act of 1850 (successor to the 1793 act of the same name) later resolved the question. It declared that enslaved persons remained in servitude even if taken to a free state by their owner. It required the governments and citizens of free states to assist in the recovery effort. Abolitionists openly defied the law, and Northern states took steps to neutralize it, such as requiring a jury trial before enslaved persons could be returned. In 1855, the Wisconsin Supreme Court declared it unconstitutional, but this decision was overturned by the Supreme Court of the United States in *Ableman v. Booth*, 62 U.S. 506 (1859).

7   *The Oxford Companion to the Supreme Court* (2nd ed.), edited by Kermit L. Hall, notes: "American legal and constitutional scholars consider the Dred Scott decision to be the worst ever by the Supreme Court." Chief Justice Charles Evans Hughes used the term "self-inflicted wound." David Thomas Konig, Paul Finkelman, Christopher Alan Bracey, *The Dred Scott Case: Historical and Contemporary Perspectives on Race and Law* 229 (2014).

8   Biographer James F. Simon wrote: "Taney's place in history [is] inextricably bound to his disastrous *Dred Scott* opinion" in which he "abandoned the careful, pragmatic approach to constitutional problems that had been the hallmark of [his] early judicial tenure." James F. Simon, *Lincoln and Chief Justice Taney* 270–71 (2006). We should note that Taney considered slavery to be wrong, and he freed the slaves he inherited before he took his seat on the Supreme Court.

9   *Dred Scott*, 60 U.S. at 404.

10 It was a 7–2 decision. The two dissenting justices were Benjamin Robert Curtis and John McLean. Justice Curtis declared that there was no foundation for the claim that Black people could not be citizens, as when the Constitution was ratified, Black men could vote in 5 of the thirteen states. Justice Curtis was so angered by this opinion that he resigned from the Court. Justice McLean declared that the majority opinion lacked legal authority, and both men attacked the majority's overturning of the Missouri Compromise.

The Court may have believed that its decision would quiet the growing controversy over slavery. However, the decision "was greeted with unmitigated wrath from every segment of the United States except the slaveholding states."[11] The decision inflamed the debate over the morality of slavery, the economics of slavery, the scope of states' rights, and the potential expansion of slavery into new western lands.[12]

The Northern courts and politicians declined to accept the decision. Maine's Supreme Court announced that African Americans could vote in state and federal elections, and both the Ohio Supreme Court and the New York Court of Appeals declared that any enslaved person that entered the state with the consent of their master would become free.[13]

The *Dred Scott* decision led to a divisive presidential election, with four major candidates divided by policy and region.[14] After Abraham Lincoln was elected president in 1860 without a single supporting Southern electoral vote, the South seceded. Active war erupted in 1861, followed by four years of bloody battles. Over 500,000 Union and Confederate soldiers died in battle and from disease during the conflict. The Civil War finally ended when Robert E. Lee and other Southern generals surrendered in the spring and summer of 1865.

---

11   John E. Nowak and Ronald D. Rotunda, *Treatise on Constitutional Law: Substance and Procedure,* 5th ed. (2012), Section 18.6.

12   Frederick Douglass, perhaps the most influential African American of the nineteenth century, believed that a major conflict had become inevitable. He said, "The American people and the Government at Washington may refuse to recognize it for a time but the inexorable logic of events will force it upon them in the end; that the war now being waged in this land is a war for and against slavery." *See* James M. McPherson, *The Struggle for Equality* 62 (1964); also, *see generally, Battle Cry of Freedom: The Civil War Era* by the same author (1988). Douglass's 1845 memoir, *Narrative of the Life of Frederick Douglass, an American Slave,* is arguably the most famous narrative from an enslaved person.

13   *See Lemmon v. the People,* 20 N.Y. 562 (1860).

14   The presidential candidates included John Bell of Tennessee, a member of the Constitutional Union party; John Breckenridge, a Southern Democrat from Kentucky; Stephen Douglas, a Northern Democrat from Illinois; and Abraham Lincoln, a Republican from Illinois. Breckenridge carried most of the South and Lincoln the North, Midwest, and Western territories.

A Tainted Legacy and a Step Toward Reconciliation

On December 3, 2016, Chief Justice Roger Taney's descendants met with the descendants of Dred Scott for the inaugural "Dred Scott Sons and Daughters of Reconciliation Conference." The conference was attended by the descendants of not only Chief Justice Taney and Mr. Scott, but also by the descendants of Thomas Jefferson, the Blow Family (who first bought Dred Scott as a slave), and Jefferson Davis, who led the Confederacy during the Civil War.

The group discussed Justice Taney's historic *Scott* opinion and his infamous words that Dred Scott had no right to file suit for his freedom because Black individuals "had no rights which the white man was bound to respect." The group acknowledged that the unfortunate language became embedded in history, perpetuating racism that continues to exist in a systemic way today. The conference was so successful that it grew larger every year. In 2019, it included descendants from litigants of landmark civil rights cases such as *Plessy v. Ferguson,* 163 U.S. 537 (1896) and *Brown v. Board of Education of Topeka*, 347 U.S. 483 (1954).

FIGURE 6.3   A step toward reconciliation

FIGURE 6.4 Robert E. Lee's surrender at Appomattox

In 1864, while the war still raged, Congress passed the Thirteenth Amendment, which legally terminated the institution of slavery in the United States. In Section 1, it declares:

> Neither slavery nor involuntary servitude, except as a punishment for crime whereof the party shall have been duly convicted, shall exist within the United States, or any place subject to their jurisdiction.[15]

The ratification of the Fourteenth Amendment followed in 1868. The Fourteenth Amendment guarantees citizenship for "all persons born or naturalized in the United States, and subject to the jurisdiction thereof." Critically, the Fourteenth Amendment includes the Equal Protection Clause:[16]

> No state shall make or enforce any law which shall … deny to any person within its jurisdiction the equal protection of the laws.

---

15   Scholars and activists argue that the exception in Section 1 perpetuated slavery in the form of prison labor. A Reconstruction-era prison boom was ushered in by the introduction of "Black Codes," which allowed Black people to be charged with vague offenses such as being disrespectful. From there, convict leasing ensured that Black prisoners would once again work for white planters or plantation owners without receiving any pay.

16   It also includes the Due Process Clause, which we will explore in the next chapter.

This clause was designed to bolster the equality provisions contained in the important Civil Rights Act of 1866, which ensured rights for African Americans who had been subjected to slavery and discrimination. The Civil Rights Act of 1866 gave federal courts exclusive jurisdiction over lawsuits related to alleged violations. The act made it illegal to discriminate in housing and employment on the basis of race. Unfortunately, federal penalties were not included, so obtaining redress was left to individuals. As those encountering discrimination commonly did not have ready access to legal services, this omission left many without recourse. Nonetheless, over time, the federal courts came to serve as important forums for the enforcement of constitutional rights.

Finally, the Fifteenth Amendment was ratified in 1870, giving the franchise to all men, no matter their "race, color, or previous condition of servitude." Together, the Thirteenth, Fourteenth, and Fifteenth Amendments outlawed slavery, compelled the states to guarantee equal protection and due process to all, and required the states to permit all men to vote.

Of course, the ratification of the Civil Rights Act and the new Amendments did not instantly cure the wrongs associated with mass enslavement. Nor did the guarantee of the right to vote create ready access to Southern voting venues for Black people.[17] However, the new laws began a process that led to important changes in society. The Civil Rights Act and the Equal Protection Clause provided the means for persons to fight discrimination, using new legal tools. Major cases on equal protection were promoted and decided. Questions of equal treatment for Black individuals slowly encouraged other groups to reach for similar legal protection, and over time, areas of required equal treatment under the law were enlarged.

Equal Protection Cases

Each month, courts across the nation hear hundreds of cases alleging discrimination based upon race, gender, national origin, religion, sexual orientation, sexual identity, disability, marital status, parental status, and age. Some of the plaintiffs in these lawsuits will prevail, and some will not. In some cases, the discrimination that occurred was not severe enough to meet the legal standard necessary to win. In other cases, the defendant will successfully prove that what the plaintiff claims was discriminatory conduct was, in truth, not discriminatory. For example, the defendant may prove that plaintiff was not fired due to his religious beliefs, but because he did not complete the required work.

Finally, although it may seem wrong, some laws that discriminate are permitted. For example, laws against smoking discriminate against people who smoke. Regulations that limit certain jobs to United

---

17   States circumvented the Fifteenth Amendment through a number of tactics designed to repress the Black vote. These efforts included literacy and civics tests, poll taxes, intimidation, and violence. The "grandfather clause"—which persisted until 1915—claimed that African Americans could not vote unless their grandfathers had voted, effectively excluding descendants of slaves. The 1965 Voting Rights Act gave voters the basis to challenge such discriminatory practices, and Black voter turnout greatly increased as a result. Benno C. Schmidt Jr., "Principle and Prejudice: The Supreme Court and Race in the Progressive Era: Part 3: Black Disfranchisement from the KKK to the Grandfather Clause," 82 *Col. L. Rev.* 835, 835–905 (1982).

Burnita Shelton Matthews

United States District Judge of the District Court for the District of Columbia (1968–1988)

Burnita Shelton Matthews was the first female United States District Court judge in the nation. President Harry Truman appointed her in 1949 to the United States District Court for the District of Columbia.

After graduating from George Washington University Law School in 1920, Judge Matthews served as counsel to the National Woman's Party. There, she fought to repeal labor laws that applied only to women, and in 1923, she helped draft the core parts of an equal rights amendment. She represented the National Woman's Party when the federal government planned to condemn the building that served as its headquarters. Though the land was condemned (and later became the United States Supreme Court Building), her skilled representation led to the largest condemnation settlement awarded by the United States government at the time. Despite widespread hostility from her male counterparts, Judge Matthews determinedly supported female jurists, choosing to hire only women as her law clerks.

FIGURE 6.5   Judge Burnita Shelton Matthews

States citizens discriminate against people who are not citizens. Laws that require the payment of income taxes discriminate against people who earn income. Laws may discriminate for legitimate reasons.

In lawmaking, it is the *reason* for the discrimination that matters. As we noted in the free speech and religious freedom cases, the Supreme Court takes a careful look at regulations that intrude upon constitutional protections. The state and federal governments should ensure that the laws they enact minimize any impairment of rights. To assess how well the governments have done this, the Supreme Court created a collection of tests. These concern the legitimacy of governmental interests and the impact of the laws on the peoples' exercise of rights. We reviewed some of these tests in the last two chapters. Recall the Clear and Present Danger Test (to determine whether free speech should receive constitutional protection); the Secular Regulation Rule (if a law does not have a religious purpose, it does not violate the Establishment Clause); and the *Sherbert* Test (to assess whether a law violates the Free Exercise clause).

This strategy is perpetuated in the context of equal protection. Any law that causes or results in discrimination must be related to a legitimate governmental interest. In addition, such a law must be tailored as narrowly as possible to achieve that governmental interest. Finally, certain types of discrimination will be meticulously scrutinized because the Equal Protection Clause should not permit discrimination on these grounds to slip through under the pretense of legitimate lawmaking.

Achieving progress under the Equal Protection Clause and supporting civil rights legislation required the well-organized and determined efforts of groups of people over many decades. The next section reviews some of the struggles in the important race cases.

Discrimination and the Race Cases

Although slavery was illegal after the Civil War, there was backlash from the white establishment. Former slave states enacted **Jim Crow laws** to ensure that racial segregation continued. Black people could not attend the same schools as white people, could not eat at the same restaurants as white people, could not use the same washrooms or drinking fountains, and could not ride in public transportation with white people.

In 1892, Homer Adolph Plessy lived in Louisiana and was subject to Louisiana's racial segregation laws. Although Plessy was seven-eighths European American, under the racial policies in Louisiana, he was legally a Black person. To challenge Louisiana's segregation laws, the Citizens Committee of New Orleans recruited Plessy to deliberately violate the law. The committee retained the services of a private detective with the power to arrest. Plessy purchased a ticket for a first-class seat in a train car that was designated for "Whites only," seated himself, and was duly arrested for violating Louisiana's Separate Car Act. Thus, the case was placed in the ideal posture for a constitutional challenge.

The trial judge ruled that Louisiana's Separate Car Act was constitutional, as Louisiana had the power to regulate the railroad business within the state. The Louisiana Supreme Court affirmed, and Plessy appealed to the United States Supreme Court.

Plessy's attorneys argued that laws mandating segregation violated the Equal Protection Clause, as they inherently implied that Black people were inferior. The Equal Protection Clause required that Black people and white people receive the same benefits under the law, but Louisiana's Separate Car Act did not provide equal benefits. Black people were relegated to cars that were different from those enjoyed by white people.

In *Plessy v. Ferguson*, 163 U.S. 537 (1896), the Supreme Court roundly rejected this argument, denying that segregationist laws marked Black individuals with "a badge of inferiority." Although the Court acknowledged that "the object of the Fourteenth Amendment was undoubtedly to enforce the absolute equality of the two races before the law," it opined that "it could not have been intended to abolish distinctions based on color, or to enforce social, as distinguished from political equality, or a commingling of the two races upon terms unsatisfactory to either."[18] Laws demanding the separation of the races fell within the police powers of the state, and as long as such as law did not oppress a particular class, it was legal.[19]

Plessy v. Ferguson legitimized legislation supporting racial segregation and created the doctrine of **separate but equal**. One effect of the decision was the rapid flourishing of Jim Crow laws requiring the segregation of Black people in places of public accommodation. Because of this case, many advances in societal integration won during Reconstruction were lost.[20] Further, although *Plessy v. Ferguson* did

---

18 *Plessy*, 163 U.S. at 543–544.
19 Justice John Marshall Harlan, from Kentucky, was the lone dissenting vote. *Id.*
20 Reconstruction (1863–1877) was the period of rebuilding and reintegration of the nation and its citizens following the Civil War. Although the North won the Civil War, some have opined that the South "won" Reconstruction, as the institutions supporting the oppression of Black persons continued long after the Civil War's end.

Thurgood Marshall

Associate Justice, United States Supreme Court (1967–1991)

Thurgood Marshall was the first Black justice to sit on the Supreme Court.

Before his service on the Court, Justice Marshall made a name for himself arguing cases involving civil rights, the Fourteenth Amendment, and racial equality at all levels of the state and federal judiciary. He worked in private practice and served as counsel for the NAACP, prosecuting cases ranging from wrongful evictions and racial discrimination in education to the excessive use of force by police. While an attorney for the NAACP, Thurgood Marshall argued and won *Brown v. Board of Education*, 347 U.S. 433 (1954), the case that legally eliminated racial segregation in education.

FIGURE 6.6 Justice Thurgood Marshall

not involve education, it affirmed the constitutionality of separate school systems for white children and Black children. This paradigm sadly remained in force for fifty-eight years, until the Supreme Court issued its ruling in *Brown v. Board of Education*, 347 U.S. 483 (1954).

Brown v. Board of Education is perhaps the most important case of the last century. The National Association for the Advancement of Colored People (NAACP) played a critical role in bringing this case to the Supreme Court.[21] Among other work, it filed lawsuits challenging laws mandating segregation in public schools, helping parents to set up cases that would achieve traction. Thurgood Marshall was a leader of the NAACP's legal team and developed the legal strategy that would lead to success. He would go on to become the first African American justice of the Supreme Court.

The NAACP worked with a collection of Black parents in Topeka, Kansas, who attempted to enroll their children in nearby white neighborhood schools. The district declined to enroll all the Black children as requested, and redirected the parents to the segregated Black schools.

The lead plaintiff was Oliver Brown, a welder who worked for the Santa Fe Railroad. His daughter, Linda, walked six blocks to take a bus to her designated segregated school, while a white school was seven blocks from the family home. Twelve other parents with similar stories joined the lawsuit on behalf of a total of twenty children.

The plaintiffs argued that racial segregation in public schools perpetuated inferior education and accommodation for Black children. The schools attended by Black children

---

21   The NAACP was founded in 1909, following deadly race riots in Springfield, Illinois. Two Black men had been arrested as suspects in crimes committed against white women. A large mob of white men gathered with the intent to lynch the suspects. When the mob learned that the suspects had been transferred, they fanned out into nearby Black neighborhoods. Dozens of homes and businesses owned by Black people were destroyed, as well as the businesses of whites who were suspected of sympathizing with Black people. At least sixteen people died. *NAACP*, History (Mar. 13, 2019). https://www.history.com/topics/civil-rights-movement/naacp.

were not equal to the white schools, and this manifestly violated the Equal Protection Clause of the Fourteenth Amendment.

The federal judge agreed that segregated schools created "a sense of inferiority" in Black children that had "a detrimental effect." However, as the Black and white school systems had similar buildings, transportation, and curricula, the judge ruled against the plaintiffs. He declined to overrule *Plessy v. Ferguson*.

When the case reached the Supreme Court, it was combined with four other cases also concerning segregated education. The case was closely watched, and a collection of *amicus curiae* briefs were filed.[22] The Court conducted two rounds of oral arguments to delay the case while members of the Court worked toward a unanimous opinion. Finally, Chief Justice Earl Warren convinced everyone that *Plessy v. Ferguson* must be overruled if the Court were to retain its reputation as the enforcer of constitutional rights.

The Supreme Court's opinion found that segregation in education violates the Equal Protection Clause:

> We conclude that in the field of public education the doctrine of "separate but equal" has no place. Separate educational facilities are inherently unequal. Therefore, we hold that the plaintiffs and others similarly situated for whom the actions have been brought are, by reason of the segregation complained of, deprived of the equal protection of the laws guaranteed by the Fourteenth Amendment.[23]

This opinion did not end segregation in education. Some Southerners worked aggressively—and occasionally violently—to create obstacles to desegregation.[24]

After a period of stalled progress, new litigation was filed to accelerate the process of desegregation in the case that became known as *Brown II*.[25] The Supreme Court in *Brown II* said that desegregation must proceed "with all deliberate speed."[26] Members of the School Board of Little Rock, Arkansas, also filed suit to suspend desegregation, asserting that the rampant public hostility and opposition of Governor Orval Faubus mandated its deferral. In *Cooper v. Aaron*, 358 U.S. 1 (1958), the Supreme Court, however,

---

22   The Supreme Court received an unexpected *amicus curiae* brief from the Eisenhower Administration's Department of Justice explaining that school segregation hurt the United States in its relations with other nations of non-white peoples. *See* Mary L. Dudziak, "Desegregation as a Cold War Imperative," 41 *Stanford L. Rev.* 61, 65 (1988).

23   *Brown v. Board of Education*, 347 U.S. 483 at 495.

24   A small sampling of these efforts follows. Arkansas governor Orval Faubus enlisted the Arkansas National Guard to keep Black students from entering Little Rock Central High School. President Dwight Eisenhower responded by deploying the 101st Airborne Division from Fort Campbell to restore order. In 1963, Medgar Evers filed suit to desegregate the schools of Jackson, Mississippi. He was murdered by Byron De La Beckwith, a member of the Ku Klux Klan and White Citizens Council. In Alabama, Governor George Wallace physically prevented two Black students from enrolling at the University of Alabama in what became known as the Stand in the Schoolhouse Door. In Virginia, schools were closed as part of the Massive Resistance movement to avoid desegregation. In recognition of these important and historic struggles, the United States established the Little Rock Central High School Historic Site in Arkansas; the Brown v. Board of Education National Historic Site in Kansas; the Birmingham National Civil Rights Monument in Alabama; and the Reconstruction Era National Historical Park in Beaufort, South Carolina. *See* "Brown v. Board at Fifty: 'With an Even Hand': The Aftermath." Library of Congress, https://www.loc.gov/exhibits/brown/brown-aftermath.html.

25   *Brown v. Board of Education*, 349 U.S. 294 (1955).

26   *Brown v. Board of Education*, 349 U.S. at 301.

FIGURE 6.7   American military escorting a member of the Little Rock Nine to school

declared that it was unconstitutional to deprive Black students of their rights in order to maintain law and order in the state of Arkansas. Segregated education was to end, immediately.

There remained the question of segregation in other areas of daily life. In 1883, the United States Supreme Court had determined that Congress lacked the constitutional authority to pass legislation preventing discrimination by private individuals.[27] Accordingly, even though public schools had been ordered to integrate, racial discrimination was permitted in privately owned places of public accommodation, such as hotels, movie theaters, and restaurants. Black persons routinely were not able to access the same services in the same locations as white persons. To cure this discrimination, President John F. Kennedy proposed new civil rights legislation that would outlaw discrimination in employment and places of public accommodation. After President Kennedy was assassinated, President Lyndon B. Johnson pushed the legislation forward, and it was signed into law as the Civil Rights Act of 1964.

An immediate challenge to the Civil Rights Act came by way of a segregated motel located in Atlanta, Georgia. The Heart of Atlanta Motel was a 200-room facility that refused to rent rooms to Black individuals. The owner, Moreton Rolleston, filed suit in federal court, claiming that he did not need to comply with

27   There were five consolidated cases, collectively called the Civil Rights Cases: *United States v. Stanley*; *United States v. Ryan*; *United States v. Nichols*; *United States v. Singleton*; *Robinson et ux. v. Memphis & Charleston R.R. Co.*, 109 U.S. 3 (1883).

the new act. He cited several reasons. First, Rolleston alleged that Congress had exceeded its authority under the Commerce Clause when it enacted the legislation. Second, he claimed that discrimination based upon race, when practiced by an individual, does not violate the Fourteenth Amendment. Finally, he argued that forcing him to rent to Black patrons placed him in a position of involuntary servitude.

The Supreme Court did not agree. In *Heart of Atlanta Motel, Inc. v. United States*, 379 U.S. 241 (1964), the Court found that Congress was acting within the scope of its authority under the Commerce Clause in passing the new Civil Rights Act of 1964. Most of the motel's patrons came from outside Georgia, and so the business was tied up with interstate commerce: "We therefore conclude that the action of the Congress in the adoption of the Act as applied here to a motel which concededly serves interstate travelers is within the power granted it by the Commerce Clause of the Constitution, as interpreted by this Court for 140 years."[28] Further, the Court found "no merit in the remainder of appellant's contentions, including that of 'involuntary servitude' ... We could not say that the requirements of the [Civil Rights] Act in this regard are in any way 'akin to African slavery.'"[29]

The case confirmed that segregation or discrimination in places of public accommodation would no longer be tolerated. Jim Crow laws that prevented Black people from entering businesses were illegal. *Heart of Atlanta Motel, Inc.* determined that such laws had no place in the United States and that Congress had the authority to support Equal Protection using the broad tool of the Commerce Clause.[30]

Our final racial discrimination case is *Loving v. Virginia*, 388 U.S. 1 (1967). In the mid-1960s, over a dozen states still maintained laws criminalizing interracial marriage. One of these states was Virginia, the home of Mildred and Richard Loving. Virginia's Racial Integrity Act of 1924 declared that a marriage between a white person and a person classified as "colored" was illegal.[31] Richard Loving was a white man, and he wished to marry his girlfriend, Mildred, who was of African-American and Native American descent. They married legally in Washington, DC, and returned to their residence in Central Point, located in Caroline County, Virginia. A few weeks later, police raided their home in the early morning hours. When the officers noted that they were sleeping in the same bed, Mildred pointed out the marriage certificate on the bedroom wall. They were told that the marriage certificate was invalid and were arrested and tried. The couple pled guilty to the charge of cohabiting "against the peace and dignity of the Commonwealth." They were given a prison sentence of one year, but the trial judge agreed to suspend the sentence if the couple left Virginia.

The Lovings then moved to the District of Columbia. However, they missed their families and friends in Caroline County. Mildred Loving wrote a letter to Attorney General Robert F. Kennedy describing

---

28   *Heart of Atlanta Motel, Inc.*, 379 U.S. at 261.

29   *Id.*

30   Supported by the First Amendment Freedom of Association, private clubs argued that they could discriminate in membership. The Supreme Court found that the Boy Scouts of America could decline to extend membership to openly gay men in *Boy Scouts of America v. Dale*, 530 U.S. 640 (2000). Since this case, the Scouts have changed policy, ending the ban on gay membership.

31   The Racial Integrity Act of 1924 defined a white person as someone "who has no trace whatsoever of any blood other than Caucasian." This came to be called the one-drop rule. This act was supported by Walter Plecker, a physician and a leader of the Anglo-Saxon Club of America, a white supremacist organization. *See* Patrick Wolfe, *Traces of History* (2016). *See also* Michael Yudell, "A Short History of the Race Concept" in *Race and the Genetic Revolution: Science, Myth and Culture* 19, 1971.

their situation, and the attorney general referred her to the American Civil Liberties Union (ACLU).[32] The ACLU took up the case, challenging the criminal conviction, and eventually brought a class action suit in the United States District Court for the Eastern District of Virginia. The case worked its way to the Supreme Court.

By this time, the Supreme Court had determined that statutes that impacted fundamental rights or suspect classes of citizens (those that had historically been subject to discrimination) should be strictly scrutinized. They must be narrowly tailored to serve a compelling government interest. Further, they must not have an alternative formulation that was less restrictive.[33]

In *Loving*, the Court confirmed that race-based classifications in the law require strict scrutiny. The Court noted that anti-miscegenation laws prohibiting marriage between persons of different races are rooted in invidious racial discrimination. This, the Court said, meant that it was impossible to establish a compelling government interest. Accordingly, the conviction of the Lovings was overturned, and anti-miscegenation laws were found universally unconstitutional. The Supreme Court said, "There can be no doubt that restricting the freedom to marry solely because of racial classifications violates the central meaning of the Equal Protection Clause."[34]

The *Loving* decision remains a key component of the civil rights movement. It foreshadowed other cases relating to the rights of couples to marry, no matter their sexual orientation.

Gender-Identity and Sexual Orientation Cases

In contrast with the race cases, the important cases involving discrimination, sexual orientation, and gender identity are all notably recent, arising after the turn of the century.

Lawrence v. Texas, 539 U.S. 558 (2003), is a key Supreme Court case addressing the constitutionality of laws criminalizing same-sex relations. The case had its genesis in a weapons disturbance call received by police officers in Houston, Texas. The officers responded and entered an apartment rented by John Geddes Lawrence. There, they discovered him engaged in a sexual act with another man, Tyron Garner. The men were arrested for violating a provision of the Texas Penal Code that stated, "A person commits an offense if he engages in deviate sexual intercourse with another individual of the same sex."[35]

---

32   The ACLU was founded in 1920 during the first Red Scare. It is a nonprofit legal organization whose stated goal is to defend and preserve the individual rights and liberties guaranteed to all people in this country by the Constitution and the laws of the United States. *See About the ACLU*, ACLU, https://www.aclu.org/about-aclu.

33   This contrasts with the rational basis test, where the statute must simply be reasonably related to a legitimate governmental interest.

34   388 U.S. at 11–12.

35   Tex. Penal Code Ann. §21.06(a)(2003). The statute goes on to define "deviate sexual intercourse" as "any contact between any part of the genitals of one person and the mouth or anus of another person; or … the penetration of the genitals or the anus of another person with an object." *Id.*, § 21.01(1).

To advance the key issue raised by the case to a higher court, gay rights advocates from Lambda Legal convinced the men to plead no contest rather than contest the charges.[36] With legal support, they appealed their conviction up to the United States Supreme Court. In a 6–3 opinion, the Supreme Court found that the statute was an unconstitutional intrusion into their personal lives. Justice Anthony Kennedy wrote the majority opinion, which declared "The Texas statute furthers no legitimate state interest which can justify its intrusion into the personal and private life of the individual."[37]

Lawrence v. Texas rendered unconstitutional laws criminalizing sexual relations between members of the same sex. However, it did not give the right to same-sex couples to marry. That required another case, *Obergefell v. Hodges, 576 U.S. 644 (2015)*.

Like *Brown v. Board of Education*, *Obergefell v. Hodges* involved a group of people. All the plaintiffs were same-sex couples who were in committed relationships. All of them wanted the state benefits and sanction of marriage, but had been denied those rights.[38]

The Supreme Court's 5–4 opinion was again authored by Justice Kennedy. The Court ruled that the right to marry is guaranteed to same-sex couples by the Fourteenth Amendment's Equal Protection Clause (and also by the Due Process Clause). The implication of this ruling is that all states are required to issue marriage licenses to same-sex couples. Further, under the Constitution's Full Faith and

Anthony Kennedy

Associate Justice, United States Supreme Court (1988–2018)

Justice Anthony Kennedy was a conservative jurist nominated by Ronald Reagan. His legacy and influence were both unexpected and significant.

In both *United States v. Windsor*, 570 U.S. 744 (2013) and *Obergefell v. Hodges*, 576 U.S. 644 (2015), Justice Kennedy constituted the swing vote, leading to rulings that supported LGBTQ rights. But he went further than simply offering his vote: in both *Windsor* and *Obergefell*, Justice Kennedy authored the majority opinions, using the Equal Protection Clause to strike as unconstitutional Section 3 of the Defense of Marriage Act and certain state laws.

FIGURE 6.8   President Ronald Reagan and Justice Anthony Kennedy

---

36   Lambda Legal Defense and Education Fund is an American civil rights organization that supports LGTBQ communities and gives legal support to members of those communities. *See About US*, Lambda Legal, https://www.lambdalegal.org/about-us.

37   *Lawrence v. Texas*, 539 U.S. at 578. The Court decided the case largely on due process grounds. *Id.*

38   Many governmental benefits attach with marriage. For example, married persons can file joint income tax returns; can inherit a share of their spouse's estate by operation of law; can receive Social Security, Medicare, and disability benefits for spouses; can receive spousal military benefits; can obtain spousal insurance benefits; and can apply for joint foster care rights.

Credit Clause,[39] they are also required to acknowledge the validity of same-sex marriages performed in other jurisdictions.

Finally, we reach a key equal protection opinion, *Bostock v. Clayton County*, 590 U.S. __ (2020). The plaintiff in the case is Gerald Bostock, who worked for Clayton County, Georgia, as an officer in the juvenile court system. Georgia has no laws protecting persons from discrimination based on sexual orientation.

In 2013, Bostock joined a gay softball league. He talked about it at work, and several months later, Clayton County conducted an audit of funds Bostock controlled. Subsequently, the county fired him for conduct "unbecoming an employee." Bostock thought that Clayton County had sought a pretext to fire him for being gay and filed suit in federal court. The court dismissed the case, asserting that the provisions of the Civil Rights Act do not protect against sexual orientation discrimination. Although he lost again in the Eleventh Circuit Court of Appeals, the Supreme Court accepted Bostock's case for review. His case was consolidated with another case involving apparent sexual orientation discrimination,[40] and their oral arguments were heard with yet another case involving alleged discrimination against a transgender person under Title VII of the Civil Rights Act.[41]

Justice Neil Gorsuch wrote the majority opinion. In it, the Court held that the applicable provisions of the Civil Rights Act extend to cover sexual orientation and gender identity:

> An employer who fires an individual for being homosexual or transgender fires that person for traits or actions it would not have questioned in members of a different sex. Sex plays a necessary and undisguisable role in the decision, exactly what Title VII forbids. Those who adopted the Civil Rights Act might not have anticipated their work would lead to this particular result. But the limits of the drafters' imagination supply no reason to ignore the law's demands. Only the written word is the law, and all persons are entitled to its benefit.[42]

Bostock v. Clayton County is one of the most important decisions regarding the rights of LGBTQ persons. It provides security in the job arena, an important benefit that had been missing from the Equal Protection jurisprudence.

Conclusion and Introduction of Law Lab

Over long years, the Equal Protection Clause, supported by civil rights legislation, has yielded important rights. Schools have been integrated, persons of all races have been given access to public accommodations,

---

39   U.S Const. Art. IV, § 1.
40   *Altitude Express, Inc. v. Zarda*, 590 U.S.__ (2020).
41   *R.G. & G.R. Funeral Homes, Inc. v. Equal Employment Opportunity Commission*, 590 U.S. __ (2020).
42   *Bostock*, 590 U.S.__.

and the rights of all persons to work and marry have been guaranteed, no matter their race, sexual orientation, or gender identity.

Because advocates have chosen cases carefully, and also because the Supreme Court may select the cases it wishes to review, some discrimination cases have not risen to the Court for review. However, human opinions and experiences are widely variable. New conflicts will continue to arise, become cases, and the courts of this nation will address the issues they present.

After Chapter 4, you may have wondered what happens when a person's religious beliefs support the unequal treatment of others. This type of case—where two fundamental constitutional rights are in direct conflict—is especially challenging. This week's Law Lab presents you with such a case.

You work in the Human Rights Commission of the State of Franklin. Two complainants have come forward, alleging that they were not offered service in a place of public accommodation due to their sexual orientation. The respondent has asserted that he could not offer them the personal services they desired, as this would conflict with his First Amendment right to practice his religion as he wishes.

In this case, there is no dispute as to what happened. Both sides tell the same story. The case concerns discrimination and also religious freedom. It is your job to adjudicate it.

What analytical process will you use to determine who should prevail? What legal elements will be part of that process? What facts will be most important to your analysis as you decide this case?

Administrative Law Judge Law Lab

MEMORANDUM

To: The Administrative Law Judges of the State of Franklin Human Rights Commission

From: The Summer Associates of the Human Rights Commission

Re: *Stonecypher and Sommers v. Silas Toppen, dba[1] Toppen Tuxes*, on Cross Motions for Summary Order (56 Frank. Admin Code, Chapter XI, Section 5300.735)

Your Honors:

Please allow this summary to assist you as you prepare for deliberations in the above-referenced matter.

The State of Franklin Human Rights Commission is the state agency with the responsibility of making impartial determinations of whether there has been unlawful discrimination, as defined by the Franklin Human Rights Act and other applicable laws.

The Commission has been presented with a case of first impression by claimants Stonecypher and Sommers. As the Commission's judges, you will determine if there has been a violation of the law by tuxedo shop owner Silas Toppen.

Factual Background

The facts in this matter are undisputed and were presented by both parties in affidavits. They are summarized below.

Toppen Tuxes is a clothing store located in Liberty Springs. It is owned by Silas Toppen. The store sells both ready-made and custom-made tuxedos and therefore offers residents a variety of choices for wedding attire. Customers can select different fabrics and designs, and have tuxedos

---

1   *dba* means "doing business as."

custom made for special occasions. Mr. Toppen employs ten people (some part time and some full time) to help him run the shop and sew custom tuxedos.

Carrie Stonecypher and Molly Sommers met when they were both studying at Liberty Springs College and began dating their junior year. After graduating, they both obtained jobs in technology companies in Liberty Springs. Their relationship flourished, and last year they decided to marry.

After booking a local church and reception venue, they considered what to wear to their marriage service. They viewed the website of Toppen Tuxes and decided on a pair of custom-made tuxedos. Using the store's web interface, Ms. Sommers made an appointment so that she and Ms. Stonecypher could get measured for their tuxedos and discuss their custom options.

On the day of the visit, Ms. Stonecypher and Ms. Sommers entered Toppen Tuxes and were greeted by Mr. Toppen. When they explained that they wanted a pair of custom tuxedos for their wedding, Mr. Toppen informed them that he would not work with them. His religious views, he explained, prevented him from engaging in activities that support same-sex marriage, including

FIGURE 6.9 Interior of Toppen Tuxedo Shop

making custom tuxedos for same-sex couples. He advised them that they could select any off-the-rack ready-made tuxedos they wished, but that he would not assist by sewing any custom clothing for them.

Ms. Sommers and Ms. Stonecypher left the store and contacted the Franklin Office of Human Rights.

Relevant Federal Law

The First Amendment Religious Freedom Clauses of the United States Constitution declare:

> Congress shall make no law respecting an establishment of religion, or prohibiting the free exercise thereof ...

The Fourteenth Amendment of the United States Constitution provides, in pertinent part:

> No state shall make or enforce any law which shall abridge the privileges or immunities of citizens of the United States; nor shall any state deprive any person of life, liberty, or property, without due process of law; nor deny to any person within its jurisdiction the equal protection of the laws.

Relevant State Law

The Human Rights Act of the State of Franklin was enacted to give the residents of Franklin a readily available state law remedy in the event that they suffered illegal discrimination. It permits people who have been the victim of discrimination to commence an action with the Franklin Office of Human Rights. The office's website provides forms to facilitate the process, with instructions as to how to complete them. Cases are adjudicated by special administrative law judges. The relevant portions of the Franklin Human Rights Act provide:

> Sec. 1-120. Declaration of Policy.
>
> Freedom from Unlawful Discrimination. It is the public policy of this State to secure for all individuals within Franklin the freedom from discrimination against any individual because of his or her race, color, religion, sex, national origin, ancestry, age, order of protection status, marital status, physical or mental disability, military status, sexual orientation, pregnancy ... real estate transactions, access to financial credit, and the availability of public accommodations.
>
> Public Health, Welfare, and Safety. It is the public policy of this State to promote the public health, welfare, and safety by protecting the interests of all people in Franklin in maintaining personal dignity, in realizing their full productive capacities, and in furthering their interests, rights, and privileges as citizens of this State. ...

Procedural Posture

Ms. Sommers and Ms. Stonecypher filed a formal complaint with the Franklin Office of Human Rights, alleging that Mr. Toppen violated the above-noted provisions of the Franklin Human Rights Act by declining to provide service to them at a place of public accommodation due to their sexual orientation.

Mr. Toppen filed an answer to the complaint, alleging that the Free Exercise Clause of the First Amendment of the United States Constitution guarantees his religious freedom. He asserts that requiring him to construct custom-made tuxedos for the marriage of Ms. Sommers and Ms. Stonecypher violates his First Amendment rights, as his religion believes that same-sex marriage is morally wrong. Mr. Toppen has identified himself as a member of a Protestant denomination that rejects same-sex marriage and regards sexual relations between members of the same sex as sinful.

Both parties have filed a Motion for a Summary Order in the pending action pursuant to Section 5300.735 of Section 56 of the Franklin Administrative Code. This provision states:

> a) Motion for Summary Order. At any time after the service of a complaint and prior to service of a decision, the complainant or the respondent may move, with or without supporting affidavits, for a summary Order in the moving party's favor as to all or any part of the relief sought.

b) Procedure. The non-moving party may file counter-affidavits prior to the time of the ruling on the motion. The Order sought shall be rendered without delay if the pleadings and affidavits, if any, show that there is no genuine issue as to any material fact and that the moving party is entitled to a recommended Order as a matter of law.

Issue: Religious Freedom vs. Equal Protection

In this pending matter, the Respondent business proprietor alleges that the First Amendment of the United States Constitution ensures his freedom to practice his religion. The Respondent's religion does not support same-sex marriage.

The Complainants are a same-sex couple who sought the services of the Respondent in constructing custom tuxedos for their same-sex marriage. They contend that the Respondent's determination not to provide them with the services that they would have otherwise received violates the law of the State of Franklin, as well as the Equal Protection Clause of the Fourteenth Amendment.

Federal Cases

There is no binding federal authority that is directly on point on this matter. The case *Masterpiece Cakeshop v. Colorado Civil Rights Commission*, 584 U.S. __ (2018), involved a baker who refused to prepare a cake for a gay couple. The case was decided on the narrow ground that the Colorado Civil Rights Commission did not employ religious neutrality when it adjudicated the case, citing the fact that the Commission had compared the religious views of the baker to the defense of slavery or to the Holocaust.[2] Such comparisons, said the Court, are "inappropriate for a Commission charged with the solemn responsibility of fair and neutral enforcement of Colorado's anti-discrimination law."[3]

Nonetheless, the majority opinion in *Masterpiece Cakeshop* includes the following:

> The case presents difficult questions as to the proper reconciliation of at least two principles. The first is the authority of a State and its governmental entities to protect the rights and dignity of gay persons who are, or wish to be, married but who face discrimination when they seek goods or services. The second is the right of all persons to exercise fundamental freedoms under the First Amendment, as applied to the States through the Fourteenth Amendment. ... One of the difficulties in this case is that the parties disagree as to the extent of the baker's refusal to provide service. If a baker refused to design a special cake with words or images celebrating the marriage—for instance, a cake showing words with religious meaning—that might be different from a refusal to sell any cake at all ...

---

2   *Masterpiece Cakeshop, Ltd.*, 584 U.S. __.

3   *Id.*

The same difficulties arise in determining whether a baker has a valid free exercise claim. A baker's refusal to attend the wedding to ensure that the cake is cut the right way, or a refusal to put certain religious words or decorations on the cake, or even a refusal to sell a cake that has been baked for the public generally but includes certain religious words or symbols on it are just three examples of possibilities that seem all but endless.[4]

The Supreme Court seems to concede that everyone should be able to come into a store, or a place of public accommodation, and purchase ready-made items/hotel rooms/tickets to events without impediment. If we permit people to opt out of this type of service, civil rights laws will be materially impacted. But the closer an action comes to personal service that counters individual beliefs, the greater the concern about violating personal freedoms.

Left unanswered are the following questions:

Should Equal Protection in public accommodation ever give way to religious freedom? If so, what process should be deployed to make this determination? Finally, what elements of the case matter for the decision-making process?

As judges serving on the State of Franklin Human Rights Commission, you must decide if either party to this matter is entitled to prevail on their Motion for a Summary Order. The facts are not disputed. It is how the law should apply that is debated. Your opinion must consider Franklin law, as well as the opinions of the United States Supreme Court. The order that you issue in this case will guide the operation of businesses throughout the state.

Conclusion

We hope that this short memorandum has assisted with your preparations. Please let us know if we can provide any additional information to assist with your deliberations.

We look forward to your ruling in this interesting and important matter.

---

4   *Id.*

CHAPTER 7

Due Process of Law

Whatever disagreement there may be as to the scope of the phrase "due process of law," there can be no doubt that it embraces the fundamental conception of a fair trial, with opportunity to be heard.
—Oliver Wendell Holmes

Introduction

As we noted in Chapter 1, mere legislative enactments cannot guarantee justice. Even where substantive laws are fair, judicial procedures may not adequately protect the rights of persons pursued by the government. History is sadly replete with examples of the show trial, where guilt was predetermined and execution the inevitable outcome.[1]

Accordingly, the rule of law requires fair and well-administered procedural laws along with equitable substantive laws. The concept of **due process of law** drives fairness in procedure and protects individuals from the improper exercise of governmental power.

The decree that the government shall observe due process of law appears twice in the Constitution. It appears twice to safeguard the people from inadequate, abusive, or capricious actions by both the federal and state governments.

First, the Fifth Amendment of the United States Constitution provides:

> [N]or shall any person ... be deprived of life, liberty, or property, without due process of law ...

This is the clause that binds the national government. The federal government may not operate against the people by wrongfully depriving them of their property or their rights.

---

1   For example, the Moscow Trials that occurred during the Great Purge under Joseph Stalin are considered show trials. These are described at length in the interesting and troubling book edited by Ron Christenson, *Political Trials in History: From Antiquity to the Present* 307 (1991).

Louis Brandeis

Associate Justice, United States Supreme Court (1916–1939)

FIGURE 7.1   Justice Louis Brandeis

As a lawyer, Louis Brandeis made his name as a champion of social justice and equity. He fought railroad monopolies and other large corporate entities and argued in favor of workplace and labor laws that improved the quality of life for industrial workers. In *Muller v. Oregon*, 208 U.S. 412 (1908), Brandeis submitted a brief that included social science research. The use of data to support a legal argument was a novel concept; prior opinions of the Court had been decided on theory, without the use of any statistics. Subsequent filings that included arguments using scientific information became known as Brandeis briefs in his honor.

President Woodrow Wilson nominated Louis Brandeis to the Supreme Court in 1916. He became the Court's first Jewish member and formed a coalition with two other justices, Benjamin Cardozo and Harlan F. Stone. The group became known as the Three Musketeers, and they supported many of the New

At the time of its enactment in 1791, the Fifth Amendment Due Process Clause was not meant to apply to enslaved persons.

The Fifth Amendment did not apply to the states until the passage of the Fourteenth Amendment, following the American Civil War. The objective of the Fourteenth Amendment was to protect the civil rights and liberties of Black Americans from infringement by the states, addressing the racial inequity that lingered after the Civil War. Section One declares:

> [N]or shall any State deprive any person of life, liberty, or property, without due process of law …

This clause requires state governments to follow just procedures when they proceed against the people. A series of Supreme Court cases has interpreted this clause to mean that the states, as well as the federal government, must extend to the citizens most of the rights and liberties set forth in the Bill of Rights. Through this process of "incorporation," the Fourteenth Amendment's Due Process Clause requires the states to honor the Bill of Rights. This means that the states must guarantee to the people the right of free speech, assembly, and religious freedom.

As the result of this incorporation, for most personal rights and liberties, the scope of federal and state obligations is the same. Moreover, the Supreme Court interprets both the state and federal clauses identically,[3] distinguishing two kinds of due process.

First, the clauses have come to mean that the rules governing proper procedures must be followed in every governmental action, legal case, or administrative proceeding. This is **procedural due process**. Courts must observe the rules of procedural law that define just processes. The government

---

3   "To suppose that 'due process of law' meant one thing in the Fifth Amendment and another in the Fourteenth is too frivolous to require elaborate rejection." *Malinski v. New York*, 324 U.S. 401, 415 (1945) (Frankfurter, J. concurring).

(continued)

must act with fairness and regard for your rights before you are executed or imprisoned or before you lose your property or rights. As noted in the chapter's opening quote by Supreme Court Justice Oliver Wendell Holmes, among other things, procedural due process means that you have the opportunity to be heard and present your side of the story when you are involved in a legal action. Procedural due process embodies a commitment to adhere to protocols that support just outcomes, a commitment that is unquestionably required by the rule of law.

In addition, over time, due process also has come to mean that the government may not burden individual liberty and rights with overreaching or unfair regulations and legal restrictions. The government must not infringe upon privacy, property, and liberty interests by establishing policies or passing laws that are irrational or unreasonable. Thus, the Due Process Clause protects persons from governmental policies that exceed the government's authority. This is called **substantive due process.** Under this doctrine, for example, the states may not infringe upon the right of parents to decide how to educate their children by forcing parents to send them to public schools.[4] This idea is distinct from procedural due process. Even though a governmental regulation might be properly enacted, if it overreaches and violates substantive due process, it is unconstitutional.

This chapter will focus on procedural due process rather than on substantive due process. It will review the history behind the concept and then consider the critical questions: what precise process is needed? How and when should that process occur? What does the rule of law require?

Finally, in the chapter's Law Lab, you will serve as state supreme court justices. You will assess whether the State of Franklin followed due process in a case involving civil forfeiture, where property was seized by law enforcement because of its connection to criminal activity.

Deal policies implemented by President Franklin D. Roosevelt.

Brandeis was known for his eloquent opinions and vigorous dissents, many of which later became majority opinions. He joined the majority in decisions incorporating portions of the Bill of Rights against the states. A titan of the law, Justice Louis Brandeis is remembered as "the most powerful moral teacher ever to have sat on our highest court."[2]

---

4   *See Pierce v. Society of Sisters*, 268 U.S. 510 (1925). Some Supreme Court justices, including Byron White and Antonin Scalia, have been critical of the concept of substantive due process. Justice Clarence Thomas rejects it entirely: "I do not regard the Fourteenth Amendment's Due Process Clause as a secret repository of substantive guarantees against 'unfairness'..." *BMW of North America, Inc. v. Gore*, 517 U.S. 559, 598 (1996).

2   Joel K. Goldstein and Charles A. Miller, "Brandeis: The Legacy of a Justice," 100 *Marquette Law Rev.* 461, 463 (2016).

The following key terms are defined in this chapter. They are also defined in the Glossary.

Due Process of Law
Procedural Due Process
Substantive Due Process

Historical Foundation of Due Process Clauses

The concept of procedural due process goes back to the ancient legal codes. In Chapter 1, we noted that the Code of Hammurabi declared that accused persons were presumed innocent and were entitled to present evidence in their defense. The Mosaic Code declared that a trial must occur before any execution and set forth the parameters for conducting a trial.[5] In addition, the Twelve Tables of Rome required trials to be publicly conducted, with citizens as jurors.

However, the wording in the United States Constitution's two Due Process Clauses traces back to the Magna Carta. In Chapter 2, we discussed the Magna Carta and its key clauses. The key provisions of Clause 39 declare that no free man:

> shall be seized or imprisoned, or stripped of his rights or possessions, or outlawed or exiled, or deprived of his standing in any way, nor will we proceed with force against him ... except by the lawful judgment of his equals[6] or by the law of the land.[7]

During the reign of Edward III, Parliament promoted a series of statutes that defined with greater precision the guarantees of liberties in the Magna Carta. The statutes defined the phrase "the law of the land" to mean judicial procedures and protocols that protect a person's liberty. One of these, a statute enacted in 1354, uses the phrase "due process of law" to describe those procedures and protocols. The appearance of "due process" in this statute was its first in the history of Anglo-American law. It reads:

> III. None shall be condemned without due Process of Law.

> ITEM, That no Man of what Estate or Condition that he be, shall be put out of Land or Tenement, nor taken, not imprisoned, nor disinherited, not put to Death, without being brought in Answer by due Process of the Law.[8]

---

5   *See generally* Richard H. Hiers, "The Death Penalty and Due Process in Biblical Law," 81 *U. Det. Mercy L. Rev.* 751 (2004).
6   Note, however, that those "equals" referenced in this clause were other noble lords of the kingdom. The practice of excluding members of society from jury service based upon gender or race has, sadly, been a common practice. Although the Civil Rights Act of 1957 gave women the right to serve on juries, it was not until 1968 that Mississippi passed a law permitting women to serve. Black people continued to be excluded from jury service in Southern states, even after the Supreme Court ruled that this was unconstitutional in *Norris v. Alabama*, 294 U.S. 587 (1935). *See* S. Jonathan Bass, *He Calls Me by Lightning*, Liveright (2017).
7   John, king of England, *Magna Carta Libertatum*, Clause 39 (1215).
8   Liberty of Subject, 28 Edw. 3.

The early American colonists were interested in legal order, and many of their colonial charters included due process protections. Nathaniel Ward, a Puritan minister who immigrated in 1634, drafted "The Body of Liberties" summarizing the Magna Carta's due process guarantees and other privileges to be enjoyed by the colonists. They included the right to notice of the charges filed, the right to a hearing before the court, and the right to a jury trial. Ward's work was incorporated into Massachusetts law and served as the first legal code in New England.[9]

Some colonies simply incorporated the English common law and statutes as their governing colonial law. South Carolina chose this option after it separated from North Carolina in 1712. It incorporated the English common law and statutory law—including the Magna Carta—as its own body of law. South Carolina thus achieved the first legislative enactment of the Magna Carta in the New World.

Although the Magna Carta and subsequent English statutes provided the foundation for early due process law in the United States, American and English law swiftly diverged. The English embraced the concept of parliamentary supremacy, which holds that the authority of the legislative branch is greater than that of the other branches of government. Accordingly, the United Kingdom historically rejected the broad power of judicial review enjoyed by the United States courts. This means that the United Kingdom did not enlarge due process rights through judicial rulings.[10] Therefore, the United States' body of law on due process has become quite distinctive from its English roots.

What Process Is Due?

In the 1855 case *Murry v. Hoboken Land*, 59 U.S. 272 (1855), the Supreme Court announced that, to determine what process is due, one should look to the Constitution and "see whether this process be in conflict with any of its provisions. If not found to be so, we must look to those settled usages and modes of proceeding existing in the common and statute law of England."[11] This technique would have the courts scan the Constitution's provisions and the common law procedures, and then arrange procedure to comply with identified protocols. This means that due process includes traditional methods of ensuring just outcomes.

While this might be a good start, this approach is incomplete. In a particular case, due process may demand more than adherence to existing procedures and requirements. When established procedures are unfair, due process requires that they be amended. Indeed, as ideas evolved about the nature of justice,

---

9   John D. Bessler, "The Anomaly of Executions: The Cruel and Unusual Punishments Clause in the 21st Century," 2 *Br. J. Am. Leg. Studies* 315 (2013).

10 The English Parliament's House of Lords functioned as the Supreme Court of England for centuries. However, under the Constitutional Reform Act of 2005, the judicial power of the House of Lords was vested in a new Supreme Court of the United Kingdom. The Supreme Court has the authority to determine whether executive and legislative authorities have acted within the scope of their authority. Notably, the Supreme Court decided in 2019 that Prime Minister Boris Johnson overreached when he prorogued (suspended) Parliament to shorten the period of debate before England exited the European Union. See *R (on the application of Miller) v. The Prime Minister; Cherry v. Advocate General for Scotland* (2019) UKSC 41 (24 September 2019).

11 *Murry*, 59 U.S. at 277.

the Supreme Court issued rulings requiring state and federal governments to change the way cases were managed and governmental proceedings conducted. These rulings adjusted the type of processes that must occur and the timing of when they must take place.

Until the twentieth century, governments imprisoned people or took property at the conclusion of criminal proceedings. The Constitution's Bill of Rights set forth protocols that must be followed for criminal cases, based upon the English common law tradition. The Supreme Court's rulings in criminal procedure cases often reference those provisions. Much of the law of criminal procedure, explored in Chapter 14, concerns the operation of those processes. In addition, Chapter 11 reviews the law of civil procedure, describing how a civil action proceeds through court.

Whether civil or criminal, there is a general consensus about minimum process rights that courts of law must honor. One distinguished jurist, Judge Henry Jacob Friendly,[12] distilled these to a useful and influential list that he believed should apply to every civil and criminal case.

Judge Friendly maintained that every case should have these features:

1. An unbiased tribunal.
2. Notice of the action and the grounds asserted in it.
3. The opportunity to argue that the action should not be taken.
4. The right to present evidence and call witnesses.
5. The right to know opposing evidence.
6. The right to cross-examine adverse witnesses.
7. A decision based only on the evidence presented in the case.
8. The opportunity for representation by counsel.
9. The requirement that a record be made of the evidence presented.
10. The requirement that the tribunal provide written findings of fact and explain the reasons for its decision.[13]

FIGURE 7.2 Judge Henry J. Friendly

In other words, at every critical step in a proceeding, due process dictates that there be an opportunity for meaningful engagement. Further, when a proceeding is concluded, due

---

12 Henry Friendly graduated from Harvard Law School *summa cum laude* in 1927 and clerked for Supreme Court Justice Louis Brandeis. Following a time in private practice, he was appointed to the United States Court of Appeals for the Second Circuit. His work encompassed a broad range of opinions, and his influence was remarkable. Following his death, Chief Justice Warren Burger described Friendly as "a very remarkable man," noting "I have never known a judge more qualified to sit on the Supreme Court." *See A Solemn Tribute to Henry Friendly, a Quiet Giant of the Appeals Bench,* the New York Times, June 10, 1986. For more information about this influential jurist, *see* David M. Dorsen, *Henry Friendly, Greatest Judge of His Era* (2012).

13 Henry J. Friendly, *Some Kind of Hearing*, 123 U. Pa. L. Rev. 1267 (1975).

process demands that there be a written record of what has occurred.

The state, federal, and Tribal courts of today generally adhere to the requirements on this list. Before property or liberty interests are taken or withdrawn, there should be a hearing before an impartial judge, the opportunity to present argument and evidence, the chance to examine and refute adverse evidence, and representation by counsel. In addition, a record sufficient for appellate review must be made. Even small claims courts, which usually resolve disputes of $10,000 or less, include these features. These requirements are now so firmly embedded in American procedural law that it would be startling to hear of their omission.

However, Judge Friendly's ten-item list of rights does not apply to administrative proceedings. Administrative proceedings can terminate benefits (such as Social Security) or revoke a license (such as a driver's or business license). Administrative proceedings are nonjudicial, conducted by governmental agencies (or military institutions). As they are not courts, when administrative agencies impose fines, revoke licenses, or terminate benefits, they have not been required to adhere to the same due process requirements as judicial proceedings. The question of what process is due in the context of administrative actions is, therefore, of special interest. When a person may lose a property interest, but the government is not taking them to court, what does justice require?

To see how the Supreme Court has responded, we will now look at the law addressing the requirements of due process in administrative proceedings.

Due Process at School

In 2015, a high school student in Tennessee was involved in a hazing incident. The school administration held a hearing to discipline the student. However, the administration failed to give the student's father notice of the date and time of the hearing and also failed to give the accused student notice of the allegations against him. The discipline committee found the student responsible and suspended him for one year.

At this point, the student asked a federal court to step in. A federal magistrate determined that the school's failures amounted to a denial of due process rights. She ordered the student's record expunged.[14]

At least seven United States Federal Courts of Appeals have heard cases involving universities that have failed to follow due process protocols during investigations. Those deprivations range from preventing a case from being heard in a reasonably speedy manner[15] to denying a respondent access to evidence.[16]

While schools are not courts of law, federal judges are beginning to expect school administrations to implement some of the rights guaranteed by the Due Process Clause of the Constitution when students face serious disciplinary charges.

FIGURE 7.3 Due process at school

14   *John Doe v. Washington County Department of Education*, et. al., 2:16-CV-00272-CRW (E.D. Tenn. 2020).

15   *John Doe v. Oberlin College*, No. 1:2020cv00669 (N.D. Ohio 2020).

16   *J. Lee v. University of New Mexico*, No. CIV 17-1230 JB/LF Memorandum Opinion and Second Amended Order (D.N.M. 2020).

Procedural Due Process in Administrative Cases

In early cases, the United States Supreme Court maintained that a hearing was not required before the termination of property rights in administrative cases. The Court adopted the viewpoint of Judge Washington in *R.A. Holman & Co. v. SEC*, 299 F.2d 127 (D.C. Cir. 1962) (cert. den. 370 U.S. 911 1962): "In a wide variety of situations, it has long been recognized that, where harm to the public is threatened, and the private interest is reasonably deemed to be of less importance, an official body can take summary action pending a later hearing."[17] Even if the termination of rights led to irremediable consequences, hearings could be held afterward.

The Court's policy changed in *Goldberg v. Kelly*, 397 U.S. 254 (1970), a landmark case involving welfare recipients. A collection of residents living in New York City received aid under the Aid to Families with Dependent Children (AFDC) program, a federally funded assistance program administered by the states under guidelines supplied by the United States secretary of Health, Education and Welfare. Other residents received benefits under New York's Home Relief program. Home Relief assists those who are unable to support themselves or obtain support from other sources. It is sponsored and administered by New York State.

Fourteen residents had been (or were about to be) cut off from AFDC aid and six from Home Relief support. Federal regulations required advance notice before benefits are reduced or terminated. However, New York State's regulations did not require prior notice or a hearing of any kind before benefits were terminated.

The twenty residents filed suit on due process grounds. After the case was filed, New York State and the City of New York amended its procedures to better protect recipients' rights. The new procedures required a caseworker to first discuss any doubts about eligibility with the recipient. If the caseworker decided that the recipient was no longer eligible, the caseworker recommended termination of benefits to the unit supervisor. If the supervisor concurred, the supervisor sent a letter to the recipient advising of the decision and informing the recipient that they could submit a written statement asking for review from a higher official within seven days. If the reviewing official confirmed termination of benefits, aid was

---

17   *Goldberg v. Kelly*, 397 U.S. 254 (1970), quoting *R.A. Holman & Co.*, 299 F.2d 127, 131 (D.C. Cir. 1962).

immediately stopped. The recipient had a post-termination right to a final hearing before a state officer where they could present evidence and witnesses. If they prevailed at that hearing, funding was reinstated.

These changes, however, were not enough for the residents. They pressed on, claiming that, before aid was stopped, they should have 1) the right to personally appear before the reviewing official; 2) the right to present oral evidence; and 3) the right to confront and cross-examine adverse witnesses. In short, they claimed that the Due Process Clause requires that a benefits recipient be afforded an evidentiary hearing before the termination of benefits.

The federal trial court agreed with the residents, noting:

> While post-termination review is relevant, there is one overpowering fact which controls here. … A welfare recipient is destitute, without funds or assets … [T]o cut off a welfare recipient … without a prior hearing of some sort is unconscionable unless overwhelming considerations justify it.[18]

The Supreme Court noted that the type of welfare benefits involved in the case "are a matter of statutory entitlement for persons qualified to receive them."[19] Their termination by the state is an adjudication of an important right. Quoting *Sherbert v. Vernor*, 374 U.S. 398 (1963), the Court found that constitutional restraints apply "as much to the withdrawal of public assistance benefits as to disqualification for unemployment compensation."[20]

Having established that termination of benefits was a governmental action that should be filtered for constitutional violations, the Court next considered what methodology should be used. It began with an assessment of the nature of the government function involved and then considered the private interest affected by the government's action. Under this analysis, the Court quickly concluded that a hearing prior to terminating aid was constitutionally required. Affording welfare recipients a hearing before terminating their benefits serves an important governmental interest: fostering "the dignity and wellbeing of all persons within its borders."[21] Welfare can help the poor reach opportunities, participate meaningfully in society, and guard against societal malaise. The same governmental interests that support providing welfare confirm that those eligible to receive it should do so without interruption. Further, termination of benefits prior to a hearing could deprive a recipient of the means to live before they could obtain proper redress. Certainly, those who have lost housing usually find it difficult to meet case filing deadlines.

The Court was careful to note that the purpose of the pre-termination hearing was simply to produce an initial assessment of the validity of the grounds to discontinue payments to protect a recipient from an erroneous termination of benefits. A complete and comprehensive opinion, such as those issued by courts "to facilitate judicial review and guide future decisions" would

---

18   *Goldberg*, 397 U.S. at 261.
19   *Id*. at 262.
20   *Id*. at 262, citing *Sherbert v. Verner*, 374 U.S. 398 (1963).
21   *Id*. at 265.

not be required.[22] However, the hearing should be conducted before an impartial officer, with the right to assistance from counsel, and the right to review the material relied upon by the government. In addition, at the hearing, there must be the opportunity to present evidence and argument and the right to cross-examine any adverse witnesses. Finally, following the hearing, the hearing officer's written opinion should state the reasons for his conclusion, citing the evidence. These procedures "have ancient roots" and "the Court has been zealous to protect these rights from erosion" not only in criminal cases, but "in all types of cases where administrative ... actions [are] under scrutiny."[23]

Accordingly, the Supreme Court found that determining what process is due requires consideration of the rights involved, as well as the process already in place. Different types of rights have different values, and the strength of different procedures varies. Depriving an accountant of their professional license or revoking a person's driver's license is more serious than suspending a child for one day from school, and the processes involved in all three situations should reflect that discrepancy. A universal methodology is needed to assess what process is due in the wide variety of proceedings conducted throughout the nation.

Mathews v. Eldridge, 424 U.S. 319 (1976), provided the Supreme Court with the opportunity to create that methodology. *Matthews* involved the termination of social security disability benefits. Under Title II of the Social Security Act,[24] the government provides benefits to workers during the term of their disability. Eldridge was disabled and awarded disability benefits. Several years later, the state agency charged with monitoring his medical condition sent him a questionnaire about his condition and identifying the physicians and psychiatrists he had consulted. The state agency considered these reports and other information in his file and made a tentative decision that his disability had ended. The agency sent Eldridge a letter telling him this and informing him that he could ask for a reasonable amount of time to submit additional information to the agency.

After Eldridge replied, the agency then made its final determination that he had ceased being disabled and that his benefits would terminate. The agency's letter told him of his right to seek reconsideration within six months.

Eldridge did not seek reconsideration. Instead, he filed an action challenging the constitutionality of the procedures used by the agency to assess his disability.

Relying upon *Goldberg*, he argued that he had the right to an evidentiary hearing before the termination of his disability benefits. Because they had been terminated without a hearing, he believed that his due process rights had been violated.

---

22   *Id.* at 267.
23   *Id.* at 270, citing *Greene v. McElroy*, 360 U.S. 474, 496–497 (1959).
24   70 Stat. 815, 42 U.S.C. Section 423.

When the Supreme Court received the case, it acknowledged that due process, "unlike some legal rules, is not a technical conception with a fixed content unrelated to time, place and circumstances."[25] Instead, due process is flexible, calling "for such procedural protections as the particular situation demands."[26]

The Supreme Court stated that, before the initial termination of benefits in a case such as Eldridge's, three factors should be considered. First, what is the nature of the injury threatened by the governmental action? Second, what is the risk of error using existing procedures, and will any additional procedural safeguards reduce that risk? Third, what are the government's interests, including the administrative costs and the need for efficiency?

Applying these three factors, the Court first noted that Eldridge's private interest was less substantial than Goldberg's. The Court believed that a person who has been provisionally denied disability benefits would likely find it easier to locate other sources of income than a person who has provisionally been denied welfare benefits. The Court then determined that the risk of error in using written procedures to provisionally deny disability benefits is not great, and adding further procedures, including an adversary hearing, would be unlikely to reduce that error. Documents may be enough to assess medical conditions, and Eldridge had access to the agency's files and the opportunity to present additional material. Finally, the Court noted that social welfare funding is not unlimited, and the government has an interest in preserving funding for those who deserve benefits, rather than spending it to support hearings and continued payments for persons ultimately determined to be ineligible.

These criteria may be thought of as a template for any attorney who wishes to argue for or against the propriety of an existing procedure under the Due Process Clause.

---

25   *Mathews v. Eldridge*, 424 U.S. at 334, citing *Cafeteria Workers v. McElroy*, 367 U.S. 886 (1961).

26   *Id.* at 334, citing *Morrissey v. Brewer*, 408 U.S. 471 (1972).

Who Watches the Watchers?

Every federal executive agency has in-house judges to adjudicate matters over which the agency has regulatory authority. Of course, those judges sometimes make mistakes. When this happens, parties may appeal their cases to the federal court that hears such appeals.

There is one court that hears more cases involving federal agencies than any other. That court is the United States Court of Appeals for the District of Columbia Circuit.

This federal Court of Appeals sits in the same city as a large number of federal agencies. During the first part of 2020, the court heard cases from the Federal Energy Regulatory Commission, the Department of Homeland Security, the Department of Justice, the Postal Regulatory Commission, and the Federal Labor Relations Authority. For the federal appellate court with the smallest geographic jurisdiction, it sees a lot of the good, the bad, and the ugly that make up federal dockets.

This court also has provided more than its share of Supreme Court justices: since its creation, eight of its judges (Wiley B. Rutledge, Antonin Scalia, Clarence Thomas, Ruth Bader Ginsburg, and Brett Kavanaugh) were elevated to the Supreme Court, and three of them (Fred M. Vinson, Warren Burger, and John Roberts) became chief justices.

FIGURE 7.4 Judges

Following *Eldridge*, the advocate attacking an administrative process as unconstitutional has a ready-made checklist. First, they must reach for arguments confirming the significance of the interest under scrutiny. Second, they must explain the inadequacy of existing procedures, and suggest changes or substitutions that will meaningfully improve those procedures without raising costs too much. Finally, they should articulate how the government's interest in efficiency will not be compromised by their suggested changes. Advocates in these situations may offer plans that are used in other contexts and jurisdictions to gain traction and support the legitimacy of suggested changes.

Conclusion and Introduction to Law Lab

You have now reviewed Judge Friendly's list of required rights in civil and criminal cases. He noted that, before property or liberty interests are taken or withdrawn in court proceedings, there must be an opportunity to present argument and evidence (and refute adverse arguments and evidence) to an impartial judge. You have also noted the Supreme Court's three-part metric for assessing what process is due in administrative proceedings. You know that procedural due process requires consideration of the value of the interest at risk, of the nature and adequacy of existing procedures, and of the government's interest in efficient management of its operations.

Your next Law Lab involves a civil forfeiture case. Such cases are civil actions, not criminal cases, but they are not filed against persons. They are brought against property seized by government agents (usually law enforcement personnel). The property is most often associated with criminal activity of some kind. For example, the government does not file a civil forfeiture case against a drug smuggler, but against the car that the smuggler drove across the border. In civil forfeiture cases, the government argues that the seizure should be permanent.

Supporters of civil asset forfeiture argue that it is an essential tool for fighting crime. It reduces the profitability of criminal activity and deprives criminals of assets (cars, boats, and planes) needed to commit crimes. Critics assert that the reduced due process protections they feature make it far easier for governments to acquire assets in such cases. In addition, critics note that law enforcement agencies have a strong incentive to reach for assets, even in marginal cases, in order to generate revenue for their agencies.

Civil forfeiture cases may be thought of as hybrid actions. They are court cases, but they are filed against property. In this new setting, what does the Constitution require? *What process is due?*

State Supreme Court Justice Law Lab

MEMORANDUM

To: The Honorable Chief Justice & Associate Justices of the Supreme Court of Franklin

From: Law Clerks of the Supreme Court of the State of Franklin

Re: *Dockson v. Franklin*, On Appeal

Your Honors:

Please allow this summary to assist this court as it considers the appeal in the above-referenced matter. In this case, the court is asked to determine whether the seizure of a vehicle under the State of Franklin's civil forfeiture law violated the Due Process Clause of the United States Constitution's Fourteenth Amendment. The court's opinion will be binding on all Franklin courts.

Factual Background

Methamphetamine

Methamphetamine is a potent stimulant that directly affects the central nervous system. In lower doses, the drug reduces fatigue, elevates mood, and moderates appetite. In higher doses, it causes psychosis, seizures, and brain bleeds. Further, methamphetamine is toxic to certain types of brain neurons, causing changes in brain structure and function and reducing the volume of gray matter. It is highly addictive, and withdrawal symptoms can be very acute, lasting months longer than is typical for other drugs. There are few medically sanctioned uses for this drug.[1]

---

[1] In the United States, the compound dextroamphetamine hydrochloride, under the trade name Desoxyn, has been approved by the FDA for treating obesity and ADHD. However, the FDA strongly cautions that the limited therapeutic value of the drug should be weighed against the inherent risks associated with its use.

FIGURE 7.5 Packages of illegal drugs

Methamphetamine addiction has become a problem in the United States. Unfortunately, the drug may be compounded from ingredients that are not hard to find. Methamphetamine can be produced in home laboratories using pseudoephedrine, found in Sudafed and Contac, combined with other ingredients. As a result, many retailers and states have implemented policies regulating the sale of products that contain pseudoephedrine. Methamphetamine is now regulated under the Controlled Substances Act, listed under Schedule II.[2]

Civil Forfeiture

In order to deter criminal activity and to raise revenue to help fight certain crimes, the federal government and the states have enacted civil forfeiture laws. These permit law enforcement to seize assets of persons involved with crimes or illegal activity. Civil forfeiture laws vary from state to state, but they most often involve civil actions brought against property. The property is the defendant in such cases, and no criminal charge against its owner is required.

In the State of Franklin, the civil forfeiture rule is found in Franklin Code Title 19: Foods, Drugs, Oils, and Compounds, §19-03.1-36. Forfeitures. This law states, in pertinent part:

> The following are subject to forfeiture:

> a. All controlled substances which have been manufactured, distributed, dispensed, or acquired in violation of this chapter.

---

2   The Controlled Substances Act is the federal statute through which the manufacture, importation, possession, use, and distribution of certain substances is regulated. The 91st United States Congress passed it as Title II of the Comprehensive Drug Abuse Prevention and Control Act of 1970.

b. All raw materials, products, and equipment of any kind which are used, or intended for use, in manufacturing, compounding, processing, delivering, importing, or exporting any controlled substance in violation of this chapter.

c. All property which is used, or intended for use, as a container for property described in subdivision a or b.

e. All conveyances, including aircraft, vehicles, or vessels, which are used, or intended for use, to transport, or in any manner to facilitate the transportation, for the purpose of sale or receipt of property described in subdivision a or b, but:

... (2) No conveyance is subject to forfeiture under this section by reason of any act or omission established by the owner thereof to have been committed or omitted without the owner's knowledge or consent. ...

A 2019 state law[3] says that the government must obtain a conviction to acquire assets by forfeiture. However, if the person is dead, has been deported, has disappeared, or has abandoned their property, no conviction is required before forfeiture.

Reeve Dockson and Methamphetamine

The following information was pieced together by investigators in this matter.

Reeve Dockson lived with his parents, Amy and Darron, in Liberty Springs, located in Liberty County, in the State of Franklin. He turned twenty-one last year. Reeve lived in a single trailer next to his parents, who lived in a ranch house in the middle of a small development. Reeve's parents are both employed by the local school district. Amy works in the elementary school cafeteria, while Darron is the chief maintenance worker for the school.

Reeve is the Docksons' only child. Reeve had a few brushes with the law in his past. When he was seventeen, he was found guilty of possession of more than three ounces of marijuana in violation of the law[4] and spent time in jail for that offense.

When Reeve graduated from high school, his father and mother bought him a truck to use. To save on the cost of insurance, they took title in the vehicle together.[5] Reeve found a job working as a salesperson in a large sporting goods store. He used the truck that his parents provided to travel to and from work.

Unfortunately, Reeve was not a particularly good employee, and he lost his job after six months. He had trouble showing up on time for work and seemed uninterested in the job. Based upon conversations

---

3   Franklin's law mirrors that of North Dakota. *See* North Dakota HB 1286.

4   In Franklin, the criminal laws relating to marijuana are relatively severe, and even the possession of less than half an ounce of the herb is punishable by up to thirty days in jail and/or a fine of up to $1,000. Possession of more than one ounce bumps the charge up to a felony, while the sale of more than 100 pounds can result in a prison term of up to twenty years.

5   Insuring young male drivers as sole owners/drivers of a vehicle can be more expensive than insuring a family of drivers for the same vehicle.

with his fellow employees and friends, and later with Reeve himself, the investigator concluded that Reeve had begun to use methamphetamine a few months after he started his job at the sporting goods store.

Reeve did not tell his parents that he had lost his job. He later said that he hoped to find another one quickly, and then tell them that he had changed jobs.

In March of last year, about a month after he had been fired, Reeve was driving his truck over the speed limit and came to the attention of Officer Taylor of the Liberty County Highway Patrol. A brief chase ensued, but after about a mile, Reeve pulled over. Officer Taylor called for backup. The second responding officer, Officer Mayhew, had some experience with people under the influence of methamphetamine, and he thought that Reeve had several symptoms: Reeve was irritable, his facial expression was odd, and he seemed confused. Then, through a rear window of the vehicle, the police officers found twenty cartons of Sudafed. They knew that people do not usually purchase

FIGURE 7.6   Officer Taylor's cruiser

FIGURE 7.7   Reeve's truck

Sudafed in bulk except to make methamphetamine. The officers gave Reeve the *Miranda* warning[6] and asked Reeve to submit to a drug test. Reeve agreed, and he tested positive for meth. After being read his *Miranda* rights, Reeve acknowledged that he was driving the Sudafed to a friend's house, where there was a small lab used to make the drug.

Reeve was charged with violating Franklin's state drug laws. In addition, the truck was confiscated and seized, pursuant to Franklin's forfeiture law.

Reeve pled guilty as part of a plea bargain and will spend three years in a state prison.

Of course, Reeve's parents are very troubled by their son's situation. They informed the court that they wish they had known what was really going on and had been able to help him.

---

6   From *Miranda v. Arizona*, 382 U.S. 436 (1966). Before custodial interrogation, officers must advise that the defendant has the right to remain silent; that any statement made can be used against them in court; that they have the right to an attorney during questioning; and that an attorney can be appointed if they cannot afford one.

Procedural Posture

After Reeve's plea was entered, his parents filed a motion with the trial court, seeking return of the truck. They argued two points: first, that the seizure itself was improper as it was not supported by the statute; and second, that they were entitled to a hearing expressly addressing their interests in the seized property under the Due Process Clause of the Fourteenth Amendment.

The court denied the motion, finding that the seizure was proper under the statute. The court made the following findings:

> Reeve was an owner of the seized vehicle.
>
> Reeve had pled guilty to violating Franklin law outlawing a) the ownership of drug supplies used to make an illegal substance; and b) using that illegal substance (methamphetamine).
>
> Reeve's guilty plea is deemed a conviction by law.
>
> Under these facts, the provisions of the civil forfeiture statute permit seizure.
>
> The statute does not preclude seizure, or require return of property, where there are owners of that property that are not implicated in a criminal case.
>
> The Due Process Clause of the Fourteenth Amendment does not require a hearing inquiring as to property rights held by owners other than the named criminal defendant prior to or subsequent to a proper forfeiture of property that has been legally seized.

In short, the trial court concluded that Reeve's parents' interests in the vehicle were immaterial under the wording of the statute. The court rejected their claim that forfeiture without a hearing violated their due process rights. Reeve's parents appealed, and the court of appeals affirmed. Reeve's parents then appealed the case to this court.

Issue: Forfeiture Rights for Jointly Owned Vehicles in Franklin

Does the forfeiture of a vehicle that was owned jointly by three people violate the Fourteenth Amendment's Due Process Clause, where no evidentiary hearing was conducted, and only one of the three people had knowledge of the criminal use of the vehicle, but that one person pled guilty to a drug offense?

Relevant Authority

The Due Process Clause of the Fourteenth Amendment says: "[N]or shall any State deprive any person of life, liberty, or property, without due process of law."

The Eighth Amendment to the United States Constitution says: "Excessive bail shall not be required, nor excessive fines imposed, nor cruel and unusual punishments inflicted."

There is a recent Supreme Court case, *Timbs v. Indiana*, 586 U.S. __ (2019) that concerns the civil forfeiture of a vehicle owned by Tyson Timbs. The car, a Land Rover, was purchased with a portion of a cash settlement from Timbs received after his father died. Timbs had been a drug addict, and after his father died, Timbs fell back into the drug habit. He spent most of the remaining settlement money on drugs and began selling drugs to support his habit. He was arrested by undercover officers after he sold them drugs worth about $225. He pled guilty to the charges and was sentenced to house arrest, probation, and payment of $1,200 in fines.

As Timbs had used his Land Rover to transport drugs, the State of Indiana also seized the car pursuant to its forfeiture law. In response, Timbs sued the State of Indiana, arguing that its seizure of the vehicle violated the Eighth Amendment's prohibition against excessive fines, which applied to the states under the Fourteenth Amendment's Due Process Clause.

The trial court ruled for Timbs, noting that the Land Rover's value was in excess of four times the greatest penalty that could have been assessed against Timbs ($10,000) and that it was over thirty times the amount that Timbs actually paid. The Indiana Court of Appeals affirmed the trial court. The Supreme Court of Indiana reversed, however, noting that the Excessive Fines clause of the Eighth Amendment only applied to the federal government, not to state governments. Timbs filed a Petition for Certiorari, and the United States Supreme Court took the case.

The Supreme Court found that the Fourteenth Amendment's Due Process Clause incorporates the Excessive Fines Clause and renders it applicable to the states. The Excessive Fines Clause "carried forward protections found in sources from the Magna Carta to the English Bill of Rights to state constitutions from the colonial era …" Accordingly, excessive fines are unconstitutional, whether the state or federal government applies them.

Note several key differences between the *Timbs* case and the *Dockson* case. First, the Supreme Court's opinion did not include any tests that may be used to determine when fines are excessive. The majority opinion suggested that the seizure of the Land Rover was disproportionate to the crime, but the job of making that determination will fall to the trial court on remand.

More significantly, the Supreme Court's opinion did not address the due process issue that this case presents. *Timbs* did not involve the property interests of any persons other than the defendant who had been criminally charged and convicted. *Dockson* does involve the interests of third parties who are innocent of any crime.

Conclusion

The law clerks remain available to answer any questions that may assist the court in addressing this civil forfeiture case. We look forward to the opinion of the court in this interesting matter.

CHAPTER 8

Property Law

The future of the nation depends in no small part on the efficiency of industry, and the efficiency of industry depends in no small part on the protection of intellectual property.

—Richard Posner, judge of the U.S. Court of Appeals for the Seventh Circuit, in *Rockwell Graphic Systems, Inc. v. DEV Industries*, 925 F.2d 174 (1991).

Orientation

In the first six chapters of this book, we traveled far in time and place. We journeyed from the legal codes of ancient Mesopotamian kings to the modern era of constitutional legal rights in the United States. We explored the rise of the English common law and its influence on the American legal system. We reviewed the creation of the United States Constitution and assessed its guarantees of free speech, religious freedom, due process, and equal protection. We noted some key Supreme Court rulings that address free speech, religious freedom, equal protection, and due process rights. We considered the methods the Court used to resolve these cases and thought about how their rulings support the modern rule of law.

For the purposes of this book, we have concluded our formal historical exploration of the foundations of American law and key concepts enshrined in the United States Constitution. We will now turn to defined areas of substantive and procedural law. In the next chapters we will review property law, contracts, and torts.

Even though our focus is shifting away from the Constitution, its provisions remain vitally relevant. A court of law can declare void any governmental action or rule in any area of substantive or procedural law that violates the United States Constitution. This is also true if a rule or procedure violates the governing state's constitution. Our federal and state constitutions are always running in the background, shaping the legal rules under which we live. From time to time, they step forward, affirming their authority and mandating a legislative or judicial response.

The following key terms are defined in this chapter. They are also defined in the Glossary.

Adverse Possession	**Fee Simple**	**Grantor**	**Personal Property**
Arbitration	**Determinable Estate**	**Infringement**	**Property Law**
Conservation Easement	**Fee Simple Estate**	**Intellectual Property**	**Real Property**
Copyright	**Fee Simple Subject**	**Intestate**	**Tenancy at Sufferance**
Defeasible Estates	**to a Condition**	**Joint Tenants with a**	**Tenancy in Common**
Easement	**Subsequent**	**Right of Survivorship**	**Tenants by the Entirety**
Eminent Domain	**Fee Tail Estate**	**Leasehold Estate**	**Trademark**
Equitable Estate	**Finite Estate**	**Life Estate**	**Trust**
Escheat	**Freehold Estates**	**Mediation**	**Trustee**
Estate for Years	**Future Interest**	**Patent**	
Estates in Land	**Grantee**	**Periodic Estate**	

Introduction

This chapter's focus is on property law. Property law is tied up with property rights, the way property can be owned, how ownership can be conveyed, and how disputes about ownership and rights may be resolved.[1] Like other areas of law, its annals include some sad features. For much of human history, portions of the population were denied property ownership rights. Enslaved persons in colonial times could not, by law, own property (and indeed, were deemed property themselves).[2] Until the middle of the nineteenth century, women's property rights were also severely limited. When a woman married, all her property became her husband's. She was entitled only to dower rights, an interest in her husband's property if he died without leaving a will.[3] Through the passage of time and legislation, these limitations

---

1   The rich historical scholarship on the law of property includes Baron Samuel von Pufendorf, a German scholar from the 1600s. He maintained that rights in property were derived from physically taking it and obtaining governmental acknowledgment of that seizure. English philosopher John Locke thought that contributing labor to property was a prerequisite to ownership, and English jurist and political philosopher Jeremy Bentham maintained that property ownership is an expectation created by settled practice and by operation of law. All three believed that governments should support property interests.

2   Delores Jones-Brown, *The System in Black and White* 142. Michael Markowitz, Ed. (2000).

3   The legal doctrine declaring that a woman's legal rights were subsumed by her husband upon marriage is called *coverture*. New York State's Married Women's Property Act of 1848 (passed April 7, 1848) permitted women to control their own property and give it to others by gift or bequest. This law became a template for others enacted by other states. In addition, Spanish law on community property shaped women's property rights in many Western states after the Mexican-American War (1846–1848). Sex discrimination continued to threaten women's property interests until a series of legislative protections were granted in the late twentieth century. One such protection was the 1974 Equal Credit Opportunity Act, which guaranteed that women could not be denied credit based on gender or marital status. This

have been corrected. However, as the result of this historical legacy, staggering racial and gender disparities in property ownership remain.[4]

The Importance of Property Law

Property comes in many shapes and sizes. It may be tangible, such as a house, a guitar, a cat, or a field of corn. Property also may be intangible, such as a patent, a copyright, or a trademark.

For our purposes, we will divide property law into three areas: **real property** (land and the things permanently attached to it); **personal property** (such as funds in the bank, items in your home, cars, mobile homes, livestock, and pets); and **intellectual property** (patents, copyrights, and trademarks).

No matter the type of property under consideration, we must have formalized rules supporting ownership rights. Legal acknowledgment of these rights encourages security, savings, and investment. If you are confident that your assets are safe, you will be more likely to work to increase them. You will be more likely to seek economic security by accumulating reserves that can be used in times of need. All over the world, people purchase needed goods and services during regular times, and in times of crisis, savings can serve as a buffer against disaster.

In addition, a stable set of rules concerning property rights supports the growth of business. Real, personal, or intellectual property can be sold or leveraged to raise capital to start or sustain useful endeavors. Businesses can offer stock to those who might wish to invest, merge with other enterprises to expand, or divest themselves of assets to streamline operations. Without the support of property law (and other areas of law, such as contracts), these arrangements would be impossible.

On a more personal level, formalized rules about property rights can improve happiness. People can purchase things that they like and engage in activities that are important to them. They can live in safe rental housing without fear of eviction or can purchase housing and make it comfortable for their families. In addition, when people's property rights are supported by the government, they will be more inclined to invest in their communities. They will wish to support long-term goals, such as quality education, social and infrastructure improvements, and environmental remediation. They

---

act also protected women from discriminatory bank practices that required a woman to get a father or husband's signature to open an account or obtain a credit card.

4   In 2016, the net worth of a typical white family was nearly ten times greater than that of a Black family. *See* McIntosh, Moss, Nunn, and Shambaugh, *Up Front: Examining the Black-white Wealth Gap* (Feb. 27, 2020). In addition, women in the United States own thirty-two cents for every dollar owned by men. *See* Janice Traflet and Robert Wright, "America Doesn't Just Have a Gender Pay Gap. It Has a Gender Wealth Gap," the *Washington Post* (April 2, 2019). One contributing factor to this phenomenon may be that women faced barriers to business ownership and control that were meaningfully addressed for the first time in 1988. Until the introduction of the Women's Business Ownership Act (1988), women often could not obtain a business loan without a male relative's signature. Women's Business Ownership Act of 1988, 15 U.S.C. 401 (1988).

Grumpy Cat and Meme Rights

A meme is a comedic image shared by thousands—sometimes millions—of people. "Grumpy Cat" is one of the most famous memes, and it became a herald of "meme culture" on the internet.

The Grumpy Cat meme is simply a picture of a grumpy-looking cat. In real life, the cat was named Tardar Sauce. Her appearance made her famous, and Grumpy Cat became one of the first memes to reach millions of viewers. Grumpy Cat now has her own verified Instagram account with over 2.5 million followers. The cat's owner created a company, Grumpy Cat Limited, which licenses the right to use her face to other entities. One such deal led to a federal lawsuit in 2015 over copyright infringement when a company used Grumpy Cat's image for more products than they had paid for. Grumpy Cat, however, had the last laugh: the federal court awarded over $700,000 in copyright infringement damages.

Not all memes are treated equally. Meme culture has blurred the lines between original and reimagined work. Since memes are generally photos taken by someone else and often involve stills from movies, they should be protected by the copyright owned by the original owner. However, there is uncertainty about how such images may be legally used. While scholars argue about what *should* be the law, it is likely that unless a meme changes the underlying photo drastically, the meme is protected by copyright or privacy laws. Thus, it is best to use images in the public domain or that the owner has given permission to share.

FIGURE 8.1 A cat meme created from a picture in the public domain

also may be more likely to engage in the political process and work to make their towns safer and more pleasant places to live.

Finally, as noted by Judge Posner in the chapter's opening quote, without the legal system's support of intellectual property rights, investments in important innovations—medical, mechanical, industrial, electronic, and agricultural—would quickly wither. As new technologies develop, the law must work to define and defend them so that their benefits can be realized. Whether it be a new vaccine, a new medical device, a type of grain that is drought tolerant, or environmentally friendly sources of energy, we rely upon property law to secure and nurture innovations that will benefit the world.

Real Property Assets and Different Types of Estates in Land

We will begin our tour of the substance of property law with real property. The English common law defined real property[5] as things that could not be moved, such as the land and permanent structures built upon it.

For most of human history, real property was the dominant source of personal wealth. If you owned the land, you owned the means of production and commerce. You could grow crops for food and herbs for health; you could raise animals for consumption and transportation; you could mine minerals for metal-making; and you could maintain wooded areas for lumber.

To understand the different types of real and other property interests, we will engage in some storytelling.

First, let us agree that you are a member of a notable and landed family. You personally own 10,000 acres[6] in

---

5   The word "real" descends from the Latin *res*, meaning *thing*. It was used in contrast with *in personam*, meaning "against a particular person." *See Concise Oxford English Dictionary* 1192, 10th Ed. (1999).

6   This is about 15.5 square miles.

FIGURE 8.2   The Bighorn National Forest

the Big Horn Mountains of Wyoming. You inherited this land at a young age, and you hold title to it in your own name.

It is a unique and beautiful parcel of land, running from a lush meadow in the high country of Wyoming, to open fields and sagebrush flats.

You built a spacious lodge near a branch of the scenic Morn Creek that meanders through part of the parcel. Your land hosts abundant wildlife, including elk, deer, and antelope, as well as a variety of birds. As a hobby (and with the help of local ranchers), you run a small herd of cattle on the lower flats.

You are married but have no children. Your spouse, Dana, took this picture, looking down toward the creek after climbing Hero's Point. Your lodge is located on the right side of the photo, hidden by the outcropping of rock.

You work full time as a judge in the town of Liberty Springs in the state of Franklin, serving in the Chancery Division. As you may remember from Chapter 2, Chancery Division cases involve matters of equity. Your powers as a judge sitting in equity are considerably greater than those of judges who preside in regular courts of law. In a court of equity, a judge can issue an injunction (an order that a party stop or start doing something) or make a finding about rights, if the interests of justice so require. In courts of law, judges usually issue monetary damage awards.

You have a reputation for fair dealings, and you work hard for the citizens whose cases come to your court.

One of America's Most Influential Legal Scholars

Richard Posner, former chief judge of the United States Court of Appeals for the Seventh Circuit, is one of the most cited legal scholars of the twentieth century. Judge Posner is most famous for his work in law and economics, a field that applies economic theory to explain and analyze the effects of laws. His book, *An Economic Analysis of Law*, has gone through nine editions and continues to be used in American law schools. This book and other writings have made a significant contribution to the dialogue about the best methods for lawmaking.

Some of his arguments have stirred controversy. Critics argue that typical economic analysis, which focuses on efficiency, lacks the tools to address concerns about human rights and the just allocation of resources. However, the field of law and economics continues to develop, with increasing use of econometrics, statistics, game theory, and behavioral economics.

FIGURE 8.3 Judge Richard Posner

You own a townhome near the Liberty County courthouse in Liberty Springs. However, each summer, you vacation in your lodge. Your work permits you to spend about a month each summer in Wyoming. While in residence, you invite friends to visit, and everyone enjoys the idyllic scenery. You and Dana swim in the winding creek, ride horses around the woods, and observe the wildlife that frequents your property.

You are a thoughtful person, and you recognize that you have lived a life that is out of reach of all but the most affluent Americans. You and your spouse have decided that it is time to think about your options concerning the disposition of your property. However, you have some concerns as well as some priorities. You want to preserve the beautiful land that your family has enjoyed. You also want to find a way to contribute toward endeavors that are important to you and Dana.

Your cousin, Marshall Godequin, is a transactional attorney with a practice focused on real property. You invited your cousin to lunch at your favorite restaurant to review your understanding of property law, as it has been a while since you graduated from law school. In addition, you have a property case pending in your docket, and you want to thoroughly understand it. (Marshall always could explain things well.)

You first asked Marshall to give you an overview of different types of legal **estates in land**, interests in real property. He explained that in property law, interests in real property can be thought of as a "bundle of rights" that come with property. These rights can include ownership, possession, use, and conveyance (the right to sell or give the property to someone else). Some types of estates in land include all the rights in the bundle. Other types of legal estates, such as leases, only come with some of the things in the bundle.

Marshall encouraged you to think of three categories of estates in land: **freehold estates**, **leasehold estates**, and **equitable estates**. To help you understand the different types of estates, Marshall wrote them out for you.

```
                        Estates in Land
Freehold Estates

    Fee Simple Estates  (Bundles ownership, possession & right to convey)
    Defeasible Estates (Can revert to granter if conditions are not met)
        Fee Simple Determinable (Bundle includes ownership and possession,
        but states a condition that must be met for continuing ownership)
        Fee Simple Subject to Condition Subsequent (Bundle includes
        ownership and possession, but something must happen or not happen)
    Finite Estates (Limited in duration)
        Life Estates (Bundles ownership & possession, but not right to convey)
        Fee Tail Estates (Bundles ownership & possession, but not right to convey)


Leasehold Estates (Includes right of occupancy, but not ownership or right to convey)

    Estate for Years
    Periodic Estates
    Tenancy at Sufferance


Equitable Estates (Includes only a partial right or interest in the property)

    Future Interests (Holder will acquire property or some interest in it)
    Easements (Includes a defined right to enter, but no ownership)
        Conservation Easement (restricts usage of land to protect & preserve it)
```

FIGURE 8.4   Types of estates in land

Marshall started the conversation with freehold estates. These come with the most rights in the bundle, including ownership and possession. There are three main types of freehold estates: **fee simple estates, defeasible estates,** and **finite estates.**

You told Marshall that you hold your Wyoming land in <u>fee simple</u>, the broadest type of freehold estate. Thus, you may use and possess the property, and you have the right to convey the property to whomever you wish. (Marshall, who helped with the property transfer, reminded you that there is one limitation that impinges upon a portion of your land. You had forgotten about it, but Marshall promised to talk about it a bit later.)

Although most people would like to own their land as you do, in fee simple, Marshall has worked with clients who hold their land as a <u>defeasible estate</u>. This means that the land is theirs, as long as certain specific conditions are met. Marshall had one client who deeded the family farm to her son, with the caveat that the land must remain in cultivation and not be sold to a developer. This created a **fee simple determinable estate**: the estate remains with the person who received it (the **grantee**) as long as the condition is met. So, as long as the son continues to make sure the land is farmed, he will be able to keep it. Otherwise, it could return to his mother, the **grantor.**

Marshall also knows of estates that were conveyed with the condition that if a certain future event happens, then the estate reverts (goes back) to the grantor. Marshall tells you about a particularly interesting defeasible estate that he helped set up. The grantor gave 500 acres to a city for use as a zoo.

FIGURE 8.5   Golden lion tamarins

However, the conveyance documents included the caveat that at all times, there must be 50 monkeys in the zoo. That created a **fee simple subject to a condition subsequent**, and if the zoo's monkey count ever drops below 50, the grantor could get the land back. (Marshall advises you that the zoo's primatologists were careful about their monkey count, keeping a few extra golden lion tamarins on hand.)[7]

Marshall has also worked with clients who needed to create <u>finite estates</u>. These estates are, from the outset, limited in duration. He had one client who wanted to create a will that would convey the family home to her husband for him to live in for the rest of his life. After his death, the home was to go to their only child. Marshall helped her draft a will that set up a **life estate**, which gave the home to the husband as long as he lived. He had the right of possession, but no right of conveyance: thus, he could enjoy the property for the remainder of his life, but he could not sell it.

Marshall also remembered a rather odd client who wanted to set up another kind of finite estate, a **fee tail estate**. He thought of himself as a particularly important individual, and he wished to create a legal document that would ensure his property remained in his personal family line forever, going from oldest son to oldest son. This was common in England, where fee-tail-male estates would automatically pass the property to the next male heir upon the death of the current male owner. This practice kept large estates intact and supported primogeniture, the feudal rule that required succession of the eldest male child. Marshall explained to the client that the fee tail estate has been abolished in most of the United States, and the attempt to

---

7   This has a real-world parallel. When Joseph Prentice founded the Santa Ana Zoo at Prentice Park in Southern California, he required that there be fifty monkeys on the zoo property at all times. *See* https://santaanazoo.org/.

create it usually results in a fee simple estate, without restrictions on subsequent conveyances. Marshall laughed as he explained that the client was quite annoyed at hearing this.

You and Marshall also discussed leasehold estates. Marshall advised that these estates come with the right of occupancy and possession but do not include ownership or the right of conveyance. One common leasehold estate is the **estate for years**, which includes a lease of property for any length of time that has a definite beginning and end date. When you were in college, you often signed leases and gained occupancy and possession rights in apartments. Marshall explained that leases that automatically renew, with no specific end date, are **periodic estates**. While attending the University of Illinois, you had such an arrangement with a landlord. The lease required you to give thirty days' notice before termination.

You also mentioned a different arrangement that your spouse worked out with a landlord while in school. Dana is a physician, educated at the Perelman School of Medicine at the University of Pennsylvania. Dana signed a one-year lease for an apartment close to campus. After that term expired, Dana continued to live in the apartment with the landlord's consent, paying rent as before. Marshall explained that this was technically a **tenancy at sufferance** because Dana was a "holdover tenant." As long as the landlord remained content with the arrangement and Dana continued to pay the rent, it would be a recognized leasehold estate. Marshall suggested that it is better to solidify arrangements in writing to affirm everyone's obligations. Some landlords feel they are entitled to become abusive if their obligations are not spelled out in a current contract. Likewise, some tenants do not take good care of the property unless penalties are spelled out in a current lease.

As it is of special significance to you, Marshall also informed you about **equitable estates**. Here, a person has neither ownership nor possession, but still has an interest in property that a court will recognize. The son of Marshall's client who will inherit the house upon the death of his father has such an interest; in that case, it is a **future interest** in land. Mineral rights can be separated from other rights in land, and those are equitable interests.

Easements are common types of equitable estates. An easement is the right to enter or use someone else's property in a certain way. No ownership interest accompanies that right. Marshall explained that utility companies usually have easements in residential and commercial parcels so that they can maintain their pipes and wires. In addition, individuals can be given easements to fish in private lakes, walk on private beaches, or hunt in private woods. Easements are handy tools to create limited entry rights in land that people do not wish to sell.

Marshall reminded you that 300 acres of your land in the Bighorn Mountains are subject to a **conservation easement.** This legal agreement permanently limits land use in order to protect and preserve it. When you acquired your acreage in the Bighorn Mountains, it came with this conservation easement, held by the Nature Conservancy.[8] Thus, some of your land cannot be developed, although

---

8   The Nature Conservancy is a nonprofit company, founded in 1951 to protect land and water, provide food and water sustainably, build healthy cities, and tackle climate change. *See Who We Are*, the Nature Conservancy, https://www.nature.org/en-us/about-us/who-we-are/.

Eminent Domain

Even if you own your land free and clear, the state or federal government has the right to buy it from you under certain circumstances. By exercising the right of **eminent domain**, the government can take your property if it is needed for a public purpose. Such purposes typically include the creation of important infrastructure, such as roads, hospitals, schools, and parks.

In *Clark v. Nash*, 198 U.S. 361 (1905), the Supreme Court acknowledged that "what is a public use largely depends upon the facts ... with which the people and the courts of the state must be more familiar than a stranger to the soil." Thus, the definition of a public use may vary from one locale to another, and the Supreme Court largely permits the states to make their own determinations. In *Kelo v. City of New London*, 545 U.S. 469 (2005), the Supreme Court extended the doctrine of eminent domain, finding that a government could use it to take unblighted homes and other private property and transfer them to a private developer to increase tax revenue. Most states have now passed laws ensuring that the power of eminent domain cannot be used in this way.

FIGURE 8.6 Private residential property

you may enjoy it in other ways. Marshall notes that the Nature Conservancy easement constitutes an equitable estate in that portion of your land.

Different Types of Real Property Ownership

In addition to describing the different types of ownership interests in land, your cousin gave you a quick overview of the various ways that title to real property can be held. An estate in land may be owned by multiple persons, or by a single person, or by corporations or other business associations. These different flavors of ownership can have different characteristics.

You and Dana own your townhome in Chicago as **tenants by the entirety**, which is only available for spouses. The property is owned by both spouses jointly, as if they were a single person. This means that when one spouse dies, there is no need to reconvey; the other spouse remains the owner, and ownership continues uninterrupted. This type of tenancy requires the spouses to manage their property jointly, and you and Dana have always worked together to care for your townhome.

A similar option exists for people who are not married. They can become **joint tenants with a right of survivorship**. This is like a tenancy by the entirety, with the same joint obligations. The tenancy is broken if one of the co-owners transfers their interest to a third party. Marshall set up such a tenancy for a pair of hairstylists who set up a business in a Victorian home. They both had invested in the home and in the business, and it was a prudent option.

Marshall reminded you that there is another popular flavor of tenancy: **tenancy in common**. In this tenancy, each owner has an equal but separate share of the property, although all the owners have the right to use the entire property. This estate is popular because owners may sell their shares to third parties without breaking the tenancy. If an owner dies, their heir (rather than the other owners) inherits their portion and then becomes a new tenant in common.

Marshall set up such a tenancy for a group of siblings who inherited a family farm. Eventually, some of the siblings thought they would buy out the interests of the other siblings, but to keep the farm operational until the details were worked out, they opted for a tenancy in common.

All these ways of holding property have features that are helpful when thinking about estate planning. Under many circumstances, estate taxes can be reduced or avoided entirely if no formal transfer of ownership occurs. This means that some types of tenancy can yield important benefits. You think about this, mentally bookmarking its importance.

Personal Property: Tangible and Intangible Assets

During the course of your lunch, Marshall noted that he intends to continue to practice law for about ten more years and then will retire (he is a bit older than you). You remarked that you have been thinking about cutting back a bit; you are financially secure and do not need to work. You and Dana also have been thinking about charitable endeavors you might pursue.

Marshall asked whether, in your retirement, you will move to Wyoming and keep the small herd of cattle that you have been running on your property. You told him that you are not certain. You have not decided what to do during your retirement. You are not sure that you will keep all your real property (the land and the town house), and your personal property also requires some consideration.

Marshall asks about your personal property. In addition to the cattle, you own some fine antique furniture and several works of art, including pieces by Cecilia Beaux (such as the picture shown here), currently on loan to the National Gallery of Art.[9]

---

9   Cecilia Beaux (1855–1942) was a portraitist who painted prominent members of American society.

Changing Property Rights Due to Rising Sea Levels

Due to climate change, rising sea levels threaten human health and safety. Another effect of this phenomenon is the strain it places on property rights. Planning decisions regarding coastal infrastructure often fall on local governments. In communities where sea level rise threatens welfare, local officials must contend with property owners who are unwilling to permit the buildup of beach infrastructure.

In *Stop the Beach Renourishment, Inc. v. Florida Department of Environmental Protection*, 560 U.S. 702 (2010), owners of beachfront properties alleged that their local government's beach nourishment program—which involved adding dry sand to eroded beaches, creating a strip of land at the edge of the water—had violated their perpetual right to beachfront property that touched water. The United States Supreme Court eventually affirmed the Florida Supreme Court, holding that there was no unconstitutional taking by the beach restoration program. Instead, restorative efforts like this program were covered by the Florida doctrine of avulsion, which provides that the owner of the seabed (the state) owns any land created by a sudden event.

FIGURE 8.7   Sunset and the sea

Adverse Possession in the Law

Adverse possession is an unusual legal process through which a person gains ownership to a parcel of real property. The rules vary from state to state, but a person making a claim of adverse possession must generally prove the following:

- That they have taken possession of the land and are using it (they are not merely walking through it or occasionally using it). This usually means living on it and paying the required taxes.

- That they do not have permission from the owner.

- That they are using the land in an "open and notorious way," meaning that the use is not covert or hidden.

- That they use the land continuously for a certain time period (the statutes vary, but the range is from five to thirty years).

- That the use of the land deprives the true owner of its use.

If all these conditions are met, then a court could grant you the legal title to your own parcel of oceanfront.

You have been considering donating the artwork to a museum. In addition, your personal property includes considerable investments in stocks and mutual funds. As the markets have been volatile, you are not certain of their current value, but you believe they total about $3 million.

Your last major asset of personal property is a yacht that is moored in a slip in nearby Pleasant Lake Harbor. You and Dana sail on the weekends when you are in town and the weather is pleasant. You think the yacht is worth about $300,000. (Marshall raises his eyebrows again at this. He tells you he thinks your estimate may be low, reminding you that it is a well-furnished vessel.)

FIGURE 8.8 Cecilia Beaux's portrait of her cousin, Sarah Allibone Leavitt

Intellectual Property and Your Family

You and Marshall also discussed the intellectual property that you own. It was the original source of your family's wealth, and he has benefited from it, too.

First, you (and Marshall) inherited some **patents** relating to a unique, nearly frictionless engine developed by your grandparents. They were notable engineers, and the engine they invented continues to have wide application. Its nearly frictionless quality means that it is quite durable, as parts do not wear out quickly. Your grandparents promptly registered their invention with the United States Patent and Trademark Office[10] and were given several patents. These patents provided them with exclusive rights to make, use, and sell the invention for twenty years.

When your grandparents retired, your parents continued to invest time in upgrading and refining the engine. They obtained successive patents that lasted throughout their working careers. Funds from the sales of the patented engines enabled your parents to purchase the Wyoming parcel. (Using his share of money from your grandparents' patents, Marshall purchased land in Florida. He always preferred beaches to mountains.)

Marshall reminded you that his son, Neville, has intellectual property of his own. During the course of Neville's career as a park ranger, he published a book describing his experiences with particularly difficult members of the public. The book recounts his efforts to keep park visitors safe from the elk, bison, and bear that some members of the public were determined to encounter at close range. Neville's book, *A Ranger's Tale*, is registered with the United States Copyright Office.[11] You know that songs, photos, videos, paintings, sculptures, and audio recordings can also be protected by a **copyright**, which preserves the creator's right to sue for **infringement.**

While Marshall talked about intellectual property, you noted a bottle of mineral water on the table. It had the curving word "Perrier," which you recognized as a **trademark.** Trademarks are words, symbols, emblems, or sounds (including songs) used in connection with a product or service. They belong to the company that manufactures the product and may be registered with the United States Patent and Trademark Office. You refilled your glass with the Perrier and pondered the reach of intellectual property in the modern world.

FIGURE 8.9 Your yacht

---

10   The patent process with the United States Patent and Trademark Office may be expensive and can take some time. Persons may patent real inventions (not ideas) that are novel, nonobvious, and original. Those who have inventions they wish to sell are wise to seek patents. In most disputes, the earliest to file will be given the rights to use and sell. *See General Information Concerning Patents*, USPTO (Oct. 2015), https://www.uspto.gov/patents-getting-started/general-information-concerning-patents.

11   Readers interested in this subject might try *Ranger Confidential: Living, Working, and Dying in the National Parks*, by Andrea Lankford (Globe Pequot, 2010).

The Estate of the Musician Prince Goes to Probate

Prince may have been a music virtuoso, but genius only goes so far: the artist forgot to write a will. With no clear direction and no immediate surviving relatives, his $300 million estate ended up in probate court.

As with many estates in probate—both large and small—a collection of people stepped forward, claiming to be heirs to the fortune. Millions of dollars in fees and costs have been spent trying to sort out who should get what. A judge found one full sister and five half-siblings are legal heirs. However, at least two others claim a right to inherit some of the estate, even though they are not genetically related.

Having a valid will is prudent for anyone. The lack of a will resulted in the loss of a considerable portion of Prince's estate.

FIGURE 8.10 Prince in Brussels in 1986; photo by Yves Lorson

Your Estate Planning

As you worked your way through dessert (a nice piece of your favorite pie), Marshall brought up the subject of **trusts.** He is in the process of setting up a trust for a niece who needs special services. A trust is a useful legal device that establishes a formal relationship between two people. One person can become legally entitled to manage property for the benefit of another. The **trustee** is the legal owner of the property, but they must manage it according to the terms of the trust document for the beneficiary. Marshall mentioned that his sister was investing a sum of money with a reliable banker in a local financial institution as the trustee. His niece, according to the terms of the trust, would receive periodic payments from it throughout her life. If the trustee failed to fulfill the terms of the trust, they could be brought to court and account for their failure to do so.

This gives you food for thought. You understand that any type of property interest can be placed into a trust: real property, personal property, or intellectual property. Your colleagues in the Probate Division sometimes see wills that create trusts, placing assets in the care of a chosen person until children come of age and can inherit. They tell you that thoughtful arrangements, worked out in advance, greatly reduce conflict and cost.

You know that larger estates must be probated. If there is no will—if the deceased has died **intestate**—then there are statutes that decide who gets what. The statutes attempt to follow the wishes of a majority of people. If you are married but have no children, your assets go to your surviving spouse. If you are married and do have children, your assets will be divided between your spouse and children. The divisions are dictated by statute, which can save families from open hostility. If someone dies intestate and has no locatable heirs, the property will go to the state, in a process called **escheat.**

You and Dana want to create an estate plan that fairly accommodates your desires and the reasonable expectations of your family members.

You and Dana do not have many relatives still living. You have no siblings, and Dana is also an only child, with one cousin. You may have more distant cousins in the family tree, but if so, you cannot remember them.

You and Dana have talked about several causes that are important to you. You are considering setting things up with those causes in mind. You are also considering benefiting causes while you are still living. You can then observe how things are progressing and make changes to your plans if needed.

You will soon meet with an attorney who can turn your thoughts and plans into a legally enforceable estate plan. This is a process that can take some time in larger estates (such as yours). Your spouse will also meet with an attorney, so that your plans can work in harmony to achieve the outcomes you both desire.

In advance of that meeting, however, you must resolve some important questions. What persons or causes do you want to benefit? Are there any entities outside your family that you wish to support? Do you want money or other assets to go to these causes while you are still living? Do you want your assets to go to these causes on a permanent basis or on a contingent basis? What legal tools do you think will best achieve your plans?

Conclusion and Introduction to Law Lab

You must now focus on an interesting property case that has presented itself for your review. It involves parcels owned by two families in the nearby city of Piestewa. You asked the Chancery Court law clerks to provide you with a memorandum about the case, as it is a case of first impression in

Myra Bradwell

Myra Bradwell devoted her life to promoting the acceptance of women in the legal profession. In 1868, Bradwell founded and published the *Chicago Legal News* in order to report on the law, including a special column, "Law Relating to Women." Bradwell then cowrote the Illinois Married Women's Property Act of 1861 and the Earnings Act of 1869, which allow married women to control their property.

After passing the Illinois state bar exam, Bradwell applied for admission to the Illinois bar. In 1870, the Illinois Supreme Court denied her application, and the United States Supreme Court denied her application for admission three years later. Finally, in 1890, the Illinois Supreme Court approved Bradwell's original application, and she became the first woman to be admitted to the Illinois state bar.

FIGURE 8.11 Myra Bradwell

Liberty County. The law clerks' memorandum follows. You will likely reach out to colleagues to obtain their thoughts about this case.

The lawsuit stems from a bad surveying job, resulting in incorrect mapping of a critical property boundary. The surveyor did not accurately plot the dimensions and shape of the boundary line between two parcels. Accordingly, the map that resulted was badly flawed. This, in turn, led a family to build an expensive structure on land they did not own.

The case must be adjudicated. The families involved need to obtain resolution of a serious legal problem that has greatly affected their lives. As a judge in the Chancery Division, you have broad powers to impose the relief that will be the most just under the circumstances of each case. You can, for example, determine to divide the property in a way that is equitable. You also have the power to call the parties to attend a mediation session to explore the possibility of informal resolution.

Read the memorandum provided by your law clerks, and consider your options. In this case, how will you exercise your judicial powers to address this property dispute?

Chancery Court Law Lab

MEMORANDUM

To: The Honorable Judges of the Liberty County Circuit Court, Chancery Division

From: The Chancery Division Legal Interns

Re: *Bailey v. Stanley*, pending in Liberty County Circuit Court, Chancery Division

Your Honors:

Please allow this memorandum to serve as the brief you requested in connection with the above-referenced pending action, which presents as a case of first impression in this county, as this court has not seen one like it before. You asked us to summarize the case and explore the concerns of judges sitting in equity on matters of this type in other chancery divisions.

Factual Background

The origins of this litigation date back five years, when the town of Piestewa (located in Liberty County) determined to sell some parcels of land ("the Piestewa Lots") to raise revenue to build a new community recreational facility.

The Piestewa Lots are big parcels, each around seven acres in size, although a few are around fourteen acres. All the lots are located on the Clearwater River and run down to the water. There is a twenty-five-yard public recreation easement along the Clearwater, so the lot owners do not have exclusive river access. The easement is used mostly by canoers who wish to pull to shore to rest or eat during recreational boat trips.

Each of the Piestewa Lots is distinctive, and some have wooded tracts of larger size. The parcels involved in this case all have wooded areas on the north side and slope gently down to the river. The river is prone to flooding in the spring, and accordingly, county ordinances mandate that construction is not permitted within 200 yards of its banks, except for docks and boathouses.

The Baileys purchased two adjacent seven-acre parcels, Lots 15 and 16, from the city of Piestewa. They planned on using these parcels to build a manor-style bed-and-breakfast. They wished to live on the top floor of the building, so the structure would be their residence as well as their business. It was the Baileys' dream to retire from their civil service jobs and run the bed-and-breakfast as innkeepers. They purchased two lots in order to have enough land for rose and vegetable gardens and a hiking trail through the woods on the north side of the property.

Lot 17, a larger fourteen-acre parcel to the east of Lot 16, was purchased by the Stanleys. They purchased the larger lot to build a riding stable on it at a later date. The Stanleys live in Liberty Springs, but their dream was to retire to Piestewa and operate the stable. They hoped to do this in the next few years.

The Baileys decided to build their bed-and-breakfast on Lot 16. Unfortunately, a serious mistake was made. During the planning stage of the project, the surveyor incorrectly mapped a part of the boundary between plots 16 and 17. Accordingly, a portion of the north-south boundary between plots 16 and 17 was wrongly placed to the east of the actual boundary (see map below).

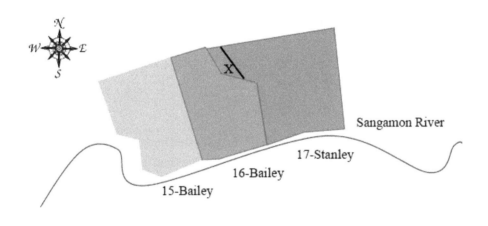

FIGURE 8.12   A marked map of the key lots

The upshot is that the contractors built the Baileys' bed-and-breakfast on Lot 17, owned by the Stanleys, instead of on Lot 16, owned by the Baileys. This was not the Baileys' fault. The mistake was discovered only when the structure was inspected by the city. The Baileys spent $300,000 (much of their retirement savings) on the bed-and-breakfast/residence.

The surveyor who made the error has declared bankruptcy. Our inquiries have confirmed that the estate in bankruptcy is worth less than $30,000 and that there are many creditors. Further, the surveyor's liability insurer has exhausted its limits of coverage in connection with another claim. Therefore, the surveyor's insurer will not be able to respond to any claim that might be presented.

After the bed-and-breakfast was built, the Stanleys learned that the Baileys had built a large structure on their property. They were particularly upset, as this construction was situated near where they planned to build a modest residence and a riding stable.

The Stanleys and Baileys informally tried to work things out, but that failed. The Stanleys finally decided to claim the bed-and-breakfast improvement as their own, but they will need money (about $100,000) to modify the structure so as to make it into a single-family residence. They then plan on building the riding stable adjacent to it.

Procedural Posture

The Baileys filed an action seeking equitable relief in the Chancery Division. They argue that they are at least entitled to $300,000, the value of the improvements that they innocently installed on the Stanleys' land.[1] The Stanleys filed a counterclaim for trespass and monetary damages. They seek $100,000, plus damages for trespass. They argue that the Baileys are trespassers and are not entitled to any relief. The Stanleys seek to recover the costs of modifying the inn to transform it into a single-family structure.

In this jurisdiction, the judge decides all cases filed in the Chancery Division. We confirm that our Chancery Division judges have broad discretion to work equitable relief. As the United States Supreme Court said in *Willard v. Tayloe*, 75 U.S. 557 (1869), "relief is not a matter of absolute right to either party; it is a matter resting in the discretion of the court, to be exercised upon a consideration of all the circumstances of each particular case."

Issue: Finding the Most Equitable Remedy in a Property Dispute

What remedy in equity should be applied where one party innocently improves the real property of another, in a way that is contrary to the usage plans of the second party? In addition: how can the parties be induced to work together to find a path forward that will optimize the outcome for everyone?

Common Law Concerns

In most jurisdictions, the following considerations are relevant to the decision of an equitable court:

1. Who are the innocent party(ies)?
2. If relief is not awarded, will a party be unjustly enriched?
3. Has someone innocently benefited another, and what is the extent of the benefit?
4. What precedent should the court establish?
5. Should one who mistakenly improves the land of another be allowed compensation?
6. What about the rights of the property owner, who has particular plans for the property? Should property owners not be allowed to feel secure in those plans?
7. What relief best serves the interests of justice?

---

1   The Baileys' theory of relief is called *restitution*. The focus of restitution is the recovery of unlawful gains. When a court orders restitution, the defendant must give up their wrongful gains to the plaintiff. This is different from compensating a plaintiff for their losses.

The common law, as declared in the Restatement of the Law of Restitution,[2] encourages a balancing of good cause and hardship in light of the degree of the parties' fault in the matter. When required by the interests of justice, judges hearing cases in matters of equity can seek creative solutions in demanding situations.

The Role of Arbitration and Mediation in Dispute Resolution

In this case, the Stanleys and the Baileys have asked for court assistance, and your law clerks confirm that the judges of Chancery Court have the jurisdiction to resolve their case. In addition to judicial resolution of this case, however, the court may wish to consider whether **arbitration** or **mediation** may serve the parties' interests. Through these processes, parties involved in legal conflict may be able to resolve their differences outside the courtroom, saving themselves time, money, and inconvenience.

In the process of arbitration, members of the legal profession serve as adjudicators. The parties submit legal briefs to explain their positions, and the arbitrators conduct a hearing on the disputed issues. After the hearing, they render a decision on how the case should be resolved.

In mediation, a neutral legal professional conducts settlement negotiations, working with each side separately to see if the case can be settled out of court. Mediators are often retired judges or experienced attorneys who have no prior relationship with the parties.

In most jurisdictions, arbitrations and mediations can be either binding or nonbinding. If the proceedings are binding, then the parties will be bound to whatever outcome results. If the proceedings are nonbinding, then the parties can freely try these methods of alternative dispute resolution, but return to court if their case does not resolve in a way that they can tolerate.

In Liberty County, binding mediation or arbitration can only be arranged if all the parties in the case agree in advance. However, Liberty County Chancery Court judges may order the parties to participate in nonbinding arbitration or mediation. Finally, the determination of which cases are suitable for mediation or arbitration is left to the discretion of the judge.

Conclusion

Please let your legal interns know if we can be of assistance as you consider how to address this matter. We look forward to the court's decision in this unusual and difficult case.

---

2   *See Restatement of the Law of Restitution*, Thomson Reuters (2011).

CHAPTER 9

Contract Law

FIGURE 9.1 American astronaut Alan Shepard

It is a very sobering feeling to be up in space and realize that one's safety factor was determined by the lowest bidder on a government contract.
—Rear Admiral Alan Bartlett Shepard Jr., American astronaut, naval aviator, test pilot, and businessman

Introduction

Each day, people purchase and sell goods and services. They enter into leases and employment agreements, they sign insurance contracts to protect property, and they execute loan documents to purchase residences. Companies enter into contracts to raise capital and launch businesses, and governments finalize agreements to procure goods and services for public agencies (including

NASA, the National Aeronautics and Space Administration, former employer of Alan Shepard, quoted above). Each of these endeavors requires the support of **contract law**, the backbone of modern business and personal enterprises.

The Framers of the United States Constitution recognized the importance of commercial and personal contracts. The Constitution of the United States declares in Article I, Section 10, Clause 1, that "No State shall ... pass any ... Law impairing the Obligation of Contracts." The rights of individuals, organizations, businesses, and governments to negotiate and enter into contracts undergirds the free enterprise system. Contract Law supports that system by providing uniformity and stability in transactions. Businesses need to know that the terms of their agreements will be enforced and that they will be enforced the same way throughout the United States. Accordingly, nearly all the states have adopted the **Uniform Commercial Code**, a comprehensive set of laws regulating commercial business dealings.[1] In addition, the American Law Institute developed a **Restatement of the Law of Contracts** that provides judges and lawyers with guidance in managing contracts and commercial transactions.[2]

Contract law, however, does more than simply ensure the uniformity and enforceability of agreements. It also addresses public policy concerns that are tied up with agreements. These concerns include making sure the parties understand the terms of a contract and are free to decide whether to enter into it; protecting minors and other vulnerable persons from the consequences of imprudent agreements; voiding unconscionable agreements and those made under circumstances we recognize as duress; and establishing protocols that protect individuals and those less well versed in business dealings from the consequences of ill-considered assumptions.

These concepts, like many ideas we have reviewed, have ancient roots. The Greek philosopher Plato wrote about contracts. He maintained that if someone failed to honor an agreement, suit could be brought by the party harmed by the default. However, performance should be excused if the contract required something to be done that was forbidden by law, or if consent to the agreement was obtained by undue pressure, or if an accident of some kind prevented performance.[3] Modern Contract Law addresses similar concerns.

In the next section, we will review the required components of a valid contract. We will then look at the reasons why performance may be excused and who has the right to enforce a contract. Finally, in this week's Law Lab, you will consider what provisions should be included in a contract that the attorney general of the State of Franklin is preparing for public use.

---

1   The Uniform Commercial Code was a joint project of the National Conference of Commissioners on Uniform State Laws and the American Law Institute. It was not entirely adopted by Louisiana. Puerto Rico and American Samoa have not adopted any of its articles. *See* Robert K. Rasmussen, "The Uneasy Case Against the Uniform Commercial Code," 62 *La. L. Rev.* (2002).

2   The current second edition was finished in 1979 and published in 1981. *See Restatement (Second) of Contracts* (Am. Law Inst. 1981).

3   Plato, *The Laws*, Book 11, Section 23, Contracts, Internet Encyclopedia of Philosophy, https://iep.utm.edu/pla-laws/.

CONTRACT LAW KEY TERMS

The following key terms are defined in this chapter. They are also defined in the Glossary.

Acceptance

Adhesion Contract

Bilateral Contract

Browsewrap Contract

Clickwrap Contract

Concurrent Conditions

Condition Precedent

Condition Subsequent

Consideration

Contract Law

Contractual Conditions

Covenant of Good Faith and
   Fair Dealing

Fraudulent Contract

Mutual Mistake

Offer

Privity of Contract

Promissory Estoppel

Rescind

Restatement of the Law of
   Contracts

Statute of Frauds

Third-Party Beneficiary
   Contracts

Unconscionable Contracts

Unenforceable Contracts

Uniform Commercial Code

Unilateral Contracts

Types of Contracts

You may recall your alternate identity as a judge in the Chancery Division of Liberty County Circuit Court. In that role, you thought about the different types of property you possess, and you began to consider the legal and financial estate planning arrangements you might make to benefit people and causes that are important to you. Your financial arrangements will, of necessity, implicate the law of contracts, as your plans will need to be transformed into formal and enforceable legal agreements. Your estate planning attorney has encouraged you to begin to think about the contracts that you and your spouse, Dana, will need to execute.

Does the Coronavirus Excuse Performance of a Contract?

Events like the coronavirus pandemic can make it difficult for businesses to perform their contractual obligations. Many have attempted to evade contract obligations by invoking *force majeure*, a provision that excuses one or both parties from performance in the face of circumstances that render it impossible (or highly impractical). When enumerated in contracts, force majeure circumstances typically include:

1. Acts of God, such as severe weather or natural disaster;

2. War, terrorism, and epidemics;

3. Governmental acts such as expropriation, condemnation, and changes in laws and regulations; and

4. Strikes and labor disputes.

In determining whether force majeure applies, courts consider whether nonperformance was unforeseeable and unpreventable, and whether compliance with the terms of the contract has been rendered truly impossible. In June of 2020, a bankruptcy court in Illinois determined that a restaurant tenant could be relieved of a portion of its rent obligations during the months of the Illinois stay-at-home order. The court in *In re Hitz Restaurant Group*, 616 B.R. 375, 2020 WL 292453 (Bankr. N.D. Ill. 2020), reasoned that the stay-at-home order applied to the "governmental acts," relying on the force majeure provision in the tenant's lease.

Contract law is on your mind for another reason. The daughter of a family friend is a 1L[4] student in the University of Franklin College of Law. Although her first-year courses in other subjects are making sense to her, contract law is giving Naomi a bit of trouble. She has reached out, and you have agreed to meet her for coffee at your local Starbucks and provide her with a simple overview of the law of contracts.

On the designated Saturday morning, you arrive at your Starbucks, purchase your favorite beverage, and find a table next to the window.

Naomi arrives a few minutes later, purchases a vanilla latte, and sits down. She thanks you for meeting with her. You reassure her that you enjoy thinking about the law and spend many Saturday mornings at Starbucks. (Next week, you are going to give a presentation on the law of torts to a group of college honors students. Later this morning, you will spend more time working on your talk.)

You first explain to Naomi that formal and informal contractual arrangements permeate our society. Her purchase of the vanilla latte involved a contract, and you will soon get to the specifics of that.

But for now, Naomi should think of a contract as an agreement between two or more parties that is enforceable by law.

FIGURE 9.2   Starbucks coffee

Such agreements may be **bilateral,** or they may be **unilateral.** You tell Naomi that you are working on personal financial planning and estate contracts. These will be bilateral, as the parties will establish their identities, negotiate in advance about their terms, and exchange promises about the obligations they will fulfill. However, your personal lawn-mowing arrangements involve a unilateral contract. You have a standing offer to pay $25 to the first neighborhood youth who mows the lawn around your townhouse Saturday after 9:00 a.m. (She asks if this works, and you tell her that it does; the money most

---

4   A 1L is a first-year student in law school. A second-year student is a 2L, and a third-year student is a 3L.

often goes to Blaise, who has the habit of rising early. You implemented the 9:00 a.m. rule to keep him from showing up at dawn.) Once the mowing is done, you pay the money to the person who did it. The contract is unilateral, because you have made a promise to pay whoever performs. There is no identified person on the other side that has a duty to perform the obligation.

Contract Requirements and Conditions

You remind Naomi that all contracts require at least three things: 1) an **offer** to tender a good or service; 2) **acceptance** of that offer by someone who wants that good or service, and 3) **consideration**, which is, loosely, something of value. Naomi's purchase of the vanilla latte included these three elements. Starbucks <u>offers</u> tasty beverages. She walked up and <u>accepted</u> that offer by asking for a vanilla latte. The barista made the latte, and Naomi paid for the drink. Both sides provided the required <u>consideration</u>: Starbucks received money, and Naomi received a tasty, caffeinated beverage. Naomi smiles and concedes that caffeine is critical to most law school students.

You brought with you an example of a simple written contract. It is the contract that you and Dana signed to purchase your new puppy, an Alaskan malamute. Naomi politely asks if you have a picture. You do, and you share it with her. She laughs, and says that the puppy is ridiculously cute.

You go over the terms of the puppy contract with Naomi. The contract identifies you and Dana as the buyers, identifies the dog breeder as the seller, and includes the price for the dog. The document also contains **contractual conditions** that are binding on both sides. The seller promises that the puppy has passed a veterinary inspection before the date of sale. This is a **condition precedent**, as it specifies something that must be completed before the buyer must pay.

FIGURE 9.3 Alaskan malamute puppy

The puppy contract notes that payment will occur when the dog is given to the purchaser. These are **concurrent conditions**, as they occur at the same time. The contract also provides that if the dog develops certain illnesses within thirty days of purchase, it may be returned for a refund. This provision is a **condition subsequent** (or escape clause) that gives the purchasers the right to negate the contract if the designated event occurs. Finally, there is also a condition subsequent that binds you and Dana as the purchasers: if you find you cannot keep the dog, you will return it to the breeder. You agree that, under no circumstances, will the dog be sent to an animal shelter. This breeder cares about her puppies and would like the opportunity to find them another home if the initial placement does not work out.

Happily, the puppy passed his veterinary examination and seems to be thriving. Naomi asks the dog's name. You explain that you and Dana have decided to name the dog after a national park in Alaska, but you are having a disagreement about which one. Dana favors Kobuk, while you prefer Yukon. You ask Naomi which one she prefers, and she diplomatically notes that Denali would be her choice.[5]

Returning to the subject of contracts, you explain that the same requirements of an offer, acceptance, and consideration apply to larger purchases, such as cars and homes. However, with larger purchases, the process becomes more complicated. Naomi asks if you would review the process involved in purchasing a home.

When someone locates a home they wish to buy, they or their agent prepares a formal written offer. The offer is tendered to the seller, who may or may not accept it. Usually, there are negotiations about the price and the condition of the property. Buyers often want to inspect the property and will require that the seller agree that they may back out if that inspection reveals a serious problem.

The seller may respond to the buyer's offer with a counteroffer, which, in turn, may or may not be accepted. The parties may trade offers and counteroffers several times until they reach an agreement.

Once the parties reach an agreement on the sales price and other terms, everyone signs the purchase contract. The buyer agrees to purchase the house for a certain sum of money, under certain conditions, and the seller agrees to sell the home to the buyer under those conditions.

Unless the buyer has a large reserve of cash, the buyer will arrange for a loan to cover most of the purchase price. This involves more contracts, including loan documents, and an agreement that the lender has a security interest, an enforceable legal claim in the home, until the loan is repaid. Title insurance (to cover the risk of a problem with the seller's ownership interest) and property insurance (to cover the lender's financial interest in the home) may be required. At the time of closing, the money goes from the lender to the seller, and the buyer receives title to the property subject to the lender's security interest. The purchase is then complete.

You note that lawyers often structure these transactions using generally accepted forms in the real estate localities where they practice. Lawyers also deal with the problems that arise when things go wrong.

Naomi asks you about a 1954 case involving the sale of property that is coming up for discussion in her class next week. The case is *Lucy v. Zehmer*, 84 S.E. 2d 516 (1954). You smile; this case is a classic, and you learned about it when you were in law school. It involves a legal contract written on a napkin. It is a great case to frame issues that can arise in connection with a contract offer and a contract acceptance.

Naomi brought her contract law textbook, and she opens it to the page that features the case. (There is even a picture of the notorious napkin.) You ask her to remind you of the facts.

The case concerns property called the Ferguson Farm located in Virginia. The Zehmers owned the farm, and Mr. Zehmer's friend, Mr. Lucy, wanted to buy it. Years before, Mr. Zehmer had verbally agreed to sell the farm to Mr. Lucy, but he later reconsidered and declined to complete the sale.

---

5   You and Dana later decided on Katmai.

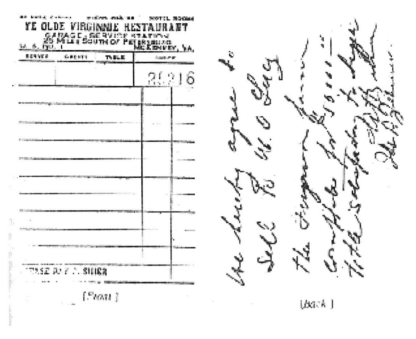

FIGURE 9.4 Contract on napkin from *Lucy v. Zehmer*

You remind Naomi about the **Statute of Frauds**, which requires that certain types of contracts be in writing.[6] The idea is that important agreements should be put in writing and signed by the parties to be enforceable. This reduces the chance that someone will falsely claim to have entered into an agreement. Contracts involving the sale of real property are covered by the Statute of Frauds, so they must be in writing. Naomi speculates that this might be why Mr. Lucy could not compel Mr. Zehmer to honor his previous verbal agreement.

You ask Naomi to continue with the story of *Lucy v. Zehmer*. She describes the momentous events that occurred at a restaurant owned by Mr. Zehmer. Mr. Lucy came to the restaurant with a bottle of whiskey in hand. He shared the whiskey with Mr. Zehmer, and they discussed the possible sale of the Ferguson farm. After discussions, Mr. Zehmer wrote the following on a napkin: "We hereby agree to sell to Mr. Lucy the Ferguson Farm complete for $50,000.00 title satisfactory to buyer." The note was signed by the Zehmers.

The next day, Mr. Lucy retained an attorney who checked on the status of the Zehmers' ownership interest in the farm. After the attorney assured Lucy that everything was in order, Mr. Lucy wrote a letter to Mr. Zehmer inquiring when he intended to close the deal. Mr. Zehmer, however, insisted that he had never really intended to sell the farm and that the note signed by him and his wife had been written in jest.

---

6   The Statute of Frauds traces back to an English act of Parliament passed in 1677 called "An Act for Prevention of Frauds and Perjuries." The statute requires a signed writing for the following contracts: 1) contracts made in consideration of marriage; 2) contracts that cannot be performed within a year; 3) contracts to transfer an interest in land; 4) contracts where the executor of a will agrees to pay an estate debt with personal funds; 5) contracts for the sale of goods valued at $500 or more; and 6) contracts through which one party acts as a guarantor for the debts of another. In the United States, the Uniform Commercial Code provides certain exceptions to the requirements of the statute. George P. Costigan Jr., "The Date and Authorship of the Statute of Frauds," 18 *Harv. L. Rev.* 329–346 (1913).

A Contractual Haunting

In 1991, Jeffrey Stambovsky was settling into his new home when he received troubling information. The house was widely known in the town of Nyack, New York, to be haunted: the seller's family had been tormented by ghosts during the last nine years of their occupancy. Stambovsky, clearly spooked, wanted out of the contract. A house is a major purchase, perhaps the biggest purchase most people will make in their lifetimes. To protect purchasers from hidden defects, contract law requires certain disclosures from sellers of residential property. Sellers must disclose some known property problems, including the existence of termites. The question of whether a seller must disclose the existence of ghosts was put before a court.

Judge Rubin of the Appellate Division New York Supreme Court wrote the majority opinion. She noted: "From the perspective of a person in the position of plaintiff herein, a very practical problem arises with respect to the discovery of a paranormal phenomenon: 'Who you gonna' call?' as the title song to the movie 'Ghostbusters' asks." *Stambovsky v. Ackley*, 169 A.D. 2d 254, 257 (N.Y. App. Div. 1991). Who can the misinformed buyer turn to but the courts? In Stambovsky's case, the court agreed that due to Ackley's failure to disclose the material fact that there were ghosts attached to the home, Stambovksy was able to rescind his purchase contract.

FIGURE 9.5   A haunted house?

Mr. Lucy was not amused. He sued to enforce the purchase agreement. At trial, Mr. Zehmer testified that everyone should have known he was too drunk to agree to the sale. The trial court agreed and found in favor of the Zehmers. Mr. Lucy appealed, and the case ended up before the Virginia Supreme Court.

The Virginia Supreme Court looked at the evidence produced at the trial and concluded that Mr. Lucy was justified in believing that the farm had been promised to him. The court noted that, where a party's words or actions indicate agreement, the actual mental assent of the party is not required; undisclosed intentions do not matter. If a party's words or actions have but one reasonable meaning—and that meaning indicates that a party intends to complete the agreement—then that party is bound by the agreement. So, the farm went to Mr. Lucy and the money to Mr. Zehmer.

You and Naomi discuss the importance of an objective standard in contract creation. If we apply an objective manifestation of intent, rather than someone's subjective interpretation, contracts will be readily enforceable, providing needed stability and security to the marketplace. If we permit people to disregard contracts by declaring that they really did not intend to be bound (despite reasonable evidence to the contrary), we inject uncertainty into an area of law that requires firmness to function.

Types of Consideration

You have now reviewed the first two elements of a contract: the offer and the acceptance. You need to spend a little time discussing the third element, the consideration.

The English common law viewed the element of consideration as necessary to confirm that the parties to an agreement intended to be bound. In early English history, coins were not in common circulation, and consideration was often an item (for barter). Today, consideration is usually monetary, although it can be other things: it can be goods or services, or some benefit to a promisor, or some detriment to a promisee. For example, you could agree to plant flowers in my garden in exchange for my agreement to fix your toolshed. Or you could agree to clean my swimming pool in exchange for my promise that you may use it every Saturday.

You advise Naomi that the law will not require me to fulfill a promise without some type of consideration. If I simply promise to fix your toolshed, and expect nothing in return, you may not compel me to do it. Gratuitous promises cannot usually be enforced. The law will not require kind people who agree to do something to fulfill their promises. While ethically perhaps they should, the law will permit them to change their minds.

Naomi asks you about the nature and adequacy of consideration. Can a promise to refrain from doing something qualify as consideration? You recall an interesting old New York case, *Hamer v. Sidway*, 27 N.E. 256 (1891), that offers an excellent answer to the question. You tell Naomi about it.

In March of 1869, William E. Story promised his nephew and namesake, William E. Story II, the sum of $5,000 if the boy would abstain from alcohol, tobacco, swearing, and card-playing until he turned twenty-one. Young William agreed to refrain from the prohibited acts, and he did give up alcohol, tobacco, swearing, and cards. But he did not forget that his uncle had promised him the money. After he turned twenty-one, William wrote to his uncle, politely requesting payment. His uncle agreed to make the payment, but asked to defer it for a time. William agreed to this. However, the senior William Story died before the money was transferred, and his estate refused to tender it, arguing that there was no binding contract because no consideration had been given.

The New York Court of Appeals[7] found that William's abstinence from liquor, tobacco, swearing and card playing qualified as consideration. Consideration is not just paying for something; it also can be refraining from something that you have the right to do. This is called the "benefit-detriment" theory of consideration. Most courts now use the "bargain theory" of consideration, which holds that a contract's consideration is the promise or performance that is bargained for in exchange. You reassure Naomi that these two theories do not often lead to different outcomes and that she should not worry about the nuances.

You note that no matter the theory of consideration, certain rules must be followed. First, if you already had an obligation to do something, you cannot use that obligation as fresh consideration. For example, if you agree to give an employee a $1,000 bonus if they work thirty overtime hours, you cannot later demand that they work fifty overtime hours to get the same money. That is fundamentally unfair.

Second, if your promise induces someone else to change their behavior because you gave it, you cannot later argue that the contract is void due to the absence of consideration. Let us say that Naomi promises to hire Marcella to work for her (fictitious) catering business during the summer. Marcella agrees to take the job and turns down other job offers because of Naomi's promise. As Naomi's promise caused Marcella to change her position, she must keep it. This is called **promissory estoppel.** It is a way to keep people from taking advantage of other people.

Along those lines, you ask Naomi if she has ever heard of the **covenant of good faith and fair dealing.** She replies that it is on the syllabus but that the class has not reached the subject yet. Naomi

---

7   The New York Court of Appeals is the highest court in New York State, analogous to other state supreme courts.

Rufus Peckham

Associate Justice, United States Supreme Court (1895–1909)

FIGURE 9.6 Justice Rufus Peckham

While serving on the United States Supreme Court, Rufus Peckham authored over 300 opinions. He wrote the opinion in *Ex Parte Young*, 209 U.S. 123 (1908), in which the Court determined that a claimant may file suit in federal court to stop state officials from enforcing unconstitutional state laws. He may be best remembered, however, for his opinion in *Lochner v. New York*, 198 U.S. 45 (1905).

In *Lochner*, a baker challenged a law which prevented his employees from working more than 60 hours a week. The baker claimed that the law violated his constitutional right to contract.

Justice Peckham agreed with Mr. Lochner and wrote the majority opinion. He declared that New York's law violated Mr. Lochner's right to contract, and did not fall under the state's police power. Justice Peckham declared that the law simply "Interfer[ed] … with the rights of the individual."

The decision sparked two dissents, and one by Justice Oliver Wendell Holmes became highly influential. Holmes argued that the state had the authority to pass the law, and it was "a proper measure on the scope of

asks you to preview it for her. You explain that the covenant of good faith and fair dealing is interesting; it is an implied provision in most contracts in the United States. Thus, it is deemed to be included in nearly all contracts, even if the contract says nothing about it. The covenant of good faith and fair dealing declares that parties to contracts must not engage in behavior that deprives other parties of their rights to receive the benefits of agreements. So, you cannot enter into a contract and then sabotage the other side's efforts to fulfill it. For example, an insurance company cannot delay payments to a policyholder who has suffered a claim in an effort to deny them the money they are entitled to have.[8]

Naomi wonders if courts ever get involved because agreements are too one-sided. You note that courts usually enforce negotiated arrangements. People are generally free to enter into the contracts they wish: good or bad, prudent or ill advised.

Some types of agreements are called **adhesion contracts** because one party presents a set of conditions that the other party must accept without negotiation. Insurance contracts, mortgages, and contracts to provide health insurance are often adhesion contracts. These are usually enforceable, and the terms have often been vetted by state or federal agencies.

Naomi asks about **clickwraps**, online agreements that require a user to click a button before using a website or making a purchase. The button confirms that the user agrees to the terms of the online contract before purchasing or visiting the website. Clickwraps are distinguished from **browsewraps** that purport to bind users just because they browse a website. Although the law is developing in these areas, courts are much happier

---

8   Most states have specific statutes that make this conduct illegal in the insurance context and spell out the penalties for engaging in it. For example, *See* Ill. Comp. Stat. 5/155 (1994); *See also* Cal. Code Regs., tit. x, Chapter 5, Subchapter 7.5, Fair Claims Settlement Practices Regulations (2013).

(continued)

with clickwraps, as the user must unambiguously signify assent.[9]

Courts do get involved, however, if a contract is so one-sided that it unconscionable. You tell Naomi you will talk about this more as you move into the next item on your list, a discussion about **unenforceable contracts**.

Unenforceable Contracts

Contracts may be entered into by parties eager to close a deal, and yet, when brought before courts, they may be found unenforceable. There are several reasons why this can happen.

First, if a party entering into a contract lacks legal capacity, the contract will be unenforceable. If a person not yet eighteen years of age signs a purchase agreement to buy a car or someone who is a ward of the state agrees to buy a house, the resulting contracts are not legally binding. However, a minor who executes a contract the day before his eighteenth birthday can reaffirm it the following day, and then it will be binding. Naomi comments that a single day can make a big difference in the law of contracts, and you agree.

A contract may also be void because it involves something illegal. A contract to sell a child is based upon an illegal act and is therefore void. Similarly, a contract to provide sexual services will not be enforced. More generally, contracts that require someone to provide personal services—to work at a certain job for a certain time—can be avoided. The alternative would require people to complete tasks that they no longer wish to complete at the behest of other people, and this draws too close to involuntary servitude.

health." Despite significant criticism, Justice Peckham's decision launched the Lochner Era, when the Supreme Court routinely struck down state regulations designed to support worker welfare on the basis that they infringed upon contract rights or economic liberty. The Lochner Era ended in the late 1930s, with the creation of a new majority that rejected Lochnerian reasoning.

---

9   *See In re Zappos.com, Inc. v. Customer Data Security Breach Litig.*, 893 F. Supp. 2d 1058, 1058–1067 (D. Nev. 2012). In the case, Zappos lost the argument that customers were compelled to arbitrate disputes. The court found that the plaintiffs did not agree to arbitrate all disputes against Zappos simply by using its website. Thus, the browsewrap agreement was not enforceable.

Fraud in Contracts

When one party does not uphold their part of a contract, the other party often sues for breach of contract. However, the failure to perform will sometimes be allowed when the party suing for breach has engaged in fraudulent behavior. A fraudulent misrepresentation is a complete *defense* to a claim of breach of contract. This means that the breaching party will not be liable if they prove that the other side committed fraud to get them to close the deal.

To succeed with this defense, the breaching party must prove that there was 1) an affirmative statement of fact; 2) that it was false; 3) that it was material; and 4) that the plaintiff reasonably relied upon it when agreeing to the contract. The law will not require persons to honor the terms of a deal premised upon materially false information.

Other types of contracts may not be enforced, even though the parties are legally competent and the contract itself is not illegal. If the parties to a contract are both wrong about an important assumption that pertains to it, the contract may be set aside on the grounds of **mutual mistake**. For example, if you ask a contractor to dig a pool in your backyard, but it turns out that three feet down your soil turns to granite (surprise!), the contract may be **rescinded**. In this case, both parties unwind the deal: the money goes back to the contractor, and the obligation to dig the pool is nullified.

Naomi had read that if a party induces the other side to agree to the terms of a contract through serious misrepresentations or deceitful acts, the contract will be voided as a **fraudulent contract**. If someone agrees to purchase a ring because the seller represents that the stones in it are real diamonds, but they are not, they need not complete the purchase. You note that, in addition, they should contact law enforcement.

Finally, a contract may also be voided on the grounds that it is profoundly unfair. The legal term for this is *unconscionable*, and it means that the contract's terms shock the conscience. A contract that overwhelmingly favors the side that had superior bargaining power may fall into this category and be found by a court to be an **unconscionable contract**. Such an agreement will not be enforced because no one who was informed and thinking clearly would agree to it, and the party that pushed the deal should not benefit from it. To determine whether a contract is unconscionable, courts look at the circumstances surrounding its creation, including the mental capacity, age, and sophistication of the bargaining parties.

Naomi mentions a 1965 case, *Williams v. Walker-Thomas Furniture Co.*, 350 F. 2d 445 (D.C. Cir 1965), and you review it with her. In that case, a furniture company extended credit to Williams for household goods. The credit agreements Williams signed with each purchase provided that none of the items would be deemed paid off until the last payment for the last item was received, no matter how low the outstanding balance. Five years after the contract was signed,

Williams defaulted, and the company attempted to repossess everything it had given to him. The Court of Appeals found that the trial court could decline to enforce the contract on the basis of unconscionability due to the inequality of bargaining power.

Contract Enforcement by Third Parties

Naomi now knows that the parties to contracts can enforce them unless the contracts are fraudulent, unconscionable, void as a matter of law, or voidable due to mutual mistake. She now wants to know if anyone who is not a party can enforce a contract.

In response, you explain how debt collection works. Credit card companies often assign the right to collect delinquent accounts to collection services. In exchange, these services receive a share of the proceeds that are finally collected. In fact, rights in commercial contracts are often assigned to other entities. Mortgages are frequently sold to other financial institutions, as the right to collect money is an asset that companies can purchase.

In addition, contracts can be written to be enforced by people who are not involved in their creation. Some contracts are created to benefit these so-called third parties. These contracts are appropriately called **third-party beneficiary contracts**. A life insurance policy is a common type of third-party beneficiary contract. Obviously, when you buy a life insurance policy that insures your own life, you do not anticipate receiving the financial benefit from it. You purchase the policy so that when you die, your loved ones will get its proceeds. So, while you and the life insurance company are the two parties who enter into the contract, the contract is for the benefit of third parties.

Naomi mentions another case in her Contracts book, *Lawrence v. Fox*, 20 N.Y. 268 (1859), that involved third parties. It is an old New York case that involved three people: Messrs. Holly, Fox, and Lawrence. You agree to go over the case with her.

The facts are simple: Mr. Holly owed Mr. Fox $300. Mr. Holly loaned Mr. Lawrence $300 in exchange for Mr. Lawrence's agreement to pay the $300 to Mr. Fox. This would resolve the debt that Mr. Holly owed to Mr. Fox.

When the time came, however, Mr. Lawrence declined to pay Mr. Fox. Accordingly, Mr. Fox sued Mr. Lawrence for the money. Mr. Lawrence argued that he did not owe Mr. Fox anything; it was Mr. Holly who owed the money. The court had to decide whether a contractual relationship, called **privity of contract**, must exist between two people in order for one to seek recovery against the other.

The Court found that privity of contract was not required to enforce the contract. Where one person makes a promise to another for the benefit of a third person, that third person may maintain an action upon that promise. This is one of the rights that goes with third-party beneficiary contracts.

On that note, you tell Naomi that you are happy to answer any questions she may have. Naomi thanks you for your time and says that she has two more questions. First, what can a court do to help someone who has suffered because of a breach of contract? In other words, what are the legal remedies for this type of claim? You explain that the type of available remedies depends upon the nature of the contract.

Student Loans and Fraud

According to *Forbes*, the year 2020 shattered the record for student loan debt. The total debt for all American students is a staggering $1.56 trillion. With an average debt burden of about $37,000, students may seek help in managing debt collectors and bankruptcy.

One student loan service company, Great Lakes Educational Loan Service, advertised that it could provide "experts" to help students pay down their loans. So, Nicole Nelson entered into a contract: she gave Great Lakes money in exchange for their expertise. The company, however, was not legitimate. It steered its clients toward repayment plans that actually harmed the students while lining its own pockets. Ms. Nelson sued under state law, asserting violations of tort law and consumer protection statutes. Great Lakes argued her case could not proceed, as educational loans are not subject to state law disclosure requirements. However, in *Nelson v. Great Lakes Educational Loan Services, Inc.*, No 18-1531 (7th Cir. 2019), the Seventh Circuit ruled that Ms. Nelson is entitled to prosecute her case. Said the court: "When a loan servicer holds itself out to a borrower as having experts who work for her, tells her that she does not need to look elsewhere for advice, and tells her that its experts know what options are in her best interest, those statements, when untrue ... are affirmative misrepresentations." Nelson was permitted to proceed with her consumer protection and tort case.

FIGURE 9.7   Tied to debt

FIGURE 9.8   Another picture of the puppy

Most often, remedies include money damages to compensate the injured party. The money damages may extend to downstream losses that occurred due to the breach. In rare cases, a court may require a party to perform a contract, particularly if the object of the contract cannot be replicated. For example, if you enter into a contract to sell a unique painting and you later decide not to sell it, a court may order you to tender the painting. In that case, money damages will not provide an adequate remedy because the object of the contract cannot be purchased using money. The law wants you to be restored, as much as possible, to your rightful position.

You tell Naomi you are ready for her second question. In response, she asks: could she see one more picture of your new puppy? You do have another photo on your phone, taken when your puppy was anticipating delivery of a treat, and you share it with her.

Conclusion and Introduction to Law Lab

Having concluded your meeting with Naomi, you open your briefcase and remove two items. The first is a draft of next week's talk on the Law of Torts. The second is an important a memorandum that you received earlier in the week. It is from the attorney general's office of the State of Franklin, and it asks for your help.

Some legal professionals (including you) have agreed to serve as members of the State of Franklin's Joint Committee on Elder Affairs. This is a bipartisan committee that explores issues relating to the health and safety of Franklin's elderly population. Among other projects, the committee has worked with state officials to promote the improvement of resident health and safety in long-term care facilities and to create and support disciplinary teams that investigate elder abuse. These are worthy causes, and you are happy to help with them.

More recently, the attorney general's office has also been considering how to regulate home health care provided to the elderly. Franklin's attorney general has asked your committee to assist with a contract law matter relating to elderly home health care. The memorandum on the next page describes the project. You and the other members of the Committee on Elder Affairs will work together to draft a contract that members of the public can use to arrange in-home care for their elderly loved ones.

As you work through this Law Lab, think about the law of contracts. What should be included in this particular contract? You need to think about arrangements that will support good in-home care for vulnerable members of the public. However, you also need to protect the interests of employees who provide that care. You must work to create a contract that is fair to all parties and sets the parameters for a safe and appropriate partnership.

Elder Care Contract Law Lab

MEMORANDUM

To: Members of the State of Franklin Joint Committee on Elder Affairs

From: Associate Attorneys in the Franklin Attorney General's Office

Re: Elder Care Contract Formation: Contract Points and Things to Consider

Dear Committee Members:

FIGURE 9.9   Elderly person

Franklin Attorney General Chris Park continues to work with state officials to address issues involving elder care. The rights and problems confronting elderly Franklin citizens are within the scope of the Attorney General's mandate, and these citizens are especially vulnerable to abuse and mistreatment.

General Park would like to create and make available a form that residents can use to help them arrange services for in-home elderly care. Accordingly, General Park would like you to generate a list of terms that should be included in any contract between a family seeking in-home elder care and the person(s) giving that care.

Please note that you are not being asked to prepare the contract itself. The attorneys in our office will do that. But all contracts begin with a list of terms that the parties want, and we hope that you can help us with that list.

The following examples should help you better understand the nature of this assignment.

People hiring caregivers for their elderly relatives should think about how many hours they want those people to work. Accordingly, a contract term would be to state the specific hours that a caregiver should expect to work, such as which days per week and which hours per day, including starting and ending times.

People should probably run criminal background checks before they hire someone to care for their elderly relatives. The prospective employee would need to agree to the background check before they were hired. Perhaps the contract should acknowledge that the caregiver agrees to a criminal background check and further agrees to advise the employer if they are arrested for anything other than a misdemeanor traffic offense.

Finally, as you know, this office represents the interests of all citizens of the State of Franklin. Accordingly, we must prepare a contract that is balanced and fair, while still supporting the special interests of the elderly. This means that you will consider the needs of the potential employees, the families seeking caregivers, and the elderly who will receive care.

The Attorney General sincerely appreciates your work on this important project.

CHAPTER 10

Tort Law and the Duty of Due Care

*Everyone owes to the world at large the duty of refraining from those acts
that may unreasonably threaten the safety of others.*
—Dissent of Judge William S. Andrews,
Palsgraf v. Long Island Railroad Company, 162 N.E. 99 (N.Y. Ct. App. 1928)

Introduction

It would be lovely to live in a world where everyone was perfectly careful all the time, and no one was ever harmed due to the carelessness of others. However, this is not the world in which we live. Some people intend to harm others, and even careful people sometimes make mistakes that cause harm. **Tort law** holds those who cause harm to others accountable in civil courts of law.

The word *tort* means *wrong* in French and comes from the Medieval Latin *tortum*, meaning *twisted* or *crooked*. Torts are actions, either intentional or accidental, that cause harm and create specific legal claims. Torts are civil and not criminal claims, although the same action can be both a crime and a tort. If someone deliberately strikes you, they commit a crime against you, and a state, federal or tribal prosecutor may bring charges against them. If convicted, your attacker may be sentenced to serve time as punishment. However, you also may file a civil suit in tort and obtain money damages from your attacker to compensate you for your injuries.

Tort law has deepened in nuance and increased in complexity over time. This is not surprising. As torts arise from breaches of the duty of care owed to others, they have evolved along with society's changing ideas about the nature of our obligations to one another. The early tort cases most often involved physical harm from tangible objects or the infringement of property rights. As new situations and emerging technologies have created new ways to harm, new duties of care have emerged. We now have torts involving defective medical devices and the nonconsensual sharing of private digital information. Breaches of the duty of care that were not possible in earlier eras now give rise to tort liability if they occur.

In addition to expanding the scope of obligations people owe, tort law has expanded to match our developing understanding about the different ways people can be harmed. We now award damages for deceptive business practices and for the emotional distress that results from seeing a loved one hurt.

These new torts—and the duties of care that support them—are useful for society. If those who commit wrongful actions are legally responsible for their consequences, they may well choose to avoid those actions. Further, relying entirely upon regulatory and administrative agencies to address misconduct is not wise. Lobbyists and other interest groups may "capture" public agencies, requiring them to further their interests instead of serving the public good. Or regulatory agencies may be starved, deprived of the resources necessary to protect the public interest. Tort law permits a legal response to misconduct that harms members of the public, even if governmental agencies cannot or will not become involved.

TORT LAW KEY TERMS

The following key terms are defined in this chapter. They are also defined in the Glossary.

Abuse of Process	**Fraud**	**Private Nuisance**
Assault	**Inducing Breach of Contract**	**Proximate Cause**
Battery	**Intentional Infliction of Emotional Distress**	**Public Nuisance**
Breach of Duty of Due Care	**Intentional Tort**	*Res Ipsa Loquitur*
Defective in Design	**Invasion of Privacy**	**Slander**
Defective in Manufacture	**Legal Cause**	**Strict Liability**
Defective in Marketing	**Libel**	**Tort Law**
Disparagement of Product	**Malicious Prosecution**	**Trespass**
Duty of Due Care	**Negligence**	
False Imprisonment	**Nuisance**	

Types of Torts

Torts may be organized in a variety of ways. We will divide them into 1) intentional torts; 2) strict liability torts; and 3) negligence torts. These can be placed on a continuum of intentionality:

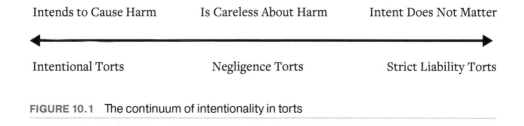

FIGURE 10.1   The continuum of intentionality in torts

At one end we have the torts where the tortfeasor (the person causing harm) deliberately acted to injure someone or infringe upon their rights. These include **intentional torts**, such as assault and battery. These torts carry a heavy burden of moral fault due to the intention to harm.

On the opposite side of the fault continuum is **strict liability**, where no carelessness or any type of moral failing is required to establish legal responsibility. We find here manufacturers of defective products that cause harm. Even if no one was careless in any way with respect to their manufacture, the doctrine of strict liability requires that manufacturers be liable for all harm caused by defective products.

The middle range is defined by **negligence**, the failure to fulfill an acknowledged duty of reasonable care. Negligence torts are as varied as human circumstances. Physicians can commit medical malpractice, a form of professional negligence; drivers may fail to stop for a red light, which is negligent driving; and restaurants may fail to deliver the nut-free dish that a customer ordered, and that, too, is negligence. In negligence cases, there was no desire to harm, but the tortfeasor did cause harm, and so the tortfeasor must bear responsibility. The moral fault in negligence cases is the lack of care, as opposed to the more culpable desire to harm in intentional torts.

Intentional Torts

We begin with intentional torts, which involve willful conduct that leads to harm. These torts often share elements with crimes, including the knowledge of wrongdoing. It is thus not surprising that intentional torts are also often crimes.

First, we have a group of intentional torts that cause physical harm or diminish a person's standing, autonomy, agency, or privacy. These include assault and battery, intentional infliction of emotional distress, false imprisonment, invasion of privacy, libel and slander, and abuse of process.

An **assault** is an intentional act that causes a reasonable fear of immediate harmful or offensive contact. If I swing my baseball bat at you, and you fear the bat will strike you, I have committed the tort of assault. My bat does not need to touch you; the point is that you feared it would. This tort includes actions against things that you are connected with, so that if I swing my bat at your laptop, and you are typing on it, I have assaulted *you*. The anticipated harm need not be painful: if I reach out to touch you in such a way that a normal person would be offended, that also is an assault.

A **battery** involves actual contact. If I swing my bat and it hits you, I have committed a battery. Further, if I touch you without your consent in a way that a reasonable person would not like, that is a battery, even if it does not hurt you. Offensive touching violates the law, along with hurtful touching. You have the right to personal integrity, and the law will support a claim against someone who touches you without your consent, even if that touching is not physically harmful.

Burdens of Proof and O.J. Simpson

In 1995, the People of the State of California charged Orenthal James Simpson with two counts of murder for the deaths of O.J.'s ex-wife, Nicole Brown, and her friend, Ron Goldman. After a spectacle of a trial, the jury acquitted Simpson on both counts.

The jury's decision, however, did not sit well with the families of the victims. In 1996, Ron Goldman's parents and Nicole Brown's father filed civil lawsuits for wrongful death. The resulting civil trial concluded with the jury finding Simpson responsible for both deaths. The jury awarded $33.5 million to the victims' families and gave the children of Nicole Brown and O.J. Simpson $12.6 million from their father's estate.

Criminal and civil cases serve different purposes. The government pursues criminal cases to vindicate the interests of society. Private parties, however, file civil actions to obtain compensation for injury. To obtain a conviction in a criminal case, a jury must decide that a defendant is guilty beyond a reasonable doubt. To prevail in a civil case, however, a party need only win by a preponderance of the evidence, just greater than a 50 percent chance. The disparity between these burdens of proof can result in different outcomes even when the same facts are at issue.

Intentional infliction of emotional distress is the original "tort of outrage." If someone behaves in an outrageous way, causing great distress, the harmed person may sue for damages. The behavior must go beyond the bounds of decency; it must be the kind of conduct that a civilized society would utterly condemn, such as telling someone falsely that a loved one is badly hurt. Maliciously used, words can cause great harm, and this tort permits a recovery for harm caused by the outrageous use of words.

I commit **false imprisonment** when I confine you to a bounded area and do not let you leave. If I lock you in a room; if I hold you so that you cannot walk away; or if I imply that you will be harmed if you attempt to leave, then I restrict your freedom of movement and commit the tort of false imprisonment. The confinement can occur anywhere, including a moving vehicle, and need not last for a long period of time. Physical force is not required. If I coerce you to stay by holding your laptop or other valuables, that, too, is false imprisonment.

The law also protects your privacy interests, so you can sue for **invasion of privacy** under several theories. If someone places a camera in your hotel room, violating your right to privacy, or publicizes private facts about you, or appropriates your likeness without your consent, you may sue them for damages. You are entitled to your privacy. However, if you step into the public or political arena, your privacy rights may be more limited, as the public has an interest in knowing what you are up to.

The defamatory torts of **libel** and **slander** involve conveying untrue harmful information that causes reputational damage. If I falsely announce in a business meeting that a particular law firm has "lawyers" that are not licensed to practice law, that is slander. (If it is true, it is not slander, but I would do better to bring my thoughts to the state bar association.) If I write those words in an online forum, that is libel. Libel traditionally involved the printed word, while slander referred to the spoken word. As new technologies have begun to merge print and speech, these distinctions have become less clear and also less important. The key to these torts remains the reputational damage caused by the spread of false information.

If I intentionally pursue a legal action against you that is clearly without good cause and it is dismissed in your favor, you may sue me for **malicious prosecution**. You may add an **abuse of process** claim if I misuse the tools of the law to harm you in the pending action. The justice system should not abide those who wrongfully use it to harm others.

Next, we have a category of intentional torts that have to do with land. There are torts that arise from interference with your possession of land and torts that occur when people are harmed due to a condition of your land.

The torts that arise from interference with your land are **trespass** and **nuisance**. An intentional **trespass** is an intrusion on your land without your consent. If I see some fine apples growing on a tree in your yard and enter your property and take them, I have committed a trespass (along with a theft). Simply entering your land without your consent is a trespass, and courts have awarded damages for this violation of rights even if no physical harm resulted.

When I do not enter your property but instead do something that interferes with your right to enjoy your property, I have committed a nuisance. If I routinely conduct night-time concerts in my side yard, next to your home, and they are noisy enough that any reasonable person would find them vexing, that is a private nuisance. If my concert is so astonishingly loud that many homeowners are disturbed, that is a public nuisance.

The court may order me to stop my concerts, or to limit their hours, or to reduce their volume as you are entitled to enjoy your property without interference from unreasonable disturbances. Nuisances can come in many forms, including smells, sounds, and even unusual traffic.

In addition, torts can occur if people are harmed on your property. While homeowners generally need only warn guests of unsafe conditions, business owners must keep their commercial establishments safe for customers. Customers should not be at risk simply by patronizing a business establishment.

The last category of intentional torts consists of economic or business torts. I can tortiously **induce a breach of contract**, which involves my knowingly tampering with an existing contractual relationship to cause its termination. The notion behind this tort is that contract rights are entitled to legal protection.[1]

I commit **fraud** when I induce you to do something, such as enter into a contract, by being untruthful in my representations or promises to you. If we agree that you will pay me money to paint your house, and I pocket the money and never do the work, I have breached our contract. But if you discover that it was never my intent to do the work, that is fraud, and you may sue me for fraud as well as breach of contract. Finally, if I engage in certain unfair business practices, such as **disparaging your product** by spreading false information about it, you may sue me for damages. Businesses can be libeled and slandered, just like individuals.

---

1   Economics scholars who posit that efficient breaches of contract are desirable may protest that this tort impairs market efficiency.

The Tort of Outrage

In *Wilkinson v. Downton*, 2 QB 57 (1897), the English courts first recognized the tort of intentional infliction of emotional distress. In that case, Mr. Downton told Mrs. Wilkinson that her husband had broken both legs in an accident on the way home from a day at the horse races.

This false statement induced severe distress and serious illness. Mr. Downton protested that he did not mean to cause any serious harm.

But the judge said: "It is difficult to imagine that such a statement, made suddenly and with apparent seriousness, could fail to produce grave effects ... and therefore an intention to produce such an effect must be imputed, and it is not an answer in law to say that more harm was done than was anticipated."

Mrs. Wilkinson recovered £100 as damages for her injuries.

FIGURE 10.2 Woman in distress

Strict Liability Torts

Strict liability torts reside at the far end of the continuum opposite intentional torts. Those who commit these torts are absolutely liable for the harm that they cause, even if they did not intend to harm, are saddened that it occurred, and were not the least bit careless. Instead of basing liability on harmful intent or carelessness that causes injury, strict liability torts represent decisions society has made about shifting the cost of harm in certain contexts.

One example concerns the keeping of wild animals. If I choose to keep a lion on my land, and it harms you, I am strictly liable for your injuries. (I am also likely violating state law in keeping such an animal.) Wild animals (*ferae naturae* in the law) are legally different from domesticated animals (*mansuetae naturae*). Wild animals are deemed dangerous, and under the doctrine of strict liability, their owners will be liable for injuries they cause.[2] We want the owners of wild animals to have a strong incentive to keep the public safe.

Similarly, if a person or business engages in certain types of very hazardous activities, the law will hold them

FIGURE 10.3 A lion in captivity

---

2   This rule applies to wild animals kept in private settings. Public zoos are not strictly liable for harm caused by the wild animals they care for.

liable for any damage that occurs, even if they did not mean to cause it. If I decide to use explosives to conduct blasting activities on my property, and an explosion shatters your windows, I should be responsible for the damage. It does not matter that I took precautions to keep your property safe; when I chose to begin blasting, I became liable for the consequences. Such hazardous activities include the transportation, storage and use of explosives, radioactive substances, and toxic chemicals. The people who engage in these activities, with potentially devastating consequences, must understand they are responsible for all the harm they cause. They alone know what they are planning, and therefore they are uniquely positioned to take the precautions necessary to accomplish the work safely. Strict liability in tort law encourages people to avoid bad choices that could lead to catastrophe.

Finally, strict liability is imposed on manufacturers, distributors, wholesalers, and retailers of defective products that cause harm. If someone sells a defective product to a consumer and that defect causes harm, the consumer can recover. The consumer may recover even if the manufacturer took reasonable steps to ensure that the product was not defective and had no knowledge of the defect.

Products can be defective several ways. They can be **defective in design** because they are unreasonably dangerous to use. They can be **defective in manufacture** because there was an error in the fabrication process. They can even be found **defective in marketing** because they were sold with insufficient or incorrect instructions. Although the consumer may sue anyone in the chain of distribution, ultimate liability will rest with the manufacturer, who will have to indemnify (cover the costs of) the distributor or retailer. The manufacturer of a product is best placed to protect the public from shoddy practices, and so the law requires the manufacturer to design, fabricate, and market products to avoid harm.

The Case of the Exploding Phone

In August 2016, Samsung released the Galaxy Note 7 cell phone. Samsung designed this phone with a number of improvements, and it sold well. However, some consumers soon discovered a flaw when their phones spontaneously ignited. Samsung responded by voluntarily recalling the Note 7, hoping to forestall further problems. This was prudent: from a product liability standpoint, Samsung may be strictly liable for any physical damage caused by their defective product.

FIGURE 10.4   Phones and fire

Harm Avoidance and Strict Liability

Guido Calabresi is an American legal scholar, senior United States Circuit Court judge and former dean of Yale Law School. Along with Ronald Coase and Richard Posner, he is a key founder of the field of law and economics.

Calabresi argues that the optimal tort liability regime will minimize the sum of the costs of accidents and the costs of avoiding accidents while also considering the administrative costs of the tort system. By making manufacturers strictly liable for the harm caused by defective products, the law has adopted a version of Calabresi's regime. Products manufacturers are best situated to minimize harm to the public while also controlling the costs they incur in doing so. So, the burden should be upon them to control these costs.

FIGURE 10.5 Judge Guido Calabresi

Negligence

Between the extremes of intentional torts and strict liability torts is the broad tort of **negligence**.

Negligence cases arise from the failure to exercise due care when it was required. This failure is the genesis of every negligence claim. Examples include the driver who ran a red light, the school district that did not properly screen personnel, the rancher who failed to maintain fencing, the attorney who did not file an appeal in a timely manner, and the maintenance engineer who did not properly ground an electrical circuit. If their failures to exercise reasonable care caused harm, they have all committed the tort of negligence.

To succeed in a claim for negligence, you must show the following elements:

1. That a duty of reasonable care (*duty of due care*) was owed;

2. That there was a *breach of that duty*;

3. That the breach of the duty of care would foreseeably cause harm (this is also called *proximate causation*);

4. That the breach of the duty was the *legal cause* of the harm (without the tortfeasor's actions, the person would not have been harmed); and

5. That harm actually resulted.

These elements are worth further discussion.

Duty of Due Care

The general principle is that bystanders owe strangers no duty of care. You are not *legally* obliged to keep someone else's toddler from walking off a cliff; to intercept a visually impaired stranger heading for a busy intersection; or to call for help when you encounter someone who has been badly beaten. While you may well have a moral obligation to intervene, the law has traditionally not held you legally responsible for your failure to do so. The notion is that you should have agency to live your own life as you wish, free from the obligation to save others who are heading for difficulties.[3]

Notwithstanding this general principle, the law recognizes that proximity or certain relationships create an obligation to avoid harm. The attorney acting to protect her client's interests, the nurse giving medication, the driver approaching a crosswalk, the lifeguard on duty at the swimming pool—all must act with due care to avoid harm. The nature of the duty of care depends upon the situation, and the law does not require perfection, just reasonableness. So, if a driver could not reasonably have avoided a collision, that is not negligence, even if the accident could have been avoided by an excellent driver on a good day.

If the claim is against a member of a learned profession and involves professional negligence, a plaintiff must show that the defendant's actions did not conform to the standard of care required of that professional. The location of the professional, as well as the nature of the profession, is relevant to this analysis. Cardiac surgeons in New York City must meet the standard of care provided by other qualified cardiac surgeons in New York City. Nurses in rural communities must provide the same caliber of care as other nurses in similar rural communities. Each profession has its own skills and training, and they may vary by locale.

Breach of Duty

When the obligation to avoid harm exists and harm could have been prevented with reasonable care, the failure to prevent that harm breaches that obligation. When a cab driver drifts into another lane of traffic and causes an accident, that is a breach of the duty of care. When a hauler fails to properly tie down a load of tires and they roll onto the freeway

A New Tort

In 1976, the California Supreme Court created a new obligation: the duty to warn of credible harm disclosed during a mental health therapy session. At the same time, it created a new negligence tort for the failure to fulfill this duty.

Tarasoff v. Regents of the University of California, 17 Cal. 3d 425 (1976) involved two college students, Mr. Poddar and Ms. Tarasoff. They met during dance classes. Ms. Tarasoff told Mr. Poddar that she did not want to date him, and he became depressed. He sought psychological treatment, and during a therapy session, he stated that he intended to kill Ms. Tarasoff.

Ms. Tarasoff was not advised of this threat. After Mr. Poddar murdered her, her parents sued, claiming their daughter should have been warned about Mr. Poddar's plans. When the California Supreme Court reviewed the case, it found that a mental health professional has a duty of care not only to the patient, but also to those individuals who are credibly targeted for serious harm by the patient.

After this case, many states enacted "Tarasoff Laws" that permit or require reporting when mental health practitioners learn of a serious, credible threat to a specific individual.

FIGURE 10.6 Let's talk

---

3   Happily, there are studies that show most people will offer help or at least call for help if they themselves cannot provide it. *See* R. Philpot et al., "Would I Be Helped? Cross-National CCTV Footage Shows That Intervention Is the Norm in Public Conflicts," *Am. Psychologist*, 71(1), 66–75 (2020).

and cause an accident, that is a breach of the duty of care. When a factory manager forgets to shut off an exhaust valve and a repairman inhales toxic gases, that is a breach of the duty of care. The possibilities are as endless as the variety of human endeavors.

Of course, there are things that can only occur if someone breached a duty of care. For example, a breach of the duty of care is inferred if a surgeon leaves a surgical instrument inside a patient. Surgical instruments should never be left inside people, and the fact that it happened means that negligence occurred. This is called **res ipsa loquitur**, Latin for "the thing speaks for itself." The unhappy patient will be able to establish a breach of the duty of care simply by presenting evidence that the instrument was left inside their body.

Foreseeability/Proximate Causation

There is a limiting factor on the duty of care, as not all harms can be foreseen and prevented. I owe a duty of care only to prevent those harms that I may reasonably foresee: my duty of due care and my legal responsibility are not limitless. So, if I fail to properly hitch my boat to my trailer and it breaks away at speed on the freeway, careening into the lake by the side of the road and striking a swimmer, I am liable. It was foreseeable that my boat would harm someone nearby if it broke loose. But if that same boat causes a flock of geese to rise from the water and fly in the path of an aircraft, causing the plane to make a rough emergency landing that harms people onboard, I am not liable. Although my negligence precipitated the entire chain of events, it was not foreseeable that my escaping boat would hurt people on a plane.[4]

Cause-in-Fact

This element is also called the "but-for" test: but for my actions, the harm would not have occurred. So, if my actions and the actions of another person combine to cause harm, I may still be found liable. I may share that liability with others who are also responsible, and a jury may decide how much injury may be attributed to each defendant.

Damages

Finally, for the tort of negligence to become a viable legal claim, there must be an actual injury. Breaches of the duty of care that do no harm are not actionable. A near-miss that causes distress and anxiety may

---

4   The economic consequences for limitless liability would be financially devastating, and as they are not foreseeable, they are not prevent-able. Accordingly, there is no incentive for the legal system to impose them.

support a claim for negligent infliction of emotional distress. However, there are specific rules on when such damages may be collected.

Among all the areas of law, torts may be the most malleable, as its scope is directly shaped by the variety of activities in modern society. As our world has grown more complex, we have come to recognize fresh legal obligations that create novel duties of care. When those newly-recognized duties are breached, injured persons may pursue claims and seek damages. They may do so even if their particular type of claim has not been presented in court before. The justice system will address their claims using the traditional tools of court, judge, and jury, following the standard rules of civil procedure.

Conclusion and Introduction to Law Lab

Having delivered your presentation on Tort Law, you will now leave behind your prior judicial persona.

This week, you will be a law firm summer associate. Many law students work in law firms during the summers between their years of formal study in law school. This job is often their first meaningful introduction to the profession. If performed well, it can launch their legal careers.

This week's Law Lab asks you to think about a tort claim in a setting involving a service dog. It is a legally important case: you will be seeking to enlarge existing law to support a new type of negligence claim. It is also a very compelling case, as the client has sustained a terrible loss. Read the Law Lab, and think about how to best frame your arguments and use existing law to advocate for your client.

Advocacy Law Lab

MEMORANDUM

To: Summer Associates of the Firm

From: J. Marshall, Senior Trial Attorney

Re: *Jenkins v. Strathe*

Client: Jessie Jenkins

Dear Summer Associates,

As you have now completed some formal legal training, the firm hopes you can assist with a new matter. Its circumstances may yield a unique claim, and we would like your assistance with it. I have met with our client and her family, and my paralegal has completed some preliminary research, which is included in this memo.

Factual Background

Jessie Jenkins and Hercules

This negligence tort case arises from an accident that killed a service dog belonging to our client, Ms. Jessie Jenkins. Jessie lives with her sister and parents in our city of Liberty Springs, in our State of Franklin. She works from home as a part-time painter, specializing in portraiture.

Jessie, now twenty-three years of age, was diagnosed in early childhood with epilepsy. Epilepsy is a medical condition associated with seizures. Unfortunately, Jessie's seizures are not entirely controllable with medication. Occasionally, she endures a grand mal seizure, which induces several minutes of unconsciousness. In order to better manage her life, Jessie and her family decided to try and find a service animal, and through the Epilepsy Foundation of Franklin, they learned about the process to obtain a seizure dog. Acquiring a seizure dog takes a great deal of time and special training. After completing the required training, Jessie and her family brought home Hercules, a large Alaskan malamute.

Hercules provided Jessie with a variety of services. He was one of those remarkable dogs that seem to be able to sense an impending seizure.[1] If Jessie was about to have a seizure, Hercules would rub her leg, encouraging her to lie down. If a seizure occurred too suddenly for a warning, Hercules placed his body between Jessie and the floor, easing her down. During her seizures, Hercules rested with Jessie, keeping her safe.

FIGURE 10.7 Hercules the dog

In addition, Hercules was a companion to Jessie and came on all the family camping trips. He would guard her tent when she rested, as shown in this family photo. Jessie also took walks with Hercules in their neighborhood. The Jenkins family confirms that Hercules was a popular dog with all their acquaintances, as well as a beloved family member, and he and Jessie were inseparable.

There is no question that Hercules materially improved the quality of Jessie's life.

The Accident

On October 15 of last year, around 3:00 p.m., Jessie was walking Hercules on the sidewalk of Applevale Drive, near its intersection with Orange Grove Street in Liberty Springs. She was on the west side of the road, heading south toward her home. At that time, Mr. Tarley Strathe was driving home from Wilson

---

[1] There is evidence that the canine detection of epileptic seizures occurs because of a group of odor chemicals that people emit before a seizure occurs. *See* Amélie Catala et al., "Dogs Demonstrate the Existence of an Epileptic Seizure Odour in Humans," *Scientific Reports*, 9:4102 (Mar. 28, 2019), https://doi.org/10.1038/s41598-019-40721-4.

High School, also heading southbound on Applevale. He has conceded that he was texting as he drove, which is against the law in Franklin. It is also likely that he was speeding. In any event, as he approached Orange Grove, Tarley lost control of his vehicle, and it drove off the road on the west side toward Jessie and Hercules.

Hercules alerted at the last minute to the threat that the vehicle presented and shoved Jessie further to the west, barely out of the way. However, the right front bumper of the vehicle struck Hercules, fatally injuring him. A neighbor called for help, and the police came to the scene. The police report describes the accident and also what the officer observed when he arrived on the scene: Jessie, kneeling next to Hercules, petting him. The officer notes that the dog licked her hands, but died within a few minutes of the accident. At that point, Jessie collapsed with a grand mal seizure and was taken to the Liberty County Medical Center. Her physician opined that the seizure was most likely a response to the mental trauma she had just undergone. She made a good recovery from that seizure and was sent home the day after the accident.

The loss of Hercules hit Jessie very hard. She and Hercules had enjoyed three years together. Since the accident, Jessie's seizures have increased in frequency, and she has treated with a mental health professional. At some point, she may decide to try and get another seizure dog, but she does not feel ready yet.

Tarley Strathe was uninjured, and the damage to his vehicle was minor. He has expressed sincere regret at the loss of Hercules. His insurance company, Allgood Insurance Company, has offered to pay the medical costs associated with Jessie's seizure immediately following the accident and has also offered to pay the fair market value of an Alaskan malamute of Hercules's age. The total offer from Allgood Insurance is $2,500. The law firm partnership feels that this figure does not adequately compensate Jessie for her injuries, and with her permission has declined the offer. This case is now set for trial before Judge Randall Markham, an experienced jurist who currently has the civil docket in Liberty County Circuit Court. For various reasons, including cost savings, the parties have waived a jury in this case. Thus, Judge Markham will make findings of fact as well as rulings of law. We note that Judge Markham owns three champion bird dogs and is an avid outdoorsman.

Issue: Award of Damages for Negligent Infliction of Emotional Distress

We believe that, in this action, Jessie Jenkins should be able to recover:

1. Economic damages[2] representing the medical bills that result from her accident, as well as the loss of Hercules; and

2. Non-economic damages[3] for her emotional distress in watching her dog die due to Tarley Strathe's negligence.

---

2   Economic damages are compensation injured persons receive for monetary losses. These include lost wages, medical costs, and the value of property damage by the defendant.

3   Non-economic damages are compensation injured persons receive for non-monetary losses. These include pain and suffering, loss of enjoyment of life, and damages for emotional distress.

Relevant Authority

Service animals, like all other animals, are considered the property of their human owners. Their loss due to the carelessness of others is a compensable injury, although recovery is nearly always limited to the animal's objective value. In this case, we will argue that Jessie is entitled to claim a higher level of damages due to Hercules's special training as a seizure dog and the rather unique services he provided. We anticipate presenting expert testimony outlining the special training and financial resources that were expended to instruct Hercules and to train Jessie to work with Hercules. We think we can show that his value should include much of these costs. We will argue that the judge should permit this higher amount of damages, along with her medical bills.

The second proposed category of damages, for Jessie's own emotional distress, will be more difficult to pursue. A very few states have enacted laws that permit the recovery of non-economic damages for the loss of a companion animal. Tennessee has passed a law permitting the recovery of emotional damages for the death of a companion animal if it was killed negligently, but the law limits the total amount of recovery to $5,000. Illinois also has a law that permits the recovery of emotional damages for the loss of a companion animal, but only for animals that were subjected to acts of cruelty or torture or who were taken in bad faith. Some scholarly articles have argued for an enhanced recovery if a service animal is negligently killed, but that argument has not gained much traction in the courts.

Like most other states, Franklin has never permitted recovery for "loss of companionship damages" for the death of an animal: recovery has been limited to an animal's fair market value. Franklin also does not have a law permitting the recovery of emotional damages for the loss of a service animal. Accordingly, we anticipate some difficulty in convincing our judge in this case that he should permit this recovery. But we feel that, under the unique facts of this case, an attempt should be made, and we intend to ask the judge for emotional distress damages. Hercules was more than a companion animal; he was part of Jessie's medical support team. He was with her 24 hours a day and slept in her room at night. Jessie will testify that he was "a member of her family," a "special guardian that helped her navigate life with epilepsy." His loss caused great emotional distress, and there should be a remedy in civil litigation for this harm. After all: "The purpose of damages is to put the aggrieved party in the position, as near as possible, as he or she would have been without the injury ..."[4] Without an award of damages for emotional distress, our client will have sustained an uncompensated loss.

The fact that Jessie watched Hercules die will help support this claim, although it will require an extension of existing law. The law now permits a recovery of damages for emotional distress when a plaintiff suffers trauma from witnessing the serious injury or death of a person they loved. In some states, like the State of Franklin, the person making the claim must demonstrate physical symptoms of trauma or distress and have been at the accident scene. Franklin's law on this was modeled after California law, based upon the case *Dillon v. Legg*, 68 Cal. 2d 728 (1968). In that case, a mother saw her

---

4   *MCI Communications Services v. CMES, Inc.,* 728 S.E. 2d 649, 652 (Ga. 2012).

daughter run over by a negligent driver, and the court permitted her to recover for her own emotional distress. Other states followed that rule, and it is widespread law—but not with respect to animals that are harmed.

In fact, there is a considerable legal authority rejecting an award of damages for emotional distress due to the loss of animals. One court noted: "... Humans have an enormous capacity to form bonds with dogs, cats, birds and an infinite number of other beings that are non-human ...We are particularly concerned that were such a claim to go forward, the law would proceed upon a course that had no just stopping point."[5] Another court noted: "[S]uch an expansion of the law would place an unnecessary burden on the ever-burgeoning caseloads of the court in resolving serious tort claims for injuries to individuals."[6] The clear weight of authority is against awarding emotional distress damages for the loss of animals. In this case, we will be asking the judge to do something that has not been done before in this state. But we think that this is the right case to promote this argument.

Assignment

Please work collaboratively to prepare a draft Findings of Fact and Conclusions of Law to present to Judge Markham at the end of the trial. These Findings should support the plaintiff's claims and the court's decision to award emotional distress damages, based upon the unique factual elements of this case.

As there is no jury in this case, the judge will make both rulings of law and factual findings. If the trial judge agrees with our position, and Jessie does receive an award of damages for her emotional distress, it is likely that we will need to defend that ruling on appeal. To have the best chance of this, we need to make sure that the Findings and Conclusions underpinning the damages claim are as strong as possible.

A Note on How to Write Findings of Fact and Conclusions of Law

The Findings of Fact should tell the story of the case, chronologically. Begin with the names of the parties, and then list the facts in short paragraphs, with one statement of fact per paragraph. The Findings of Fact should sequentially describe how the events giving rise to the case occurred. They should set forth the facts that demonstrate our client met the burden of proof for her claim of negligence against Tarley Strathe. They should also set forth the particular facts that support her entitlement to damages for negligent infliction of emotional distress.

At the conclusion of the Findings of Fact, add the Conclusions of Law through which the judge finds that Jessie Jenkins is entitled to a recovery of damages for negligent infliction of emotional distress. These Conclusions should explain the elements of the claim for negligence and why they were satisfied.

---

5   *Rabideau v. City of Racine*, 627 N.W. 2d 799 (Wis. Sup. Ct. 2001).
6   *Harabes v. Barkery, Inc.,* 791 A.2d 1142, 1144 (Superior Ct. of N.J. 2001).

I have attached a sample Findings of Fact and Conclusions of Law that was prepared for use in a medical malpractice case. (This document was only roughed out, as the case settled before trial.) You may find the format helpful as you move forward with this assignment.

Thank you for your assistance, and I look forward to reviewing your work.

SAMPLE FINDINGS OF FACT AND CONCLUSIONS OF LAW

Medical Malpractice Claim

Findings of Fact

1. Plaintiff Jonas Greane ("Mr. Greane") is a citizen of the State of Franklin and resident of the City of Liberty Springs.

2. Defendant Sarah Smith ("Dr. Smith") is a surgical physician licensed to practice medicine in the State of Franklin, with admitting privileges at Liberty County Hospital.

3. Mr. Greane presented for medical treatment at Liberty County Hospital's emergency room on March 23, 2020, at 8:00 p.m., complaining of acute abdominal pain. At that time, Mr. Greane was diagnosed as suffering from acute appendicitis.

4. Plaintiff was taken into surgery at Liberty County Hospital the morning of March 24, 2020. Dr. Smith there and then performed an appendectomy upon Mr. Greane.

5. Mr. Greane was discharged from Liberty County Hospital on March 26, 2020. At the time of discharge, Mr. Greane complained of abdominal pain. Dr. Smith inspected Mr. Greane, attributed the pain to the recent surgery, and authorized Mr. Greane's discharge.

6. On March 28, 2020, at 1:00 p.m., Mr. Greane called Dr. Smith's office, complaining of severe abdominal pain. He was advised to return to the Liberty County Hospital.

7. At 2:00 p.m. on March 28, Mr. Greane presented for medical treatment at Liberty County Hospital's emergency room. The attending physician documented a fever of 102 degrees, and Mr. Greane's abdomen was found to be exquisitely tender. Mr. Greane submitted to an X-ray, and a foreign object was located in the vicinity of the appendectomy incision.

8. Mr. Greane was taken to surgery at 5:00 p.m. on March 28. During that operation, the surgeon, Dr. Gabriel Sanchez, removed a small surgical retractor from the appendectomy site. Dr. Sanchez noted that the area around the retractor was inflamed and infected.

9. Mr. Greane endured a lengthy recovery from the second operation, during which he experienced significant pain and could not continue with his employment or other activities. His recovery period lasted for four months.

Conclusions of Law

1. Jurisdiction and venue are proper in this matter pursuant to Franklin Code of Civil Procedure §110-2.

2. As a practicing physician, Dr. Smith owed plaintiff, her patient, a duty of care to use the skills and care ordinarily used by reasonably well-qualified surgeons practicing in Liberty County. See: Franklin Statutes Annotated, §520(A).

3. By leaving a surgical retractor inside Mr. Greane during the course of an operation, Dr. Smith breached that duty of care, committing professional negligence. The Court finds that this misconduct constitutes *res ipsa loquitur* negligence under the facts of this case. See: Restatement (Second) of Torts, §328D and Franklin Statutes Annotated §320(D).

4. Mr. Greane sustained and is entitled to recover economic and non-economic damages due to the harm he sustained from Dr. Smith's breach of the duty of care. These damages include:

    a. Loss of income;

    b. Medical costs, including the costs associated with the remedial operation and aftercare; and

    c. Pain and suffering and loss of enjoyment of life.

CHAPTER 11

Civil Procedure and Remedies

It is procedure that marks much of the difference between rule by law and rule by fiat.

—Supreme Court Justice William O. Douglas, Wisconsin v. Constantineau, 400 U.S. 433 (1971)

Introduction

During their lifetimes, people may be harmed by others and also inadvertently cause others harm. The criminal justice system deals with those who commit crimes. However, those who are injured by non-criminal actions must pursue their own claims to obtain compensation. The law of **civil procedure** governs how they do this, and the law of **remedies** dictates the relief they can get.

The rules of engagement in civil litigation are important. Before litigants find themselves enmeshed in contentious proceedings, they must agree on how that litigation will be conducted. There must be fair procedural rules that are more likely to produce just outcomes. Those rules must observe the requirements of due process, with appropriate opportunities to present evidence and arguments. The parties must have confidence that the legal professionals in the courthouse will treat them fairly, following procedures that are just. They should understand that if the case is ultimately tried, a neutral judge and an impartial jury will determine its outcome. With a robust set of fair procedural rules in place, litigants will enter the court system knowing that their interests are appropriately protected, whether they are suing or being sued.

Further, the interests of society as well as the interests of justice require the imposition of a legal remedy when a wrongful act has caused serious harm. People are less likely to take matters into their own hands if they see a clear path to meaningful relief. In the first chapter, we noted that members of early societies often resorted to vigilante justice in response to injury. Legal codes were, in part, established to secure appropriate redress for harm to stop destructive feuding and other types of extrajudicial violence.

Today, the law of **remedies** offers different forms of relief tuned to different types of wrongs. An award of **monetary damages** offers financial remuneration to compensate for harm, an **injunction** requires others to undertake actions demanded by the interests of justice, and a **declaratory judgment** clarifies a right or obligation that is in dispute. Whether a claim involves the violation of patent rights or a personal injury, redress is available.

CIVIL PROCEDURE AND REMEDIES KEY TERMS

The following key terms are defined in this chapter. They are also defined in the Glossary.

Abuse of Discretion	**Direct Examination**	**Motion**	**Restitution**
Affirmative Defense	**Discovery**	**Motion in Limine**	**Rules of Evidence**
Answer	**Evidence**	**Motion to Compel**	**Sanctions**
Burden of Proof	**General Damages**	**Objection**	**Service of Process**
Causes of Action	**Hearsay**	**Opening Statement**	**Special Damages**
Civil Procedure	**Injunction**	**Personal Jurisdiction**	**Status Conference**
Closing Statement	**Interrogatories**	**Plaintiff**	**Subject Matter**
Complaint	**Judgment**	**Prayer for Relief**	**Jurisdiction**
Cross-examination	**Judgment**	**Privilege**	**Subpoena**
Declaratory Judgment	**Notwithstanding the**	**Punitive Damages**	**Subrogation**
Defendant	**Verdict**	**Record**	**Voir Dire**
Deliberations	**Legal Guardian**	**Remedies**	
Demand for Inspection	**Liability**	**Requests for**	
Deposition	**Monetary Damages**	**Production**	

The Genesis of Litigation: A Problem or Dispute

A lawsuit arises from a dispute or a problem that people have been unable to solve themselves. Such disputes can involve tangible property, intellectual property, the breach of a contract, a personal injury, or the violation of some other right or duty. The causes of litigation are as varied as human experience. A person may need the court's help to establish their ownership of a pet, or a multinational corporation may need the court to decide how a billion dollars of insurance coverage should be allocated to hundreds of thousands of injured individuals.

Let us now pretend that we are members of a group of new attorneys practicing with a well-established law firm in Liberty Springs, in the state of Franklin. Last summer, we worked as summer associates with the firm, and our work made an interesting change in tort law. We received an offer of employment, and after passing the bar examination, we began to work with the firm as new attorneys. The firm, Living & Justice, handles plaintiffs' cases and other legal matters.

One day, we received a phone call from a Mr. Jaime Soto. Months ago, on July 9, he was injured at a carnival ride, and he would like to talk with us about it. We check our calendars and find a convenient date to meet with him.

During that meeting, we learn that Mr. Soto is a single father; sadly, his wife died unexpectedly of a wide-ranging infectious disease a few years back. Mr. Soto has two young children, Roberto and Sara, whom he clearly loves very much.

Mr. Soto tell us that, last summer, he took his children to the annual Liberty County carnival. One of the rides at the carnival featured six oversized spinning teacups. Each teacup could seat up to three patrons. Once the ride began, the teacups rotated around each other, picking up speed. In addition to the large circular rotation, each teacup spun on its own central axis. The rate of spin could be accelerated if the patrons turned the wheel that rose from the floor of the teacup. Roberto and Sara were fascinated and could hardly wait to try it.

Mr. Soto and his children boarded the ride without difficulty. When the ride started up, the children excitedly turned the wheel on their personal teacup, accelerating its spin. Everything was going well until, about a minute into the ride, there was a loud "crack," and their teacup disconnected from its base. Due to the rotation of the ride, the teacup with Mr. Soto and his children was flung off the platform and rolled about fifteen feet. Mr. Soto grabbed his children and protected them from physical injury, but he sustained a significant break in the tibia and fibula of his lower right leg. This injury explains the cane that he used to walk into our law office. The broken leg required major surgery, and sadly his physicians have told Mr. Soto that his leg will never be as good as it was before.

Once Mr. Soto was released from the hospital, he reached out to the registered owner of the carnival. He did not receive a response. His medical bills were covered by his employer's insurance, but he had to take two months' uncompensated time off work. Sadly, Mr. Soto continues to experience pain, and staying on his feet for longer than half an hour is difficult. More troubling to Mr. Soto is the fact that his two children were traumatized by this accident and have had difficulty sleeping. Mr. Soto wonders what can be done.

FIGURE 11.1 Teacup ride

The Initial Stage of Litigation: Pleadings

All cases begin with the filing of a **complaint**. This is a formal document that sets forth the plaintiff's legal claims. In some jurisdictions, this can be done in a summary fashion with few embellishments. Other jurisdictions require a more detailed accounting of the events giving rise to the lawsuit and how those events constitute a legal claim. In the State of Franklin, complaints must state in detail the facts supporting the case, as well as the legal theories of **liability**.

Before we agree to represent Mr. Soto, we make sure that his story is true. Lawyers have an ethical obligation to perform due diligence before they proceed with litigation. We ask Mr. Soto for relevant documentation and invite him to come back with his children. We review the dates of the carnival's visit to Liberty County, read through Mr. Soto's medical records, and look through the incident report filed by the police who responded to the carnival accident. We speak again with Mr. Soto and chat briefly with his children. Everything supports Mr. Soto's story.

We discuss representation arrangements, including our ethical work principles, the fees involved, and the professional ground rules of legal practitioners. When Mr. Soto has had some time to think about it and is certain that he would like our help, he signs a retainer agreement confirming that he is engaging us to represent his legal interests and establishing the financial details of that representation.

Now that we formally represent Mr. Soto and his children in connection with their accident, we begin our work. We determine that the carnival is owned by a closely held corporation named Merry Times Carnival, Inc. We learn that the company is owned by Mr. B. Merry. He is also the designated agent to receive legal documents on behalf of the corporation. We write to Mr. Merry, noting that we represent Mr. Soto, and stating that we would like to talk about the accident and Mr. Soto's injuries. We also give Mr. Merry formal notice that he must not destroy or tamper with any of the evidence that could relate to this claim. We send this letter out via certified mail. Unfortunately, but perhaps not surprisingly, we receive no response.

We have now made a reasonable effort to invite Mr. Merry to work things out without involving the court system. We will now proceed with a lawsuit to help Mr. Soto and his children get the relief they are entitled to have.

We prepare our complaint against Merry Times Carnival, the **defendant**. We consider the causes of action that we should assert against Merry Times Carnival and whether other persons or entities should be sued. We do not know if the accident resulted from insufficient maintenance, or a defect in the teacup ride, or from some other cause. We will need to have the equipment and the ride's maintenance records inspected by an expert to learn why the accident occurred. Once that is done, we can amend our complaint if this inspection shows that other parties are at fault.

We name Mr. Jaime Soto as the **plaintiff** in our complaint. It states that he is filing suit on his own behalf and also on behalf of his two children, Sara Soto and Roberto Soto. As they are minors, their **legal guardian** must assert their rights for them in courts of law. Our complaint asserts claims for negligence and negligence *per se* on behalf of all three plaintiffs. The complaint's charging allegations describe how

Merry Times Carnival owed a duty of due care to its business invitees to furnish rides that were safe. It breached that duty because the teacup ride was unsafe.

After stating the supporting facts, our complaint finishes with a formal **prayer for relief**, which asks the court to award damages to the plaintiffs for their physical and psychological injuries. Our law firm is careful in drafting this part of the complaint, as we want to be sure to ask for all the relief that Mr. Soto and his children should receive. We include a request for monetary damages for pain and suffering, loss of enjoyment of life, emotional distress, and disability, which are all types of **general damages**. We also ask for **special damages**, which in this case are Mr. Soto's enumerated medical expenses and lost wages. For the children, we also ask for general damages for emotional distress and for loss of care and support due to their father's injury and disability, and for the costs of the counseling sessions they are now receiving and will continue to receive. We also request costs of suit and any other relief in our clients' favor that the court might wish to award.

Once our complaint is drafted, we have Mr. Soto sign it for himself and for his children. We also sign it. We then send our law clerk to file it with the Court Clerk of Liberty County Circuit Court, located in Liberty Springs. We can file the case in our city because the accident occurred here, because Mr. Merry lives here, and also because the carnival operated for two months in Liberty Springs. Liberty County Circuit Court can exercise **personal jurisdiction** over the defendant because of these extensive contacts with Liberty Springs. We could not file this lawsuit in a place where it would be unfair for the defendant to have to come to court, as the rules governing personal jurisdiction require that

FIGURE 11.2 The courthouse

there be contacts between the defendant and the place the case is filed. Further, the Liberty Springs Circuit Court is the proper court to hear claims for personal injury, so there is **subject matter jurisdiction**. Finally, the Liberty County Circuit Court in Liberty Springs is the correct venue, as it is convenient for the parties.

Once the case is filed, we must see to it that Merry Times Carnival receives it. We cannot conduct litigation against someone without telling them about it, as that violates their due process rights. Since Mr. Merry is the designated agent for Merry Times Carnival, Inc. to accept **service of process**, we arrange to transmit the complaint to him in such a way that receipt is confirmed. Then, we file proof of service with the court, documenting that he has received it.

Now, we wait the required thirty days to see how the defendant responds to the complaint. A defendant can **answer** a complaint, challenging the claims asserted and perhaps making claims of his own. Alternatively, a defendant can challenge the sufficiency of the complaint and argue that it is so flawed that it should be dismissed. A defendant can also challenge the court's jurisdiction to hear the case or the way that the complaint was served.

Our complaint was well crafted, the defendant was served, and the case may be properly heard by the Liberty County Circuit Court, so Merry Times Carnival, Inc. files an answer to the complaint through its retained counsel. In its answer, Merry Times generally denies the claims that we have made against it. The answer also asserts **affirmative defenses**, including the allegation that the injury was caused by Mr. Soto's negligence. We were expecting this allegation, as such defenses are commonly included. More interestingly, Merry Times also files a third-party complaint, bringing in another entity, Festival Maintenance, Inc. Merry Times Carnival argues that Mr. Soto's accident was not the result of any negligence on its part but rather resulted from the carnival maintenance contractor's failure to properly perform required maintenance work. Merry Times seeks **subrogation** from Festival Maintenance for any damages it must pay as the result of Mr. Soto's injury.

Our lawsuit has increased in complexity. We think about whether we wish to sue Festival Maintenance ourselves and decide to proceed. We file a cross-complaint against Festival Maintenance, asserting that improper maintenance harmed our client.

Through its attorney, Festival Maintenance files an answer to the third-party complaint and to the cross-complaint. It denies that it is in any way at fault for Mr. Soto's injuries, and it alleges that all injuries resulted from Merry Times' operation of the ride. Festival Maintenance also asserts that Mr. Soto's injuries were due to his own negligence. We are not surprised by these allegations, as it is typical for the parties in litigation to blame one another for what has occurred.

Discovery: Gathering Information

Now that the parties have answered, we can begin **discovery**. Discovery is the formal process of gathering information while a case is in litigation. We would like to learn more about the facts of the case, and develop a better understanding about precisely why the accident occurred. This could lead us to amend our complaint, adding new claims and perhaps new parties, if we find they are responsible for our clients' injuries.

Written Discovery Requests

We prepare special discovery documents to file with the court and serve on Merry Times and on Festival Maintenance. We start by serving **requests for production**. These ask for documents (physical or electronic) that we think the other parties may have that relate to the facts and legal claims in the lawsuit. We ask for any records, photos, or other materials relating to the specifications, purchase, and maintenance of the teacup ride. We ask for any materials relating to the ride's operation, including the training given to its operators. We also ask for materials relating to any incidents or accidents that have occurred in the past five years relating to the teacup ride.

We also file and serve **interrogatories**. These are a set of formal questions that must be answered in writing, under oath. We ask for a list of the people who have worked on or with the teacup ride. We also ask if other people have been injured on the ride. If the teacup ride has injured many people, we might explore with Mr. Soto the possibility of a class action lawsuit. Finally, we ask the other parties to list the factual reasons supporting their claims that they are not at fault and that Mr. Soto's actions led to his injuries. This will help us understand how the other parties intend to defend the case.

The other parties in the case also serve discovery requests upon us. They require us to forward the medical and employment records for Mr. Soto, the counseling records for his

Class Action Lawsuits

When many people have suffered the same type of harm, a class action lawsuit may be a useful option. Class actions allow plaintiffs to batch their claims to lower the costs of litigation and get traction against well-funded defendants. A named group of plaintiffs prosecutes the case on behalf of all similarly situated individuals, who form the class of plaintiffs.

There are special rules and requirements for class actions. All locatable potential claimants must be given notice of the action, and the class must be formally certified by the court. Claimants may opt in and receive the specified class remedy or opt out and pursue individual actions.

The Supreme Court addressed class action certification in the 2011 case *Wal-Mart Stores, Inc. v. Dukes*, 564 U.S. 388 (2011). The lawsuit challenged Wal-Mart policies that arguably caused nationwide gender, pay, and promotion inequalities. The Court rejected the request for certification, unanimously holding that the six identified individual plaintiffs had not adequately shown that they could properly represent 1.5 million class members.

FIGURE 11.3 Judge's gavel

children, and any other documents we have pertaining to the accident, our clients' injuries, and incurred expenses and damages. We comply with these requests, as we want the defendants to have information about our clients' injuries and monetary damages. The other parties will forward this information to their insurers, who will most likely end up paying for any **judgment** or settlement in this case. As those insurers cannot pay claims without supporting evidence, they need our records.

After some time, we receive the responses to our discovery requests. The responses contain helpful information about the teacup ride and its management. We learn that this teacup ride was manufactured by Westsea Amusement, Inc. We learn the names of the maintenance personnel who serviced it and the names of the operators who ran it. This is important, as we will want to talk with these people about their jobs as well as about the accident.

Inspections

We take care to update Mr. Soto on our work. He is our client and should approve of the things that we are doing. Further, we have decided to recommend hiring an expert. We need Mr. Soto's approval for this step, as it will result in additional expenses that he will pay.

We locate an amusement park safety expert. Denise Santiago, PhD, has twenty years' experience performing and supervising safety inspections, maintenance, and repairs at prominent theme parks. We are pleased that she has hands-on experience as well as academic experience. She is qualified to help us: she is a member of the ASTM[1] F24 Committee on Amusement Rides and Devices, has industry-related certifications with key trade organizations, and has assisted with creating ride and inspection protocols and operating procedures. She has done a mix of plaintiff and defendant work, so she has no apparent bias. In addition, she is personable, so we think a jury will easily relate to her.

After Mr. Soto agrees that we should proceed, we arrange to retain Dr. Santiago. We send her the police report about the accident and Mr. Soto's statement about how it occurred. We also send her copies of the responses to the discovery requests that we served. She will need this information to help her prepare for her inspection of the teacup ride. We want her to look closely at the ride and hopefully tell us why the accident occurred. She can only do these things after she has familiarized herself with the key information about the accident, including information about the teacup, its maintenance, and its operation.

We file a **Demand for Inspection**, asking that the teacup ride and the specific teacup that Mr. Soto and his children rode in be made available so that our expert can inspect it. Merry Times' attorney advises that the traveling carnival has moved on from Liberty County but that the teacup involved in the accident was replaced. The original teacup is now in a storage unit in Liberty Springs. The storage unit is owned by Merry Times Carnival and is used for storage of supplies, spare parts, and other goods.

On the day of our inspection, we go with our expert to the storage unit where the teacup is located. The lawyers for all the parties as well as any retained experts usually attend such inspections to make sure that things are done properly. No one wants a critical piece of **evidence** to be damaged, as that

---

[1]   Formerly the American Society for Testing and Materials.

FIGURE 11.4 The orange teacup before the accident

could result in **sanctions** against the party that damaged it. We are told that an expert for Merry Times will also attend.

Counsel for Merry Times arrives with the key to the storage unit's lock. Our expert enters the large unit and locates the cup, which is lying on its side. Dr. Santiago inspects it carefully from all angles, noting its condition, and photographing the dents and scrapes. She then looks closely at the section where the teacup connected to the base. She observes that the bolts connecting the base of the teacup to the platform have been sheared off; she tells us that it looks as though they snapped in half. The other expert present also takes notes but does not say anything about his observations. Dr. Santiago then takes out some tools. The other expert asks Dr. Santiago what she is planning on doing with the tools, and Dr. Santiago confirms that no destructive processes will be used; she is simply taking measurements. A few minutes later, Dr. Santiago takes us aside and tells us that the bolts that connected the teacup to the base are not the size that the manufacturer's equipment specifications manual states they should be. It appears that the original bolts were replaced with bolts that were not as thick. She also tells us that she will need to perform some calculations but that using nonstandard, thinner bolts to join parts subjected to significant torque could well have been the cause of the accident. Dr. Santiago completes her inspection, and we ask her to work up a report that will detail her findings and expert opinions.

Depositions

While we wait for the expert report, we deploy another discovery tool: the **deposition**. A deposition is a formal question-and-answer session, where a person must respond to a lawyer's verbal questions under oath and in person. The answers are recorded in writing (and sometimes are also videotaped) and become evidence in the case. In most lawsuits, the key players are all deposed. At some point, Festival Maintenance and Merry Times Carnival will want to depose Mr. Soto. We have decided to depose Mr. Merry. We send out a notice of his deposition.

An **objection** is filed to our request; it seems that Mr. Merry does not want to be deposed. He claims that he has very limited knowledge about the accident, as he was not on-site the day it occurred. This may be true, but we still want to question him. We therefore file a **Motion to Compel**, which asks the court to intervene and order compliance with our discovery request. Before that **motion** can be heard, however, Mr. Merry's attorneys contact us, and inform us that he has agreed to be deposed. We wonder at this change; is it because Mr. Merry can offer no reason to evade the deposition that the court would respect? In any event, we are glad to proceed. We coordinate with the other attorneys and find a date that will work for all of us. We will hold the deposition in the large conference room in our office.

On the day of his deposition, Mr. Merry arrives with the attorney representing Merry Times Carnival. Mr. Merry is a middle-aged man with a distinctly unfriendly demeanor. The attorney for Festival Maintenance also arrives, and we begin proceedings. The court reporter, who will type out Mr. Merry's testimony, administers the oath, and Mr. Merry swears that he will tell the truth. We first ask for some background information, and Mr. Merry tells us that he was born in Liberty Springs. After graduating from the University of Franklin with a degree in business, he decided to look for a new startup operation to purchase. He has always liked carnivals and traveling, and so he moved in that direction, acquiring the carnival using an inheritance from an aunt. We ask him detailed questions about how ride maintenance is managed, and he tells us that ten years back he signed a comprehensive maintenance contract with Festival Maintenance, which handles everything—routine maintenance and emergency repairs.

We had already received the contract with Festival Maintenance in response to our discovery requests, and we review it with Mr. Merry. We point out the provision that states Mr. Merry was required to advise Festival Maintenance of any problems with any rides as soon as feasible so that repairs can be made. Mr. Merry says that whenever anyone told him about a problem with a ride, he would immediately tell Festival Maintenance about it. He also states that he made all his rides available at the manufacturer's specified inspection and repair intervals. We ask about any documentation he has that supports this statement, and he simply refers us to the repair logs that Festival Maintenance has on hand. He is clearly impatient, but we take our time and require him to review all the important documents we received and explain how they fit into the picture.

Mr. Merry's testimony takes about three hours, and by the end of it we have developed our sense of him as a person, and of his approach to the operation of his carnival. In particular, we wonder if the things he said about ride maintenance are true. We decide that we next want to depose the person who was managing the teacup ride when Mr. Soto was hurt. From Mr. Merry's testimony and the responses to our interrogatories, we know that the operator of the ride was Ms. Sally McDermott. She is no longer employed by Merry Times Carnival, but she does live in the nearby city of Aspen Creek in our state of Franklin. So, we set a date for her deposition.

Ms. McDermott is not a party to this case, and so we must serve her with a **subpoena** so that she will appear for her deposition. A subpoena is a court order that requires someone to present themselves and/or deliver records or other items to someone at a particular time and place. Because we are courteous, we reach out to Ms. McDermott, tell her about the lawsuit, and ask her if May 1 will work for her deposition. Like most people, Ms. McDermott is not delighted that she will be deposed, but she tells us she is not surprised, as she knew that Mr. Soto had been hurt.

We serve Ms. McDermott with a subpoena *duces tecum*, which asks her to bring any documents she might have that pertain to the accident or to her work for Merry Times Carnival. This way, we are making sure that we will capture not only her testimony but can review any materials she has that might give us more information. She calls us before her deposition, and we learn that she does have relevant documents. We learn that she keeps a diary, which contains her personal reminiscences about her job and her life. We agree that she should make copies of the pages that include information about her job. We also agree to strike from those pages any parts that concern only her personal matters so that we can preserve her privacy as much as possible.

We take Ms. McDermott's deposition in an office in Aspen Creek. We use a conference room in the court reporter's office for this deposition. After Ms. McDermott is sworn in, we ask her some general questions about her educational background and employment history. We want the witness to feel relaxed about responding to our questions. We then ask her about Mr. Soto's accident. Ms. McDermott testifies that she remembers the accident quite well. She was the primary operator of the teacup ride during the month that Mr. Soto was injured. About two hours into her shift, there was a loud noise. At that point, Mr. Soto's teacup detached from its platform and rolled away. She describes her shock and concern and how she immediately stopped the ride and ran to see if she could help. She called 911 and then called her boss, Mr. Merry. Mr. Merry told her not to talk with anyone. The attorney representing Merry Times Carnival states an objection to this question and its answer, but at this deposition Ms. McDermott is permitted to answer it anyway. The **rules of evidence** decide what testimony can be admitted at trial,

FIGURE 11.5   Listening to deposition testimony

but there is wider latitude for testimony gleaned during discovery. Mr. Merry's attorney will probably object to this question again if it is asked during the trial.

Ms. McDermott is also able to offer some testimony about ride maintenance. She testifies that maintenance usually occurred during the early morning hours so as not to interfere with the operation of the carnival. The primary maintenance person for the teacup ride was Mr. George Nabby of Festival Maintenance. We already knew about Mr. Nabby from the responses to our interrogatories, but it is good to see the stories line up. Ms. McDermott met Mr. Nabby once or twice but did not know him well. We ask about her opinion of the maintenance protocol. Counsel representing Festival Maintenance objects, as this question may require her to offer an expert opinion that she is not qualified to provide. We amend our question to ask Ms. McDermott if she ever brought concerns about maintenance to her boss, Mr. Merry. She replies that, in fact, she quit her job because Mr. Merry was not interested in hearing about any employee concerns, and she was terribly upset about Mr. Soto's accident. There are more objections, but we persist, and Ms. McDermott advises that the teacup ride had been making periodic crunching sounds that alarmed her. She testifies that she had told Mr. Merry about those sounds, but he told her that George Nabby would attend to the problems during the next scheduled maintenance. This contradicts Mr. Merry's prior testimony.

We ask Ms. McDermott about any documents she may have collected in response to the subpoena. She pulls out the pages from her diary. We knew these pages would be presented today, but opposing counsel did not.

The portions that pertain to her work are relevant, and we are glad to have them. Four entries in particular are important to us:

> July 2: Still working the teacups. Ride sounds terrible—I hear a loud crunching sound on cockpit four, the orange teacup. Told Merry, he said ignore it, George will deal with it when the ride is serviced as scheduled. Typical!

> July 5: Asked George about the sound. He promised he would check it out "soon," whatever that means.

> July 7: Asked to be moved from teacups because I cannot stand the infernal sound. Merry says he will work on reassignment for August. But I think I should look for other work. This whole thing is pathetic, and I really hate the smell of popcorn and cotton candy.

> July 9: There was a terrible accident—with the orange teacup! That poor man and his children! I am quitting this job tomorrow!

During the deposition, we ask Ms. McDermott to explain each diary entry. Counsel for Merry Times Carnival objects to the contents of the diary, claiming that they are **hearsay**. Hearsay is an out-of-court statement (which can be in writing) introduced in court as evidence of the truth of what it says. As we are not now in court and are conducting discovery, Ms. McDermott is allowed to answer. She describes the crunching sound, how loud it was, and how it bothered her. We ask her what she meant by her comment "Typical!" on the July 2 entry. Over continuing objections, she testifies that Mr. Merry did not, in her opinion, seem interested in employee concerns. We ask her for specifics, and she states that she had raised other issues about problems with rides with him in the past. We press her for details, which are particularly important to establish credibility. Ms. McDermott says that in March and in April, she was worried about problems with the Dragon Ride, which she was then supervising. The Dragon Ride was a small roller coaster for young children. The cars were molded to look like dragons, and glided slowly on an elongated track. One of the dragons seemed to jerk back a bit every time it climbed the small rise in the ride. Mr. Merry did not want to hear about her concerns, but we are quite interested.

We decide that we should depose the maintenance worker who performed routine maintenance on the teacup ride. We have some rather pressing questions for him. George Nabby lives in Liberty Springs, and we serve the parties with a notice of deposition. As Mr. Nabby still is employed by Festival Maintenance, he will be represented by the attorney for Festival Maintenance at his deposition.

On the day for Mr. Nabby's deposition, Mr. Nabby comes to our law office with two lawyers: Festival Maintenance's attorney and also his own personal attorney. Mr. Nabby has retained private counsel to protect his personal interests. This is a wise decision where there is a conflict of interests between what an employer might wish a person to say and what the employee should say to protect their own interests. We wonder why this has occurred and are even more eager to depose George Nabby.

We all settle into our conference room. The court reporter administers the oath to Mr. Nabby. He seems nervous and is constantly looking at his personal attorney. After obtaining some background information, we begin to ask about his maintenance work for Festival Maintenance. We ask him if he performed maintenance work on the teacup ride for Merry Times Carnivals, and he answers "yes." We ask about the nature of his maintenance work, and at this point, he looks at his lawyer, who nods back at him, and responds: "I am exercising my Fifth Amendment right to remain silent." We are surprised at this, but know that the United States Supreme Court has ruled that the constitutional privilege against self-incrimination applies to civil proceedings as well as to criminal cases.[2]

We then ask a collection of questions about Mr. Nabby's work for Festival Maintenance and determine that he will not answer any further inquiries. It is important that we do this to make a **record** so that the court can review the deposition later and make rulings on the propriety of Mr. Nabby's exercise of his right to remain silent for all questions we asked.

Mr. Nabby's deposition performance is thought provoking. He is clearly worried about something he did—or did not do—in the course of his maintenance work for Festival Maintenance. We think about this information, along with Mr. Merry's deposition, Ms. McDermott's deposition, and Dr. Santiago's

---

2   *See McCarthy v. Arndstein*, 266 U.S. 34 (1924).

analysis. Dr. Santiago determined that the wrong bolts had been used to anchor the teacup to the base. We are developing a theory about who is at fault in this case.

We send the deposition transcripts to Dr. Santiago. The following week, we speak with her, and she tells us that her report is nearly ready. She has looked at all the discovery in the case, including the deposition transcripts. She has also performed a deep review of the maintenance records for the teacup ride and compared those records with the recommendations for maintenance by the manufacturer of the ride and the measurements she took when she inspected the teacup. She tells us that it is clear the wrong-size bolts were used, and also that the maintenance intervals were too infrequent. Industry standards and the manufacturer's own instructions were not followed. Further, she tells us that the sounds Ms. McDermott heard were likely the result of the bolts beginning to fail. Had the orange teacup been properly serviced at that point, the ride most likely would not have failed. She will send the report to us in a few days.

We reflect on Dr. Santiago's conclusions. It is sad that the serious oversight in maintenance was not corrected before the accident. In fact, there are governmental agencies that are supposed to inspect traveling carnivals to ensure that the rides are safe. We know, however, that the doctrine of sovereign immunity makes it difficult to obtain a meaningful monetary award from the state or the federal government. Suits against sovereign entities can only be filed in courts where those entities agree to subject themselves to the jurisdiction of the court. These special courts consistently set a limit on the amount of monetary damages that may be recovered. We recommend that Mr. Soto not pursue any claim he might have against the State of Franklin for any failure to properly inspect the teacup ride.

We receive Dr. Santiago's formal report, and we send it to the other parties. The report concludes that improper maintenance, specifically the wrong-size bolts, coupled with the circular action of the ride, led to the catastrophic equipment failure. It notes that the impending failure of the bolts was most likely the cause of the sound Ms. McDermott heard and that emergency repairs should have been made at that time.

Festival Maintenance and Merry Times Carnival have also asked to depose Mr. Soto. We prepare Mr. Soto for his deposition in a meeting at our firm. We tell him that he should take his time in answering, and that he should take care to answer only the question that is asked. He should not volunteer information; he must make the lawyers ask for it. And, of course, he must tell the truth.

Mr. Soto's deposition goes very well. He provides clear testimony about what happened on the day of the accident. He talks about his course of medical treatment and about his rehabilitation. He offers compelling testimony about how his life has become much more difficult due to his limited mobility. He describes the pain in his leg and how it keeps him awake at night several times a week. He testifies about how, as a single parent of young children, he feels especially vulnerable because his children will continue to need him for a long time. He is a particularly good witness on his own behalf.

Dispositive Motions

We are soon to return to court for a **status conference**, a check-in session where the judge asks the parties how the case is progressing and when it might be ready for trial. We would like to increase the pressure on the other parties, and after talking with Mr. Soto, we file a Motion for Partial Summary Judgment on the issue of liability. This document asks that the judge review the evidence and make a finding that Merry Times Carnival and Festival Maintenance are jointly liable for the accident. We can make this motion because we now have clear evidence about how the accident occurred, and that evidence confirms that it was the defendants' fault: the defendants did not follow the manufacturer's recommendations about maintenance for the ride. We have no evidence indicating that the manufacturer of the teacup is responsible; the only entities that are at fault are the two defendants in the case. Our motion argues that the accident resulted from lax and improper maintenance, and these things were in the defendants' exclusive control. Accordingly, there is no dispute of fact about what happened. If our motion is successful, the only issue remaining is the amount of monetary damages that should be awarded to Mr. Soto and his children.

Our Motion for Partial Summary Judgment will be helpful to our case even if it is not granted. First, our judge will learn more about the litigation. In addition, in order to oppose our motion, Merry Times Carnival and Festival Maintenance will have to file a formal opposition. They could argue that our motion was filed too soon (claiming we don't yet have all the relevant information about the accident), or they could present other evidence (perhaps from their own expert) that contradicts the factual evidence we presented. This is useful, as we will then learn how the other parties are planning on defending the case.

The Law of Evidence

In every endeavor—from track competitions to trial proceedings—there are rules governing what may and what may not be done. The Law of Evidence establishes what testimony and physical evidence can be admitted and presented to the jury during trial.

The Federal Rules of Evidence were drafted after Chief Justice Earl Warren impaneled a committee to create a set of advisory rules in 1965. President Gerald R. Ford signed the first federal rules into law in 1975, and those rules became the foundation for many state evidentiary rules. As the law develops, they continue to be amended.

The Rules of Evidence clarify what evidence may be admitted in court and define how admissible evidence may be used. Accordingly, the rules support fairness in the justice system: they ensure relevance, limit prejudice, protect due process and reliability, and support efficient case management. They also ensure that constitutional mandates, such as the privilege against self-incrimination, are enforced.

Mediation, Arbitration, and Settlement

A week after we file our Motion for Partial Summary Judgment, we go to court for the status conference. Judge Niles Patel presides over the civil litigation docket in Liberty County Circuit Court, and he will be our trial judge. On the day of the status conference, there are many attorneys in the courtroom waiting for their cases to be called. Happily, our case is one of the first ones to be called. We approach the bench where the judge sits. The court bailiff stands to the side, and the court reporter is ready to transcribe what is said. We introduce ourselves, and Judge Patel notes that he received our Motion for Partial Summary Judgment. He then asks whether the parties are interested in working toward a settlement. We say that our clients may be interested, and the defendants' attorneys say that their clients would be willing to try and get the case resolved. The judge asks if all the parties would agree to mediation. We tell the court that we would recommend mediation to Mr. Soto on two conditions: first, that all the parties agreed to participate, and second, that it would go forward in the next 90 days so that we do not waste a great deal of time. The court asks us to check with Mr. Soto within the next few days and call back with the conversation's outcome.

We talk with Mr. Soto about mediation. We explain that mediation involves an attempt at negotiating a settlement with the help of a neutral third party. Mr. Soto asks about alternatives. We explain that the parties can always conduct settlement negotiations without outside assistance, but it is often better to have a skilled professional on board. In addition to mediation, the parties can agree to (or the court can order) arbitration, which involves an arbitrator reviewing presentations, and then deciding about liability and damages. Resolving a case before trial can be good; it saves time and expenses and eliminates the uncertainty that surrounds any trial. Mr. Soto says that he is happy to give mediation a try, as he would prefer not to take more time off work for trial. Further, he would like to avoid having his children deposed or testify in court, which may well happen if this case goes forward. Since Sara and Roberto have spent time in counseling, they have been sleeping better, and he would like to minimize their stress.

We tell the court that our client is willing to try mediation. The court says we can all agree upon a mediator within one week, or he will assign one to our case. Several retired judges work as mediators in Liberty Springs. After conferring, the attorneys agree to use retired judge LaShawna Levitt, an experienced and fair-minded jurist.

We meet with Mr. Soto and talk about how the mediation will work. The mediator will first visit with both parties together briefly and then meet with each party separately. She will discuss the case and its features with the parties separately until a resolution of the case occurs, or until it seems that a settlement is not achievable on that date. We offer our law firm's offices as a mediation venue.

On the day of our mediation, the lawyers for the other parties come to our office. Representatives of the insurance companies for Merry Times Carnival and Festival Maintenance also come. Most of the time, it is the insurers that pay damage awards and negotiated settlements. Having them here makes it more likely that we will achieve a settlement in our case.

Judge Levitt introduces herself and then greets everyone present. She makes a point of thanking Mr. Soto for coming and asks how his children are doing. They are in school and will not attend, but as Mr. Soto is their legal guardian, he can make settlement decisions on their behalf.

All the parties have sent Judge Levitt mediation briefs. These are advocacy briefs that explain the case from each party's point of view. Judge Levitt tells us that she has read them, and we are glad to hear that she is prepared. The parties are splitting the cost of her time, and we want her to be efficient.

Judge Levitt meets separately with each party and its legal representative (and also with the insurance representatives of Merry Times Carnival and Festival Maintenance). At our first individual meeting with Judge Levitt, we confirm that Mr. Soto's medical bills total about $75,000, and that the financial loss due to missed work is $10,000. We make sure Judge Levitt has read our clients' deposition testimony and the key report from Mr. Soto's physiatrist (rehabilitation physician). This report concludes that, due to substantial muscle and ligament damage, Mr. Soto will likely not ever be able to walk any distance comfortably. This is a significant physical disability, particularly difficult in a young father. We are glad that Judge Levitt appears thoughtful as she receives this information. Any appropriate settlement proposal must include a substantial award for this permanent injury.

Judge Levitt spends considerable time talking with the defendants. She returns to us and advises that Festival Maintenance has offered double the medical costs, or $150,000, but that Merry Times Carnival is only offering $25,000. We advise Mr. Soto that a total settlement of $175,000 for his case is not in line with jury verdicts in our county for plaintiffs with similar injuries. We know that Merry Times maintains that the accident was caused by Festival Maintenance's poor maintenance efforts. We also know that Festival Maintenance is asserting that Merry Times would not permit Festival Maintenance to inspect and repair the ride at appropriate intervals. Festival Maintenance further claims that Merry Times failed to tell them that there was a known problem with the orange teacup. Thus, each party is blaming the other for what occurred. Although Judge Levitt discusses our clients' injuries in detail, emphasizing the seriousness of the case, she makes no meaningful progress toward resolving the case. We conclude that the case will not resolve by settlement, at least on that day.

At a meeting the following week, we discuss the case further with Mr. Soto. As mediation was unsuccessful, we need to prepare for the hearing on our Motion for Partial Summary Judgment. If that is denied, we will need to think about who else we should depose and what other claims we need to assert based upon the evidence we have gathered. Finally, we will need to prepare for trial.

Trial Proceedings

Mr. Soto asks what will happen at trial. We start with the big picture: the trial is where the parties present their stories in court and see who is believed. The process is highly structured, and the plaintiff has the **burden of proof**: the plaintiff must present evidence to establish the facts supporting the claims they have asserted in their lawsuit. To win our case, the jury must find, by a preponderance of the evidence,

Hearsay

Hearsay, as defined by the Federal Rules of Evidence (FRE), is an out-of-court statement that is used to prove the truth of the matter asserted. For instance, if a witness testifies that "my father told me he saw the defendant strike the victim," a court would likely strike the testimony from the record because it is 1) a statement made outside of the courtroom; and 2) being used to prove the truth of the assertation that the defendant struck the victim.

However, there are many exceptions to the Hearsay Rule. Some of the more notable exceptions include:

- A Record of Regularly Conducted Business, FRE 803(6). This exception, known as the Business Records Exception, allows documents that were created in the ordinary course of business to be entered into evidence. The rationale behind this hearsay exception is that routinely created business documents are usually reliable. Examples of admissible business records would include monthly bank statements, inventory reports, and tax returns.

- An Excited Utterance, FRE 803(2). This exception allows into evidence statements that were made immediately after the speaker experienced a stressful event. People who make such spontaneous comments are not likely to be lying, and so they are admissible. An example of an excited utterance would be a person saying, immediately after an accident: "Did you see? That blue van just ran through the crosswalk and struck that poor child!"

that the claims asserted by Mr. Soto are true. The jury will set an award of monetary damages to compensate Mr. Soto and his children for their injuries. As Mr. Soto's attorneys, our job is to present the evidence in the light most favorable to our clients. As officers of the court, we are not allowed to lie while we do this.

We explain that trials begin with **voir dire**, the process of asking jurors questions to find any bias or other reason why they should not hear the evidence in the case. Once a jury has been selected, the court reads the jury instructions, which tell the jury what they are to do in the case. The instructions are tailored to each case. The court may be presented with **motions in limine**, which seek to restrict the admissibility of certain testimony or other evidence.

Mr. Soto asks how trials begin. We tell him that once the jury has been instructed and all pretrial motions are decided by the court, the attorneys give **opening statements**. These explain what the evidence will show, according to the attorneys on each side. The opening statements are particularly important, as this is where the attorney will have the first opportunity to tell their client's story. Opening statements must give the jurors a preview of the evidence supporting the client's case. They should be interesting and compelling so that the jury can understand the significance of the case to the client.

After the opening statements are concluded, plaintiffs present evidence and witnesses that support their side of the story. All relevant evidence can be admitted in this effort unless it is more prejudicial then probative, or unless it is hearsay, or violates a **privilege** or other rule of evidence. Sometimes, evidence needs a foundation or authentication before it can be admitted; for example, documents should be shown to be authored by the appropriate people, and a chain of custody should be established to confirm that a particular piece of evidence comes from where it supposedly originated. In addition, expert witnesses must be shown to be qualified before they present their opinions.

(continued)

Mr. Soto has heard about **cross-examination** and wants to know more about it. We explain that once the testimony of each plaintiff's witness has been introduced by **direct examination**, the defendants may complete a cross-examination of that witness. Cross-examinations are designed to highlight inconsistencies, bias, a lack of foundational information or knowledge, or any other quality about the witness or the testimony that will help the defendant's case. A plaintiff may seek to repair any damage done during cross-examination through redirect examination.

When a plaintiff has finished presenting all their witnesses and evidence, the defendants will present their cases. The plaintiff's attorney now may cross-examine any witnesses or otherwise challenge any testimony in the same way that the defendants could during the plaintiff's case.

We next tell Mr. Soto about **closing statements**. After all the parties' witnesses and evidence has been presented, the attorneys give their closing statements. The attorney for each party sums up the evidence, highlighting the most helpful parts, and explaining why their client should win.

At this point, the jurors receive final instructions from the judge and then begin **deliberations**. This is the process where the jury discusses the case and decides if the plaintiff has proven the claims asserted. At the end of this process, we tell Mr. Soto, we would hope for a **verdict** in his favor and in favor of his children. We would hope for a damage award that properly compensates his family for their injuries.

Sometimes, judges think that juries have made a mistake. A judge can then issue **a judgment notwithstanding the verdict**, setting the verdict aside. But we tell Mr. Soto that this is rare, as our system gives great deference to the findings of juries.

Posttrial Proceedings

Mr. Soto asks if a jury verdict is the end of a case. We explain that the losing party has the right to an **appeal**. In an appeal,

- A Statement Under Belief of Imminent Death, FRE 804(2), also known as a dying declaration. If an individual believes they are dying and makes a statement relating to the event that caused the threat of death, that statement is admissible. In this situation, the speaker is unlikely to lie, and therefore the statement is sufficiently reliable to be admitted. Dying declarations are favorite tools of screenwriters, but they also are important in real life. On February 18, 2018, a woman was found dying from multiple stab wounds on a road in Alameda County, California. Before she died, she told the responding officers about the people who had attacked her. They were arrested for her murder.[3]

The Hearsay Rule is one of the most complicated parts of the Law of Evidence. However, it ensures that testimony presented in courts of law is reliable.

---

3   Angela Ruggiero and Aaron Davis, Outbursts from Family Disrupt Court Appearance of Livermore Stabbing Suspects, East Bay Times (Feb. 14, 2018).

The Hidden Costs of Litigation

The National Center for State Courts found that, on average, tort cases take sixteen months to resolve. In addition to taking a long time, the litigation process can be expensive. Even plaintiffs who secure contingent-fee attorney representation will pay court costs and perhaps expert witness fees.

The process can also be stressful. Litigants may be required to recount their narrative before the case begins, during the discovery process, and during trial, when a jury will decide if their story is true. Most plaintiffs find that participating in the litigation process is time-consuming and emotionally difficult.

Experienced attorneys know that the emotional costs for their clients can be too high to ignore. Careful attorneys prepare clients for the realities of how long their case may take and what they may experience in the process. This permits clients to make well-informed decisions at every phase of litigation.

FIGURE 11.6   Litigation

the losing party will claim that something went wrong during the trial that led to an unjust outcome. They may say that some evidence was not admitted that should have been admitted, or vice versa. Or, they will say that a jury instruction incorrectly stated the law.

Appellate courts address trial court errors that impinge substantially on the fairness of the trial process or cause results that are inconsistent with the substantive law. A decision that was clearly arbitrary, unreasonable, or erroneous and led to an unjust outcome is an **abuse of discretion**. Judges that make harmful erroneous rulings put the integrity and consistency of the judicial system at risk, and so those rulings should be reversed on appeal. This can even result in a new trial, depending upon the nature of the error.

FIGURE 11.7   New York Court of Appeals hearing oral arguments

Remedies

Mr. Soto is curious about what he could receive as monetary damages at the end of his case. We tell him about the remedies that we have asked for: monetary damages for pain and suffering, for loss of enjoyment of life, for emotional distress and disability, and for his medical expenses and lost wages. For the children, we remind him that we have asked for damages for emotional distress and for loss of care and support due to his injury and disability. We explain that these damages are typical for his case. Had this been a case for violating the rights of a patent holder, we would have asked for different remedies, including **restitution**, which requires a defendant to return the monetary gains they have unlawfully acquired. Had this been a case about property ownership, we could have asked for a declaratory judgment confirming that the property belonged to us.

We tell Mr. Soto that based upon the deposition of Mr. Merry, we will amend our complaint to include claims of gross negligence against Merry Times Carnival and Festival Maintenance. Ms. McDermott's testimony shows that Mr. Merry knew the ride had a safety issue but chose to ignore it. From our expert's report, it appears that Festival Maintenance used the incorrect bolts to anchor the orange teacup to the ride platform. These actions show a careless indifference to harm, a recklessness which is morally repugnant. As we now have facts to support claims of gross negligence, we can now ask for **punitive damages**. These are damages assessed against a party to punish them for reprehensible behavior that causes harm. Punitive damages can range up to several times the amount of actual monetary damages.

Mr. Soto has no further questions. We will continue to stay in contact as his case moves forward. Merry Times Carnival and Festival Maintenance will file their briefs opposing our Motion for Partial Summary Judgment in the next two weeks, and the court has set a hearing date in one month. Our fingers are crossed that we will prevail on our motion.

Conclusion and Introduction to Law Lab

We have now proceeded from our initial introduction to potential clients to the adjudicative phase of their case.

We began by meeting with someone who had been harmed, Mr. Jaime Soto, and learning about his possible

When the Trial Court Gets It Wrong

When a party to a legal proceeding believes that a trial judge or jury made a mistake, they may be able to appeal to a higher court. Appellate courts are typically made up of a panel of judges. They usually hear cases involving legal questions that the lower court answered incorrectly. Perhaps the trial court allowed a coerced confession into evidence or permitted a lay witness to testify about a matter requiring expert qualifications. In both instances, the lower judge made an error of law. If such an error caused an incorrect outcome, then an injustice has occurred that should be corrected on appeal.

After hearing an appeal, a panel may reverse the trial court, affirm the trial court, reverse in part and affirm in part, or reverse the decision and remand it back to the trial court for further proceedings.

If a party feels that the appellate court erred, they may then appeal to an even higher court. In the federal system, this is the United States Supreme Court, and in the states, this is often the State Supreme Court (although the high courts of some states have different names). These appeals to the highest court are often discretionary: the higher court may decide not to hear the case.

FIGURE 11.8 Judges of the United States Court of Appeals for the Federal Circuit

claim. After performing due diligence to make sure that the case had merit and after reviewing the terms of our representation with Mr. Soto, we decided to proceed. He signed a retainer agreement for himself and his two children, and we completed the initial research needed to begin litigation.

After concluding our research, we filed a formal complaint against Merry Times Carnival, as we believed it was responsible for the harm that was done to Mr. Soto and his children. We sought the remedy of monetary damages for the costs they incurred and also for the pain, suffering, and disabilities that they have endured. We then served the complaint on the company. When its answer was filed, we learned about another party that was potentially responsible, Festival Maintenance. Accordingly, we amended our complaint to include new claims against this new party.

During the discovery process, we served written interrogatories and requests for production of documents. We also found an expert witness, Dr. Denise Santiago, to conduct an inspection of the carnival ride that harmed our clients. We deposed Sally McDermott and George Nabby, key witnesses to the events leading to our clients' injures. From the depositions, we learned what they saw, heard, and thought and obtained important information about our clients' claims.

After the discovery process was complete, we filed a Motion for Partial Summary Judgment, asking the court to review the evidence and make a ruling that our clients' injuries were caused by the defendants. While that motion was pending, we proceeded with mediation. Sadly, the mediation was not successful.

At every stage of the litigation process, we have been both driving the actions of the other parties and responding to their actions. We have both served pleadings and responded to pleadings. We have sent out our own discovery requests and we have produced witnesses and information in response to the other parties' requests. The exchange of information and requests is an important part of the process: it ensures that all parties can find out what has occurred and appropriately assess the merits of the case. Most cases resolve by settlement, based upon information gained through the discovery process.

We have also responded to commands and requests by the court. The judge presiding over the case must see to it that it progresses appropriately. Parties in cases that are not properly monitored are at risk of sustaining unnecessary legal fees, costs, and delays. Sometimes, parties will try and stall the processing of cases for tactical reasons, seeking to wear out adversaries. They may initiate frivolous proceedings, such as unnecessary discovery requests or motions, in order to burden the other side with heightened legal fees. The ethical rules that govern the work of attorneys and judges, which we explore in Chapter 16, condemn such actions. Justice is imperiled when a case is inappropriately delayed. A plaintiff who has filed suit should either get relief within a reasonable time or find out that they are not entitled to it.

In this week's Law Lab, you will learn what happened in response to the Motion for Partial Summary Judgement that we filed. You will also be asked to assist with one of the most important tasks that a litigator can perform for their client. The task will require your knowledge of the case, your personal talents, and your ideas about the needs of your clients and the interests of justice. As you read the Law Lab, consider how you will advocate on your clients' behalf.

Advocacy Law Lab

MEMORANDUM

To: Associates of Living & Justice

From: J. Justice

Re: *Soto v. Merry Time Carnival, Inc. and Festival Maintenance, Inc.*

Clients: Jaime Soto; Roberto and Sara Soto

Dear Associates:

This memorandum will bring you up to date in the above-referenced matter and seek your assistance with a critical part of our upcoming trial.

First, we must advise you that Judge Patel denied our Motion for Partial Summary Judgment. In opposition, Mr. Merry filed a declaration stating that he always saw to it that maintenance occurred on a timely and regular basis. Festival Maintenance claimed that neither Mr. Merry nor anyone else working for the carnival ever pointed out any problem with the teacup ride. Festival Maintenance further claimed that it occasionally had problems accessing the carnival rides at the proper intervals, which Mr. Merry contests. As there is a dispute of fact concerning fault, the judge determined that any summary judgment motion should be denied. Accordingly, we must now prepare for trial.

We are hoping that you can assist with the opening statement that we will give to the jury at the beginning of the case. We would like you to prepare a draft opening statement that we can review and refine in the coming weeks.

Please bear in mind the following as you work up your draft:

The opening statement should tell the jury what evidence will be presented and what this evidence proves. It should introduce the jurors to our clients' perspectives sympathetically.

229

The best opening statements *tell stories* and *have themes* to help the jury determine how to view the case as a whole and connect to the plaintiffs and their troubles.

The opening statement should be *organized*. Think about where key information should go and what should be emphasized. We know from social science research that information is remembered best when it is encountered first or last.

The opening statement should call into question the credibility of opposing witnesses.

Most importantly, the opening statement should be *persuasive* and *confident*, using powerful language to make it memorable. We want the jurors to remember our descriptions of the evidence as the case unfolds before them.

The partnership looks forward to reviewing your draft opening statement.

Thank you for your assistance.

CHAPTER 12

Family Law

If you have a caring life partner, you help the other person when that person needs it. I had a life partner who thought my work was as important as his, and I think that made all the difference for me.

—Ruth Bader Ginsberg, Supreme Court justice, from an interview with Katie Couric for Yahoo, July 30, 2014

Introduction

Family Law regulates the important relationships at the core of our personal identities. It is, therefore, an area of law that touches everyone. It governs the creation and termination of familial bonds and the rights and duties of persons living with others in family groups. As these relationships can be complicated (and occasionally unfortunate), the Family Law umbrella is large, and the laws that fall under it are complex.

When people think of Family Law, they most often think of marriage, and Family Law is indeed concerned with marriage, annulment, and divorce.[1] Family Law also governs the management and treatment of children, and therefore it addresses paternity, adoption, surrogacy, parental rights, custody, and guardianship. In addition, Family Law covers the economics involved in family relationships, and so Family Law and Property Law overlap. Family Law courts routinely adjudicate the correct division of assets upon divorce, the proper amount of child support, and the custody rights of divorcing persons.

There is also an overlap between Family Law and Criminal Law. Sadly, people living in family units can become abusive or violent toward others in their households. They can also fail to fulfill their legal responsibilities to their dependents. Thus, Family Law is concerned with domestic violence, elder abuse, juvenile delinquency, and also with child abuse and child neglect.

---

1   Religious institutions and their codes also address marriage, divorce, annulment, and the law of the family. A review of how religious institutions treat Family Law is beyond the purview of this chapter.

To summarize, Family Law concerns our relationships with 1) persons we love and live with; 2) persons we may love but cannot live with; and 3) persons we no longer like at all, but must continue to deal with. It is not surprising that family courts are among the busiest tribunals in the nation,[2] and the cases they adjudicate can be emotionally difficult.[3]

In this chapter, we will survey the key Family Law topics noted above. Then, in your Law Lab, you will work as lawmakers to craft new legislation to protect the health and safety of children who are at risk due to their parents' actions.

FAMILY LAW KEY TERMS

The following key terms are defined in this chapter. They are also defined in the Glossary.

Abused Child	**Fault-Based Divorce**	**Permissive Reporter**
Annulment	**Joint Custody**	**Physical Custody**
Child Abandonment	**Legal Custody**	**Prenuptial Agreement**
Child Sexual Abuse	**Legal Guardian**	**Presumption of Legitimacy**
Common Law Marriage	**Legal Separation**	**Shared Parental Responsibility**
Dissolution	**Mandatory Reporter**	**Ward of the State**
Divorce	**Neglected Child**	
Domestic Violence	**No-Fault Divorce**	

Marriage, Annulment, and Divorce

From the earliest times, young people have been expected to marry and have children, and the law has regulated this process. The ancient Code of Ur-Nammu references marriage, and the Code of Hammurabi describes the rights of husbands and wives.[4] The Mosaic code addresses the management of both marriage and divorce.[5]

Until the twentieth century, women in Anglo-American society lived under the authority of their fathers (or other male relatives) until given in marriage to men chosen by members of their families. The

---

2   For example, in New Jersey, family law cases accounted for 41% of the state's total case filings in 2006. During the same period, that number was 58% in Nebraska, 49% in Nevada, and 46% in Maryland. *See* Barbara Babb, "Reevaluating Where We Stand: A Comprehensive Survey of America's Family Justice Systems," 46 *Family Court Rev.* (2008).

3   *See* Esther Rosenfeld et al., "Confronting the Challenge of the High-Conflict Personality in Family Court," *Family Law Quarterly* (2020); *see also* Kathryn Abrams, "Barriers & Boundaries: Exploring Emotion in the Law of the Family," 16 *Virginia J. of Social Policy & the Law* 301 (2008).

4   *See* Elizabeth Meier Tetlow, *Women, Crime and Punishment in Ancient Law and Society* 14 (2014); and *Code of Hammurabi*, Rules 128–153.

5   *Mishnah Torah*, 15: 8–15.

historical purposes of marriage were pragmatic rather than romantic. They included unifying families to increase wealth and security and producing children to continue the family line.[6]

In Roman times, a man and woman who lived together and had consensual sexual relations were considered married. The English common law also recognized informal marriages where a man and a woman lived together in a committed relationship, and some of the colonies recognized a version of the **common law marriage**. Where a couple has lived together but not purchased a marriage license, some states continue to acknowledge the couple as married. However, the common law marriage as a legal institution is fading. In its place, states have passed laws regularizing the requirements and benefits of marriage. These establish a minimum age to marry, impose limitations on marriages among close kin, and identify the rights and benefits that accrue to marital partners. In addition, Arizona, Arkansas, and Louisiana have created laws supporting the legally distinct covenant marriage, where the spouses commit to premarital counseling and agree to divorce only under limited circumstances.[7]

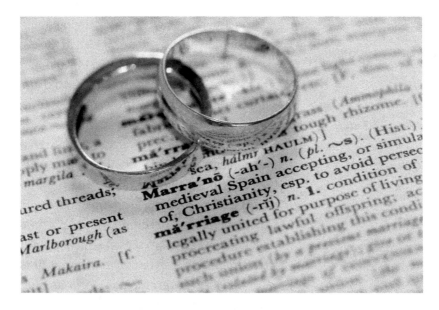

FIGURE 12.1 Symbols of marriage

Today, a valid marriage changes the legal status of those who marry, bestowing upon them a collection of rights supported by the government and the courts. Accordingly, people now marry because they want to obtain the legal benefits that come with marriage, as well as because they care for each other and wish

---

6   *See Women's Writing of Ancient Mesopotamia: An Anthology of the Earliest Female Authors*, Mesopotamian Women 18 (2017).

7   In covenant marriages, a spouse wishing to divorce must prove that the other spouse committed adultery or a felony, is engaging in substance abuse, has abused the spouse or a child, or has lived apart for a period of time.

The Power of Oaths

An oath can be a *performative utterance*. A performative utterance is different from normal speech: it is a phrase that not only describes reality but also affects it in some way. For example, by taking the oath of office, the president not only agrees that he is the new president, but he also *becomes* the new president. Performative utterances appear in many places. The phrase "You are under arrest" said by a police officer is such an utterance. When those words are spoken, the suspect is not only advised of the arrest but also becomes an arrested person. More benevolently, the words "I do" uttered in response to the phrase "do you take this person to be your lawful wedded spouse?" both signal an agreement to marry and facilitate matrimony.

to formally acknowledge a cherished relationship. Marriage is now celebrated as a meaningful enterprise that confers specific legal rights as well as important intangible benefits.

The Legal Requirements and Rights of Marriage

Despite the warmth and optimism that suffuses most new marriages, the rate of divorce in the United States is high.[8] Accordingly, no matter how confidently they view their upcoming union, people with substantial assets may choose to enter into legal arrangements to protect those assets in the event that their marriage fails. Without these advance arrangements, state distribution laws can dictate how marital assets will be divided in the event of divorce.

To ensure that personal assets avoid statutory distribution, marital partners sign a **prenuptial agreement**. This is a contract that confirms each person's property rights before the marriage and provides that each person will retain their own property if the marriage ends. As prenuptial agreements are legal contracts, the rules of Contract Law apply. To be legally binding, both parties must disclose their assets honestly before entering into the agreement so that there is no fraud. In addition, if one party has a bargaining advantage that makes the agreement patently unfair under the circumstances, the court will set aside the agreement.[9]

To obtain governmental recognition of their union, a couple must meet certain legal requirements. First, a marriage cannot be performed between parties that are too closely related or between parties who are already married

---

8   American families marry, divorce, and cohabit more frequently than in most other Western countries. *See* Andrew Cherlin, *The Marriage-Go-Round* 3 (2010).

9   An example of such an unfair agreement is found in *Petracca v. Petracca*, 956 N.Y.S. 2d 77, 77-9 (NY 2012). The case involved a contract entered into a few months after the couple married. It dictated that the jointly owned marital residence would go to the husband and denied the wife any interest in his business or his estate. The husband's net worth was valued at $22 million. The wife signed the agreement under duress and without legal representation, and the court readily set it aside.

to someone else. In addition, in every state and territory, there is an age requirement. An individual can marry without parental consent when they reach eighteen years of age in every state except Nebraska, where that age is nineteen, and in Mississippi, where the age is twenty-one. In most states, you may marry at a younger age if your parents provide written consent. Most states have passed legislation that sets an absolute minimum marriage age to prevent forced and child marriages.[10]

Since June 26, 2015, same-sex couples have been permitted to marry in the United States. On that date, the United States Supreme Court ruled in *Obergefell v. Hodges*, 576 U.S. 644 (2015) that bans on same-sex marriage are unconstitutional. Accordingly, partners in same-sex as well as traditional marriages may now receive the same important legal rights that flow from marriage. These include the right to open a joint bank account, the right to take title to real property as tenants by the entirety, and the right to file a joint tax return. In addition, married partners have the right to receive a spouse's worker's compensation, disability, pension, and social security benefits and have the right to recover monetary benefits upon a spouse's injury. Spouses also have the right to receive the support of state inheritance laws. Finally, spouses have the critical right to make certain medical decisions for their married partners, to visit them in the hospital, and to speak with their physicians when others may not do so.

Annulment, Separation, and Divorce

Marriages end for a host of reasons.[11] Even with the best of intentions and goodwill, some couples cannot successfully navigate their relationship through troubled waters. When it is necessary, marriages can be

FIGURE 12.2   A broken marriage

---

10   Unchained, an advocacy organization dedicated to ending forced and child marriage, estimates that 248,000 children as young as twelve were married between 2000 and 2010 in the United States. The overwhelming majority were female, married to adult men. *See* https://www.unchainedatlast.org/.

11   One research study found the major contributors to divorce were a lack of commitment, conflict, and infidelity. Infidelity, domestic violence, and substance abuse were the most common precipitating causes. The study also found that most people believed the persons most at fault for the divorce were their partners. Scott, Rhoades, Stanley, Allen, and Markman, "Reasons for Divorce and Recollections of Premarital Intervention: Implications for Improving Relationship Education," 2 *Couple Family Psychol.* 131, 131–145 (Jun. 2013).

legally terminated or undergo **dissolution**. Marriages are dissolved through the process of **annulment** or by **divorce**.

An annulment is a legal invalidation of a marriage, and it requires a finding that a marriage was void from the start. Annulments most often result where there was a defect in the way the marriage was contracted. For example, until a prior order of divorce is finalized, a couple is still legally married. So, if one of them marries again before their divorce is finalized, the new marriage should be annulled. A marriage may also be annulled if a party were not of marriageable age or not mentally competent.

Sometimes, spouses will decide to live apart for a time, commencing a **legal separation** while they consider their next steps. In some states, this is a required step prior to obtaining a divorce.[12] Such separations do not alter the spouses' legal rights and responsibilities to each other. The terms of the legal separation are often put into an agreement that is filed with the court. Legal separation agreements address the division of debts and assets and often establish child custody, visitation, and support arrangements. During times of legal separation, the spouses' health care and other benefits usually continue. Depending upon the state, spouses may still be responsible for each other's debts and can still make medical decisions for each other.

Many couples who legally separate end up proceeding with a divorce. The legal requirements involved in obtaining a divorce have changed substantially in the last forty years. For much of the nation's history, divorce was an intentionally difficult process, viewed as compromising the public interest of supporting families and children. Accordingly, until the 1970s, divorces were only granted if one spouse could meet extremely specific and difficult statutory requirements. This was known as the **fault-based divorce**. Essentially, a divorce was only granted if one party had behaved so badly that the other party was excused from continuing the marriage. Grounds for divorce typically included adultery, habitual intemperance or bad temper, extreme cruelty, abandonment, impotency, or insanity. If both parties were guilty of bad behavior, no divorce was permitted. The responding partner in the divorce case had the options of 1) agreeing that the allegations were true; 2) challenging the allegations as untrue; 3) saying that the spouse was just as guilty; or 4) showing that the spouse condoned the bad behavior, and so the behavior could not support dissolution of the marriage.

If the divorce was contested, a trial followed. These were often lurid, and as court proceedings are open to the public, quite newsworthy.[13] It was not uncommon for people to agree to pay money to avoid the public airing of their personal problems. Following the trial, the court would rule in favor of the party who was not "at fault."

In the 1960s, states began to move to a concept of **no-fault divorce**. This enabled spouses to end a marriage without becoming adversaries and eliminated the accusations they were forced to make against each other to terminate their marriages. In a no-fault divorce, there is no need to tender evidence

---

12   Lawrence Ganong and Marilyn J. Coleman, Eds., *The Social History of the American Family* 369 (2014).

13   Some of these are collected in Naomi Cahn's article, "Faithless Wives and Lazy Husbands: Gender Norms in Nineteenth Century Divorce Law," GW Law Faculty Publications & Other Works, Faculty Scholarship at Scholarly Commons (2002).

concerning adultery, intemperance, cruelty, impotency, and insanity. The parties can work together on custody and child support arrangements without first enduring nasty court proceedings.

Today, parties usually terminate their marriages with the aid of experienced divorce attorneys. Divorce attorneys counsel their clients on the best path forward, negotiate and draft their final agreements, and present them to family court judges. Family court judges review the agreements and if appropriate, enter judgments affirming them. If matters are too complex and no agreement is possible, family courts hold proceedings to work out financial and custodial matters. Judges conduct evidentiary hearings to obtain the correct information about joint and personal assets, the status of the children, and any potential challenges to resolution of the divorce proceeding. After gathering evidence and hearing from counsel, the court will work toward a fair and equitable division of assets and determine proper arrangements concerning the custody and support of children.

Children, Marriage, and the Family

In Roman times, a man exercised broad and absolute control over his children and grandchildren. It extended to deciding whether an infant born in the family should be allowed to live.[14]

Today, the government supports the legal rights of children as well as the legal rights of parents. Parents are required to maintain and nurture their children from the moment of birth until they become adults. It is illegal to neglect or abuse a child. Parents who harm their children may have their parental rights terminated and will likely find themselves subject to criminal prosecution.

Paternity and Adoption

Legal rules have evolved to support the rights of children and to safeguard their health and welfare. All states have passed statutes recognizing that children have the right to physical, mental, emotional, and financial support from their parents. These laws declare that the obligations arising from the parent-child relationship extend to both parents, no matter what their legal relationship is with each other. Parents are their children's legal guardians and are responsible for their health and safety.

Some laws reflect the common law tradition from which much of American law derives. For example, any child born to a married woman is presumed to be legitimate. Likewise, any child born before a parent's divorce is finalized is presumed to be legitimate. This **presumption of legitimacy** dates back to feudal times and remains a strong presumption. Historically, it could be rebutted only by proof that

---

14   This power is the *ius vitae necisque*, the right of life or death. *See* W.V. Harris, *The Roman Father's Power of Life and Death,* in Studies in Roman Law in Memory of A. Arthur Schiller (Bagnall and Harris, Eds., 1986). Some scholars, however, think that this right has been misinterpreted. *See* Brent D. Shaw, "Raising and Killing Children: Two Roman Myths," 54 *Mnemosyne* 31–77 (2001).

Harry Blackmun

Associate Justice, United States Supreme Court (1970–1994)

Supreme Court family law cases do not often make the news. Justice Blackmun, however, left an indelible mark on the jurisprudence of parental rights, childcare, and family planning.

In the area of parental rights, Justice Blackmun wrote for the Court in *Santosky v. Kramer*, 455 U.S. 745 (1982) when it determined that New York's evidentiary standard for terminating parental rights violated the Due Process Clause. He also wrote for the majority in *Stanton v. Stanton*, 421 U.S. 7 (1975), which struck down a Utah law that imposed differentiated definitions of adulthood for men and women.

But perhaps Justice Blackmun's lasting impact on family law comes from his writing of the Court's opinion in *Roe v. Wade*, 410 U.S. 113 (1973). After surveying a wide swath of history, spending a summer researching the medicine behind abortions and navigating the politically contentious topic, his decision garnered the votes of seven other justices. In *Roe*, the Court held that a woman's right to privacy protects her choice to terminate a pregnancy. The Court, however, found that this right is balanced against the government's broad interest in protecting the health of women and its interest in the "potentiality of human life."

FIGURE 12.3 Justice Harry Blackmun

a man was incapable of procreation or that he and his wife lived in separate locations during the time the child could have been conceived.

The English kingdom did not want children declared illegitimate for several reasons. First, an illegitimate child was deprived of the right of succession and inheritance and could well end up a **ward of the state**, which required the government to take care of their needs. In addition, the kingdom had an interest in promoting marriage and families, and facilitating lawsuits seeking to declare children illegitimate did not serve that interest. Finally, illegitimacy was viewed as a stigma that could blight lives.[15]

The presumption of legitimacy and the state's right to protect the family relationship remains a feature of American law. In 1989, the United States Supreme Court upheld a California law that created an irrebuttable presumption that a husband is the father of a child born into his family, even when blood tests showed he was not the father, and the child's mother had lived with the biological father.[16]

Although adoption is now a worldwide institution, it contradicted the customary English common law rules of inheritance. In fact, adoption was not legally permitted in Great Britain until 1926.[17] Adoption was also historically

---

15   Not only was an illegitimate person denied inheritance rights, but they were locked out of certain professions and denied pension benefits. This was true in the United States as late as the mid-twentieth century. In *Jung v. St. Paul Fire Dept. Relief Ass'n*, 27 N.W. 2d 151, 151–155 (Minn. 1947), a statute required pension benefits to be paid "when an active member of a relief association dies ... [and leaves] a child or children. ..." The Minnesota Supreme Court determined that the word *child* meant only a legitimate child, finding itself bound to follow "the harsh rule of the common law." *Id.* at 155. The father had made a written statement declaring himself to be the father of the child in question, but the Minnesota Supreme Court ruled that the declaration did not change the outcome. *See also* "Bastards—Illegitimate Child's Right to Pension Payable to 'Child' of Deceased Member of Beneficial Association," 5 *Wash. & Lee L. Rev.* 73 (1948).

16   *See Michael H. v. Gerald D.*, 491 U.S. 110, 110–163 (1989).

17   In 1926, the first Adoption of Children Act was passed that regulated adoption in England and Wales. Before then, adoption was usually secretly managed, and the adoptive parents had no legal rights. *See* Jenny Keating, *A Child For Keeps: The History of Adoption in England, 1918–45* (2008).

disfavored in civil law countries. Under the old Napoleonic Code, adoption was especially difficult: children were ineligible for adoption, adopters had to be over the age of 50, and they could have no children or legitimate descendants of their own. Further, adopters had to be older than the adopted person by at least fifteen years, and the adopted person must have been fostered for at least six years by the adopting party.[18] Adoptions of minors in the modern sense began in France in 1923, following amendments to the French Civil Code.

In contrast, the first United States legislation concerning adoption was passed in Massachusetts in 1851. This legislation required a judge to determine that the proposed adoptive parents had the means to bring up the child and that "it is fit and proper that such adoption take effect."[19] Every state now has laws that support and regulate adoption. They vary somewhat but usually provide that the adopting parent(s) must declare the desire to adopt and make a showing that they will be able to take care of the needs of the child. In addition, courts must usually find that the adoption will be in the best interests of the child.

Before children may be adopted, the rights of their biological parents should be legally terminated. There is a collection of particularly sad cases that revolve around this topic. Children have been ordered returned to biological parents after living for years with putative adoptive parents because biological parents' rights were not properly terminated.[20]

Most of the time, however, adoptions are not complicated. The parents stand up in court, formally acknowledge their responsibilities toward their new child, and the judge presiding over the adoption case issues the order of adoption.

Open and Closed Adoptions

The relationship between birth families and adoptive families is dictated by whether an adoption is deemed *open* or *closed*. Until the mid-1970s, nearly all adoptions were closed. In closed adoptions, the adoptive and birth families do not contact one another prior to or after the adoption. Typically, the adoptive family does not know the identity of the birth family, and vice versa. In these cases, adoption records are sealed so that adoptees cannot learn about their birth parents.

Courts have determined that unsealing adoption records may injure the rights of biological parents, adoptive parents, and even a state's interest in encouraging future adoptions. This reasoning was cited in the case *In re R.D.*, 876 N.W. 2d 786 (2016), in which the Supreme Court of Iowa affirmed a juvenile court's decision to deny the request of an adult adoptee to unseal her adoption records, despite her urgent desire to discover her family's health history.

The common practice of closed adoptions began to shift following public consumption of research that suggested that an alternative—open adoptions—would prove beneficial to children. Open adoptions, in which adoptive and birth parents maintain a level of communication prior to and after the adoption, now make up the majority of adoptions. The terms of open adoptions vary greatly, as both parties decide on the level of communication that they feel most comfortable with. Birth parents may also exercise control in finding a home for their child by selecting a family.

---

18   *See* French Civil Code, Book I, Title VIII, Chapter 1, Section I, Provisions 343–346.

19   The Adoption of Children Act of 1851, found in *Acts and Resolves Passed by the General Court of Massachusetts*, Chap. 324, (1851).

20   One example is *In Re Clausen*, 442 Mich. 648, 648–739 (1993), which involved a custody battle between the biological parents of a child and her would-be adoptive parents, with whom she lived for over two years.

Surrogacy

FIGURE 12.4 A surrogate mother

Surrogacy agreements, in which a woman consents to carry a child for another person, are still not regulated by any federal laws. Parties seeking these arrangements must look to state laws, which vary widely. Generally, states are considered "surrogacy friendly" if they have an existing legal framework that governs 1) the surrogacy agreement, a contract that establishes the responsibilities of the surrogate mother and intended parents; 2) the Pre-Birth Order, a court order that directs a hospital to list the name of the intended parents on the birth certificate rather than the surrogate mother; and 3) the Post-Birth Order, which determines the parentage of the baby after birth if a Pre-Birth order is not established.

These items are complicated by whether the surrogacy is traditional or gestational. Traditional surrogacies involve the surrogate's own egg. Gestational surrogacies do not, and so there is no biological relationship between the surrogate mother and the child. Many states do not address gestational surrogacies in their statutory law. In these states, birth orders are determined on a county-by-county basis. However, Illinois has a statute that dictates the process of gestational surrogacy from contract formation to birth certificate and is therefore considered more "surrogacy-friendly" than many other states.

The vast majority of adopted children fare very well with their new families.[21]

Children and Divorce

The United States Department of Justice reports that more than 1,000,000 children in the United States have been affected by divorce, and that half of all children born to married couples are likely to experience a divorce before their eighteenth birthday.[22] Marriages are legally terminated in family courts, and family courts also address the living and financial arrangements for children when couples divorce. This is vitally important work, and it requires not only the support of determined jurists but of well-crafted legislation.

The English common law, consistent with its patriarchal paradigm, initially required custody of all children to be granted to the father in the event of marital dissolution.[23] Over time, this doctrine was abandoned, especially for very young children, who still required care from their mothers. By the early twentieth century, with the rise of social welfare legislation, the courts began to think about which parent who could best serve the interests of the child on a daily basis. That parent would receive **physical custody**, which covers where a child will live and who will care for them. In addition, that parent (or both parents) would receive **legal custody** and have the right and obligation to make decisions about the child's upbringing, schooling, and health care.

Changes in society drove other changes in custody determinations. Mothers began to work outside the home in greater numbers, and fathers began to share household

---

21   According to one study, 85 percent of adopted children were reported to be in good health and doing well socially and emotionally. *See* Sharon Vandivere, Karin Malm, and Laura Radel, *Adoption USA, A Chartbook Based on the 2007 National Survey of Adoptive Parents*, by the U.S. Department of Health and Human Services.

22   *See Office of Juvenile Justice and Delinquency Prevention*, United States Department of Justice Juvenile Justice Bulletin 1 (2001).

23   For an interesting exploration of the roots of patriarchy and its effects, *see* Charis Kramarae and Dale Spender, *Routledge International Encyclopedia of Women* (2004).

FIGURE 12.5   A child with toys

duties. Accordingly, courts began to explore the question of child custody in a more nuanced way. Judges began to consider which parent would be more likely to allow the child frequent contact with the non-custodial parent. They began to inquire as to the physical, mental, and moral health of each parent and the quality of their emotional ties with their children. In addition, courts began to ask about the fitness of the custodial home and the ability of the parents to provide medical care and support their children's education. Even more recently, courts began to ask about children's preferences as to where and with whom they wished to live.

As these changes occurred, the courts began to issue orders of **joint custody**, in which both parents share responsibility for living arrangements and upbringing. Courts also introduced more novel arrangements, such as **shared parental responsibility**. Orders governing shared parental responsibility recognize that both parents have the obligation to rear their children. This requires them to work together. Although one parent may provide the primary physical residence of the child, both will retain parental rights and responsibilities. This means both parents will participate in decisions relating to education, health, and upbringing.

As the population has become more mobile, the courts have had to deal with a new problem: interstate child custody disputes. Parents have sometimes exploited the law to draw out litigation, obtain conflicting custody orders, and deny custody and visitation rights. In response, the National Conference of Commissioners on Uniform State Laws created the Uniform Child Custody Jurisdiction and Enforcement Act.[24] The purpose of the act is to avoid jurisdictional competition and conflict among courts. It requires any litigation concerning child custody to be adjudicated in the "home state" of the child, the state where the child lived within six months before child custody proceedings began.[25] The act also provides that,

---

24   This 1997 act has been adopted by 49 states, the District of Columbia, Guam, and the US Virgin Islands. Massachusetts is the only state that has not adopted the act. *See Id; Office of Juvenile Justice and Delinquency Prevention.*

25   If no state falls within that definition, the litigation will proceed where the child and at least one parent have significant connections and there is substantial evidence to support a determination of custody. *Id.*

if a child is in danger and needs immediate protection, a court in any state may take appropriate action to safeguard the child, including issuing an emergency order.[26] In addition, in 1980, Congress enacted the Parental Kidnapping Prevention Act[27] to help resolve jurisdictional problems in custody cases and discourage interstate child abductions. It requires courts to honor custody determinations issued by courts in other states or Tribes. It also authorizes emergency jurisdiction so that courts can help abandoned children, or children or their parents who are threatened with mistreatment.[28]

All states now have guidelines that describe how much financial support is to be given for housing, food, clothing, education, and medical care. Sadly, despite the entry of child support orders, timely payments might not be made. When this occurs, custodial parents return to court. Family court judges have various remedies that can be used to solve the problem. Defaulting parents can be found in contempt of court; their wages may be collected; and even criminal sanctions may be imposed. The Uniform Interstate Family Support Act[29] permits parents to compel assistance from those who might otherwise evade compliance by providing support across state lines. In addition, most jurisdictions also have Child Support Enforcement units in their state attorney's offices that can push cases forward where defaults in child support payments are serious or recurring.

Finally, the federal government has also offered support. In 1992, Congress passed the Child Support Recovery Act,[30] which provides that anyone who willfully fails to pay a support obligation for a child and who resides in another state may be guilty of a federal offense if the obligation is more than $5,000 or has been unpaid for a year. A person may be found in violation of the statute not only if they had the money and refused to tender it, but if they declined to accept gainful employment. United States attorneys prosecute these actions, and the Office of the Inspector General of Health and Human Services helps with investigations.

Domestic Violence, Child Abuse, and Child Neglect

Domestic violence is a depressingly widespread problem in the world today. The National Coalition Against Domestic Violence[31] provides sad statistics: in the United States, nearly twenty people a *minute* are physically abused by intimate partners, exceeding more than 10 million women and men each year.[32]

---

26   *See* The Uniform Child-Custody Jurisdiction and Enforcement Act, Articles 1, 2, and 3. Patricia M. Hoff, *The Uniform Child-Custody Jurisdiction and Enforcement Act*, Department of Justice Juvenile Justice Bulletin 4 (2001).

27   The Parental Kidnapping Prevention Act (PKPA), 28 U.S.C. §1738A (1980).

28   When a victim of domestic violence flees across state lines, PKPA provides that a court in the refuge state may issue protective orders if a parent or sibling has been abused or threatened. *Id.*

29   The Uniform Interstate Family Support Act was first drafted in 1992 and reviewed in 1996 and 2001. It was most recently amended in 2008. Every state has now adopted a version of it.

30   The Child Support Recovery Act of 1992, 18 U.S.C. §228 (1992).

31   The National Coalition Against Domestic Violence (NCADV) is a 501(c)(3) nonprofit organization founded in 1978 to support and advocate for victims of domestic violence. The National Coalition Against Domestic Violence, https://ncadv.org/about-us.

32   *See National Statistics*, the National Coalition Against Domestic Violence, https://ncadv.org/statistics.

These numbers are appalling, and the economic impact is staggering: victims of intimate partner violence collectively lose millions of days of paid work each year.[33]

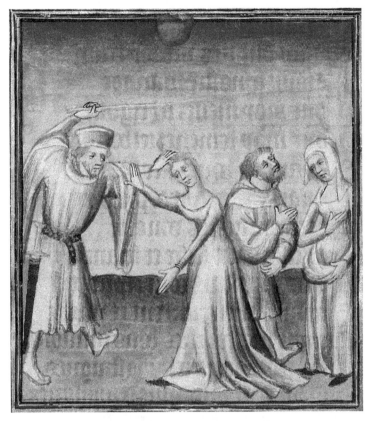

FIGURE 12.6   A medieval husband beating his wife

Domestic violence includes not only physical violence but also behavior patterns through which an abuser gains control of their victim. In addition to physical abuse, abusers often commit psychological and emotional abuse. These include threats, isolation, humiliation, and deprivation of food, money, and other needed resources. The goal of the abuser is to deprive the victim of agency and control, and abusers use the means most likely to achieve that end.[34]

Children, too, suffer from emotional and physical abuse in the United States, and from neglect when their parents or others fail to properly tend to their needs. The terms "abuse" and "neglect" are defined by statute in each state. Generally, an **abused child** is a child who suffers death, disfigurement, impairment

---

33   *See* E.F. Rothman et al., *How Employment Helps Female Victims of Intimate Partner Violence: A Qualitative Study,* 12 J. *Occupational Health Psych.,* 136, 136–143 (2007).

34   When victims of domestic violence decide to leave, they begin a perilous journey. They are exercising autonomy, and many batterers react violently in response. This is called "separation assault." When a victim leaves a batterer, their risk of death increases sixfold. Jennifer Hardesty, "Separation Assault in the Context of Post-divorce Parenting," 8 *Violence Against Women* 601 (2002).

of physical or emotional health, or loss or impairment of any bodily function. This includes excessive corporal punishment, torture, and female genital mutilation. A **neglected child** is a child who has not received the proper or necessary nourishment or medically indicated treatment or remedial care for their child's well-being, including adequate food, clothing, and shelter. A child may also be abused or neglected if the child's blood, urine, or feces contain any amount of a controlled substance. Further, those who have the responsibility to care for a child commit **child abandonment** when they leave a child under a certain age alone without proper supervision for a certain amount of time.[35] The United States Administration for Children & Families found that about 678,000 children[36] were victims of abuse and neglect in 2018.[37] This is a dire statistic, particularly as the actual number is likely significantly underreported.[38]

Child sexual abuse is a form of child abuse that occurs when an older adolescent or adult uses a child for sexual stimulation. Its legacy can result in chronic and complex trauma in the child. Every state has passed laws making the sexual abuse of children illegal, and incest is a criminal offense. Although minors cannot give legal consent to sexual acts, many states have passed laws creating exceptions that lower the legal age for consent for sexual acts to sixteen or seventeen years of age.[39] Criminal penalties for child sexual abuse depend upon the nature of the offenses committed but may include imprisonment, registration as a sex offender, and loss of custody or parental rights.

The best way to stop all types of child abuse is to bring its occurrence to the attention of law enforcement agencies. Accordingly, states have passed legislation requiring people whose jobs bring them into regular contact with children to report instances of suspected child abuse. A child's teacher, medical care provider, daycare worker, or social worker is a **mandatory reporter**. If they suspect that a child has been abused, they are required to report that abuse, and their failure to do so violates the law. As long as the report is made in good faith, the reporter has immunity if it turns out that they were wrong. Other people can also report, and most state laws encourage persons other than mandatory reporters to reach out if they believe that abuse or neglect has occurred. Thus, a neighbor or family friend is a **permissive reporter**.

When abuse and neglect come to the attention of the state, intervention is required. When law enforcement personnel learn of suspected abuse or neglect, they refer the case to a state social agency who will investigate, and if appropriate, commence child protective proceedings. Family courts will then

---

35   In many states, that age is thirteen and that amount of time is twenty-four hours. For example, *See* Illinois code on Child Abandonment, 720 ILCS 5/12C-10.

36   In 2018, according to statistics from the United States government, there were about 73 million children living in the United States. *See* childstats.gov.

37   National annual child abuse statistics are cited from U.S. Administration for Children & Families, Child Maltreatment 2018. This data, released annually, is the most current federal data available. *See Child Maltreatment*, Children's Bureau: An Office of the Administration for Children and Families, https://www.acf.hhs.gov/cb/research-data-technology/statistics-research/child-maltreatment

38   Donileen Loseke et al., *Current Controversies on Family Violence* 300 (2005).

39   The most common age for consent for heterosexual sex is sixteen years. In Illinois, the age is seventeen years, and in California it is eighteen years. *Age of Consent by State 2020*, World Population Review, https://worldpopulationreview.com/state-rankings/age-of-consent-by-state.

issue the orders necessary to secure the safety of affected children. One of the most important jobs of courts across the nation is to intervene to ensure the safety of the most vulnerable members of our society.

Conclusion and Introduction to Law Lab

Family Law has a broad sweep. It swings from the happy laws establishing legal marriages to the necessary laws requiring people who work with children to report suspected child abuse. At its core are the rights of couples, parents, and children.

As we noted in Chapter 7, the United States Constitution's Due Process Clause supports the rights of parents to bring up their children as they wish. This right includes raising children under the parents' chosen religious faith.

This week's Law Lab asks you to consider the plight of children living with parents who will not seek necessary medical treatment due to their religious faith. Courts of the nation can issue emergency orders to preserve the health and safety of children when their parents fail to meet their legal responsibilities, including their medical needs. Courts can only do so, however, when people with the authority to act are made aware of situations that require intervention.

As law clerks working with the General Assembly of the State of Franklin, you are tasked with shaping legislation that will support reporting by those who encounter seriously ill children in this situation. It is hoped that this legislation will give people who find children in distress the tools that they need— and the confidence required—to reach out and report. Your work is important; the General Assembly believes that this legislation could save lives.

Lawmaking Law Lab

MEMORANDUM

To: Law Clerks of the General Assembly of the State of Franklin

From: The State of Franklin General Assembly Committee on Health; and also from the Subcommittee on Children and Families

Re: *New Legislation for the Promotion of Child Health and Welfare*

Sadly, in Franklin and in other states, children have died because their parents failed to seek timely medical care due to their personal religious beliefs. Accordingly, the General Assembly is considering new Good Samaritan legislation that will empower and protect people who act to support the health of children against their parents' religious beliefs. Members of the General Assembly Committee on Health would like to receive your recommendation as to how the new legislation should best be framed.

This memorandum will provide background information concerning state and federal law protecting the exercise of religion in the context of child health care. It also notes certain issues that other lawmakers have addressed when drafting similar legislation.

Introduction

Many sick or injured children in the United States have died because their parents did not seek medical attention due to their personal religious beliefs. This is contrary to the ruling of the United States Supreme Court, which has found that the Free Exercise Clause of the First Amendment does not permit parents to make religious choices that damage the health of their children. As their legal guardians, parents are charged with supporting their children's health and well-being, and every state has laws requiring parents to provide their children with appropriate medical care when they are ill.

Notwithstanding the Supreme Court's ruling and state laws addressing parental obligations, federal and state religious exemption laws provide parents (or legal guardians) with immunity from prosecution if their dependent children are harmed because of religious choices.

Supreme Court Decisions and Federal Law

In *Reynolds v. United States*, 98 U.S. 145 (1879), the Supreme Court addressed the question of whether a religious belief takes precedence over a generally applicable law. The Court upheld federal antipolygamy laws that conflicted with religious beliefs, finding that Congress could not intrude into the areas of speech or opinion, but that legislation could "reach actions which were in violation of social duties or good order."[1] This doctrine remains essentially unchanged today.

In *Prince v. Massachusetts*, 321 U.S. 158 (1949), the Court extended the ruling in *Reynolds* to include the well-being of children. The Court determined that the nation has an interest in safeguarding children's welfare, and the state has the authority to achieve that goal. *Wisconsin v. Yoder*, 406 U.S. 205 (1972), decided two decades later, did not change this determination. The Court in *Yoder* found that permitting Amish children to stop attending high school at the age of sixteen did not, in fact, harm them. In *Employment Division Department of Human Resources of Oregon v. Smith*, 494 U.S. 872 (1990), the Court found that religious figures are not entitled to religious exemptions from general laws. Justice Scalia wrote that such religious exemptions would make each citizen "a law unto himself."[2]

FIGURE 12.7 Children deserve support

---

1   *Reynolds*, 98 U.S. at 169.
2   *Employment Division*, 494 U.S. at 879, quoting *Reynolds v. United States*, 98 U.S. 145 at 166 (1879).

Despite these rulings, when Congress enacted the Child Abuse Prevention and Treatment Act ("the Act") in 1974, it included a provision exempting parents from civil and criminal prosecution if they did not provide children with needed medical care because of their religious beliefs.[3] Critically, the Act stipulates that to qualify for federal funds to fight child abuse, a state must include a similar religious exemption to its child welfare laws. Federal power thus tips in favor of parents who deny children medical care due to religious beliefs.

State Law and Child Outcomes

Nearly all states have religious exemptions from preventive and diagnostic measures, such as immunizations, metabolic testing, blood lead-level tests, newborn hearing tests, and other screenings.[4] However, statutory religious exemptions for the medical care of sick children vary greatly. Some states permit parents and guardians to rely only upon prayer in cases of trivial, self-limiting illnesses. Other states have broad laws that, in effect, permit parents to withhold life-saving medical care from children who are desperately ill without facing any consequences.[5] In Idaho, a collection of children have died due to the absence of medical care.[6]

The story of Clayton Scott Zimmern, age nine, is particularly troubling. He died in Park Forest South, Illinois, of injuries sustained when he was struck by a car while riding his bicycle. Following the accident, the driver of the car immediately called the police. By the time they arrived, Mr. Zimmern had taken his son home, and he told police that his son did not require medical attention based upon his religious beliefs. He repeated this when police called him later that evening. When Mr. Zimmern finally did call the police to his house, the boy had died.[7] Sadly, the true number of children like Clayton is impossible to determine due to problems in reporting and in cause-of-death assessments.[8]

---

3   The Christian Science church lobbied to include this provision.

4   For example, as promoted via Senate Bill 1410, Illinois supports exemptions from vaccinations for religious reasons. However, parents who want to cite religious belief as a reason not to vaccinate must complete a Certificate of Religious Exemption and have it signed by a health care provider. *States with Religious and Philosophical Exemptions From School Immunization Requirements*, National Conference of State Legislatures, https://www.ncsl.org/research/health/school-immunization-exemption-state-laws.aspx.

5   Section 18-1501 of Chapter 15 (Children and Vulnerable Adults) of Idaho's Crimes & Punishments statutes states: "Any person who willfully causes or permits a child to be placed in a situation that its person or health is endangered could spend 10 years in prison." But it also says: "Prayer or spiritual means alone shall not for that reason alone be construed to have violated the duty of care to the child." Brian Morrin, "Idaho Laws Protect Faith Healing Even When Children Die," *Idaho News* (Nov. 25, 2013), https://idahonews.com/news/truth-squad/idaho-laws-protect-faith-healing-even-when-children-die.

6   These children include Arrian Granden, aged fifteen, who died in 2012 after days of nausea and vomiting due to food poisoning. Micah Eells, four days old, died in 2013 of a bowel obstruction. Pamela Eells, aged sixteen, died in 2011 of untreated pneumonia. Stephen Hughes, aged four, also died of pneumonia. He was born with spina bifida and never saw a doctor. Cooper Shippy, nearly two, died in 2010 of untreated diabetes. The total number of such children is not known. *See Child Abuse in Idaho: Deadly and Legal*, Idaho Children, http://idahochildren.org/articles/a-few-of-the-children/.

7   Clayton is included in one list of child fatalities due to religious beliefs, found here: https://www.masskids.org/index.php/religious-medical-neglect/cases-of-child-deaths.

8   One county coroner in Idaho conceded she does not autopsy the children of faith healers who die without medical care. Further, public officials take no action about these deaths; charges are not filed. Garna Mejia, "Tammy Daybell Investigation: Idaho Law Allowed Her Burial Without Autopsy," *East Idaho News* (June 23, 2020).

Legislative Considerations

Religious exemptions can discriminate against children, violate their human rights, and deprive them of protections the state extends to others. Lawmakers have discussed repealing religious exemptions in childcare laws. However, no state legislature can repeal a federal act. Further (and perversely), due to provisions in the Act, erasing existing exemptions in state law may also eliminate funding to help stop child abuse.

Some states have decided that, as a first step, legislation should be enacted to protect those who intervene to provide health care to children who otherwise would not receive care due to their parents' or guardians' religious beliefs.[9] The General Assembly believes that such Good Samaritan legislation would benefit children in Franklin.

Several facets to this new legislation need particular attention. First is the question of **who should receive legal protection**. Should the new legislation be broadly drawn and include any adult who comes within the orbit of a child in need of medical care? Should it be narrowly drawn and include only health care workers? What about including teachers and social workers? Cafeteria and food service employees? Neighbors? Members of the child's extended family?

Second, the legislation must clearly define **which actions will be protected**. The broadest language would extend protection to those who take actions reasonably necessary to provide medical care. Narrower language would extend protection only to emergency medical care required to save a child's life following an accident.

Finally, the legislation should specify **the type of protection that is to be offered**. Should it extend total immunity from all lawsuits that could be brought by the child's parents or legal guardians? Or should it be restricted and extend immunity only under certain circumstances? If so, how should those circumstances be defined? Most state laws protect those who, in good faith, file a report based upon *reasonable* suspicion. If reporting is done for reasons other than concern for a child, or if there is no reasonable basis to think that any neglect has occurred, there would be no legal protection. Thus, if someone files a report just to create trouble for someone else, they could be sued.

Alternatively, a law could say that legal protection will be extended if the person making the report *subjectively* believes that neglect is occurring. This means that, even if it was not reasonable to think that a child was being neglected, the reporter will be protected if they honestly thought neglect was occurring. This option would increase the protection reporting persons receive and likely encourage more reports of neglect. It would also increase the likelihood of false reports, and it might also shield some persons who filed a report for malicious reasons.

We look forward to receiving your recommendations.

---

9   The General Assembly understands that this legislation may intrude upon the parents' constitutional rights. However, the lawmakers would like to proceed and have the issue go to the courts for review.

CHAPTER 13

Criminal Law

To ignore evil is to become an accomplice to it.

—Martin Luther King Jr. (1929–1968) at Hearings Before the Subcommittee
on Executive Reorganization of the Committee on Government Operations,
United States Senate, Eighty-Ninth Congress, Section Session, December 15,
1966

Introduction

We have now traveled some distance in our journey across the legal landscape.

We began with a review of the ancient legal codes and then turned to the rise of the English common law. We explored the creation and purpose of the Constitution of the United States, reviewed the different structures of the state and federal governments that it established, and considered the responsibilities it endowed to the different branches of government. We then focused on key constitutional rights, such as free speech, religious freedom, and equal protection, and considered how those rights have evolved over time. Our review of Constitutional Law introduced us to the realm of **public law**, which concerns the relationship between the government and the people.[1]

We then turned to Property Law, Contract Law, Tort Law, and Family Law, all areas of **private law**. Private law addresses the relationships between private persons and entities. When conflicts in the private law arena result in litigation, one person or entity sues another without the involvement of the government's representatives.

In this chapter and in the two following chapters, we return to public law. Criminal Law is public law, and criminal defendants are accountable to the community for their crimes. Criminals are prosecuted by society's designated representatives rather than by the persons who have been harmed.

---

1   Public law divides readily into three categories. The first is the work of governmental entities, such as the three branches of federal and state governments. The second concerns the relationships between the government and private persons or entities and includes the law defining the scope of governmental interference in private endeavors. The third category is the relationships among private persons or entities where they involve matters of governmental concern. In this last category, we find the parts of Constitutional Law that address the rights of individuals to receive services at places of public accommodation under the Equal Protection Clause.

The English common law viewed crimes as offenses against the king's law and order, and criminal cases were prosecuted on the king's behalf. For example, one famous English cannibalism case was styled *Her Majesty The Queen v. Tom Dudley and Edwin Stephens*.[2] Today's English prosecutors continue to pursue cases in the name of the Crown, and the cases are denominated *R* [for *Rex* or *Regina*] *versus* [*Defendant*].

The United States, however, is a federal republic, and its citizens are its sovereigns. Accordingly, criminal cases are brought on behalf of the people (in state court) and on behalf of the United States (in federal court). The Illinois case against serial killer John Wayne Gacy was styled *People of the State of Illinois v. John Wayne Gacy*.[3] However, the lawsuit brought against the murderer of Chinese scholar Yingying Zhang was filed in federal court and was therefore entitled *United States of America v. Brendt A. Christensen*.[4]

Tribal courts similarly acknowledge that crimes are offenses against the Tribal community and prosecute criminal litigation on behalf of members of the Tribe. Thus, a criminal case against a Navajo committed on Tribal lands is styled *Navajo Nation v.* [*Defendant*].

Whether state, federal, or Tribal, crimes are offenses against society. As a result, the victims of crimes stand in the role of witnesses. The prosecution may call victims to court, even though they may not wish to testify.[5]

As state and federal criminal laws run to hundreds of thousands of pages, this chapter offers a very broad overview. The chapter begins by noting the sources of American Criminal Law. It then reviews the differing mental states that support distinct levels of criminal culpability. The chapter then turns to specific crimes, beginning with crimes against persons, such as murder and assault. It thereafter focuses on crimes against property, vice crimes, crimes that violate the public order, and environmental crimes. In the following chapters, we review the procedural law involved in prosecuting and punishing crimes. We also consider several of the important and controversial issues that trouble America's criminal justice system today.

Finally, in this week's Law Lab, you will step into a new role. While serving as state's attorneys for Liberty Springs, you and your colleagues must decide whether to prosecute the parents of a boy who died

---

2   *Her Majesty the Queen v. Tom Dudley and Edwin Stephens*, (1884) QBD 273 DC, concerned survival cannibalism following a shipwreck. It established the legal precedent that you cannot kill and eat someone to avoid starvation and then plead necessity as a defense to the subsequent murder charge. Queen Victoria was on the throne when this case was prosecuted; she is "the Queen" referenced in the complaint.

3   John Wayne Gacy was a prolific serial killer convicted of murdering thirty-three young men in 1980. He was executed by lethal injection in 1994.

4   Yingying Zhang was a Chinese national studying at the University of Illinois. Christensen kidnapped, assaulted, and murdered her. On July 18, 2019, Christensen was sentenced life in prison without the possibility of parole. *See United States of America v. Christensen*, Case No. 17-cr-20037-JES-JEH.

5   The National Conference of Commissioners on Uniform State Laws drafted the Model Victims of Crime Act, which provides some rights to victims of crimes. These include the right to appear in proceedings regarding the sentencings of those who committed crimes against them. The Model Act also supported the creation of a fund to provide some money to the victims of certain crimes. All states have passed legislation that seeks to give victims a role in criminal proceedings, recognizing that they should have a voice in cases arising from harm they have endured. *See* Harvey S. Perlman and Josephine R. Potuto, "The Uniform Law Commissioners' Model Sentencing and Corrections Act: An Overview," 58 *Neb. L. Rev.* 925, 925–964 (1979).

due to their failure to obtain medical care. You have broad discretion to decide whether to prosecute, and as an agent of the State of Franklin, it is your duty to exercise that discretion properly.

KEY TERMS FOR CRIMINAL LAW

The following key terms are defined in this chapter. They are also defined in the Glossary.

Actus Reus	Cyberstalking	Kidnapping	Sex Trafficking
Arson	Disorderly Conduct	Larceny	Sexual Battery
Assault	Doctrine of the Public Trust	Looting	Solicitation
Attempt	Drug and Alcohol Offenses	Manslaughter	Stalking
Bad Check Laws	Embezzlement	*Mens Rea*	Statutory Rape
Battery	Extortion	Misdemeanor	Theft
Burglary	Felony	Murder	Unlawful Assembly
Child Abuse and Neglect	Felony Murder	Organized Crime	Vandalism
Conspiracy	Forgery	Private Law	Vice Crime
Corporate Crime	Homicide	Prostitution	White-Collar Crime
Credit Card Fraud	Identity Theft	Public Law	
Crime of Fraud	Illegal Gambling	Rioting	
Criminal Harassment	Inchoate Crime	Robbery	

Criminal Law in the United States

When British rule ended, each colony established public prosecutors to charge and try those who violated the law. County attorneys were responsible for state law violations, and town prosecutors addressed ordinance violations. In addition, United States attorneys were appointed by the president to prosecute federal crimes in each district. In 1861, Congress gave the United States attorney general the authority to supervise the work of the United States attorneys. There are now 94 United States attorneys, one for each of the federal judicial districts.

Like other branches of law, American criminal law largely comes from the English common law. State legislatures enacted statutes that broadly adopted the common law definitions of crimes. Over the years, however, the states' criminal statutes drifted apart, leading to inconsistencies. To support the standardization of American penal law, after ten years of effort, the American Law Institute[6] published its Model

---

6   The American Law Institute was founded in 1923, and its members include law professors, attorneys, judges, and other legal professionals. The ALI's headquarters are in Philadelphia, Pennsylvania.

Penal Code. The Model Penal Code is a comprehensive criminal code, and two-thirds of the states have enacted statutes that borrow from its provisions. Legal professionals regularly use it to guide their work in interpreting criminal regulations.[7]

At the outset, the federal government stepped in a different direction from the states. It did not adopt the common law definitions of criminal offenses. Instead, Congress passed federal statutes to define the actions that would constitute federal crimes. Federal criminal laws address immigration, naturalization, military service, crimes that cross state lines, and federal civil rights violations. Federal offenses include mail fraud, carjacking, kidnapping, bank robbery, child pornography, identity theft, counterfeiting, and tax evasion. Federal law also addresses organized crime, and the important Racketeer Influenced and Corrupt Organizations (RICO) Act allows leaders of criminal syndicates to be tried for crimes that others commit on their behalf.

Elements of Crimes

The old Latin legal saying *actus non facit reum nisi mens sit rea* means that, for an action to be illegal, it must be done with a guilty mind. This aphorism captures the two components that are required for most crimes: 1) a voluntary illegal physical act, called the **actus reus**; and 2) the requisite mental state, called the **mens rea**. Our system of criminal justice is based upon the notion that individuals are responsible for what they do, and when their actions harm others, they should be held accountable. To justify imposing punishments on persons convicted of most crimes, their actions must be both voluntary and knowing. The government has the burden of proving, beyond a reasonable doubt, that the defendant committed the charged crime with the requisite criminal intent.

Actus Reus, *the Voluntary Act*

The *actus reus* requirement means that a person accused of committing a criminal act must have been acting of their own volition. The Model Penal Code states that, to qualify as a voluntary act, the bodily movement constituting the crime must result from "the effort or determination of the actor, either conscious or habitual."[8] Any type of voluntary physical behavior can support this element, from a computer keystroke to a jerk of a steering wheel. The focus is on voluntariness; involuntary movements will not support criminal liability. Accordingly, someone enduring a convulsion or epileptic seizure will not be held responsible for any

---

7   *See* Paul Robinson and Michael Cahill, "Can a Model Penal Code Second Save the States from Themselves?," 1 *Ohio St. J. Crim.* L 169, 169–177 (2003).

8   Model Penal Code, Section 2.01(2)(d) (Am. Law Inst., Proposed Official Draft 1962).

resulting harm.[9] Courts have found that this is also true of sleepwalkers acting without conscious intent.

In addition, if a person had a duty to act, the failure to act will also serve as the *actus reus*. For example, if a parent sees their child badly injured and fails to procure medical assistance, that omission can result in criminal charges. Or, if a person has a duty to file a tax return but fails to do so, that failure will support the government's case. Further, if a person had a duty to slow down at a school crossing and did not, that, too, will support criminal charges. The Model Penal Code notes that for liability to be based upon an omission to act, there must be a law defining the offense, or the duty to perform the omitted action must be otherwise legally recognized.[10]

Mens Rea, *the State of Mind*

The second element, *mens rea*, is more challenging to define. Different crimes require different mental states, and statutes have not always clearly explained what must be proven for each crime. To clarify matters, the Model Penal Code settled on four different terms describing different states of mind, and most of the states adopted them. They are 1) purposely; 2) knowingly; 3) recklessly; and 4) negligently. These different mental states correlate with different levels of moral guilt and therefore with different degrees of criminal culpability. They also require different evidentiary proofs to achieve a conviction, although the intent may be inferred from the circumstances surrounding the crime.

Purposeful behavior is the most culpable mental state. It means that the person not only had the intent to complete the criminal act but that they also intended its result.

The Murderous Sleepwalker

FIGURE 13.1 Restless slumber

The Canadian Supreme Court case *Her Majesty the Queen v. Kenneth James Parks*, 2 S.C.R. 87 (1992), is a key decision on the application of the automatism (sleepwalking) defense.

Kenneth Parks drove to his in-laws' house and used a tire iron to kill his mother-in-law. Thereafter, he tried to choke his father-in-law to death. He then drove to a nearby police station and declared to law enforcement personnel, "I think I have just killed two people." Parks was acquitted based upon a physician's evidence that he had a sleep disorder and was sleepwalking at the time of the homicide. The Canadian Supreme Court upheld the acquittal, finding that the evidence presented a reasonable doubt that Parks had acted voluntarily.

---

9   There have been exceptions. If a person knew that they were subject to seizures and drove a vehicle anyway, they could be found liable for the resulting harm. *See* Ronald P. Smith, "Criminal Law—Criminal Responsibility of Epileptic Driver Who Causes Death When Stricken With Sudden Epileptic 'Blackout,'" 32 *Notre Dame L. Rev.* 688, 698 (1957).

10   Model Penal Code, Section 2.01 (3).

If I take a gun, drive to someone's house, and shoot them, then my action was purposeful: I intended to shoot my gun, and I intended that they be harmed. Similarly, if I see someone I loathe and deliberately run them down, I acted purposely; I meant to run them over, hoping that they would be harmed.

Knowing behavior is a small step down in moral culpability. It means that the person who committed the crime intended both the criminal action as well as its *probable* consequences. The defendant acted with the awareness that when they engaged in the conduct, the harm was quite likely to occur.[11] Knowing behavior differs from purposeful behavior only in the degree of certainly of the resulting harm. If I see a group of people at a large street demonstration and drive my car into the crowd, I acted knowingly: I was practically certain that someone would be badly harmed.

Reckless behavior is yet another step down the continuum. Crimes involving reckless intent are not as common as crimes involving purposeful or knowing conduct. A defendant is criminally reckless if they engaged in the prohibited action and consciously disregarded a substantial and unjustifiable risk that the harm would occur. Note that there are three parts to this definition: 1) the defendant completed the criminal act; 2) the defendant consciously disregarded the potential for harm; and 3) the risk of harm was unjustified.[12] If I drive my car through a school crosswalk because I want to scare children, I engage in reckless behavior. I consciously disregarded the risk of harm, and my action was unjustifiable, as there was no reason to speed through the crosswalk.

Finally, we reach negligent criminal behavior. This is a less culpable state of mind, and negligent intent crimes are much less common. Defendants committing crimes with negligent intent are unaware of the "substantial and unjustifiable risk" that their actions pose, even though a reasonable person would be aware of the risk.[13] Someone who quickly shoots a firearm at movement in the forest during deer hunting season and ends up killing another hunter may be criminally negligent. A reasonable person would be sure that they were shooting at game rather than another person before they discharged their weapon. If a state statute permitted a charge of homicide based upon negligent intent, the hunter could be found guilty.

Criminal Liability Without Mens Rea

There are some criminal offenses that do not require a *mens rea* element. In such cases, the government must only establish that the defendant engaged in the behavior. It does not matter what the defendant was thinking at the time, and so no proof regarding state of mind is needed to establish guilt. **Statutory rape** (sexual relations with an underage person) is one such offense. It does not matter how old the

---

11   *See* Model Penal Code Section 2.02(2) (Am. Law Inst., Proposed Official Draft 1962).

12   The Model Penal Code requires that the risk be "of such a nature and degree that ... its disregard involves a gross deviation from the standard of conduct that a law-abiding person would observe in the actor's situation." *See* Model Penal Code Section 2.02(2)(c) (Am. Law Inst., Proposed Official Draft 1962).

13   *See* Model Penal Code Section 2.02(2)(d) (Am. Law Inst., Proposed Official Draft 1962).

person looked, or how old they said they were, or how old the defendant thought they were. If a person was underage and the defendant had sexual relations with them, the defendant committed the crime.[14]

Some economic regulations and public health and safety laws also may not require *mens rea*. If you fail to pay your taxes on time, if you drive while intoxicated, if you pollute a waterway, your intent usually does not matter. Requiring the government to show intent in such cases would make the laws unenforceable. Instead, the law imposes strict liability for these crimes, and must only prove that you committed them.

Types of Crimes

In the following sections, we will survey different types of crimes, as they are generally defined in the United States.[15] Before we begin, however, we should note that our society's ideas about permitted and illegal behavior have evolved substantially since the nation's founding. This is particularly true in the area of social regulations. In Chapter 5, we saw that same-sex relations used to be subject to criminal penalties and that Jim Crow laws made it illegal for Black individuals to use the same public conveyances and accommodations as whites. Today, racial segregation in education is illegal and same-sex marriage is legal. In addition, we have laws that prohibit discrimination against students based upon sexual orientation and gender identity, as well as regulations that protect students from cyberbullying.[16]

Health and safety regulations have also shifted. We have come to understand how certain products adversely affect public health and welfare, and we have passed regulations that limit their use. In addition, as new products and technologies have developed, the law has responded to the threats presented by their abuse. Many states and municipalities have banned tobacco smoking in enclosed areas,[17] and minors may not purchase alcohol.[18] Using a cell phone while driving[19] is also a crime in many states. Further, as we develop safeguards to protect public health, we have implemented laws supporting their

---

14   There are good reasons for this policy. We want to keep minors from enduring a "what did you say about your age" inquiry. If a person could say that the minor told them that they were of legal age to avoid conviction, then pressure would frequently be brought to bear on the minor to say just that. Minors should not be responsible for dealing with adults who know how to take advantage of them and then avoid the consequences.

15   Note that the definitions of state crimes vary state to state, as does the terminology that defines them. This survey presents general definitions and terms.

16   All fifty states have passed anti-bullying legislation. An Illinois anti-bullying statute requires that all school districts, charter schools, and nonpublic, nonsectarian elementary or secondary schools implement a policy on bullying. The policy must include a detailed procedure for reporting, investigating, and parental contact following an incident. The policies must also encourage restorative measures, and the district or school is required to provide the victim with information regarding counseling and support services. 105 ILCS 5/27-23.7.

17   Since January 1, 1995, smoking has been prohibited in all enclosed workspaces in California. In Illinois, the Smoke Free Illinois Act (effective January 1, 2008) bans smoking in all enclosed workspaces, including restaurants and bars. 410 ILCS 82/1. By contrast, Texas has no statewide ban, but many municipalities (including Houston, Austin, and Fort Worth) have enacted smoking bans in workspaces, including bars and restaurants. Aman Batheja, "As Statewide Smoking Ban Burns Out in Capitol, Cities Go it Alone," *Texas Tribune* (Dec. 19, 2014).

18   The National Minimum Drinking Age Act (passed in 1984) set the minimum legal age to purchase alcohol as twenty-one. 23 U.S.C. § 158.

19   Texting while driving is illegal in most states. In 2010, the United States Department of Transportation's Federal Motor Carrier Safety Administration implemented a rule that prohibits truckers from texting while driving. *See* 75 Fed. Reg. 59118 (proposed Sept. 27, 2010).

Fatou Bensouda

Chief Prosecutor of the International Criminal Court (2012–present)

FIGURE 13.2 Chief Prosecutor Fatou Bensouda

Fatou Bensouda has served as the chief prosecutor for the International Criminal Court since 2012. The International Criminal Court (ICC) is a permanent international court established to bring to justice individuals who are not prosecuted by their home countries and who have been accused of the most serious crimes. These include crimes against humanity, genocide, war crimes and other crimes of aggression. To have jurisdiction over an individual, the ICC prosecutor must prove the individual has committed crimes in a country that is party to the Rome Statute, which established the ICC, and that the United Nations' Security Council has recommended the case to the ICC. The United States is not a party to the Rome Statute.

After Ms. Bensouda began considering an investigation into war crimes by US troops in Afghanistan, President Donald Trump threatened the court with sanctions. However, the prosecutor remained firm in her commitment to seek the truth, decrying interference "with the rule of law and court's judicial proceedings."

use. Federal law requires people to wear hard hats on certain construction sites, and failing to wear a seat belt is against the law in many states.

Finally, our ideas about illegal behavior in the environmental sphere have also changed. Over the past fifty years, we have come to recognize that clean air and pure water are resources that we must protect. We now have regulations that criminalize polluting and require the remediation of contaminated properties.[20]

As we review different categories of illegal actions, we will consider both traditional crimes and some of the newer crimes that have been identified. We begin with incomplete crimes: crimes that were intended but not accomplished.

Inchoate Crimes

An **inchoate crime** is committed when a person takes a punishable step toward an illegal act. Not every step toward an illegal act is punishable: purchasing a handgun is not a punishable act, but taking that handgun to someone's home to shoot them is punishable, even if you are stopped from pulling the trigger. Offering someone else's child an ice cream is not a punishable act (although children should not take food from strangers). However, offering another person's child an ice cream to lure them into your vehicle is a punishable offense. Trying to abduct a child is a crime, and the law will prosecute a person for simply beginning to undertake it.

Solicitation and **conspiracy** are common inchoate crimes. The crime of solicitation consists of commanding, encouraging, or requesting another person to commit a

---

20   The key federal environmental regulations were passed between 1960 and the early 1980s. These include the Clean Air Act of 1963 (42 U.S.C. § 7401); the 1972 Clean Water Act (33 U.S.C. §§ 1251–1387), officially called the Federal Water Pollution Control Act; and the 1980 Comprehensive Environmental Response, Compensation, and Liability Act (42 USC §§ 9601, *et. seq.*) also known as CERCLA, or the federal Superfund law.

crime. A conspiracy consists of two or more people agreeing to commit a crime.

The most frequently charged inchoate crime is **attempt**. Generally, any crime a person can be charged with if completed will also support a charge of attempt. A person can be charged with the attempt to commit a robbery; the attempt to commit arson; and the attempt to commit an assault. A person can also be charged with the attempt to commit murder.

To sustain a charge of criminal attempt, the government must prove that the defendant had the required intent (*mens rea*) to commit the crime. For example, to sustain the charge of attempted first-degree murder, the defendant must be shown to have acted purposely or knowingly. The government must also prove that the defendant took steps to complete the crime. This requirement ensures that we are not simply punishing people for their thoughts. In some jurisdictions, if a defendant took steps but then canceled their plans, they may raise the fact that they abandoned the endeavor as a defense. The public policy reason for this is clear: we want to encourage people to stop before they complete a crime. In addition, we want would-be criminals to know that if they abandon their effort before harm is done, they have a viable defense to offer in court.

Offenses Against Persons

In the public mind, the most compelling and notorious crimes are those committed against persons. Since the 1950s, popular televisions programs such as *Dragnet*, *Columbo*, *CSI*, and *Criminal Minds* have featured law enforcement officers and lawyers who bring to justice those who kidnap, kill, and assault others.

Crimes of Attempt

FIGURE 13.3 The White House, venue of a presidential assassination attempt

There are many famous crimes of attempt. One notable case was prosecuted against Francisco Martin Duran, who fired twenty-nine rifle rounds at the White House. He was attempting to assassinate United States President Bill Clinton, whom he thought was standing nearby. A group of citizens tackled Duran and held him until law enforcement arrived. No one was injured in the assassination attempt. Duran was charged with attempted murder and with four counts of assaulting a federal officer (the Secret Service agents who responded). He pleaded not guilty based upon insanity, but his defense gained no traction, as more than sixty witnesses testified that Duran hated both the current government and President Clinton. It took less than four hours for the jury to find him guilty. Duran is serving his sentence at the Federal Correctional Institution's complex in Florence, Colorado. He is expected to be released in 2029.

Offenses against persons are also the most severely punished crimes. The penalty for homicide can include execution under federal law and the laws of a majority of states.[21]

An **assault** is an attempt to inflict bodily injury upon another person. A **battery** is an unlawful use of force against another person that entails injury or offensive touching. Someone commits an aggravated assault or an aggravated battery if they inflict serious bodily injury or used a deadly weapon. A person also commits a battery when they strike something that another person is holding or touching, such as a backpack. In addition, a person can commit a battery with something that they are using. For example, a driver commits vehicular battery by striking someone with their car.

The most serious crime that can be committed against a person is **homicide**. Homicide is the unlawful killing of another human being, and the term comes from the Latin *homo* (human being) and *caedere* (to cut or kill). In the common law tradition, **murder** was the "unlawful killing of another with malice aforethought." This terminology has been largely abandoned in favor of the Model Penal Code's four states of mind: purposely, knowingly, recklessly, and negligently.

Manslaughter is a homicide committed "under the influence of extreme mental or emotional disturbance for which there is a reasonable explanation or excuse."[22] **Felony murder** is the unintentional killing of a person during the commission of (or attempt to commit) a **felony**. A felony is a crime punishable by death or more than a year's imprisonment. If a crime is punishable by less than one year in prison, it is classified as a **misdemeanor**. Most states have identified specific felonies that will support felony murder, and they usually include robbery, rape, arson, and kidnapping.

Additional Terms

The term *felony* came to the English common law from the old French word *felonie*. A felonie was a crime that, at a minimum, would require the defendant to give up their lands and personal property. The word appears in the Year Books of Edward II, dating to 1309. In many states, if a person commits a felony, they lose the right to vote. They may also be excluded from jury duty and lose the right to own firearms.

Under the English common law, rape was forced sexual intercourse of a woman by a man who was not his wife.[23] In the United States today, **sexual battery** is recognized as a gender-neutral offense. The

---

21 The Federal Death Penalty Act of 1994 made capital punishment available for a collection of criminal offenses, most of which require a concomitant homicide. In addition, the death penalty can be imposed in federal cases of treason, espionage, or the attempted murder of a witness, juror, or court officer. It can also be imposed in aggravated drug trafficking cases. *See* 18 U.S.C. §§ 3591–3598.

22 Model Penal Code, Section 210.3 (Am. Law Inst., Proposed Official Draft 1962).

23 This is called *Hale's rule*. Sir Matthew Hale declared in his *Historia Placitorum Coronae*, "the husband cannot be guilty of a rape committed by himself upon his lawful wife, for by their mutual matrimonial consent and contract the wife hath given herself up to her husband, consent to which she cannot retract." *See* Paul Finkelman, *Encyclopedia of American Civil Liberties* 961 (Routledge 2006). In 1992, the English House of

severity of the offense varies in most states, depending upon the type of conduct, the force involved, and the age and vulnerability of the victim.[24] Sadly, sexual violence remains a significant problem in American society.[25] There is now a network of organizations throughout the nation that offer confidential support and referrals to victims of sex crimes.[26]

Kidnapping is a serious crime against persons under both state and federal law. It involves taking and transporting someone without their consent. Many states distinguish kidnapping from aggravated kidnapping, which involves kidnapping a child, kidnapping with a firearm or other weapon, or intending to obtain ransom as part of kidnapping.[27] The Federal Kidnapping Act, popularly known as the Lindbergh Law,[28] assumes that someone who has been kidnapped and not returned within twenty-four hours has been moved across state lines. This provides a basis for federal law enforcement to exercise jurisdiction.

From Chapter 12, we know that laws prohibiting **child abuse and neglect** criminalize the mistreatment of children. The definition of abuse varies state to state, as does the idea of what constitutes abusive behavior. For example, in Illinois, corporal punishment is not allowed in public

The Crime of the Twentieth Century

FIGURE 13.4   Charles Lindbergh Jr. on Times cover

The Lindbergh Law was passed following the kidnapping and death of the oldest child of prominent aviator Charles Lindbergh and author Anne Morrow Lindbergh. The twenty-month-old boy was taken from his crib on the second floor of the family home, and a ransom note was left on the windowsill. The child's remains were found months after the $70,000 ransom was paid. Law enforcement tracked some of the ransom bills to a German immigrant, Bruno Richard Hauptmann. Hauptmann had items that connected him with the crime in his possession, including a sketch of a ladder similar to the custom ladder found at the Lindbergh home. Hauptmann was tried and executed for the crime.

Lords determined that there is no exception for husbands in the law of rape. *R v. R* (1992) 1 AC 599. By the mid-1990s, the United States had also eliminated exceptions for marital rape, although some states treat spousal rape differently from non-spousal rape.

24   For example, in Illinois, a person commits criminal sexual assault if that person "commits an act of sexual penetration and 1) uses force or threat of force; 2) knows the victim lacks capacity to give consent; 3) is a family member of the victim and the victim is under eighteen years old; or 4) is at least seventeen years old, holds a position of trust over the victim, and the victim is between thirteen and eighteen years old." 720 ILCS 5/11-1.20.

25   Nearly one in five women and one in seventy-one men have endured sexual violence in their lives. *See* Michelle C. Black et al., *The National Intimate Partner and Sexual Violence Survey: 2010 Summary Report*, Centers for Disease Control and Prevention (2010).

26   VictimConnect is a nationwide helpline that provides information and support to victims of all types of crimes, including sexual assault. Its website, and information about how to get help, is here: https://victimconnect.org/.

27   The Illinois kidnapping law is found at 720 ILSC 5/10-2.

28   The Lindbergh Law, or Federal Kidnapping Act, 18 U.S.C. 1201 (1932).

schools, and physical force may only be used in the defense of students or personnel.[29] By contrast, Alabama passed legislation in 1995 that allows schools to use corporal punishment, although it prohibits excessive force or cruel and unusual punishment.[30]

Criminal harassment is a newer crime, and it entails intentionally targeting someone with harmful, annoying, or terrorizing behavior. The behavior must be severe enough that it causes the targeted person (or their family) to feel that their health or safety is at risk. Harassing behavior can be accomplished using phone calls, text messages, emails, and other forms of communication.

California passed the first law criminalizing **stalking** in 1990.[31] All states now have anti-stalking laws. The Illinois statute provides that a person commits the crime of stalking if they knowingly engage in conduct directed at a specific person that would cause a reasonable person to fear for their safety (or the safety of another) or suffer emotional distress. A person commits the crime of stalking if they follow or surveil on at least two occasions without justification.[32] Since 2018, stalking has been a federal crime if it occurs across state lines.[33] **Cyberstalking** laws prohibit stalking someone electronically, through the internet, email, text messages, or other online means. Cyberstalking is a federal crime, as it is an interstate activity. It is also a crime in some states, including Illinois.[34]

Property Crimes

In addition to protecting the rights of persons, the English common law greatly valued private property rights. American law follows this tradition, and there are many state and federal penal provisions that address property crimes.

Theft is a general term that includes the specific property crimes of **robbery**, **burglary**, and **larceny**. All thefts involve the intentional and permanent taking of property without the owner's consent. Larceny consists of what we think of as a simple theft, while robbery involves theft using the threat of force. Robbery, therefore, is punished more severely than larceny. Burglary is defined as breaking and entering another's property with the intent to commit a felony.

A defendant commits the property **crime of fraud** when they use deception for gain or to deprive someone of their rights. A person may fraudulently obtain goods, services, or benefits, such as insurance proceeds, assets from an estate, or a driver's license. **Identity theft** is a modern crime of fraud that involves one person pretending to be another person in order to obtain property by using their name. Identity theft violates federal law and the laws of all the states.[35]

---

29   *See* 105 ILCS 5/24025.
30   Alabama Code, Title 16, Education, § 16-1-24.1.
31   *See* California Penal Code (CPC) § 646.9(a).
32   *See* 720 ILCS 5/12-3.2.
33   *See* 18 U.S.C. § 2261A.
34   The citation for the federal statute is 47 U.S.C. § 223. Illinois' statute is found at 729 ILCS 5/12-7.5.
35   The Identity Theft and Assumption Deterrence Act of 1998, 18 U.S.C. § 1000, 112 Stat. 3007.

Forgery consists of creating or altering a document in order to defraud someone. Forgers have created false checks, passports, security passes, wills, artwork, and artifacts. Creating counterfeit money and "other security of the United States" with the "intent to defraud" violates federal counterfeiting laws.[36]

Modern payment systems have led Congress and the state legislatures to define new crimes. Someone who makes a purchase on a credit card that they do not have the legal authority to use commits **credit card fraud**. **Bad check laws** criminalize presenting a check for payment when the remitter knows the account has insufficient funds to cover the amount of the check.

Extortion consists of obtaining something of value from someone by causing that person to think that they will be exposed to ridicule, disgrace, or physical injury. Extortion threats that involve the mail or interstate communications are federal crimes.[37]

If you intentionally damage someone else's property, you may commit the misdemeanor of **vandalism**, depending upon its value. **Arson** is the crime of intentionally setting fire to structures or personal property.[38] The modern statutes punish arson of inhabited residential structures and churches most severely. Scorching property or introducing smoke is included in the definition.

White-Collar and Organized Crimes

In contrast with the arson and vandalism, which can be committed anywhere by anyone, **white-collar** (or **corporate crime)** is an offense committed in the course of a person's work, using resources available because of their job. This

---

36 *See* 18 U.S.C. Chapter 25, Counterfeiting and Forgery.
37 *See* 18 U.S.C. Chapter 41, §§ 871 *et seq.*
38 California also has the offense of "reckless burning," which may be charged when a fire is set recklessly rather than willfully. *See* California Penal Code § 452.

The Death Penalty for an Arsonist

FIGURE 13.5 Esperanza Fire as seen from space

In 2006, Raymond Lee Oyler intentionally started the Esperanza Fire, a large fire that burned over 41,000 acres near Palm Springs, California. Oyler was a serial arsonist and set as many as twenty-five fires throughout the summer. As the fires grew larger and more difficult to control, Oyler bragged to his girlfriend about setting them but complained that they were not causing enough damage.

In the course of containing the Esperanza Fire, five firefighters lost their lives. Oyler was tried for murder and sentenced to death. He was the first citizen of the United States to receive the death penalty for a wildfire started by arson. Oyler remains in custody in San Quentin, awaiting execution.

Al Capone, Chicago's Public Enemy Number 1

FIGURE 13.6   Al Capone

Al Capone was the head of a Chicago criminal syndicate that operated a bootlegging business. Bars that refused to do business with him risked being bombed.

Capone used bribery and intimidation to take over elections in the town of Cicero, which he made his home base. He supported the campaign of William Hale Thompson, bombing the voting booths of Thompsons's opponents.

Capone survived several assassination attempts by rival gangs. He sought to eliminate Bugs Moran, the head of the rival North Side Gang, but instead seven Moran affiliates were killed in what became known as the St. Valentine's Day Massacre of 1929.

He was eventually tried and convicted of tax evasion and sentenced to a term in federal prison. Capone was paroled from the Federal Correctional Institution at Terminal Island (Alcatraz Prison) in 1939 after syphilis rendered him confused and disoriented. He died in 1947 at his home in Florida, and his remains are interred in Hillside, Illinois.

includes **embezzlement** (stealing money or other assets from the employer) and also bid-rigging, price-fixing, insider trading, money laundering, Ponzi schemes,[39] and tax fraud.

Organized crime is usually committed by groups who victimize businesses through the use of theft or extortion. Sometimes organized crime groups engage in insurance or stock fraud, taking money from legitimate business enterprises. Crime groups also victimize individuals by establishing auto theft rings, committing burglaries and bank robberies, engaging in identity theft, and other fraudulent activities.

Some organized crime groups defraud governmental organizations by bid-rigging public projects, counterfeiting money, smuggling drugs or other goods, or manufacturing and selling untaxed alcohol (called bootlegging). One hundred years ago, Al Capone ran a notorious bootlegging gang in Chicago.

In addition, organized crime groups may also seek to corrupt public officials in executive, law enforcement, and judicial roles. Sometimes they seek special treatment, and sometimes they hope to receive early warnings about law

---

39   A Ponzi scheme pays "profits" to investors using funds from later investors. Investors believe the money they are receiving is coming from sales (or other legitimate sources) of the business in which they invested, but it is actually coming from new investors. As long as there are enough new investors to pay earlier investors, the scheme can continue. Bernard Madoff operated the most notorious Ponzi scheme in modern times, defrauding investors of tens of billions of dollars. Madoff and his affiliates pled guilty to a collection of federal felonies, including security fraud, wire fraud, money laundering, and theft from an employee benefit plan. Madoff was sentenced to 150 years in prison and died in federal custody on April 14, 2021.

enforcement investigations.[40] They may secure political influence or favors using bribery and threats of violence.[41]

Vice Crimes

Vice crimes are different from other types of crimes. They are illegal because they are morally offensive and also because their proliferation leads to situations society has decided to address. Vice crimes include **illegal gambling**, **drug and alcohol offenses**, and **prostitution**.

Gambling was legal under the common law, but after the Revolutionary War, the states widely criminalized it. It is now legal in many venues but highly regulated by both state and federal law. Similarly, although the common law did not directly address drug or alcohol abuse, we now recognize the adverse consequences of chemical dependency of all kinds. Federal and state laws classify and regulate controlled substances, and alcohol sales to minors are universally prohibited.

Prostitution is pervasive in the world today, driven by demand.[42] Exchanging money for sex among adults is legal in many countries. In the United States, it is legal only in several counties in Nevada.

The crime of prostitution is often described as "victimless," as no one involved is supposedly unwilling. However, a wide-ranging academic study concluded that prostitutes are routinely abused and subjected to violence, and the vast majority of women engaged in prostitution do not desire to continue.[43] This suggests that prostitution is neither voluntary nor consensual. Further, there is a strong link between prostitution and **sex trafficking**, illegally transporting people from one area to another for the purpose of sexual exploitation.[44] Sex trafficking is a federal crime in the United States, and the sex trafficking of American children and foreign national children is equivalently criminalized.[45] If the victim is under fourteen years of age, or fraud, force, or coercion were used, the crime carries a minimum sentence of fifteen years and a maximum sentence of life in prison.

---

40   In the 1980s, the FBI, the IRS Criminal Investigation Division, the US Postal Inspection Service, the Illinois State Police, and the Chicago Police Department Internal Affairs Division One conducted a major investigation into the corruption of the judiciary in Chicago. The investigation was called "Operation Greylord," and it led to the indictment of ninety-three people: forty-eight lawyers, seventeen judges, ten deputy sheriffs, eight policemen, eight court officials, and James DeLeo, a state legislator. Most were eventually convicted, either at the end of trial or by entering a negotiated plea. Two men committed suicide shortly before they were to be indicted. Maurice Possley, "Archives: Operation Greylord: A Federal Probe of Court Corruption Sets the Standard for Future Investigations," *Chicago Tribune* (Jan. 19, 2017).

41   Public corruption has been a problem in the United States. Over a six-year period, more than seventy-five public officials were convicted of public corruption offenses in just the Southern District of West Virginia. *See* Michael W. Carey et al., "Federal Prosecution of State and Local Officials: The Obstacles to Punishing Breaches of the Public Trust and a Proposal for Reform" (pt. 1), 94 *W. Va. L. Rev.* 302 (1991).

42   *See* Michael Shively et al., *A National Overview of Prostitution and Sex Trafficking Demand Reduction Efforts, Prepared for the National Institute of Justice*, United States Department of Justice (Apr. 30, 2012), Grant #2008-IJ-CX-0010.

43   Melissa Farley et al., "Prostitution and Trafficking in Nine Countries," 2 *Journal of Trauma Practice* 3–4, 33–74 (2004).

44   A 2012 study found that countries with legalized prostitution have more trafficking than countries where prostitution is illegal. *See* Seo-Young Cho et al., "Does Legalized Prostitution Increase Human Trafficking?," 41 *World Development* 67–82 (2013).

45   *See* 18 U.S.C. §1591; *See also* 18 U.S.C. §§ 2421, *et seq.*

Antonin Scalia

Associate Justice, United States Supreme Court (1986–2016)

FIGURE 13.7 Justice Antonin Scalia

As a Supreme Court justice, Antonin Scalia was known for his fiery rhetoric, his scrupulous prose, and his charismatic presence.

Perhaps lesser-known, however, was Justice Scalia's vigorous defense of the rights of those accused of crimes. Writing for the majority, he railed against the use of thermal imaging by police in *Kyllo v. United States*, 533 U.S. 27 (2001) and warrantless GPS tracking of cars in *United States v. Jones*, 565 U.S. 400 (2012). In a dissent he took the majority to task for allowing police to take DNA samples when booking suspects in *Maryland v. King*, 569 U.S. 435 (2013) and for allowing officers to pull over cars based solely on anonymous tips in *Navarrete v. California*, 572 U.S. 393 (2014).

Justice Scalia demonstrated another trait worth mentioning: collegiality. He routinely disagreed with Justice Ruth Bader Ginsburg, but they remained good friends. As he said, "I attack ideas. I don't attack people."

Public Order and Safety Offenses

Under the English common law, **rioting**, **unlawful assembly**, and **disorderly conduct** were outlawed as violations of the king's peace. The Model Penal Code criminalizes disorderly group activity where persons intend to commit a felony or misdemeanor or prevent lawful official action.[46] In many jurisdictions, the disorderly conduct must occur in a public place, which the Model Penal Code defines as "affecting or likely to affect persons in a place to which the public or a substantial group has access." This would include "highways, transport facilities, schools, prisons, apartment houses, places of business or amusement, or any neighborhood."[47] To qualify as a riot under the Model Penal Code, three or more persons must participate in the disorderly conduct.[48] However, in many jurisdictions, the crime of riot also includes the requirement that the defendants cause or risk causing public terror or alarm.[49] During the summer of 2020, there were protests against the deaths of George Floyd and others in police custody in cities throughout the United States. While the majority of those protests were peaceful, some demonstrations escalated to riots where there was **looting**, the theft of goods from places of business.

Americans are highly mobile, and there are many millions of registered motor vehicles in the United States. The states have all adopted a collection of laws regulating their use. Among these are laws against speeding, driving under the influence, driving without a license, and failing to obey traffic signals. Motor vehicle laws are relatively uniform across the states, which is important for a society that is highly mobile. New laws prohibit texting or otherwise using a handheld device while driving.

In addition to owning many cars, Americans own many guns. In 2008, the Supreme Court affirmed that the Second Amendment of the United States Constitution guarantees

---

46   *See* Model Penal Code, § 250, *et seq.*
47   Model Penal Code, § 250.02.
48   Model Penal Code, § 250.01.
49   *See* Alabama Criminal Code § 13A-11-3.

citizens the right to bear and keep arms for personal home protection.[50] However, federal and state laws regulate the manufacture, trade, transfer, and possession of firearms and ammunition.[51]

Environmental Crimes

Environmental laws and regulations are largely modern developments. However, the common law included the torts of trespass and nuisance to protect private property rights, and the **doctrine of the public trust**, which maintains that some national resources belong to the public. In the United States, this doctrine has supported the public's right to clean drinking water and access to lakes and some navigable waterways. American law today supports lawsuits for nuisance and trespass when the activities of others injure private resources.

Most federal and state environmental regulations were enacted in the last fifty years. The broad statutory scheme now includes laws protecting water, air, land, and migrating birds, marine mammals, endangered animals, along with other natural resources. Current federal laws regulate the interaction of humans and the environment and seek to conserve and manage resources. Substantial criminal penalties attach for many violations.[52]

The Lacey Act

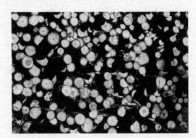

FIGURE 13.8   Cut timber

The Lacey Act of 1900 prohibits the interstate sale of illegally taken wildlife, fish, and plants. For Lumber Liquidators' import of prohibited timber in violation of this act, in 2016 the company was convicted of a felony and sentenced to pay $7.8 million in criminal penalties. In addition, the company paid nearly $1 million in criminal forfeiture and $1.23 million in community service payments. This was the largest fine ever imposed under the Lacey Act.

---

50   *Dist. of Col. v. Heller*, 554 U.S. 570 (2008). The Supreme Court incorporated the Second Amendment against the states in *McDonald v. City of Chicago*, 561 U.S. 742 (2010).

51   The federal laws go back to 1934, when the National Firearms Act was passed. This act requires that certain weapons be registered, such as explosive ordnance, machine guns, and short-barreled rifles. There are many federal laws affecting weapons. Some of the more notable laws include the Brady Handgun Violence Prevention Act of 1993 that mandates background checks for most persons who purchase firearms. The Gun-Free School Zones Act of 1990 prohibits most persons from taking a firearm into a school zone, and the Law Enforcement Officers Safety Act of 2004 gives law enforcement officers (and former law enforcement officers) the right to carry a concealed firearm in any jurisdiction in the United States, with some exceptions.

52   A list and description of the current statutes may be found on the EPA's website. *See* epa.gov/laws-regulations.

Conclusion and Introduction to the Law Lab

The broad sweep of state and federal criminal law in the United States supports our social order, ensuring that those who violate others' rights will be penalized. Our criminal laws reflect our own ideas of what is right and what is wrong, as our representatives enact criminal laws based upon our community's ideas of decency and integrity. Accordingly, a jury's finding of criminal guilt is also a pronouncement of moral condemnation by the community.

In the following Law Lab, you are working in the office of the state's attorney of Liberty County, the county in which our city of Liberty Springs is located. A member of the community, young Adam Garçon, has needlessly died from dehydration because his parents did not obtain medical care for him on a timely basis. Adam's parents did not seek medical care for their son due to their religious beliefs, even though they thought it likely he could die. Under the circumstances, may you charge them with homicide? Does their state of mind—*mens rea*—support the charge? How do their religious beliefs fit into your analysis? The state's attorney has great discretion to determine which charges to file. Think about your obligations to Adam, to the community, and to the interests of justice. Which, if any, charges will you decide to file against Adam's parents?

State's Attorney Law Lab

MEMORANDUM

To: Liberty County State's Attorney

From: Legal Interns of Liberty County State's Attorney's Office

Re: *People of the State of Franklin v. Conrad and Lera Garçon*

You have asked us to provide background information concerning the death of Adam Garçon, aged nine. A physician became aware that Adam was ill and instructed Adam's parents, Conrad and Lera Garçon, to seek medical care. Unfortunately, Adam's parents did not pursue medical treatment because of their religious beliefs. They are members of the Third Temple of Hope and Glory ("the Temple"),[1] which believes in faith healing as the exclusive remedy for disease.

FIGURE 13.9 Adam Garçon

---

1   This is a fictitious religious group.

We understand that you are considering charging Adam's parents with the crime of first-degree murder and/or child neglect under Franklin law. This memorandum will provide background information about the Temple, about Adam's death, and about the relevant state and federal law protecting the exercise of religion in the context of child health care decisions.

Factual Background

Members of the Temple periodically become objects of media attention. This occurs when a child dies after failing to receive needed medical care. Sadly, this has happened a dozen times in the last few decades.

Temple churches were established in the United States in the early 1900s. Members form tight-knit family groups, and the women in the church are required to stay home to raise their children. Members call God to come forth during their services, which they attend two or three times a week. In addition, members of the Temple rely upon faith healing to cure disease. They acknowledge that some doctors and medicines can heal, but they believe that people who rely upon them lack faith. Such persons are shunned in the Temple community.

When a church member is sick or dying, members of the Temple offer prayers. They believe that their prayers can heal. However, if healing does not occur, Temple members will comfort the sick person until they die.

With the exception of one aunt, all the adults in Adam Garçon's family are members of the Temple. Adam has a large family and is one of six children.

The precipitating cause of Adam's fatal illness has not been identified. The medical examiner notes that Adam could have become ill from something he ingested, from a virus or other infectious agent, or from an undiagnosed chronic condition. At this point, it may be impossible to find the cause.

Adam's illness came on quickly, with vomiting and watery diarrhea. His parents put him to bed, thinking he had contracted a stomach flu. Unfortunately, Adam did not improve. On the third day of his illness, his aunt, Dr. Abigail Fille, came to visit her sister, Adam's mother. Dr. Fille was surprised to find Adam in bed and perceived that he had become dehydrated. She told Adam's parents that he needed medical care and offered to take him to a nearby hospital. After some discussion, Adam's parents responded that they would "certainly see that Adam received what was needed." Dr. Fille interpreted this statement to mean that they would take him to the hospital. However, they did not do so. Adam's parents later explained that, by their words, they meant that they would pray and take such care measures as they felt appropriate.

Over the next days, Conrad and Lera Garçon repeatedly brought Adam water and soup, but he remained so weak that he was unable to drink more than a sip at a time.[2] Sadly, Adam's condition worsened, and he died ten days after his illness started. The medical examiner determined that the primary cause of death was dehydration.[3]

---

2   Nausea and vomiting can be caused by many things, including gastroenteritis, poisons and toxins, food poisoning, and gastric diseases. Once a person experiences symptoms of dehydration (such as extreme thirst, dry mouth, little urination, or dizziness), they need prompt medical care. Such care could include intravenous therapy to deliver fluids and medications directly to the veins.

3   The following narrative about dying from dehydration is offered to help understand Adam's ordeal. Dying from dehydration is not pleasant. The mouth dries out and becomes coated with thick material, and the lips become parched. The eyes dehydrate and recede, and the skin becomes scaly. The urine becomes concentrated and burns when excreted. The body temperature can become very high. When brain cells lose moisture, convulsions can result, and when the respiratory tract dries out, secretions can plug the lungs. Finally, major organs cease functioning, and death occurs.

Many people from the Temple offered healing prayers for Adam during his last illness. The testimony from Adam's parents confirms that, during this time, they were very concerned that he might well die. However, they continued to hope and believe that God would save him. They have said that they regret Adam's death, and they clearly grieve for him. They have also stated that, if presented with the situation again, they would not change their actions.

State Law and Federal Law on Child Abuse

A variety of state and federal laws are relevant to the Garçon case.

First, there are federal and state laws that protect neglectful parents from prosecution if they do not provide a child with required medical attention due to their religious beliefs. In 1974, Congress enacted the first Child Abuse Prevention and Treatment Act (CAPTA). CAPTA's purpose was to provide state funding to fight child abuse and neglect, and it has been periodically reauthorized and amended. Importantly, CAPTA includes a provision exempting parents from civil and criminal prosecution if they fail to provide a child with needed medical care because of their religious beliefs.[4] To qualify for federal funds to fight child abuse, CAPTA requires a state to include a similar religious exemption in its child welfare laws. Accordingly, nearly all states now incorporate religious exemptions that permit parents to waive otherwise mandated preventive and diagnostic measures for their children, including immunizations, metabolic testing, blood lead-level tests, newborn hearing tests, and other screenings.[5]

Second, there is a relevant Franklin law addressing child neglect. The governing Franklin statute states:

> A "Neglected Child" means any child who is not receiving … medically indicated treatment … as determined by a physician acting alone or in consultation with other physicians, or otherwise is not receiving the proper or necessary support or medical or other remedial care as necessary for a child's well-being …

Following the requirements of CAPTA, the Franklin statute also provides:

> A child shall not be deemed neglected or abused for the sole reason that the child's parent … depends upon spiritual means through prayer alone for the treatment of disease. …[6]

However, Franklin's Abused and Neglected Child Reporting Act declares that relying upon prayer alone to cure a disease does not extinguish a claim of neglect. This Act states:

> A child whose parent, guardian, or custodian in good faith selects and depends upon spiritual means through prayer alone for the treatment or cure of disease or remedial care may

---

4   Lobbying efforts by the Christian Science church led to the inclusion of this provision.
5   Franklin supports exemptions from vaccinations for religious reasons. However, parents who want to cite religious belief as a reason not to vaccinate must complete a Certificate of Religious Exemption and have it signed by a health care provider.
6   Franklin's laws are very similar to those of Illinois. *See* 325 ILCS 5/3, *et seq.*

be considered neglected or abused, but not for the sole reason that his parent, guardian, or custodian accepts and practices such beliefs.

Thus, under Franklin law, a claim of neglect may not be based only upon the fact that a child's parents depend upon prayer to treat disease. A further showing of facts supporting abuse or neglect is required. Finally, the relevant parts of Franklin's law defining first-degree murder provide:

> A person who kills an individual without lawful justification commits first degree murder if, in performing the acts which cause the death:

> He either intends to kill or do great bodily harm to that individual or another, or knows that such acts will cause death to that individual or another or;

> He knows that such acts create a strong probability of death or great bodily harm to that individual or another ...

The statute for second degree murder under Franklin law is not a good fit for this situation.[7]

Issue: With Which Crime(s) Should the Defendants be Charged?

As in other jurisdictions, in Liberty County, the determination of which crime(s) a defendant should be charged with rests entirely with the State's Attorney. In this case, there are several options to consider.

First, you could decide to charge Conrad and Lera Garçon with first-degree murder. Franklin's first-degree murder statute permits a finding of guilt based upon "performing acts which cause ... death" where "such acts create a strong probability of death or great bodily harm." This statute could well apply to the failure of Adam's parents to seek medical help for their critically ill son. The fact that Adam's parents were advised of that necessity by a physician supports the claim that they knew their son was very ill. The countervailing consideration is that Adam's parents hoped and believed that he would not die.

Second, you could decide to charge Conrad and Lera Garçon with child neglect. Franklin's child neglect statute could support this charge. The legislation confirms that claims of neglect are not excused simply because the parents relied upon faith-based treatment.

---

7   Franklin's second-degree murder statute is very similar to Illinois Law 720 ILCS 5/9-2. It provides:
    (a) A person commits the offense of second-degree murder when he or she commits the offense of first-degree murder ... and either of the following factors are present:
    (1) at the time of the killing he or she is acting under a sudden and intense passion resulting from serious provocation by the individual killed or another whom the offender endeavors to kill, but he or she negligently or accidentally causes the death of the individual killed; or
    (2) At the time of the killing he or she believes the circumstances to be such that, if they existed, would justify, or exonerate the killing ... but his or her belief is unreasonable.

Third, you could decide to charge Conrad and Lera Garçon with both crimes. Many prosecutors include multiple charges to gain leverage in plea negotiations with criminal defendants. However, multiple charges can be confusing for juries, and can make lower-level criminal defendants look like egregious offenders.

Finally, you could determine that no criminal charges should be filed in this matter. This alternative, of course, permits Adam's parents to avoid all criminal responsibility.

Again, the authority for making this decision is vested solely with the State's Attorney.

Conclusion

The legal interns await word on the charging decision. Please let us know if we can assist in any other way in connection with this sad and troubling case.

CHAPTER 14

Criminal Procedure

If the government becomes a lawbreaker, it breeds contempt for law; it invites every man to become a law unto himself; it invites anarchy. To declare that in the administration of the criminal law the end justifies the means—to declare that the government may commit crimes in order to secure the conviction of a private criminal—would bring terrible retribution.
—Louis Dembitz Brandeis, associate justice of the United States Supreme Court, dissenting in *Olmstead v. United States*, 277 U.S. 438, 485 (1928)

Introduction

Criminal Procedure is the law that regulates the actions of government agents as they pursue, detain, arrest, and prosecute criminal defendants. It determines when and how the government can act against people who may have committed crimes and defines the path to and through their trials.

The law of Criminal Procedure is not new. In Chapter 1, we noted that the ancient Code of Hammurabi decrees a presumption of innocence for criminal defendants, and Mosaic Law requires a trial before an execution can occur. The rules of Criminal Procedure in today's United States are largely derived from the express rights declared in the Constitution, as shaped by the common law and interpreted by the Supreme Court.

Most criminal cases begin with criminal investigations conducted by law enforcement. Accordingly, this chapter begins with a brief review of the development of law enforcement in the United States. Then, we will walk a simple case down the path that Criminal Procedure defines, beginning with the identification of criminal activity and ending, as most cases do, with a plea agreement. We will review pretrial procedure and consider the roles of counsel and the court. We will look at the rights that the United States Constitution provides to criminal defendants and note where those rights have been defined by several important Supreme Court decisions.

In this chapter and the following chapter, we will also observe several places where the American criminal justice system's use of the rules of Criminal Procedure and punishment of offenders has fallen short of the constitutional guarantees of equal protection and due process of law. One critical problem involves racial disparities, incongruities between the treatment of racial groups. These disparities are evident at every procedural stage of the criminal justice system's operation.[1]

Finally, in this week's Law Lab, you will reprise your prior role as a state court judge. This time, however, you have shifted dockets: you will now be presiding over a criminal case. You must assess whether certain evidence should be admitted in support of the case's prosecution or should be excluded as improperly obtained. Your ruling will either confirm that persons who broke the law may be prosecuted or require that the case against them be dismissed.

CRIMINAL PROCEDURE KEY TERMS

The following key terms are defined in this chapter. They are also defined in the Glossary.

Arraignment	**Grand Jury**	**Public Defender**
Bail	**Hot Pursuit Exception**	**Right to a Speedy and Public Trial**
Chain of Custody	**Indictment**	**Search Incident to Arrest**
Challenge for Cause	**Peremptory Challenge**	**Search Warrant**
Criminal Procedure	**Plain View Exception**	**Warrant Requirement**
Emergency Search Exception	**Plea Bargaining**	
Exclusionary Rule	**Probable Cause**	
Fruit of the Poisonous Tree	**Prosecutor**	

Law Enforcement in the United States

In medieval England, it was the duty of constables and watchmen to maintain order with help from the adult men in the community. If patrolling watchmen encountered trouble, they would summon assistance by sounding a "hue and cry" until the criminal defendant was apprehended. By law, all able-bodied men were required to respond to the hue and cry and assist in pursuit of criminals.[2] Over time, this form of community policing has given way to government law enforcement agencies who employ armed officers to patrol public areas and investigate crimes.

Development of State Law Enforcement

In 1631, when Boston was a Puritan settlement of under 200 persons, it established a formal watch to protect its citizens from fire, crime, and dangerous animals. Two hundred years later, the City of Boston

---

1   *See* Margaret Bull Kovera, "Racial Disparities in the Criminal Justice System: Prevalence, Causes, and a Search for Solutions," *Journal of Social Issues*, Vol. 75 No. 4 (2019).

2   *See* the Statute of Winchester of 1285 (1 Edw. I, ccs 1 and 4).

founded the first dedicated police force in the United States. It was modeled after London's Metropolitan Police Service, now informally known as the Met or Scotland Yard. In 1844, New York founded its police department, and over the next decades the cities of New Orleans, Cincinnati, Philadelphia, Chicago, and Baltimore followed suit. Over time, American police officers began to carry and use firearms instead of the clubs borne by their British counterparts. In 1896, New York City became the first city to issue standard sidearms to its officers.

The rise of automobiles resulted in additional changes in law enforcement. Statewide police forces such as the California Highway Patrol came into being to serve a public that used state highways. Modern state police forces have the authority to conduct criminal investigations throughout their states. In addition, state troopers enforce traffic laws on state highways, support local law enforcement, and serve where the jurisdiction of county sheriffs ends. The role of county sheriffs varies from state to state, but sheriffs have the power to make arrests, serve warrants, transport prisoners, and manage county jails. Today's sheriff's departments range in size from just a few persons to the over sixteen thousand members of the Los Angeles County Sheriff's Department.[3]

Development of Federal Law Enforcement

The United States government supervises a large collection of law enforcement agencies that address matters of federal law and order. We will confine our review to those that fall under the control of the United States Department of Justice, which has historically served as the key federal law enforcement agency.

The Department of Justice was founded after adoption of the Thirteenth, Fourteenth, and Fifteenth Amendments to the United States Constitution, which extended civil and legal protections to formerly enslaved persons. The department's initial mandate was to subdue groups, including the Ku Klux Klan, that had been using violence and intimidation to keep Black persons from exercising their rights to vote, run for public office, and serve on juries.

The oldest federal law enforcement agency is the United States Marshals Service, which was founded in 1789. Today, the US Marshals protect federal judges and courthouses, apprehend federal fugitives, seize assets involved in federal crimes, and transport and house federal prisoners. The US Marshals also operate the federal Witness Security Program, popularly called the "Witness Protection Program." This program protects persons whose lives are endangered due to their cooperation with the federal government in criminal cases.

The Federal Bureau of Investigation (FBI) is the principal federal law enforcement agency in the United States, with jurisdiction over hundreds of federal crimes. It maintains field offices in major cities and resident agencies in other areas. The FBI traces back to the National Bureau of Criminal Identification, founded in 1896 to distribute information about known criminals. Over time, its role expanded, and in

---

3   Interestingly, Alaska has no sheriffs, as it has no counties and therefore no county law enforcement. Instead, state troopers provide law enforcement outside city limits.

The FBI and J. Edgar Hoover

Director, Federal Bureau of Investigation (1924–1972)

FIGURE 14.1 Former FBI director J. Edgar Hoover

During his tenure as the first director of the FBI, Mr. Hoover presented himself as a driven, ambitious, and transformative force in the field of federal law enforcement. Among other advancements, he helped to create a national fingerprint database, pushed to upgrade the national crime lab, and devised the first type of database to locate potential terrorists.

In 1941, Attorney General Robert Jackson gave Mr. Hoover a blank check to conduct warrantless wiretaps. Hoover proceeded to conduct hundreds of illegal wiretaps, collecting information on a group of prominent Americans. Hoover compiled a list of over 12,000 Americans whom he considered to be subversive, and, at the outbreak of the Korean War, he encouraged President Harry S. Truman to suspend the writ of *habeas corpus* and detain the individuals on the list. The President, however, declined to do so.

As one result of Hoover's abuses of power, FBI directors are now limited to serving one ten-year term. Any extensions must be approved by the United States Senate.

1933, it received its present name. Its long-term director, J. Edgar Hoover, was instrumental in shaping it into the robust crime-fighting agency that serves the public today. He created its famous Scientific Crime Detection Laboratory to professionalize the investigation process. J. Edgar Hoover became a highly controversial figure when his secret and severe abuses of the agency's power came to light.

The Department of Justice also administers the Bureau of Alcohol, Tobacco, Firearms and Explosives (ATF) and the Drug Enforcement Administration (DEA). The ATF investigates federal offenses involving the unlawful use and possession of firearms and explosives. It also investigates arson, bombings, and illegal trafficking and tax evasion of tobacco and alcohol products. It often works with state law enforcement on joint endeavors to locate those who violate firearms, alcohol, and tobacco laws.

Finally, the DEA is the federal law enforcement agency that combats illegal drug distribution and trafficking in the United States. It is the lead agency responsible for enforcing the Controlled Substances Act, though it shares jurisdiction for this effort with the FBI and several other federal agencies. The DEA employs nearly five thousand special agents and has an Aviation Division to provide air support for its mission. It also has a Special Operations Division that forwards information from wiretaps and databases to federal and state law enforcement.

While new branches of law enforcement were certainly created to meet the needs of the public, some forces have been used for less noble purposes. For example, in Pennsylvania, the primary missions of the Coal and Iron Police were to bust unions and end strikes. The Pennsylvania General Assembly established it in 1865, but coal companies paid for it. The famous Pinkerton National Detective Agency, created in 1850 by Allan Pinkerton, included strikebreaking and anti-union activities among its private detective services. In addition, in some places and times there has been an unfortunate linkage between politics and law enforcement in the United States. As a result, law enforcement forces have occasionally been used for improper purposes. Two striking historic examples include the use of Arkansas state troopers to keep Black students from entering Little Rock Central High School in 1957 and the 1965 use of Alabama state troopers to forcibly break up groups of voting-rights marchers in Selma, Alabama.

Pretrial Criminal Procedure

Every criminal case begins with the discovery of a crime. When this happens, law enforcement investigates, collects evidence, and interviews witnesses. As the case progresses, law enforcement may arrest and interrogate suspects. When the evidence supports it, a state or federal prosecutor will file a criminal case (with the approval of a grand jury for federal cases and for some state cases). The criminal defendant will then be tried or the case resolved through plea negotiations.

At every point through this process, the rules of Criminal Procedure dictate what actions government agents—from police officers to court officials—may legally take. These rules are designed to support fair play and protect the people from overreach, and they are supported by procedural penalties. The failure to follow them can result in the premature termination of an otherwise meritorious case or the reversal of a conviction on appeal. In serious cases, a judge, attorney, or law enforcement officer may be suspended or fired. In the most extreme cases, they may even be charged with breaking the law. At that point, they become criminal defendants in cases prosecuted on behalf of the people they were sworn to serve.

Search and Seizure

We will now review criminal procedure from investigation to plea bargain. We here compress and combine some steps for the sake of brevity: the story told here highlights phases of the process.

The Conviction of Derek Chauvin for the Murder of George Floyd

FIGURE 14.2   Memorial at the site of George Floyd's murder

On May 25, 2020, forty-six-year-old George Floyd used a counterfeit $20 bill to purchase cigarettes at a grocery store in the Powderhorn Park neighborhood of Minneapolis. A store employee called the police, and Officers J. Alexander Kueng and Thomas Lane responded. The officers took Floyd from his vehicle, handcuffed him, and informed him that he was under arrest. Floyd told the officers that he was anxious and claustrophobic and that he did not want to get inside the police car; however, officers Kueng and Lane forced him into their cruiser. Officers Tou Thao and Derek Chauvin then arrived, and Chauvin assumed command. The officers pulled Floyd out of the cruiser, and Floyd dropped to the pavement, lying on his chest with his cheek to the ground. While in this position, Chauvin knelt on Floyd's neck, while Keung applied pressure to Floyd's body and Lane to his legs.

Witnesses to the events recorded the encounter on their cell phones. While the other officers stopped applying pressure, Chauvin continued to kneel on Floyd's neck for over nine minutes. During this time, Floyd

(continued)

repeatedly begged Chauvin to move, saying "I can't breathe." Bystanders became increasingly alarmed as Floyd became unresponsive, and the officers finally called paramedics. Floyd was taken from the scene by ambulance and was pronounced dead in the emergency room of the Hennepin County Medical Center. Two autopsies confirmed that Floyd's death was a homicide: George Floyd had been asphyxiated.

Derek Chauvin was tried for Floyd's murder in Hennepin County District Court. Video footage taken by bystanders provided critical evidence supporting the prosecution's case. On April 20, 2021, the jury convicted Chauvin, making him the first white Minnesota police officer to be found guilty of murdering a Black person.

Law enforcement officers have a duty to protect the public by pursuing those who commit crimes, and the law grants officers the authority to use force as they do so. However, officers also have a duty to exercise their authority responsibly. Chauvin's use of lethal excessive force against George Floyd violated that duty. Thus, Chauvin's actions not only broke the law but also violated the public's trust.

You will recall the sad case of young Adam Garçon, whom we met in last week's Law Lab. His parents are in custody after being charged in connection with his death.

During Adam's autopsy, the forensic pathologist took blood samples and sent them out for toxicology testing, a routine measure when a death is connected with criminal charges. The toxicology lab told the pathologist of an alarming discovery: there was a considerable amount of methamphetamine in the boy's blood.

Methamphetamine is classified as a Schedule II drug by the United States Drug Enforcement Agency (DEA). This means that it has a high potential for abuse, and its use can cause severe psychological or physical dependence.

After reviewing the toxicology report, the pathologist concludes that the methamphetamine was a contributing cause of Adam's death. Adam's dehydration likely increased its lethal effect.

The Liberty Springs police forwards the pathologist's report to the Franklin State Police and the Federal Bureau

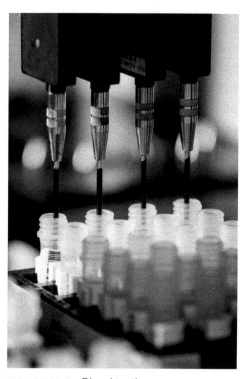

FIGURE 14.3 Blood testing

of Investigation. They also send a copy to the DEA. Both federal and state laws restrict the production, distribution, and sale of methamphetamine. After viewing the report, and the FBI and DEA tell the state police that they should proceed with the investigation and keep them informed of developments. All the law enforcement personnel who have heard about Adam's case want to know where the drug came from and how Adam ingested it.

The Franklin State Police dispatches a member of the Division of Criminal Investigations to Liberty Springs. Detective Archer Soin reviews the evidence gathered, including statements made by Adam's parents. He needs to develop a picture of the last month of Adam's life so that he can try and understand where and how the boy consumed methamphetamine. The detective knows that Adam's parents are farmers and that they have lived on and farmed the same land for twenty-five years. With their permission, their property was searched at the time of Adam's death, and no drugs were found anywhere on the premises. Detective Soin believes Adam acquired and ingested the drug somewhere else.

Adam's parents agree to speak with Detective Soin. They are still mourning their son's death and are quite bewildered by their mounting legal problems. After consulting with them, their attorneys encourage the couple to cooperate. Their cooperation could result in a more favorable outcome in the case that is pending against them.

In that interview, Adam's parents tell Detective Soin that Adam did not leave his room for the last ten days of his life. Before that, he attended school three days a week with other members of his parents' church in the large basement of his parents' home. On days when he did not have school, Adam often rode his bicycle a few miles to a farmstead shared by two uncles, Aubin ("Abe") and Alain ("Al") Garçon. The men helped their nephew with his schoolwork and let him play with the farm animals on the property. In addition, Adam helped his uncles with their business of distilling herbs into therapeutic oils for online sales. The business was very successful, and they paid Adam small sums for his help. During the last three months of his life, his parents believe that the only trips Adam made outside his home were to see his uncles on their property.

Detective Soin is very interested in Adam's uncles and their property. However, he knows that he cannot simply drive over and conduct a search. The Fourth Amendment to the United States Constitution includes the **warrant requirement**:

> The right of the people to be secure in their persons, houses, papers, and effects, against unreasonable searches and seizures, shall not be violated, and no warrants shall issue, but upon probable cause, supported by oath or affirmation, and particularly describing the place to be searched, and the persons or things to be seized.

Detective Soin knows that, to conduct a search of the uncles' home, he must either have their consent to search or obtain a **search warrant** in advance. The detective would rather conduct a search without giving advance notice to the uncles. If he asks them for permission, his request could be denied, and if there is contraband on the property, the uncles might have time to remove it before a warrant could be obtained. Therefore, Detective Soin decides to pursue a search warrant.

The detective must establish **probable cause** to get a search warrant and describe the place to be searched and the things he hopes to find. So, Detective Soin drafts a warrant that includes the address of the uncles' property and describes why he would like to search it. His affidavit explains that Adam Garçon died with a quantity of methamphetamine in his blood and that his death is implicated in a pending criminal case. The affidavit also includes information from Adam's parents, explaining that based upon information he received in the course of his investigation, the only place Adam traveled outside the home was to his uncles' property. Finally, the detective asserts that he has a reasonable suspicion that the property is in some way connected to the drug, and that the detective is looking for drug-related contraband, including the equipment needed to make or sell methamphetamine. Detective Soin signs the affidavit under penalty of perjury and takes it to the local judge assigned the duty of reviewing requests for search warrants.

The judge reviews it and then calls the detective into her chambers. She explains that she cannot issue the warrant because the detective's showing of probable cause is insufficient. While the showing to establish probable cause is lower than that required for a criminal conviction, the judge does not believe that the detective has met even the more limited requirements. Though the detective believes Adam visited the uncles' residence frequently and did not appear to travel anywhere else, it does not follow that the uncles are connected with the methamphetamine in Adam's system. The judge puts it bluntly: she requires more proof to issue a search warrant.

Detective Soin is disappointed but undeterred. He knows that if he had proceeded with a search without the warrant, any evidence he and his colleagues obtained would be thrown out of court. This could also have occurred if he had obtained a warrant if an appellate court later found that it should not have been issued. The **exclusionary rule** prohibits the use of illegally obtained evidence in a criminal trial. Ever since the Supreme Court decided *Mapp v. Ohio*, 367 U.S. 643 (1961), that rule has applied to the states as well as to the federal government.

The Reasonable Expectation of Privacy Test

The Fourth Amendment protects against unreasonable searches and seizures. To distinguish a reasonable search or seizure from one that is unreasonable, courts assess whether it violated the person's reasonable expectation of privacy.

In *Katz v. United States*, 389 U.S. 347 (1967), Justice Harlan developed a two-prong test to determine whether a search violated a person's reasonable expectation of privacy. First, an individual must demonstrate that they felt their privacy was violated. Second, their expectation of privacy must be recognized as reasonable when measured against societal standards. The expectation of privacy in one's own home satisfies both the subjective and objective standards defined by Justice Harlan. But what about public places, such as restrooms, phone booths, or even airspaces? Does a person have a right to privacy over the garbage they leave out for collection? As you read, compare your initial thoughts to the relevant law. Do you agree with the Court's interpretation of a reasonable expectation of privacy? Why or why not?

The detective will need a search warrant to enter the uncles' property unless one of the exceptions to the warrant requirement applies. The detective mentally reviews the exceptions to the warrant requirement. First, there is no need for a warrant if consent is given for a search, but Detective Soin has already dismissed this option as unfeasible. The **hot pursuit exception** certainly does not apply, as there is no fleeing felon to apprehend. The **emergency search exception** would apply if someone were calling for help or if gunshots had been heard, but that is not on the table.

Then the detective considers the **plain view exception**. If something is in plain view, there is no need to obtain a search warrant, as there is no reasonable expectation of privacy concerning it. People have no reasonable expectation of privacy in public locations, such as city streets and the lobbies of public buildings. If they engage in criminal activities in those locations, they may be arrested without a warrant, and any visible criminal paraphernalia can be seized without a warrant.

This leads Detective Soin to think about another Supreme Court case, *California v. Greenwood*, 486 U.S. 35 (1988). In this case, the United States Supreme Court held that the Fourth Amendment does not require law enforcement to obtain a warrant before searching garbage left for collection outside residential property. The Court found that people do not have a reasonable expectation of privacy in garbage left on the curb. In addition, in *Florida v. Riley*, 488 U.S. 445 (1989), the Court ruled that no warrant is required for observations made from public airspace for the same reason.

FIGURE 14.4   Drones are used by law enforcement in some investigations

Detective Soin previously drove by the uncles' property and noted the curbside trash. He arranges for it to be picked up before it can be collected. He also considers a drone or airplane reconnaissance of the property. He will ask the DEA to lend a plane or drone for this effort if the trash pickup is not fruitful.

The trash is picked up and delivered in bags to Detective Soin's temporary office in Liberty Springs. It comes with a signed document confirming who collected it and when and how it was gathered. **Chain of custody** is vitally important: at trial, law enforcement must show how and by whom evidence was gathered and confirm that it was correctly processed and managed from the moment of its acquisition to the time it is introduced as evidence at trial. A failure to maintain records demonstrating the proper management of evidence can render it inadmissible.

With the assistance of local law enforcement, the detective goes through the contents of the garbage container. It largely consists of the usual household trash, and he initially does not find anything useful in the messy bundle. However, near the bottom of the pile, there is a used coffee filter with minute traces of an odd crystalline substance. Detective Soin smiles; he has strong suspicions about the substance. He sends the filter off with a deputy for testing to a local crime lab on an expedited basis. When necessary, crime labs can now complete this testing very quickly, and Detective Soin expects results within hours.

The crime lab does not disappoint. Detective Soin soon learns that the coffee filter has not only tested positive for coffee, but it has also tested positive for methamphetamine compounds. The detective now is confident that he can obtain a search warrant, and he swears out another affidavit. He takes it to the judge, and she quickly approves it, telling the detective that the coffee filter has established probable cause to support the requested search.

Detective Soin gathers a team of officers and proceeds to the property. They approach cautiously and carry weapons; people involved in the drug trade often have firearms. However, no one is at home when they arrive. The team fans out throughout the house and the grounds, recording what they see. One team member notes a patch of dead vegetation and takes pictures and samples of the vegetation. People who make methamphetamine sometimes dump toxic compounds in their yards, and this often causes the vegetation to die. Inside the house, on the kitchen table, the team finds a box of cold medication containing ephedrine and a quantity of lithium batteries. This is highly suggestive, and the team continues to search.

The property covers about three acres. There is a large herb garden and several outbuildings, including an old grain storage silo. Detective Soin walks all around the silo; it looks normal, but he can smell a pungent odor on one side. Then the detective notices something odd: one of the rusted metal panels near the bottom of the silo has a small knob on it. Carefully, wearing gloves, the detective pulls on the knob. To his surprise, a panel opens out from the side of the silo. He calls other members of the team over, and they inspect the hidden door. After taking more photographs, the team then proceeds inside the silo.

Their flashlights illuminate glass and metal containers and jugs of compounds. The inside of the silo has been converted into a meth lab. There are beakers and hot plates, cartons of cold medication, and racks of supplies. They find a large quantity of product stored in bags and also bundles of twenty-dollar bills stored in in a large metal trunk. The officers have discovered a high-volume operation. They film and photograph everything and begin to catalog what they have found.

Detective Soin goes to his vehicle and calls the state police and federal law enforcement personnel to update everyone on what has been found. As this is a large operation, and as it is

FIGURE 14.5 Farm silo

Searches of Automobiles

FIGURE 14.6 Vehicles may be searched more readily than homes

somehow tied up with the death of a child, he anticipates that the federal government will want to prosecute it. However, his immediate concern is locating the Garçon brothers. They should be arrested before they learn that their operation has been discovered and attempt to flee.

Just as Detective Soin ends his last call, he observes a pickup truck coming down the country lane toward the property. In it are two men. The truck slows down as it nears the house, and the two men inside gaze with open mouths at the law enforcement vehicles parked in front of the house. The truck then speeds off, but not before Detective Soin has recognized Abe and Al Garçon. He starts his engine, turns his vehicle into the country lane and follows.

Detective Soin is now in hot pursuit of suspected federal felons. Using his radio, he calls other officers to join in the chase. It does not take long; there is nowhere to hide on the open country roads surrounding Liberty Springs. When the men in the truck see the fleet of vehicles pursuing them, they realize that it is hopeless and pull over. They are ordered to step away from the truck with hands raised, and they comply. They are carefully searched. A **search incident to arrest** does not require a warrant, as the officers need to know if the apprehended person has concealed weapons or contraband.

The Fourth Amendment protection against unreasonable searches and seizures extends to automobiles. However, courts have found that there is a lower expectation of privacy associated with vehicles than with residences. This means that police have broader rights to conduct warrantless vehicle searches.

In a vehicular search incident to arrest, an officer may search an arrestee's person and the surrounding area, including places around the arrestee inside a car. Along with evidence preservation, this rule is designed to protect officers by revealing weapons that may be within the arrestee's reach. Inventory searches are allowed after an officer has arrested a driver and impounded a vehicle. Finally, probable cause searches are permissible when an officer suspects (through plain view or smell, for example) that evidence of a crime will be found in the vehicle. Of course, warrantless vehicular searches may be conducted without meeting the requirements of any of these exceptions if the driver gives the officer consent to search.

The *Terry* Stop and Frisk

The 1968 case *Terry v. Ohio*, 392 U.S. 1 (1968) arose when police detective Martin McFadden conducted a pat-down search of John Terry and Richard Chilton. McFadden observed suspicious behavior from Terry and Chilton and believed that the two men were casing a store in preparation for a robbery. Upon frisking the men, McFadden discovered that they were carrying guns. Terry and Chilton were convicted for un-lawfully carrying concealed weapons. They appealed, and the case eventually reached the United States Supreme Court.

Terry argued that the evidence against him had been obtained through an illegal search and seizure. Howev-er, the Supreme Court held that stop-and-frisk encounters do not necessarily violate the Fourth Amendment. Chief Justice Earl Warren wrote that police of-ficers, in order to protect against imme-diate danger, may conduct warrantless pat-downs for weapons if they observe behavior that sparks reasonable suspi-cion based on "specific and articulable" facts. Further, the Court reasoned that the purpose of the exclusionary rule—which precludes the use of illegally obtained evidence in trial—is to deter officers from conducting unreasonable searches while gathering evidence, not while preventing crime.

Arrest and Interrogation

Abe and Al Garçon are driven to the Liberty Springs police station. From there, they are taken into federal custody. The federal authorities are now quite interested in the case, and state law enforcement will work with the United States attorney for the State of Franklin. Cooperation between state and federal agencies occurs frequently where jurisdiction overlaps.

Federal agents would like to question Abe and Al. However, before the brothers may be questioned by any government agent, they must be advised of their rights in accordance with the Supreme Court's decision in *Miranda v. Arizona*, 384 U.S. 436 (1996). The brothers are advised that they have the right to remain silent and that anything they say can and will be used against them in court. They are informed that they have the right to have a lawyer present while they are being questioned, and if they cannot afford a lawyer, one will be appointed to represent them if they wish. They are told that they can choose to exercise these rights at any time and not answer questions or make any statements. The brothers affirm that they understand their rights. They also say that they choose to exercise their right to remain silent.

The giving of the *Miranda* warning is recorded, as is the brothers' response. It is best to not take any chances with this rule. If questioning had occurred without it, any incriminating information derived from it could be thrown out as **fruit of the poisonous tree**. This doctrine extends the exclusionary rule to render evidence inadmissible if it was derived from evidence that was illegally obtained: if the "tree" was tainted by improper procedure, the "fruit" is tainted, too, and cannot be admitted in court.[4]

---

4   There are some exceptions to the doctrine. If the evidence came from a source that was independent of the illegal activity, then it can be admitted. In addition, if its discovery was inevitable—such that law enforcement would have discovered it anyway, even ignoring the illegal search, then it can be admitted. The case that created this latter exception is *Nix v. Williams*, 467 U.S. 431 (1984).

Pretrial Detention and the Charging Process

The Fifth Amendment to the United States Constitution requires the federal government to use a **grand jury** for felony cases.[5] Grand juries are composed of sixteen to twenty-three members of the community, and they decide whether criminal charges should be brought against a potential defendant. There is no presiding judge; the prosecutor explains the law and the evidence to the grand jurors and brings witnesses to testify. Grand juries have broad power: they may ask questions, reach out for new information, and hear most any evidence they feel is important. Grand jury meetings are not open to the public, and proceedings are conducted in secrecy. A grand jury may issue an **indictment** for a crime only if twelve of its members find probable cause that a crime has been committed by a criminal suspect. In the case of the Garçon brothers, the grand jury had no difficulty supporting an indictment, a formal charge of crimes allegedly committed by the defendants.

The federal indictment filed against Al and Abe is accompanied by an affidavit that lists the evidence that has been secured to support the case. Federal agents bring Abe and Al Garçon to the United States District Court for the District of Franklin, as they are facing federal felony criminal charges. Their first appearance is an **arraignment** before District Court Judge Sara Sheehan. The **prosecutor** of the case is Assistant United States Attorney Ahmed Syed, who works with the United States attorney for the State of Franklin.

Although the brothers have already received a *Miranda* warning, Judge Sheehan informs them again of their constitutional rights. Their responses are captured in the record of court proceedings. The men are asked if they can afford counsel, and they claim that they cannot. It seems that most of their assets were stored as cash in a trunk in the silo on

The *Miranda* Warning

FIGURE 14.7 Giving a *Miranda* warning

In 1963, Arizona resident Ernesto Miranda was arrested and charged with rape, kidnapping, and robbery. Miranda was interrogated for two hours and then signed a written confession. It was an open-and-shut case for the prosecution. But Miranda's defense attorney felt uneasy about the confession, and at trial asked the officers whether they had advised Miranda of his right to remain silent or have an attorney present. The officers had not, but the trial judge admitted the confession as there was no requirement that a person *be notified* of these rights. Miranda's case went all the way up to the Supreme Court. In the resulting landmark decision, *Miranda v. Arizona*, 384 U.S. 436 (1966), the Supreme Court determined that due to the coercive nature of police interrogations, no confessions could be admitted in court unless suspects were advised of their right to remain silent and their right to have an attorney present. The Court overturned Miranda's thirty-year prison sentence and threw out his confession. *Miranda* warnings thereafter became standard procedure in any custodial interrogation.

---

5   The Fifth Amendment says in pertinent part, "No person shall be held to answer for a capital or otherwise infamous crime, unless on a presentment or indictment of a grand jury ..." The purpose of this requirement is to screen out cases that are baseless or driven by a malicious motive.

Earl Warren

Chief Justice, United States Supreme Court (1953–1969)

FIGURE 14.8 Chief Justice Earl Warren

Chief Justice Earl Warren presided over some of the most momentous decisions in Supreme Court history. During his influential tenure, the Court saw the expansion of the rights of criminal defendants and a move toward a more expansive understanding of criminal procedure.

Among his Court's best-known opinions are *Gideon v. Wainwright*, 372 U.S. 335 (1963), which ruled that states must provide an attorney to defendants in criminal cases, and *Escobedo v. Illinois*, 378 U.S. 478 (1964), which confirmed a suspect's right to speak with an attorney during police interrogations. Chief Justice Warren authored a number of transformative majority opinions, including the opinion in the landmark case *Mapp v. Ohio*, 367 U.S. 643 (1961). *Mapp* applied the exclusionary rule to the states, preventing the use of evidence gathered in violation of a defendant's constitutional rights. These opinions signaled an increasing federal interest in protecting the rights of state court criminal defendants. Until this point, the field of criminal procedure had largely been left to the states to regulate.

their property, and that trunk has been seized as evidence. They mortgaged their property to get their start in the meth business, and the remaining equity in their small farm will likely not be sufficient to meet their legal costs. The brothers have filled out financial affidavits, swearing under oath that they cannot afford counsel. The Sixth Amendment of the United States Constitution guarantees them the right to counsel in federal cases, and through the Supreme Court's ruling in *Gideon v. Wainwright*, 372 U.S. 335 (1963) and other cases, it has been extended to state cases where a sentence of imprisonment could result.

Judge Sheehan calls a recess in the proceedings and reviews the affidavits submitted by the brothers. She then returns to the bench and approves their request. They are assigned representation from a **public defender**, who provides legal representation to criminal defendants who cannot afford an attorney. Assistant Federal Public Defender Alexa Petrovoka will represent them in this case.

The judge outlines the charges that have been filed against the defendants. In addition to the charges for attempting to avoid arrest (incurred because of the vehicle chase), they include, for each man, two serious drug-related counts and a third count, which is the most serious of all. The charges are:

1. A count of conspiracy to manufacture more than fifty grams of methamphetamine (and related compounds), a Schedule II controlled substance. This offense can result in a sentence of life in prison. The evidence supporting this count includes the drugs and drug-making apparatus seized on the property.

2. A count of illegal trafficking in a Schedule II controlled substance. This offense is punished more harshly than mere possession and also can result in life in prison. The evidence supporting the trafficking includes the amount of product and the money in the trunk found in the silo.

3. A count of felony murder, based upon Adam's death. The prosecutor believes he can prove that one

(continued)

precipitating cause of the boy's death was his inges-tion of the methamphetamine and that its source, beyond a reasonable doubt, was his uncles' opera-tion. This count carries with it the possibility of the death penalty.

Judge Sheehan informs the Garçon brothers of the charges against them, and of the maximum sentence for each charge. When she tells the brothers that they are facing the death penalty, they become very still and pale.

The judge then considers the question of **bail**. Bail is security, usually money, that a defendant must post before being released from custody to ensure that they will return to court when required to do so. The Eighth Amendment to the United States Constitution prohibits "excessive bail." While a judge is not obligated to grant bail for someone who has been arrested, if they do, the amount may not be unreasonable. Racial disparities are particularly notable in the bail setting. Black defendants are more likely to be denied bail than white defendants, and Black, Latino, and Native American defendants are more likely to remain incarcerated because they cannot afford bail.[6]

In the case of the Garçon brothers, the judge explains that she is not inclined to grant bail due to the serious nature of the charges. She also notes that the men already tried to evade law enforcement when pursued in their vehicle. Their attorney, Ms. Petrovoka, argues that they are not a flight risk, but the judge declines to reconsider. This means that, until their case is resolved in their favor, Abe and Al Garçon will remain in federal custody. If they do not win their case, they could remain in federal custody for the rest of their lives.

The case now formally moves toward trial. The Sixth Amendment of the United States Constitution declares that criminal defendants have the **right to a speedy and public trial**. This does not mean that the case will be tried in the following months or even in the following year. Both the assistant United States attorney and the public defender

Upon his retirement and reflecting back upon his Court's influence in expanding in-dividual civil rights, Chief Justice Warren remarked, "I would like [my] Court to be remembered as the people's court."

---

6   David Arnold et al., "Racial Bias in Bail Decisions," *Quarterly Journal of Economics*, Vol. 133 No. 4 (2018).

Kalief Browder and the Necessity of Speedy Trials

FIGURE 14.9 Riker's Island, home to New York's largest jail

In 2010, sixteen-year-old Kalief Browder was accused of stealing a backpack. Though the backpack was never found (nor was any evidence to implicate Browder), he was charged with robbery, grand larceny, and assault. Browder was sent to Rikers Island, where he spent three years awaiting trial. Browder endured two of those years in solitary confinement and suffered torture, abuse, and starvation. The charges against him were eventually dropped. Upon release, a traumatized Browder attempted to move forward and receive a college education, but the psychological toll was too great. In 2015, at the age of twenty-two, he committed suicide.

The importance of a speedy and public trial—as guaranteed by the Sixth Amendment—cannot be overstated. Speedy trials do not merely protect evidence and witness memory but may also save lives. Forty-four states have their own "speedy trial" statutes, including Browder's home state of New York. Yet many have observed that New York's "Ready Rule" (CPL §30.30) is employed unequally, pointing out the large discrepancies in trial wait time between upscale Manhattan and

(*continued*)

have much to do; major cases require a great deal of work to prepare for trial. Both the public defender and the assistant United States attorney will seek to develop the facts and legal arguments, just like in civil cases. The prosecution will assess the evidence seized at the silo and will try and figure out where the drugs went and how they were distributed. The prosecution will also consider what evidence will best support the stated charges in the eyes of the jury. The defense will file pretrial motions, including motions to dismiss charges or suppress evidence. In this case, a Motion to Sever is likely to be filed. It will require a separate trial and a separate attorney for each defendant. If either Abe or Al wishes to claim that the methamphetamine operation was conducted by the other brother, or seek to assert that the other brother was more at fault for Adam's death, they cannot be jointly represented.

The attorney currently representing Abe and Al is working for clients who are facing the death penalty. This is arguably the most serious type of case that an attorney can manage. Ms. Petrovoka consults with the brothers and talks with them about the case and their prospects. Due to the serious nature of the charges, there is a limited opportunity for **plea bargaining**. Through plea negotiations, defendants may agree to plead guilty to a lesser charge, or to a reduced number of charges, or accept a reduced sentence for the crime(s) they are accused of committing. Plea bargaining benefits prosecutors, who can resolve a case without the risk of loss at trial. It benefits judges, who have busy dockets and cannot try all the cases that they hear. It also benefits public defenders such as Ms. Petrovoka, who serve many clients. Of course, if a defendant committed the crime, plea bargaining also benefits that defendant, as they will obtain a reduced sentence.[7] Whether

---

7   Plea bargaining has been the subject of much controversy. Some argue that plea bargaining arrangements permit offenders to escape just punishment. Others note that plea bargain offers can increase the pressure on an innocent defendant to accept a plea rather than exercise their right to a jury trial. Some jurisdictions have experimented with bans on plea bargaining. *See* Robert Weninger, "The Abolition of Plea Bargaining: A Case Study of El Paso County, Texas," *UCLA Law Rev.* 35 (1987).

or not to accept a proposal made through plea bargaining is entirely up to the defendant.

Ms. Petrovoka's communications with the Garçon brothers are protected by the attorney-client privilege (just like in civil cases). Without eavesdropping on their conversations, we can surmise that her greatest priority is protecting them from execution. A successful plea bargain requires this outcome. She does have something to work with: the connection between Adam's death and the brothers' criminal activity remains opaque. To prevail on the felony murder count—the count that comes with the death penalty—the assistant United States attorney will have to prove that Adam's death was tied up with the drug operation beyond a reasonable doubt.

After protracted discussions with her clients and with the assistant United States attorney, Ms. Petrovoka advises the court that they have reached a plea agreement. In exchange for their cooperation and information about the methamphetamine network that they were part of, the Garçon brothers will plead guilty to the first two charges, and the third charge of felony murder will be dismissed. Abe and Al will not face the death penalty, but they will spend the remainder of their lives in prison. Finally, the prosecutor agrees to recommend that the brothers be allowed to serve their time at the same federal facility.

The court schedules a hearing to go over the terms of the plea bargain. This is the final—and vital—procedural safeguard in this process, and Judge Sheehan is very careful at the plea bargain hearing. Rule 11 of the Federal Rules of Criminal Procedure declares that, before the court "accepts a plea of guilty ... the defendant may be placed under oath, and the court must address the defendant personally in open court." Rule 11 also says that proceedings involving plea bargains must be recorded. By pleading guilty, defendants give up a host of very important constitutional rights. Federal judges are required to make sure that each defendant who pleads guilty is aware of these rights and has made the decision to relinquish them voluntarily.

lower-income, racially diverse communities such as the Bronx. Without equal and fair implementation of speedy trial statutes, criminal defendants may be held indefinitely under untried accusations. As in the case of Kalief Browder, the consequences of such a process may be irreversible.

These rights include 1) the right to plead not guilty; 2) the right to a jury trial; 3) the right to be represented by counsel during trial; 4) the right to cross-examine adverse witnesses; 5) the right to compel witnesses to come to court; 6) the right to be proven guilty beyond a reasonable doubt; and 7) the right to be protected from compelled self-incrimination. This last right comes from the Fifth Amendment to the United States Constitution, which contains the privilege against self-incrimination. The government must prove its case without the help of the person it has charged, and a jury may not infer guilt from a defendant's failure to testify at trial.

In addition to making sure that the men understand that they are giving up these rights, Judge Sheehan must review the nature of the charges and their possible penalties. She must review the terms of the plea agreement and make sure that there is enough evidence to support a guilty plea on the proposed charges. The judge is not required to accept the guilty plea; if she believes there is not a sufficient factual basis for it or if she thinks that improper coercion has been brought to bear, she may reject it. The judge serves as a final, critical safeguard in the plea bargain process.

Judge Sheehan speaks in court with each brother carefully. She must satisfy herself that the Garçon brothers are entering voluntary pleas and confirm their understanding about the important rights they are giving up. She must also make sure they understand that if they fail to fully cooperate with the pending investigation, their plea bargains will be revoked. At the end of the hearing, both men plead guilty to two charges each, and their sentence of life in prison is confirmed. They are remanded to federal custody and will be moved to federal prison.

We later learn that the brothers cooperated with federal authorities, fulfilling the terms of their plea bargains. They offered useful information about their drug contacts. They also offered more information about their interaction with Adam.

They confirmed that Adam worked at their farm, helping them with their online herbal business. This business was cover for their meth operation; they could purchase many of the items they needed to cook meth without raising suspicion. The brothers worked in their meth lab on the days Adam was not on the property and tended to the herbal business on the days that Adam was there. They enjoyed their time with him and did not want him involved in their criminal enterprise.

Abe shared that, about a month before Adam died, Abe caught him opening the silo door. Abe firmly told Adam that he was not to go inside. Then, about a week before Adam died, Al found Adam inside the silo. Al told Adam that his uncles were operating an illegal alcohol still. Al asked Adam to keep it secret, and Adam agreed. During the conversation, Adam asked a few questions about the operation and picked up a used coffee filter. Adam asked about the substance on the filter. Al told Adam that the crystals were a type of sugar. Later, Adam told Abe that he was thinking it would be cool to add sugar to coffee as it was being brewed. Abe did not, at that time, know of Adam's prior conversation with Al.

Adam liked to make coffee in his uncles' kitchen. He liked his coffee very sweet and added teaspoons of sugar to it before he drank it. Abe and Al now think that the boy decided to make coffee using the filter to try and "add sugar as it was being brewed." This is their best guess as to how he ingested the methamphetamine. It is noteworthy that, when Adam threw the filter out in the trash, he created the chain of evidence that led to his uncles' arrest for his murder.

Conclusion and Introduction to Law Lab

The government's case against Abe and Al included many measures designed to satisfy the requirements of due process. In fact, the rules that govern the processing of criminal cases are critically important to the rule of law. Correct outcomes are far more likely to result from fair processes. Robust procedural rules protect the rights of the accused and the rights of the government as cases moves through the legal system.

One of the most important procedural tools of justice is the jury trial. As Supreme Court Justice James Wilson remarked, "[t]o the conviction of a crime, the undoubting and the unanimous sentiment of the twelve jurors is of indispensable necessity."[8]

The English common law considered the right to an impartial jury to be vital to ensure a just verdict. Attorneys are permitted to **challenge for cause** and remove before trial any jurors who appear to be

FIGURE 14.10 Coffee filter

unable to remain fair or impartial. Lamentably, until the Supreme Court said otherwise in *Batson v. Kentucky*, 476 U.S. 79 (1986), prosecutors could use their discretionary right of **peremptory challenge** to exclude Black jurors from hearing cases.

Today, most criminal cases bypass the jury system entirely and are resolved through plea negotiations. Accordingly, the parts of Criminal Procedure that address pretrial matters have become even more important in today's legal system. The pretrial rules include important safeguards to protect criminal defendants from abuse and overreach by the government. As we noted, one important safeguard is the warrant requirement.

In the Law Lab that follows, there is a question about whether a warrant should have been issued before a particular search was conducted. You are a judge in Liberty County Court, and you must decide the matter. If you find that the search was proper without a warrant, then the evidence that was gathered during the search can be admitted in the criminal case. However, if you find that law enforcement should have obtained a warrant, then some or all of the evidence cannot be admitted. This decision will severely impair the criminal case.

You and your judicial colleagues must consider: what do the rules of criminal procedure require?

---

8   *See* James Wilson, *The Works of the Honourable James Wilson, L.L.D.* 350 (1804).

State Court Judge Law Lab

MEMORANDUM

To: The Associate Justices of Liberty County Circuit Court

From: Law Clerks of Liberty County Circuit Court

Re: *State of Franklin v. Evans*

Your Honors:

The Law Clerks of the Liberty County Circuit Court offer this memorandum, which summarizes the contents of filings made by both the State's Attorney's Office and the Public Defender's Office concerning this unusual matter.

Factual Background

Ethel Evans, a resident of Liberty Springs, was in her home one Friday afternoon, sharing a joint of marijuana with her friends George McMartin and Sally Okira. Marijuana is not legal to grow, own, or smoke in the State of Franklin. From the testimony of Mr. McMartin and Ms. Okira, all was peaceful (and very mellow) until there was a pounding on Ms. Evans's front door at about 5:30 p.m. When she opened it, a masked man burst inside, carrying a canvas bag. Ms. Evans called out, "Hey, dude!" but he did not stop. Instead, he ran down the hallway leading to Ms. Evans's bedroom. A second later, Police Sergeant Smith appeared at the door. He rushed inside, breathlessly calling out, "Police! We're chasing a robbery suspect!"

Sergeant Smith pursued the suspect into the bedroom and arrested him as he was trying to crawl outside through a window. But as the sergeant passed back through the house, suspect in tow, he noted the cloying scent of marijuana smoke. He radioed a nearby officer, Officer Lee, to come inside.

FIGURE 14.11 Joint of marijuana

The officers looked around the front room and found the mostly smoked joint. Ms. Evans, Mr. McMartin, and Ms. Okira were all arrested. At the time of their arrest, they all exhibited dilated pupils (typical of marijuana usage) and their breaths smelled of marijuana.

While in the house, Officer Lee and Sergeant Smith noted another smell. When later questioned about it, Officer Lee said that he recognized the sulfuric/rotten-egg smell associated with the production of methamphetamine.

The police officers secured the three suspects in a squad car (this took about three minutes). They then searched the house thoroughly. In the basement, they found a surprise: Ms. Evans had a meth operation underway. They also found a lockbox with over $10,000 in cash in it, labeled "Sales Money."

Ms. Evans, Mr. McMartin, and Ms. Okira have been charged with unlawful possession of less than 2.5 grams of cannabis, a misdemeanor in Franklin. In addition, Ms. Evans has been charged with the felony of manufacturing a Schedule II controlled substance, methamphetamine, with the intent to sell.

Attorneys in the public defender's office represent all three defendants. They have filed a motion to keep all the evidence that the police discovered out of court on the grounds that it resulted from an unlawful search. This evidence includes the partially smoked joint, the testimony of Officers Smith and Lee, and the evidence of meth production and sales (including the lockbox) found in the basement. The state's attorney filed an opposition to the motion, arguing that no warrant was required because Sergeant Smith was in "hot pursuit" of a suspect at the time he entered the home. Therefore, he was legally entitled to be inside the home, as was Officer Lee. Their detection of the marijuana joint occurred in the course of their presence in a lawful location, and therefore the evidence should be admitted. In addition, the state's attorney argued that the smell of the lab was in "plain view" and authorized the search of the house.

Relevant Law

The Fourth Amendment to the United States Constitution declares:

> The right of the people to be secure in their persons, houses, papers, and effects, against
> unreasonable searches and seizures, shall not be violated, and no warrants shall issue, but

upon probable cause, supported by oath or affirmation, and particularly describing the place to be searched, and the persons or things to be seized.

In *Warden v. Hayden*, 387 U.S. 294 (1967), the United States Supreme Court found that police may enter a residence without a warrant if "the exigencies of the situation made that course imperative." *See also McDonald v. United States*, 335 U.S. 451 (1948). In *Warden*, the police were informed that an armed robbery had taken place and that the suspect had entered 2111 Cocoa Lane less than five minutes before they reached it. The Court found that law enforcement acted reasonably in entering the house and searching for a man of the description they had been given and for weapons which he had used in the robbery or might use against them. "The Fourth Amendment does not require police officers to delay in the course of an investigation if to do so would gravely endanger their lives or the lives of others." *Warden*, 387 U.S. at 299.

However, if police should have a warrant for a search and fail to obtain one before searching, any evidence that they improperly seize may not be used in court against the criminal defendant. *See Mapp v. Ohio*, 367 U.S. 643 (1961).

Issue: What Evidence is Admissible?

The court must determine whether the evidence seized by the police in this case may be admitted at trial. The evidence includes the marijuana joint and items from the basement meth lab. As no warrant was issued before law enforcement gathered the evidence, exceptions to the warrant requirement must apply for the evidence to be admitted in court.

You may wish to consider each defendant's situation separately. You may also wish to consider the items of evidence individually. How do the rules of Criminal Procedure apply in this case?

Conclusion

The law clerks are available to answer any questions that the members of our judiciary may have in connection with this unusual case. We look forward to your ruling on this interesting matter.

CHAPTER 15

Crime and Punishment

Laws too gentle are seldom obeyed; too severe, seldom executed.
—Benjamin Franklin (1706–1790), writer, publisher, politician, scientist, diplomat, and Founding Father of the United States

Introduction

In the two last chapters, we explored Criminal Law and Criminal Procedure, reviewing crimes and how they are prosecuted. In the next chapter, we will move on to explore social and ethical considerations in the work of legal professionals.

First, however, we must address two more components of criminal law: defenses to crimes and the penalties for committing them. Both implicate the theories of criminal punishment. Some actions that cause injury are not punished in the American criminal justice system. Two people may commit the same act, and yet the prosecutor could decide that only one of them should be charged with a crime. Alternatively, a jury may find that a criminal defendant committed an unlawful action but should not be punished for it. The defendant may have lacked the capacity to commit the crime or had a legal justification for undertaking the action. In this chapter, we will consider the most common defenses to crimes and why they exonerate.

We will then overview the theories governing the punishment of criminal offenders in the United States. In Chapter 1, we encountered the concept of *lex talionis* (an eye for an eye), but there are other ideas about what justice requires after a crime has been committed. Some theories support the death penalty for those who take the lives of others. In the United States, however, the death penalty is only used for the most morally repugnant crimes and criminals. We will explore some of the theories guiding punishments for criminal actions, and continue to note the places where the promise of equality and due process under the United States Constitution falls short.

FIGURE 15.1 Lady Justice

Finally, in this week's Law Lab, you will once more reprise your role as a United States Supreme Court justice. You must determine whether the death penalty should apply in a case involving a young man who committed premeditated murder on his eighteenth birthday. A jury has convicted him, and the law of the State of Franklin supports his execution. You will decide if he should pay the ultimate price for his wrongful and premeditated criminal action.

CRIME AND PUNISHMENT KEY TERMS

The following key terms are defined in this chapter. They are also defined in the Glossary.

Age of Criminal Responsibility

Defense of Consent

Defense of Infancy

Defense of Intoxication

Defense of Others

Deterrence

Doctrine of Necessity

Duress

Incapacitation

Insanity Defense

Irresistible Impulse Defense

M'Naghten Rule

Penitentiary

Recompense

Restorative Justice

Retribution

Self-Defense

Stand Your Ground Laws

Substantial Capacity Test

Defenses to Crimes

Defenses to crimes are most often based upon (1) a claimed legal justification for the crime or (2) a claimed lack of capacity. Defenses based upon lack of capacity argue that the defendant did not possess the mental state required to commit the crime. This can be due to their young age or due to a condition that they were enduring at the time of the offense. This defense is often tied up with the *mens rea* (mental state) that must be established for a conviction.

In contrast, defenses asserting a legal justification acknowledge the criminal action, but argue that the offender had a legally recognized excuse for committing it. We will begin with these defenses, which include duress, consent, necessity, self-defense, and defense of others.

Defenses Asserting Excuse or Justification

The Model Penal Code provides that the defense of **duress** may be used where a defendant was coerced to engage in criminal action by the threat or use of unlawful force, such that "a person of reasonable firmness" in the situation would have been unable to resist.[1] The defense may not be used if the defendant recklessly or negligently put themselves at risk. In addition, the defense only may be used if the threatened harm is greater than the harm that would result from the criminal act. Thus, to plead duress, you must be coerced by the threat or use of unlawful force, and you may not harm someone else to save yourself.

If someone engages in criminal action to avoid greater harm, that may be a defense under the **doctrine of necessity**, also called the choice of evils defense. The Model Penal Code notes that the harm avoided must be greater than the harm committed.[2] For example, let us say

---

1   *See* Model Penal Code §2.09.
2   *See* Model Penal Code, §3.02.

Patty Hearst and Duress

FIGURE 15.2 Patty Hearst

Patricia "Patty" Hearst is an heiress of the Hearst family fortune. She was kidnapped by members of the Symbionese Liberation Army (an American domestic terrorist group), held hostage, assaulted, indoctrinated, and given a new name ("Tanya"). She was induced to renounce her friends and family and thereafter help the group build bombs and rob a bank. She was arrested along with other members of the group. While being booked into jail, she listed her occupation as "urban guerrilla" and asked her attorney to relay the following message:

> "Tell everybody that I'm smiling, that
> I feel free and strong and I send my
> greetings and love to all the sisters
> and brothers out there."

At the time of her arrest, she weighed 87 pounds. Within a few weeks, Patty Hearst had repudiated the tenets of the terrorist group.

At her trial in the robbery case, she asserted the defense of duress, claiming that she had been compelled to collaborate with her captors. The jury did not find her argument compelling; she was convicted and sentenced to thirty-five years in prison. Her term was later reduced to seven years and then commuted by President Jimmy Carter. She was finally pardoned by President Bill Clinton. Her name is now associated with Stockholm syndrome, a psychological condition in which hostages develop a bond with their captors.

that I am injured in a storm at sea, and my damaged boat washes ashore on a remote island. I break into an uninhabited cottage on the island to access a satellite communication service to call for help. I may plead the defense of necessity to the charge of breaking and entering. The minimal harm to the property owner was less severe than the imminent threat to my life. I will be required to pay the owner of the cottage for anything I used and any damage I caused. If, however, the cottage owner is in residence and declines to permit me to enter, I may not kill them to gain entry. My life is not more important that theirs, and the defense will not justify homicide.

The right of **self-defense** supports the use of force against those who seek to commit criminal acts against others. Under the Model Penal Code and the laws of most states, a person may use force against another person when it is immediately necessary to prevent the unlawful use of force by that person.[3] Generally, the use of deadly force is not permitted unless required to protect against death, serious bodily injury, kidnapping, or sexual intercourse compelled by force or threat. Deadly force is also not justified if the person knows that it can be avoided by retreating or surrendering possession of property.[4] This is a variation of the old common law rule: a person was obliged to "retreat to the wall" before using deadly force in self-defense. You are also allowed to use force to protect others from harm if, under the circumstances, you would have been justified in protecting yourself.[5] Thus, the law also recognizes the use of force in **defense of others**.

In contrast with the Model Penal Code and the common law rule, a majority of states have passed **stand your ground laws** that permit the use of deadly force when an individual is confronted with the threat of serious injury or it reasonably appears that deadly force is necessary to prevent a felony. Under these laws, there is no duty to retreat if you are in a location lawfully.[6] Critics argue that people may use their right not to retreat in an aggressive way, increasing the likelihood of assaults. In addition, some research suggests that stand your ground laws correlate with a racial bias.[7]

If someone is playing football and becomes injured as the result of a legal tackle, the tackler can establish the **defense of consent**. The defense of consent applies if the bodily injury consented to is not serious or involves the foreseeable hazards of participation in a lawful athletic contest or sport. If, however, the tackler punched the victim in the face, the defense would not apply, as that action is beyond the scope of consent provided. In addition, the consent must be given by a person who is competent to provide it and not induced by force, duress, or deception.[8]

---

3   *See* Model Penal Code, §3.04.
4   *See* Model Penal Code, §3.04.
5   *See* Model Penal Code, §3.05.
6   The history of this defense is interesting. The transformation from the common law rule that you must retreat to the American rule that you are entitled to stand your ground and use deadly force was "a combination of Eastern legal authorities and Western judges … [who thought the common law rule] upheld cowardice" and wished to create a new rule "suited to the bravery of the 'true man.'" *See* Richard Maxell Brown, *No Duty to Retreat: Violence and Values in American History* 5 (1991).
7   Ackermann, Goodman, Gilbert, Arroyo-Johnson, and Pagano, "Race, Law, and Health: Examination of 'Stand Your Ground' and Defendant Convictions in Florida, Social Science & Medicine," 142 *Social Science and Medicine* 194–201 (Oct. 2015).
8   *See* Model Penal Code, §2.11.

Defenses Asserting a Lack of Capacity

American law generally presumes that all adult persons have the capacity to commit a crime. Accordingly, prosecutors need not prove that this is true for a particular criminal defendant. Instead, it is up to the defendant to prove that they lack the legal capacity to commit the crime.

If a crime involves a person who has not reached the legal age of majority, the **defense of infancy** may apply. In the United States, we do not punish young children for crimes in the same way that we punish adults. We recognize that children are not always in control of their actions and sometimes do not comprehend the consequences of the choices they make. This defense has historical roots. Under Roman law and the English common law, a child younger than seven was presumed to be incapable of committing a crime.[9] Yet, despite these historical antecedents, most states have no established minimum **age of criminal responsibility**. Thus, children as young as six have been taken from their parents and sent to juvenile court as delinquents.[10] Rarely, children as young as fourteen have been charged with crimes as adults.[11] However, it is far more common for children who commit crimes to be placed in a juvenile detention center and enrolled in programs supported by the state juvenile justice system. These programs usually focus on rehabilitating youthful offenders by providing the individualized guidance needed to facilitate their successful reintegration into society.

In the same way that a child is not held legally responsible, a person operating with limited mental capacity due to their consumption of alcohol may plead the **defense of intoxication** to crimes requiring a specific *mens rea*, depending upon the law of the state in which they are tried. For example, if a person was so intoxicated that they did not realize they were shooting their weapon at another person, then they may bring proofs at the subsequent murder trial to establish that their actions were not purposeful or knowing. Depending upon these proofs, their actions could still support a prosecution for homicide based upon reckless or negligent conduct. Similarly, if someone repeatedly drives while

---

9   Bath and Billick, *Overview of Juvenile Law* in *Principles and Practice of Adolescent Forensic Mental Health* 337 (Benedek, Ash, and Scott, Eds., 2010).

10   South Carolina sets the minimum age of criminal responsibility at six years; thirty-five states set it at seven years. For federal offenses, eleven years is the minimum age. This is a marked contrast with many other countries. For example, Norway, Finland, and Sweden have established fifteen years as the minimum age of criminal responsibility. Anette Storgaard, "Juvenile Justice in Scandinavia," *J. of Scandinavian Studies in Criminology and Crime Prevention* 188–204 (2005).

11   The youngest person executed by a state in the United States was Hannah Ocuish, a Pequot Native American with an intellectual disability. She confessed to the crime of killing the six-year-old daughter of a wealthy farmer in New London, Connecticut. She was executed by hanging at the age of twelve in 1786. A modern case concerns the 2019 murder of Tessa Majors, an eighteen-year-old Barnard College freshman. She was stabbed to death during a robbery by three teenagers, one aged thirteen and two aged fourteen. The two fourteen-year-olds were charged with second-degree murder. Under New York law, persons as young as thirteen can be tried as adults if charged with second-degree murder. *See* New York Consolidated Laws, Part 1, Title A, Art. 10, §18.

Elena Kagan

Associate Justice, United States Supreme Court (2010–present)

FIGURE 15.3   Justice Elena Kagan

As the first female dean of Harvard Law school and the first female solicitor general of the United States, Justice Elena Kagan made quite a name for herself in the American legal community. When President Barack Obama nominated her to the Supreme Court, the Senate confirmed her with a vote of 63–37.

Justice Kagan has authored a number of influential opinions. In *Miller v. Alabama*, 567 U.S. 460 (2012), she wrote the majority opinion, holding that sentencing juveniles convicted of homicide to mandatory life in prison without parole violated the Eighth Amendment. *Miller* came under a recent attack in *Jones v. Mississippi*, 593 U.S. __ (2021), when a majority of the Court found that the Eighth Amendment does not require a sentencing authority to determine that a juvenile is permanently incorrigible before imposing a life sentence without the possibility of parole. Justice Kagan joined the dissent in *Jones*, arguing that "the distinctive attributes of youth diminish the penological justifications for imposing the harshest sentences on juvenile offenders, even when they commit terrible crimes."

intoxicated and finally kills someone, the fact that they continued to make the choice to drink and drive could support a criminal conviction.

Offenders may also argue that they are not responsible for their conduct due to mental illness.[12] The American **insanity defense** initially followed the **M'Naghten Rule**, a jury instruction that arose from Daniel M'Naghten's 1843 murder of Edward Drummond, the private secretary to British Prime Minister Sir Robert Peel. Daniel M'Naghten was operating under the delusion that the prime minister wanted to murder him. He shot Drummond, who was wearing Sir Robert's coat.

FIGURE 15.4   Sir Robert Peel and his infamous coat

---

12   Twelve states (California, Iowa, Kentucky, Massachusetts, Nebraska, New Mexico, New York, North Carolina, North Dakota, Pennsylvania, Rhode Island, and South Dakota) follow the rule that mental illness negates only specific intent crimes. *See* Robinson and Williams, *Mapping American Criminal Law: Variations Across the 50 States* 93 (2018).

Drummond died, and M'Naghten was tried for murder. The jury acquitted M'Naghten, finding him not guilty by reason of insanity in *R v. M'Naghten* 8 E.R. 718 (1843). The British House of Lords decided that, to exonerate the offender, the defense must clearly prove 1) that the accused was laboring under such a defect of reason, from disease of the mind, that they did not know the nature and quality of the act that they were doing; or 2) if they did know what they were doing, they did not know that it was wrong. The current federal rule is very close to the M'Naghten Rule.[13]

Some attorneys representing defendants diagnosed with certain mental illnesses have argued that the M'Naghten Rule did not go far enough. Their clients conceded that they knew what they were doing and even knew it was wrong, but declared that they were compelled by an irresistible impulse to do it anyway. The **irresistible impulse defense**, offered as a flavor of the insanity defense, has garnered special attention. Critics point out that murderers are eligible for the death penalty because they kill people; the fact that killing was an irresistible impulse should not exonerate. In response, the American Law Institute devised the **substantial capacity test** for its Model Penal Code. This rule combines the element of volition (the ability to control your behavior) with the M'Naghten Rule's emphasis on cognition (understanding your behavior). It states:

> A person is not responsible for criminal conduct if, at the time of such conduct, as a result of mental disease or defect, he lacks substantial capacity either to appreciate the criminality of his conduct or to conform his conduct to the requirements of law.[14]

In addition, the Model Penal Code defines "mental disease or defect" to exclude abnormalities that are shown only through repeated criminal or antisocial conduct. Accordingly, a person who repeatedly kills others cannot escape prosecution simply because he has repeatedly committed murder. More broadly put, the criminal defendant cannot show that he lacks the ability to conform his conduct to the requirements of the law just because his conduct has been unlawful.

The insanity defense has not been popular with the public, and a handful of states have abolished it entirely. In those states, mentally ill people may be convicted even if they had no control or understanding of their actions at the time that they committed the crime. Their mental condition may, however, be a mitigating factor in their sentence.[15] Finally, in *Ford v. Wainwright*,[16] a majority of the Supreme Court determined that the Eighth Amendment bars states from executing the mentally insane. This means

---

13   Believing the defense had been overused, Congress passed the Insanity Defense Reform Act of 1984, which controls in all federal courts. It declares that insanity "is an affirmative defense to a prosecution ... [if] at the time of the commission of the acts constituting the offense, the defendant, as a result of a severe mental disease or defect, was unable to appreciate the nature and quality or the wrongfulness of his acts. Mental disease or defect does not otherwise constitute a defense." *See* 18 U.S.C. §17(a).

14   *See* Model Penal Code, §4.01. Twenty-two states have adopted the Model Penal Code's provision. They are Alaska, Arkansas, Colorado, Connecticut, Hawaii, Idaho, Indiana, Kansas, Maine, Maryland, Missouri, Montana, Nevada, New Hampshire, New Jersey, Ohio, Oregon, Tennessee, Utah, Vermont, Washington, and West Virginia. Robinson and Williams, *Mapping American Criminal Law, Id.*

15   The laws of Kansas, Montana, Idaho, and Utah do not support the insanity defense. Idaho and Montana allow a verdict of guilty but insane, and Utah allows a verdict of guilty but mentally ill. *See Mapping American Criminal Law* at 94.

16   *Ford v. Wainwright*, 477 U.S. 399 (1986).

that a person who was convicted and sentenced to death, but who then become mentally ill such that they cannot understand why their life is to be ended, may not be executed.

CRITICAL THINKING   Consider the impact of <u>age</u> as a factor of charging and sentencing.

Should there be a minimum age of criminal responsibility? If so, what is that age, and by what process do you select it? Should a six-, seven-, or eight-year-old be subject to criminal legal process?

In addition, should there be a single age of criminal responsibility across the United States, or should each state be able to establish its own minimum age? How does this issue implicate provisions of the United States Constitution?

Punishment of Offenders

Our societies have always acknowledged the need to punish those who violate the law. The earliest codes focused on **retribution** and **recompense**. The ancient Code of Hammurabi demanded the death penalty for twenty-five different crimes and compensation of various forms for other offenses.[17] The Mosaic Code also required the death penalty for a collection of offenses and instructed judges to assess damages and implement rules to settle penalties in other cases.[18]

In the modern United States, executions still occur, and retribution is cited as a major factor supporting capital punishment. However, over time, more nuanced philosophies about justice have emerged. As a result, some American penal systems have moved from a strictly punishment-based paradigm to models based upon new ideas about what justice and how the system can best achieve it.

In addition, there is now a vigorous national dialogue about the roles that gender, race, and socioeconomic status play in the justice system. This is tied to continuing discussions about the death penalty and what the law should require of criminals who consciously take the lives of others. The sections that follow briefly explore these ideas.

Goals of the Criminal Justice System

In medieval England, a person convicted of a misdemeanor was sentenced to corporal punishment. This might include flogging, branding, or time in a stockade. A person convicted of a felony, however, was executed. Over time, the number of capital crimes rose until, in the 1700s, hundreds of crimes were punishable by death.[19] In colonial America, these practices were largely followed, and well into the twen-

---

17   *See* H. Dieter Viel, *The New Complete Code of Hammurabi* (2012).
18   *See* Exodus 21:18, or Commandment 481, as numbered by Maimonides.
19   The code in effect was called the "Bloody Code" because it condemned so many to die for offenses we would now categorize as misdemeanors. *See* John Walliss, *The Bloody Code in England and Wales 1760–1830* (2018).

tieth century, executions followed convictions for a variety of felonies, such as arson, murder, rape, and horse theft.

The death penalty served several early objectives of the justice system. In addition to retribution, it served the goal of **deterrence**, the notion that serious punishments incline others away from committing crimes. A third goal was **incapacitation**. Incarcerating prisoners removes them from society and prevents them from committing more crimes. Proponents of the death penalty point out that it achieves all of these goals.

In the early nineteenth century, reformers came up with the idea of the **penitentiary**: a place to do penance for crimes, where offenders could transition away from sinful deeds toward good behavior.[20] They believed that work and Bible study would lead to reformation.[21] The idea that an offender can become a law-abiding member of society is powerful: many educational, psychological, and formal training programs have been created to serve this goal. There are studies showing that prison training and educational programs can assist reentry into society when criminal offenders have finished their term of incarceration.[22]

In the 1980s, victims' rights advocacy groups led the movement toward **restorative justice**, a more victim-oriented approach to the management of criminal cases. They began to encourage legislators to pass laws giving victims more rights in legal proceedings, such as the right to be heard in court, and the right to know when an offender is to be released.[23] During court hearings, victims now can offer their perspectives concerning the crimes committed and the appropriate punishments for offenders. This permits public acknowledgment of victims' emotional and material losses, which encourages the opportunity for healing. More broadly, restorative justice seeks to repair the harm caused by the crime. The criminal is still held accountable but is also provided with an avenue to make reparations and is given the opportunity to seek rehabilitation. Studies indicate that restorative justice can hold more offenders accountable, help more victims, and reduce the costs for the government.[24]

---

20   The Quakers (members of the Religious Society of Friends) were vigorous supporters of prison reform. The Quakers are a Christian religious movement founded in 1650. They advocated for a more rehabilitative approach for criminal offenders. Rather ironically, their emphasis on prayer and reflection promoted the concept of solitary confinement. *See* Robert Alan Cooper, "The English Quakers and Prison Reform 1809–23," 68 *Quaker History* 3–19 (1979).

21   The Eastern State Penitentiary was the first of its kind in the world, and it opened October 25, 1829, in Philadelphia, Pennsylvania. It created the "Pennsylvania System," which required nearly constant separate confinement of prisoners, with frequent visits from the warden and overseers. However, the Auburn, or "Congregate System," became the model used in the Northeast, South, and Midwest. It combined physical work in groups with solitary confinement at night. Prisoners were prohibited from speaking with each other at all times. The Post-Reconstruction prison era was particularly brutal for inmates, with punishments we now would recognize as torture. Chai Woodham, "Eastern State Penitentiary: A Prison with a Past," *Smithsonian Magazine* (Sept. 30, 2008).

22   Studies show that funding education classes reduces recidivism and reduces the operational costs associated with long-term warehousing of prisoners. John H. Esperian, "The Effect of Prison Education Programs on Recidivism," 61 *J. of Correctional Ed.* 316–334 (2010).

23   Academic evaluations of restorative justice offer a positive view. Criminal offenders seem less likely to offend, and victims are more satisfied with the outcomes of cases that incorporate restorative justice features in their management. *See* Lawrence W. Sherman & Heather Strang, *Restorative Justice: The Evidence* (2009).

24   *Id.*

FIGURE 15.5 Incarceration

Perspectives on Gender, Race, Poverty, and Crime

Questions about the proper purpose and methods of punishment are particularly important in the United States, as the nation has the highest rate of incarceration in the world. In 2018, the American rate of incarceration exceeded 650 persons per 100,000 persons in the general population.[25] In addition, the nation also has a very high percentage of its population under some form of correctional supervision (such as parole). At the end of 2018, that figure was about one in forty adults.[26]

In criminal populations throughout the nation, men outnumber women by a significant percentage, often at a ratio of ten to one.[27] In addition, criminal offenders are predominantly young; the peak age for involvement in crime is younger than twenty-five for all major crimes except gambling.[28]

There is a continuing national dialogue about the relationship between race, law enforcement, and crime. In the last chapter, we noted that racial disparities are evident in the American criminal justice system. In fact, Native American and Black persons are more likely to be charged with serious offenses, and they are more likely to be convicted and incarcerated.[29] This disparity has also been the subject of many research efforts. The disproportionately high number of minority arrests may arise from police

---

25   *See States of Incarceration: The Global Context 2018*, Prison Policy Initiative (last visited Sept. 28, 2020), https://www.prisonpolicy.org/global/2018.html.

26   *See* Bureau of Justice Statistics, Correctional Populations in the United States, 2017–2018, 1.

27   *See Chart: United States Incarceration Rates by Sex*, Prison Policy Initiative (last visited Sept. 27, 2020), https://www.prisonpolicy.org/graphs/genderinc.html.

28   We define "major crimes" as those reported in the FBI's Uniform Crime Report program. *See* Jeffrey T. Ulmer and Darrell J. Steffensmeier, "*The Age and Crime Relationship: Social Variation, Social Explanations," The Nurture Versus Biosocial Debate in Criminology: On the Origins of Criminal Behavior and Criminality* 377–396 (2014).

29   *See* M. Marit Rehavi and Sonja B. Starr, "Racial Disparity in Federal Criminal Sentences," 122 *Journal of Political Economy* 1320–1354 (2014); Shamena Anwar, Patrick Bayer, and Randi Hjalmarsson, "The Impact of Jury Race in Criminal Trials," 127 *Quarterly Journal of Economics*,

practices, such as extended policing in minority communities, racial profiling, and inherent bias.[30] For example, a 2015 report prepared by the United States Department of Justice found that police officers in Ferguson, Missouri, were focused on generating revenue for the department and city and that their practices violated the law and undermined community trust. More critically, the report found that the Ferguson Police Department engaged in a pattern of excessive force that violated the Fourth

FIGURE 15.6   Black Lives Matter protest

Amendment rights of the citizens, disproportionately harmed Black residents, and was motivated by discriminatory intent.[31]

In addition, there is continuing discussion about the relationship between crime rates and economic conditions. Some historic studies indicate that deep poverty correlates with certain types of crime.[32] Other studies challenge those findings as oversimplified.[33] However, in 2018, the influential Brookings Institution published a study that found a direct connection between poverty and crime rates.[34] In addition, the United States Department of Justice has determined that, among juveniles, violent victimization is a warning sign for future violent crimes: the same young people who become victims of violent crimes are more likely to later commit these crimes.[35] Accordingly, protecting young people from crime should be a priority for many reasons, including community safety.

1017–1055 (2012); David S. Abrams, Marianne Bertrand, and Sendi Mullainathan, "Do Judges Vary in Their Treatment of Race?," 41 *Journal of Legal Studies*, 347–383 (2012).

30   *See* John Donohue III and Steven Levitt, "The Impact of Race on Policing and Arrests," 44 Journal of Law & Economics 367–394 (Jan. 1, 2001). *See also* Ching-Chi Hsieh, M.D. Pugh, "Income Inequality and Violent Crime: A Meta-Analysis of Recent Aggregate Data Studies," 18 *Criminal Justice Review* 182–202 (1993).

31   *See March 4, 2015, Report: Investigation of the Ferguson Police Department*, United States Department of Justice, Civil Rights Division (last visited Sept. 20, 2020), https://www.justice.gov/sites/default/files/opa/press-releases/attachments/2015/03/04/ferguson_police_department_report.pdf.

32   *See* E. Britt Patterson, "Poverty, Income Inequality, and Community Crime Rate," 29 *Criminology* (Nov. 1991).

33   *See* Karen Parker and Matthew Pruitt, "Poverty, Poverty Concentration, and Homicide," 81 *Social Science Quarterly* (June 2020).

34   The Brookings Institution is an American organization founded in 1916 that performs research and conducts education in the social sciences. Its work has been frequently cited by both liberal and conservative politicians. The study also found that a criminal record is a significant barrier to reemployment. *See* Adam Looney and Nicholas Turner, *Work and Opportunity Before and After Incarceration*, Brookings Institution, (March 2018).

35   Jennifer Shaffer and R. Barry Ruback, *Violent Victimization as a Risk Factor for Violent Offending Among Juveniles*, United States Department of Justice, Office of Justice Programs, Office of Juvenile Justice and Delinquency Prevention (December 2002).

Ruth Bader Ginsburg

Associate Justice, United States Supreme Court (1993–2020)

FIGURE 15.7 Justice Ruth Bader Ginsburg

Justice Ginsburg's legal career spanned several spheres: she worked in academia, participated in litigation, sat as a federal appellate justice, and later became the second woman to serve as a Supreme Court justice.

Much of the justice's career focused on advancing sexual and gender equality. She founded and became lead counsel for the Women's Rights Project at the ACLU and wrote briefs in a number of federal gender rights cases.

She also made a number of contributions to the American body of criminal law. While sitting on the US Court of Appeals for the DC Circuit, Justice Ginsburg wrote the opinion of the court in *In re Letter of Request from Crown Prosecution Service of United Kingdom*, 870 F.2d 686 (D.C. Cir. 1989), permitting law enforcement from the United Kingdom to petition a district court for help in obtaining evidence for a case. Once on the Supreme Court, Justice Ginsburg joined the majority opinion in *Law-*

(continued)

CRITICAL THINKING   For decades, there has been a vigorous debate concerning the death penalty. It is one of the places where racial disparities in the criminal justice system are most obvious. For example, 35 percent of those executed over the last forty years have been Black individuals. However, African-Americans make up only about thirteen percent of the general population.[36]

As current citizens and future leaders, you may influence decisions about the implementation of capital punishment.

What, if anything, would you change about the current system? Should the government terminate the lives of those who have catastrophically demonstrated their inability to abide by the rules governing society? How well does the death penalty fulfill the general goals of punishment? What substantive and procedural laws ensure that capital punishment complies with due process of law and other constitutional requirements?

The Death Penalty

In the words of Supreme Court Justice William Brennan, the death penalty is a punishment of "awesome" power: "The calculated killing of a human being by the State involves, by its very nature, the denial of the executed person's humanity. ... When a man is hung, there is an end of our relations with him. His execution is a way of saying, 'You are not fit for this world, take your chances elsewhere.'"[37]

From the Eighth Amendment of the United States Constitution, we know that certain types of punishments are not to be permitted. The Eighth Amendment declares that "cruel and unusual punishments [shall not] be inflicted."[38] The

36   *See NAACP Death Penalty Fact Sheet*, NAACP (Jan. 17, 2017).
37   *Furman v. Georgia*, 408 U.S. 238, 290 (1972), citing Stephen, *Capital Punishments*, 69 Fraser's Magazine 753, 763 (1864).
38   The words "illegal and cruel punishments" were originally incorporated in the English Bill of Rights of 1689, mentioned in Chapter 2. That act, in part, chronicled the failings of King James II and cited the use of cruel punishments.

Supreme Court has addressed whether a punishment is cruel and unusual on several occasions. It has, for example, found that a sentence of twelve years in chains performing hard labor was an unconstitutional cruel and unusual punishment.[39]

The Supreme Court has also considered the constitutionality of the death penalty. In *Furman v. Georgia*, 408 U.S. 238 (1972), the Supreme Court reviewed whether its use to end the lives of the defendants in three pending murder cases complied with the Eighth Amendment. Justice Brennan provided four factors to guide the analysis. The factors are interrelated, and so a convergence would support a finding of cruel and unusual punishment. First and most important, "a punishment must not by its severity be degrading to human dignity." Second, a severe punishment must not be "obviously inflicted in a wholly arbitrary fashion." Third, if the punishment were "clearly and totally rejected" by society, it could well be cruel and unusual. Finally, a severe punishment should not be "patently unnecessary"; unnecessary punishments incline toward cruel and unusual.

In a deeply divided opinion, the Supreme Court in *Furman* found the death penalty, as currently imposed in the three cases before it, failed the arbitrariness factor, as there were no rational standards to determine when it should be imposed.[40] As a result of this opinion, executions were halted across the United States.

Following *Furman*, the states of Florida, Georgia, Louisiana, North Carolina, and Texas passed amended statutes that set specific guidelines for the application of the

rence v. Texas, 539 U.S. 558 (2003), which struck down a criminal anti-sodomy law in Texas under the Fourteenth Amendment.

Justice Ginsburg was known to engage in passionate dissents, earning her the nickname "the Notorious R.B.G." This nickname reflects her lifelong fight for voting rights, women's reproductive rights, immigration, health care, same-sex marriage and other causes related to civil rights. After her death in 2020, Ruth Bader Ginsburg became the first woman to lie in state at the US Capitol.

---

39 *See Weems v. United States*, 217 U.S. 349 (1910).

40 *Furman* was a 5–4 *per curiam* opinion comprised of a one-paragraph finding that the death penalty was unconstitutional. Each of the five justices in the majority wrote their own opinion, so there was no signed opinion of the Court. However, as Justices Stewart, White, and Douglas agreed that the death penalty was being imposed in an arbitrary way, and this view is considered the controlling finding. The other two justices in the majority, William Brennan and Thurgood Marshall, argued that the death penalty was incompatible with the standards of decency in contemporary society. The dissenting justices (all appointed by President Richard Nixon) found that, as the death penalty was currently being used by the federal government and forty state governments, there was no foundation for a finding that it was contrary to any evolving standard of decency. *Furman*, 408 U.S. at 238–470.

Is a Painful Death Cruel and Unusual?

Russell Bucklew was convicted of kidnapping, rape, and murder and sentenced to death by lethal injection. Bucklew contested his execution in federal district court, arguing that lethal injection would violate the Eighth Amendment's prohibition against cruel and unusual punishments in his particular case.

Bucklew had a rare congenital condition which would likely cause him to hemorrhage and choke to death on his own blood during his execution by lethal injection. He proposed nitrogen hypoxia as an alternative execution method. But the Supreme Court decided that Bucklew had not satisfied the test to show that his execution would be unconstitutionally painful. Wrote Justice Neil Gorsuch for the Court: "The Eighth Amendment does not guarantee a prisoner a painless death—something that, of course, isn't guaranteed to many people, including most victims of capital crimes." *Bucklew v. Precythe*, 587 U.S. __ (2019).

death penalty. Thereafter, five criminal offenders convicted of murder were sentenced to die in each of those states. These five offenders appealed their convictions to the Court, asking the Supreme Court to extend its ruling in *Furman*. They wanted the Court to find that the death penalty itself violated the Eighth Amendment. The cases were consolidated, and the Court rendered its opinion in *Gregg v. Georgia*, 428 U.S. 153 (1976). The Court established two rules that legislatures must follow to create a capital punishment scheme that would be constitutional. First, there must be objective criteria to guide death sentencing discretion, and the criteria must review and apply to all death sentences. Second, the statutory scheme must permit the sentencing agent (either judge or jury) to consider the record and character of each defendant as part of the sentencing process.

The Supreme Court found that the capital sentencing schemes in Georgia, Florida, and Texas passed these guidelines but that those in Louisiana and North Carolina did not. The Georgia scheme generally followed the Model Penal Code's provisions, which included, until 2010, suggested rules for the application of the death penalty.[41] Under Georgia law, the death penalty may be imposed for murder, certain kidnappings, armed robbery, rape, treason, and aircraft hijacking.[42] The trial of the criminal offender must be conducted in two phases. The first phase establishes the defendant's guilt or innocence. The second phase assesses mitigating and aggravating circumstances to determine the defendant's eligibility for the death penalty. In order to impose capital punishment, in the second phase the jury must find the presence of at least one of ten aggravating factors. The ten factors include the following:[43]

1. The defendant previously committed a capital felony or has a history of committing serious felonies;

2. The felony was completed while the defendant was committing another capital felony or an aggravated battery;

---

41   The American Law Instituted voted in 2009 to withdraw the death penalty provisions (Section 210.6) from the Model Penal Code "in light of the current intractable institutional and structural obstacles to ensuring a minimally adequate system for administering capital punishment."

42   Ga. Code Ann. §26-1101, 26-1311 26-1902, 26-2001, 26-2201, 26-3301 (1972).

43   *See Gregg v. Georgia*, 428 U.S. at n. 9.

3. The defendant's criminal actions created a grave risk of death to more than one person in a public place by means of a weapon or device that would normally be hazardous to the lives of more than one person;

4. The defendant committed the crime to receive money or something else of value;

5. The defendant killed a judge or district attorney during or because of their exercise of official duties;

6. The defendant committed murder while an agent or employee of someone else;

7. The offense was "outrageously or wantonly vile, horrible, or inhuman in that it involved torture, depravity of mind, or an aggravated battery ..."[44]

8. The defendant murdered a police officer, prison guard, or fireman in the line of duty;

9. The defendant committed murder while in lawful custody or after escaping lawful confinement; or

10. The defendant committed murder for the purpose of avoiding arrest.

If the jury in the second phase of the trial concludes that any one of these aggravating factors was present, it may find the defendant eligible for execution.

The Supreme Court has struggled to determine the age at which persons may be eligible for execution, issuing opinions that have shifted over time. In the 1988 case *Thompson v. Oklahoma*, 487 U.S. 815 (1988), the Supreme Court determined that executing a person who was under sixteen years of age when they committed the capital offense violates the Eighth Amendment. A year later, in *Stanford v. Kentucky*, 492 U.S. 361 (1989), the Court determined that the Constitution does not forbid the execution of a murderer who was sixteen when he committed the capital crime. Then, in the landmark opinion *Roper v. Simmons*, 543 U.S. 551 (2005), a bare majority of the Court found it unconstitutional to execute persons for crimes committed when they were under the age of eighteen. Justice Anthony Kennedy's majority opinion used research studies to show that juveniles generally lack the maturity and responsibility of adults. This, said the Court, is confirmed by the fact that the states have established the age of eighteen as the age for voting, for marrying without parental consent, and for serving as jurors. In addition, the majority found that there was a national consensus against the application of the death penalty in juvenile cases, as evidenced by the fact that only six states since 1989 had executed offenders for crimes committed as juveniles.[45]

Conclusion and Introduction to Law Lab

The American criminal justice system supports and defines the punishments of those found guilty of crimes. When a person commits an unlawful action with the mental capacity to understand its

---

44   Ga. Code Ann. §27-2543.1 (Supp. 1975).
45   *Roper*, 543 U.S. at 551–630.

wrongfulness and has no legally recognized excuse, a court of law may find them guilty and impose punishment. They may be punished to achieve retribution; to deter others from committing crimes; or to remove them from the population (at least for a time), and stop them from continuing to commit crimes. In jurisdictions that support restorative justice measures, the people they have harmed will have the opportunity to engage with the court, explain the harm they have endured, and offer input on sentencing.

The death penalty is the most extreme punishment. By its nature, it is final and irreversible. By law, it is now reserved for the most heinous criminal actions, and only those who are adults are eligible to receive it. Further, the Supreme Court has determined that laws concerning its application must be carefully crafted to avoid arbitrary and unjust outcomes.

In the following Law Lab, you are again justices of the United States Supreme Court. You must decide if the person who committed the homicide described in the scenario should be executed. It is a nasty crime, and the Criminal Code of the State of Franklin permits an execution on the established facts. Think carefully, discuss your views, and render your decision.

Supreme Court Justice Law Lab

MEMORANDUM

To: The Honorable Chief Justice and Associate Justices of the United States Supreme Court

From: Law Clerks of the Supreme Court

Re: *State of Franklin v. Smythson*, On Review Following Grant of Petition for Certiorari

Your Honors:

Please allow this summary to assist you as you prepare for deliberations in this matter, which involves the imposition of the death penalty for a homicide committed by Winston Smythson.

Factual Background

In the spring of 2015, Winston Smythson was a senior at Hometown High School, located in Liberty Springs, in the state of Franklin. Winston lived with his mother and his younger brother, as Winston's father died in military service when Winston was sixteen. His father's death was difficult for Winston. Afterward, he had a few brushes with the law, which consisted of arrests for property damage (egging houses and stealing signs), shoplifting (cigarettes and alcohol), underage drinking (three arrests), and brawling (two arrests). He was also the victim of a robbery when he was fourteen. However, by his senior year of high school, Winston appeared to have turned things around and had not been involved with law enforcement for over a year. Further, he had moved from being a D student to consistently receiving good grades in all his classes.

Winston was a member of Hometown High School's track and field team, historically a strong competitor. During Winston's senior year, the team performed very well. Based upon the strength of its runners, it was poised to advance to the state-level competition, something that had not occurred previously in the history of the school. The team's prospects for the state competition would be decided at a track meet that would take place at Hometown High on March 5. March 5 also happened to be Winston's eighteenth birthday.

Under Franklin law, you are deemed to be eighteen the day before the anniversary of your birth. For example, if you were born on January 1, 2000, you would be deemed eighteen years of age at the earliest moment of December 31, 2017. Therefore, no matter what time of day Winston was born, he was legally eighteen the day before his birthday.[1]

The morning of March 5, Winston's mother cooked him a birthday breakfast and gave him several gifts. One gift was a small revolver (a Smith & Wesson model 642) that had belonged to his late father, with the correct ammunition. Winston was familiar with the gun, as he and his father had fired it at a shooting range during his father's last leave and visit home.

After breakfast, Winston drove his car to Hometown High. His mother stayed home with his brother, who was unwell. Winston brought his revolver but left it safely locked in the trunk. He was thinking of showing it to his friends later.[2] Winston was to run several races at the track meet, including his best event, the 100-meter dash. He hoped to set a new school record in the race. Winston had come very close before and had been training hard.

FIGURE 15.8 High school track

Winston's first race at the track meet was the 400-meter relay race. In that race, Winston was to run the last lap, the "anchor lap."[3] The 400-meter relay event began, and the first three Hometown High runners did well. Then, it was Winston's turn. As he took the baton from the third runner, victory seemed certain. But when Winston reached the last ten yards, he stumbled and dropped the baton, and by the time he had recovered it, it was too late. His team finished last.

---

1   This is also true under United States law.
2   Note: Bringing a gun onto school property is a crime under Franklin law.
3   A track relay race involves several racers on the same team. Each member of the team runs a certain distance, carrying a special stick called a baton, and then passes it to the next runner. The team whose member first crosses the finish line with the baton wins the race.

The track and field team's coach, Mr. Landrus Nickerby, was known to be a man with a temper. He was not pleased with Winston's performance, and he became verbally abusive. He told Winston that he was "a clumsy idiot," and that he was "sorry he had wasted his time" training him. After being yelled at for a while, Winston took a swing at the coach, striking him. Winston was then restrained. Coach Nickerby, holding an icepack on his jaw, told Winston that he was off the team and would not be allowed to run the 100-meter dash. Further, the coach said he would see to it that Winston was suspended from school. Nickerby had the officials scratch Winston's name from the competition lists, and Winston was escorted off the field.

Winston then went back to his car. Security footage shows that Winston went to the trunk of his car, removed his revolver, and loaded it with ammunition. Winston then sat in his car for an hour. At the end of the hour, he got out and put on a windbreaker. Winston put the revolver in the pocket of the windbreaker and walked back to the track meet. He walked up to Coach Nickerby, who was talking to his wife and twin daughters (aged eleven). Then, Winston pulled out the revolver and shot the coach in the head. He then attempted to shoot himself, but was restrained and arrested. Coach Nickerby was taken to the hospital, where he died two hours later.

A psychiatric evaluation was performed after Winston's arrest. The examining psychiatrist found that Winston was reactive and impulsive, that he was still grieving his father's death, and that he was very angry about his situation. Winston's IQ was tested to be in the normal range, consistent with the regular school testing that was routinely given to all students.

Procedural Posture

Hometown High School is located in the city of Liberty Springs in the State of Franklin. Franklin's Criminal Code says that capital punishment may be used in first-degree murder cases. First-degree murder is defined in the Code as "an unlawful killing when it is proven that the defendant 1) intentionally sought to bring about the death of another; 2) had knowledge that his conduct was practically certain to cause death or create a strong probability that death would result; and 3) acted with deliberation and premeditation." It is not disputed that Winston acted with deliberation.

The prosecutor for Liberty County (where Winston resides and where Hometown High School is located) sought the death penalty in Winston's trial. In accordance with the ruling of the Supreme Court in *Furman v. Georgia*, 408 U.S. 238 (1972), the trial was bifurcated, and in the first phase, the jury convicted Winston of first-degree murder. In the second phase, both aggravating and exculpating evidence was explored as the jury considered whether Winston should receive the death penalty. As the State of Franklin has passed legislation supporting victims' rights, Mr. Nickerby's wife was present during both phases of the trial. In the trial's penalty phase, she and her daughters testified about how their lives had been impacted by the loss of Mr. Nickerby. Their testimony was compelling and affecting; Mr. Nickerby had been a beloved husband and an affectionate and supportive father.

At the conclusion of the penalty phase, the jury rendered findings that confirmed the presence of two special aggravating circumstances. First, Winston's use of the handgun on school property during a track meet created a grave risk of death to more than one person in a public place. Second, Winston's murder of Mr. Nickerby in front of his family was wantonly vile and showed "depravity of mind." The jury sentenced Winston to death.

Issue: Cruel and Unusual Punishment Under the Eighth Amendment

The mandatory appeals followed, and the case worked its way up to the United States Supreme Court. This Court accepted review to consider whether the execution of Winston Smythson is permitted under the United States Constitution, looking specifically at the Eighth Amendment, which prohibits "cruel and unusual punishments."

Brief Background: Capital Punishment

In the United States, capital punishment is currently used in a majority of states. It is also used by the federal government. The United States is an outlier in its use of the death penalty among other wealthy Western nations.

This Court suspended capital punishment in *Furman v. Georgia*, finding that its application was unconstitutionally arbitrary.[4] After a collection of states amended their laws to eliminate its arbitrary application, the Court affirmed the legality of capital punishment in the 1976 case *Gregg v. Georgia*, 428 U.S. 153 (1976). Juvenile capital punishment was entirely outlawed in *Roper v. Simmons*, 543 U.S. 551 (2005).

Since 1976, more than 7,800 defendants have been sentenced to death; of these, more than 1,400 have been executed. Over 2,500 persons remain on death row.

Death sentences in the states are loosely tied to their populations. California, the most populous state, has over 700 inmates on death row. Wyoming, the least populous state, has the fewest. In addition, executions tend to be more frequent in conservative states. Texas carried out over 500 executions during the post-*Furman* era, more than a third of the national total. Minorities and males are disproportionally represented on death row.[5]

Conclusion

The law clerks are eager to be of further use to the Court in connection with this important matter. Please let us know if we can assist in any further way.

We look forward to reviewing the Court's opinion.

---

4   *Furman*, 408 U.S. 238 (1972).
5   *See NAACP Death Penalty Fact Sheet*, NAACP (Jan. 17, 2017).

CHAPTER 16

Professional Responsibility

The leading rule for the lawyer, as for the man of every calling, is diligence.

—Abraham Lincoln

FIGURE 16.1 Law books and other texts

Introduction

We have nearly finished this book's exploration of the law.

We began in Chapter 1 by observing that laws have not always served as a barrier to acts of abuse and oppression. Even in modern times, governments with comprehensive legal codes have failed to protect their citizens from injustice. Codes may be inequitable, or they may be unfairly applied. In addition, those who administer the law may not stand independent, but be subject to influence or pressure to reach convenient outcomes. They may be encouraged to disregard evidence and arguments and instead issue rulings that favor the influential.

We then considered the benefits of a true rule of law, which contemplates equitable substantive laws, impartially and uniformly administered through fair procedural laws. A key feature of any rule of law is that it restricts the arbitrary exercise of power and demands that personal and community rights be preserved until regular legal proceedings establish good cause for them to be revoked.

In the ancient legal codes, we saw the slow emergence of ideas that are now part of the modern rule of law. These codes reached for components of due process, such as the right to be heard before an impartial judge, and the insistence upon an evidentiary hearing before imposing punishment. Most of the old codes also scaled punishments for crimes, with intentional homicide demanding the most severe penalty. Attributes of some of the ancient codes (particularly Roman law) were adopted by the Framers of the Constitution of the United States when they designed the blueprint for their new nation.

We then explored the rise of the English common law. After the Norman conquest, the demands of a new central government required uniform administration of the same legal code throughout England. We noted the creation of courts of equity, with enhanced judicial discretion to address exceptional legal problems, and the capture of legal precedent in court reporters, a process that continues today. The English common law profoundly influenced American law and the legal systems of the United States.

Thereafter, we reviewed the creation of the United States Constitution and noted its key provisions. We then examined several key components of constitutional law, including the critical areas of free speech, religious freedom, due process, and equal protection. From there, we ventured on to explore other areas of substantive and procedural law, including areas of private law, such as Torts and Contracts, and areas of public law, such as Criminal Law and Criminal Procedure. We then considered defenses to crimes, explored the theories behind punishments, and considered a few of the places where the justice system is troubled by inequities.

The law is a vast and complex subject, and we have barely skimmed its surface. There is always more to learn. Moreover, its contours continue to shift. New challenges arise, and new rights, rules, and procedures must develop to meet the needs of a society that continues to evolve.

Before the end of this book, however, there is one more component of our legal system that we must address. It concerns the responsibility of the individuals who administer it and work within it. Any rule of law is only as robust as the ethics of the people who support it. Unless legal professionals—attorneys, judges, prosecutors, public

FIGURE 16.2 Judge's gavel

defenders, court clerks, bailiffs, police officers, sheriffs, and the myriad of others serving in governments and courts—enforce laws fairly and vigorously, the legal system will not operate properly. It can become distorted by the same qualities that damage lives everywhere: dishonesty, intemperance, bias, apathy, and ignorance.

In this chapter, we will explore the ethical considerations involved in the faithful discharge of the duties of judges and attorneys. Then, in the book's last Law Lab, you will serve as an officer of the Ethics Board of the Franklin State Bar Association. A young attorney has contacted you with a terrible ethical dilemma, and you must offer advice on how best to solve it, in accordance with her dual obligations to her client and to the system of justice.

PROFESSIONAL RESPONSIBILITY KEY TERMS

The following key terms are defined in this chapter. They are also defined in the Glossary.

Attorney
Duty of Zealous Advocacy
Fiduciary Duty
Judicial Independence
Officer of the Court

The Ethics of the Judiciary

Throughout the five millennia of recorded human history, there have been judges to resolve disputes. The word *judge* has ancient antecedents. It traces back to the Latin word *iudicem*, which is a compound of the word *ius* meaning "law" or "right" and the root of the word *dicere*, meaning "to say or declare." Judges have always been people who are supposed to say what is right and declare what justice requires.

Several chief justices of the Supreme Court have offered perspectives on their work. Although they had different ideas about the interpretation of the Constitution and how to apply it, they all agreed that judicial independence is critical. John Marshall noted that judges are trusted due to "their independence in office and manner of appointment."[1] Warren Burger declared that judges should "rule on the basis of law, not public opinion, and they should be totally indifferent to pressures of the times."[2] William Rehnquist stated that a "judiciary independent of the executive and legislative branches" was one of the two key ideas that the constitutional Framers devised (the other was a chief executive who was not dependent upon the legislature for political support).[3]

---

1   John Marshall, *Virginia Ratifying Convention*, 20 June 1788, Papers 1:275–285, Document 26, para 1.
2   *See* Charlotte Saikowski, "The Power of Judicial Review," Christian Science Monitor (Feb. 11, 1987).
3   William H. Rehnquist, *Judicial Compensation*, Statement Before the National Commission on the Public Service (July 15, 2002).

Shirley Mount Hufstedler

FIGURE 16.3 Justice Shirley Mount Hufstedler

Shirley Mount Hufstedler was one of only two women in her 1949 law school graduating class, and she initially struggled to find employment. She refused to be discouraged, and her unwavering perseverance led to a groundbreaking judicial career: she was appointed to the Los Angeles County Superior Court in 1961, the California Court of Appeals in 1966, and to the United States Court of Appeals for the Ninth Circuit in 1968. She was only the second woman to serve as a federal appellate justice.

On the bench, Hufstedler proved herself to be an advocate for the right of privacy as well as public education. Her contributions to education caught the attention of President Jimmy Carter, who appointed Judge Hufstedler in 1979 to be the first United States secretary of education. Hufstedler chose to focus on equal access to education, prioritizing opportunity regardless of race, gender, or ethnicity. Hufstedler's historic career earned her many honors, including the Earl Warren Medal, the Louis D. Brandeis Medal, the 1995 American Bar Association Medal, and twenty honorary degrees from universities across the nation.

The notion of **judicial independence** is perhaps the most prominent feature in the modern rules governing the conduct of judicial officers. The American Bar Association drafted Canons of Judicial Ethics to serve as guidelines for judges as they perform their judicial work. Most of the states have adopted versions of these rules.[4] The United States Courts have also established a Code of Conduct that includes ethical canons for federal judges. The state and federal canons are similar.[5]

The first of the American Bar Association's four canons addresses judicial independence. It requires judges to "uphold the integrity and independence of the judiciary," declaring that judges shall act "at all times in a manner that promotes public confidence in the independence, integrity, and impartiality of the judiciary." Indeed, unless judges act with integrity and independence, the rule of law is at risk. We must have confidence that our judges will act thoughtfully and carefully in accordance with their duties to the public. The erosion of public trust in the judiciary can lead injured parties to reach for extrajudicial resolution of their legal problems, which increases and perpetuates violence.

The Second Canon requires judges to perform their duties "impartially, competently, and diligently." A judge's judicial duties must "take precedence over all of a judge's personal and extrajudicial activities." Judges are to "uphold and apply the law ... fairly and impartially." All duties are to be performed without "bias and prejudice," and judges should require lawyers who appear before them to refrain

---

4 The American Bar Association is a national organization of lawyers and law students that was founded in 1878. It established the standards for legal education in law schools across the United States. It also formulated model codes governing professional ethics. It originally created a list of 36 canons in 1924. They were revised over time, and the newest set contains just four mandatory provisions with clarifying subparts. All references here are from its provisions. The Model Code may be found at the ABA's website, https://www.americanbar.org/.

5 The Code of Conduct for United States Judges was initially adopted in 1973 and most recently revised in March of 2019.

"from manifesting bias or prejudice." Bias is a destroyer of the rule of law, and judges have been removed for exhibiting it.[6]

The Third Canon obliges judges to conduct their extrajudicial activities so as "to minimize the rise of conflict with judicial obligations." Judges must manage their time to support the performance of their duties. Further, they should take care that their involvement in enterprises outside the courthouse do not raise questions about their ability to remain neutral inside the courthouse.

Finally, the Fourth Canon declares that judges must refrain from inappropriate political activity.[7] Judges who demonstrate political bias sow seeds of doubt about their neutrality. Elected judges are usually affiliated with a particular political party. This, however, does not permit them to act as leaders in political organizations or to make sweeping declarations about the uniquely laudable aspects of persons affiliated with a particular political party. Our judges swear oaths to serve all people equally, no matter their political affiliations.

These modern canons are consistent with another famous set of judicial guidelines crafted by Sir Matthew Hale, who served as chief justice of the King's Bench in England from 1671 to 1676. Hale's Resolutions remain relevant notwithstanding the passage of so many years. In modern English, the key rules read as follows:

> In the execution of justice, I will set aside my own passions, and not permit myself to be provoked.

> I will focus entirely upon the matter at hand.

> I will keep an open mind and reserve judgment until the entire case has been presented.

> I will reject all private solicitations that relate to a case. I will also reject all solicitations from persons whose interests are likely to come to me for adjudication in the future.

> I will not be biased. In point of justice, I will favor neither the rich, nor the poor.

> My personal behavior will be beyond reproach, on the bench and also in daily life.

---

6   On September 18, 2020, the Oklahoma State Court of the Judiciary removed Kendra Coleman from the position of District Court judge in Oklahoma County in part because she ruled in favor of a person who donated to her campaign. She also committed "oppression in office," engaging in abusive behavior toward attorneys and litigants.

7   The title of the Fifth Canon of the federal Code of Conduct declares that "Judges should refrain from political activity." This rule prohibits judges from holding political office, making speeches for political organizations, soliciting money for political organizations or candidates, and broadly prohibits "any other political activity." *See* Canon Five, *Code of Conduct for United States Judges*, United States Courts, effective March 12, 2019.

In sentencing criminals, I will not compel punishments or acts of humiliation without authority of law.

Neither commendation nor condemnation from the public or the government will affect my work in the distribution of justice.[8]

Sir Matthew insisted that those who worked in his court follow similar rules. They were not to interfere with the business of the court; they were not to accept bribes; they were not to give "undue precedence" to certain cases; and they were not to offer advice or "recommend counsel."[9]

Whether a judge serves in state or federal court, there are consequences for the failure to follow the rules of judicial conduct. In Illinois, the Judicial Inquiry Board investigates complaints against state judges. If it finds grounds for prosecution, it pursues them by filing a complaint before the Illinois Courts Commission, which has the authority to suspend or remove judges from office. The commission can also reprimand judges or retire judges who are unable to perform their duties.[10] Other states have agencies with different names, but the procedures are similar.

Federal judges appointed under Article III of the United States Constitution serve for life. Only Congress has the power to remove them. In the event of judicial abuse or neglect, the federal Judicial Conference begins an investigation. If the investigation finds grounds for impeachment, it submits a report to the House of Representatives. If the House determines to pursue impeachment, a trial follows in the Senate. In the nation's history, only 15 federal judges have been impeached, and only eight of those were convicted and removed from the bench.[11]

The Ethics of the Practice of Law

Attorneys also have a historic role that has evolved over time. The word **attorney** comes from the Old French verb *atorner*, meaning "to turn to or assign." An attorney is someone clients turn to in order to obtain assistance with their legal problems.[12]

Unlike judges, attorneys have dual ethical obligations. They must, of course, represent their clients' interests zealously and properly, in accordance with their **fiduciary duty**. In addition, as

---

8   Tom Bingham, *The Rule of Law* 20–21 (2011).
9   *Id. See also* Matthew W. Hill, "Sir Matthew Hale and Modern Judicial Ethics" 11 *Judicature* 280–282 (1971).
10   Constitution of the State of Illinois, Judicial Amendment, 1964 Art. IV Sec. 18.
11   Three judges resigned before the conclusion of their impeachment proceedings. Of the eight convictions, one was based upon mental instability and intoxication; one was convicted for refusing to hold court; two for conducting improper business dealings with litigants; one for tax evasion; and three for accepting bribes and committing perjury. The most recent to be impeached was Thomas Porteous, serving in the Eastern District of Louisiana. He was convicted of accepting bribes and committing perjury and removed on December 8, 2010.
12   Although the terms *attorney* and *lawyer* are often used in the same way, there is a small technical distinction in the United States. All graduates of law schools are lawyers. But in order to practice law, lawyers must pass the bar examination in the jurisdiction in which they wish to practice. They then become attorneys. For our purposes in this chapter, we will use the terms interchangeably.

officers of the court, they must serve the interests of justice. These two obligations generate separate professional duties. Occasionally, these duties collide, creating conflicts of interest that attorneys must carefully resolve.

A deep exploration of the moral, legal, and professional constraints that define these roles would take many chapters. Indeed, the American Law Institute's Third Restatement of the Law Governing Lawyers runs to several volumes.[13] We can, however, overview these two distinct obligations and note the key rules that shape them.

The **duty of zealous advocacy** requires attorneys to exercise their best efforts on behalf of their clients within the bounds of the law. Each state has enacted rules that detail the particular obligations of lawyers that practice in that state. They are all based upon the American Bar Association's Model Rules of Professional Conduct.[14]

Rule 1.1 of the Model Rules is a core provision, declaring that the attorney must "provide competent representation to a client." This means that the attorney must use such "legal knowledge, skill, thoroughness and preparation" as is reasonably necessary to promote the client's interests.[15] Rule 1.3 of the Model Rules requires attorneys to act with "reasonable diligence and promptness."[16] The Comment following Rule 1.3 plainly states that the attorney should "pursue a matter on behalf of a client despite opposition, obstruction or personal inconvenience … and take whatever lawful and ethical measures are required to vindicate a client's cause or endeavor." The Comment also sharply admonishes against "procrastination," noting that "unreasonable delays can cause a client needless anxiety and undermine confidence." In addition, lawyers in vulnerable positions should prepare for disaster: sole practitioners should consider planning for

---

13 Restatement (Third) of The Law Governing Lawyers § 1–2 (Am. Law Inst. 2000).

14 The American Bar Association's Model Rules have been adopted by all the states except California. However, the California Rules of Professional Conduct were derived from the ABA Model Rules.

15 Model Rules of Prof'l Conduct R. 1.1 (2020).

16 Model Rules of Prof'l Conduct R. 1.3 (2020).

Lyda Burton Conley

FIGURE 16.4   Lyda Burton Conley

Lyda Burton Conley was the first Native American woman lawyer and the first woman to be admitted to the Kansas bar. She is best known for her ardent defense of the Huron Place Cemetery in Kansas City, the burial grounds for her Tribe, the Wyandots.

In an 1855 treaty, the US government guaranteed the preservation of the Huron Place Cemetery. However, in 1906, Congress approved the sale of the land for commercial development. Conley filed an injunction to stop the sale. After an initial dismissal and an appeal, Conley became the first Native American woman to argue a case before the US Supreme Court. She is also believed to be the first plaintiff ever to argue that the federal government has a duty to protect Native American burial grounds.

Although the Supreme Court decided that Congress had the right to sell the land, a buyer for the land could not be found. Many have speculated that buyers were deterred by the national interest that Conley had generated in her case. Moreover, Conley's defense of the burial grounds was enough to compel Kansas Senator Charles Curtis to lead passage of 1916 legislation that established the Huron Cemetery as a federal park. As of 2016, the Huron Cemetery is a National Historic Landmark.

death or disability and designate another attorney to review files to determine the need for "immediate protective action" to protect the interests of clients.

In contrast with the duty of zealous advocacy, the attorney's duty as an **officer of the court** is not owed to clients. Rather, it is owed to society and requires that the attorney actively support the administration of justice.

The duty of the attorney to support the administration of justice is reflected in various places in the Model Rules. Model Rule 1.2 governs the allocation of authority between the attorney and the client, and it addresses both the duty to the client and the duty to support the administration of justice. While lawyers should consult with their clients about the objectives of the representation, they must not assist a client to accomplish "conduct that the lawyer knows is criminal or fraudulent." Further, the Comment following Rule 1.2 states that lawyers must withdraw from representation if the client persists in concealing wrongdoing.[17]

Under Model Rule 1.3, an attorney is "not bound" to push "for every advantage that might be realized," and diligence does not demand the use of "offensive tactics or preclude the treating of all persons involved in the legal process with courtesy and respect."[18] Such tactics would certainly not support the administration of justice.

Model Rule 1.6 addresses the confidentiality of client information and disclosures, and it too touches on both duties. Lawyers must keep client information confidential, but not at the expense of great harm to others. Accordingly, the rule declares that "a lawyer shall not reveal information relating to the representation of a client unless the client gives informed consent, or the disclosure is impliedly authorized ..." However, if needed to prevent "reasonably certain death or substantial bodily harm," the attorney may reveal confidential information. Disclosure may also be made to "prevent the client from committing a crime or fraud ..." and also to prevent or cure substantial "injury to the financial interests or property of another ..."

The attorney's duty as an officer of the court supports the operation of the rule of law in the United States. Commentators have waxed eloquent about the obligation, noting its connection to the loftiest of human ideals:

> The individual member of the profession who never realizes, or who forgets, that he is an officer of the Court, has missed the mark of his high calling and should seek other lines of endeavor in justice to the profession which has played a part in the development and maintenance of civilization unequaled in the affairs of men.[19]

As a preliminary safeguard against misuse of the law, before they are admitted to practice, attorneys formally swear an oath to uphold the foundation of American law, the United States Constitution. Further, the United States Code requires all federal lawyers to take an oath to faithfully execute their duties.[20]

---

17   *See* Model Rules of Prof'l Conduct R. 1.6 (2020).
18   Model Rules of Prof'l Conduct R. 1.3 (2020).
19   Isaac Meekins, "The Lawyer as an Officer of the Court—His Duty to the Court in the Administration of Justice," 4 *N.C. L. Rev.* 3 (1926).
20   *See* 28 U.S.C. §544.

Attorneys admitted to the bars of the states must, in addition, swear to serve their clients faithfully. In Illinois, before formal admission to the state bar, attorneys swear as follows:

> I do solemnly swear (or affirm) that I will support the Constitution of the United States and the constitution of the State of Illinois, and that I will faithfully discharge the duties of the office of attorney and counselor at law to the best of my ability.[21]

Finally, some states require attorneys to formally acknowledge their status as officers of the court in the oath that they swear. Attorneys in these states must swear to uphold the federal Constitution, to uphold the constitution of the state in which they will practice, to serve their clients faithfully, and also to honor their responsibilities to the justice system. Admittees to the California bar must swear:

> I solemnly swear (or affirm) that I will support the Constitution of the United States and the Constitution of the State of California, and that I will faithfully discharge the duties of an attorney and counselor at law to the best of my knowledge and ability. As an officer of the court, I will strive to conduct myself at all times with dignity, courtesy, and integrity.[22]

Conclusion and Introduction to Law Lab

Legal professionals are uniquely positioned to help individuals and organizations. In the realm of private law, critical legal problems can weigh down the operations of groups and

---

21 705 ILCS 205/4 (Westlaw 2016).
22 *California Rules of Court*, Title 9, Rules on Law Practice, Attorneys and Judges, effective May 23, 2014.

Whistleblowers: Private Citizens Reporting Corruption or Abuse

FIGURE 16.5   B-1 bomber

A whistleblower is someone who reports or reveals fraud, abuse, or corruption. Whistleblowers can reveal corruption in private organizations or in governmental agencies. Often, they work for the entity that they report.

John Gravitt served in the United States Marines during the Vietnam War, earning two Purple Hearts. Thereafter, he went to work for a GE Aircraft plant. In the 1980s, he discovered fraudulent billing in connection with GE's construction of the B-1 bomber. His complaints to his supervisors were ignored, and when he escalated the matter to management, he was promptly fired. However, his attorney helped him file suit under the False Claims Act, signed into law by President Abraham Lincoln. The act permits private citizens with knowledge of fraud to sue entities that defraud governmental programs on behalf of the United States attorney general. In these suits, whistleblowers receive a portion of the recovered damages. Gravitt's suit prospered, and millions of dollars were recovered for the United States government. In addition, his lawsuit resulted in the passage of a new 1986 law that facilitated the prosecution of lawsuits under the old act. After his death in 2001, his widow explained why Gravitt persisted: "As far as he was concerned, it was an act of treason to take an engine that cost $1 Million and make the government pay $2 Million."

impair individuals' quality of life. Resolving legal problems brings ease of mind as well as appropriate recompense. Attorneys working in the public law arena serve society as governmental and private counsel, prosecuting and defending criminal cases, supporting the work of important federal and state entities.

Whether in the public or private sphere, attorneys support endeavors that further important interests. Attorneys have served society for centuries, representing clients in cases that improved the plight of groups and individuals. Some of the legal titans profiled in this book have made remarkable contributions to the cause of justice, and every year new attorneys and judges step forward to assume the burden and the honor of that service. They swear oaths to serve their clients and the cause of justice, and they work hard to fulfill those oaths.

In the following Law Lab, a young attorney is representing a client in a serious criminal matter that is pending in court. She has received troubling information from the client indicating that other persons may have been harmed. She needs to know how to navigate the dual obligations of serving her client's interests and fulfilling her obligation as an officer of the court. As members of the Ethics Committee of the State Bar of Franklin, it is your obligation to think carefully about what the profession and the cause of justice demands. Your advice will have serious consequences for her, for her client, and (perhaps) for other individuals with much at stake.

Ethics Law Lab

MEMORANDUM

To: Members of the Ethics Committee of the State Bar of Franklin

From: Law Clerks

Re: *In Re Attorney Jane Doe*

Franklin State Bar Ethics Supervisors:

Please allow this brief summary to assist you as you consider the appropriate response to an attorney who has anonymously posed a question of legal ethics through the Franklin State Bar attorney ethics telephone line. The attorney requests that you provide guidance concerning whether she has an obligation to disclose the information revealed to her by her client.

Factual Background

Like the bar associations in other states, the Franklin State Bar Association maintains an "Ethics Infoline." Attorneys may call anonymously and receive guidance on how to best conduct themselves when ethical challenges arise.

When the Ethics Infoline opened this morning, an attorney called in. She chose to remain anonymous. She explained that she had been approached by a man seeking legal advice who believed he was about to be implicated in a criminal investigation involving two missing women. The women have been missing for two days, and a large-scale search is still ongoing in the county where the client lives. The women's families have pleaded for information on public media.

The attorney agreed to represent the client. She is a criminal defense attorney, and the case falls within her specialization. Later in the day, she received a phone call from the client. The client sounded intoxicated during this second call. He disclosed that the two missing women would likely be found dead in a shed in his yard. The attorney wondered if she had an ethical obligation to give this information to the police. She also wonders if she should recuse herself from the case. She has agreed to call back later today to receive guidance.

Review of Confidentiality Rules

Lawyers have an ethical obligation to keep their clients' information secret. This duty of confidentiality extends beyond information the client tells the lawyer directly. Any information a lawyer learns "relating to the representation of the client" must be kept confidential, including information learned from interviews, photographs, or observations. Attorneys must support the Fifth Amendment right of their clients not to incriminate themselves. In Franklin and in other jurisdictions, a lawyer who wrongfully discloses information may be subject to disciplinary proceedings, including disbarment. Thus, lawyers should not disclose information about past criminal actions that clients have shared.

Further, lawyers cannot be compelled to disclose certain lawyer-client communications due to the attorney-client privilege. "Privileged" information includes communications where a client seeks legal advice or services and provides details about the legal matter. The attorney-client privilege is supported by courts, which can quash (terminate) a request to disclose information that violates the privilege. A client should be able to speak freely with their attorney about their legal situation without fear that what they say may become part of a court record. Attorneys can best guide clients whose explanations are candid and complete.

These obligations are acknowledged through American Bar Association Model Rule 1.6 and by the Franklin Rule 1.6 governing confidentiality.

American Bar Association Model Rule 1.6 is <u>advisory</u> in the State of Franklin. It states:

> A lawyer shall not reveal information relating to the representation of a client unless the client gives informed consent, the disclosure is impliedly authorized in order to carry out the representation, or the disclosure is permitted by paragraph (b).

A lawyer may reveal information relating to the representation of a client to the extent the lawyer reasonably believes necessary:

> to prevent reasonably certain death or substantial bodily harm. ...

The Franklin Rule is <u>binding</u> on attorneys who practice law in the state, and it is different from the Model Rule. Franklin Rule 1.6(c) reads:

> A lawyer <u>shall</u> reveal information relating to the representation of a client to the extent the lawyer reasonably believes necessary to prevent reasonably certain death or substantial bodily harm. [Emphasis added.]

Whether mandatory under the Franklin Rule or discretionary under the ABA Model Rule, the threshold for disclosure of confidential information is the same: whether an attorney <u>reasonably</u>

believes that the revealing of such information is necessary to prevent reasonably certain death or substantial bodily harm.

As recognized in the Restatement (Third) of the Law Governing Lawyers §66(2000), the question of whether the disclosure of confidential information is necessary to prevent reasonably certain death or substantial bodily harm is intensely fact sensitive. Moreover, in deciding whether death or substantial bodily harm is reasonably certain to occur, Comment [6] to Franklin Rule 1.6 (c) recognizes that such harm is reasonably certain to occur if it will be suffered immediately or if there is a present and substantial threat that a person will suffer such harm at a later date if the lawyer fails to act to eliminate the threat.

To this effect, the Restatement has recognized factors to be considered in deciding whether the disclosure of confidential information is necessary to prevent reasonably certain death or substantial

FIGURE 16.6 Navigating the rules of ethics

bodily harm. The factors are as follows:

1. The degree to which it appears likely that the threatened death or serious bodily harm will actually result in the absence of disclosure;

2. The irreversibility of the consequences once the act has taken place;

3. Whether victims may be unaware of the threat or may rely on the lawyer to protect them;

4. The lawyer's prior course of dealing with the client; and

5. The extent of adverse effect on the client that might result from disclosure contemplated by the lawyer.

Examples as to whether disclosure is necessary to prevent reasonably certain death or substantial bodily harm include the following:

1. Under Franklin Rule 1.6, a lawyer who knows that a client or other person has accidentally discharged toxic waste into a town's water supply must reveal this information to authorities if there is a present and substantial risk that a person who drinks the water will contract life-threatening or debilitating disease and the lawyer's disclosure is necessary to eliminate the threat or reduce the number of victims.

2. A lawyer representing a defendant in a personal injury action learns from a consulting physician that the plaintiff has a life-threatening medical condition of which the plaintiff is unaware and which can be repaired through surgery. The lawyer may, under ABA Rule 1.6, reveal such condition to the plaintiff.

3. A lawyer whose client reveals that they have set a mechanical device to burn down a building in which people are living has the discretion under ABA Rule 1.6 to reveal such facts, even though the disclosure may result in criminal charges against the client.

Issue: May (or Must) the Attorney Disclose the Communication?

This query to the Ethics Committee poses the attorney's ethical obligation of client confidentiality against the attorney's obligation to disclose information necessary to prevent reasonably certain death or bodily harm. The wrong decision in this matter could result in serious consequences. It could subject innocent persons to grave injury, including death. Alternatively, it could severely prejudice a client's position in an important legal matter. The wrong decision could also lead to disciplinary proceedings against the attorney for failing to fulfill her required ethical obligations to the client, or her obligations to society as an officer of the court.

Please prepare appropriate advice to the attorney. When she calls back, she will then have the guidance she needs to navigate her obligations to her client and to the public.

Conclusion

The law clerks of the Ethics Committee are available to assist in any further way that might be useful. We look forward to receiving the Committee's determination as to the appropriate guidance to be offered the attorney involved in this difficult matter.

CHAPTER 17

Reflections on Legal Careers

The first reward of justice is the consciousness that we are acting justly.
—Jean-Jacques Rousseau, *Émile, or Treatise on Education* 4, 1762 (translated by Barbara Foxley, 1911)

FIGURE 17.1 Bust of Lincoln

Introduction

We have now ventured far in time, journeying from the earliest legal codes, through areas of substantive and procedural law, to the modern rules of professional responsibility. Along the way, we noted the emergence of concepts now firmly embedded in the legal systems of nations that honor the rule of law. The early codes, incomplete though they were, reached for ways to resolve conflict and stabilize society.

The early codes also defined the mission and authority of persons involved in the legal system. Their recognition of the ethical obligations of judges and lawyers is echoed in Sir Matthew Hale's seventeenth-century Resolutions and in the modern canons governing judicial and attorney behavior. Legal professionals should support the interests of justice while also serving the needs of their clients. In fact, before they are allowed to practice law, every attorney must swear an oath to uphold the United States Constitution and the constitution of the state(s) in which they practice. Additionally, they must swear to faithfully discharge their duties to their clients. In swearing this oath, new attorneys acknowledge and agree to fulfill their important role in the justice system of the United States.

Although attorneys swear substantially the same oath, they serve in many different roles. As we noted in the Introduction, the umbrella of the legal profession is quite large. With the same credential, an attorney can engage in the following work:

1. Represent multinational corporations seeking to market new technologies.

2. Represent teachers in union negotiations with school districts.

3. Prosecute those who engage in human trafficking.

4. Defend health care providers in medical malpractice cases.

5. Negotiate and finalize real estate transactions.

6. Prosecute (or defend) civil rights cases in state and federal courts.

7. Guide clients through divorces, adoptions, and estate planning.

8. Craft state and federal laws that will affect the lives of many.

9. Provide legal oversight for public agencies to ensure that personnel properly use public assets.

10. Serve as risk management counsel, helping companies define, prevent, and address legal risks.

11. Serve as court-appointed advocates for children in legal proceedings.

Attorneys also work for organizations mentioned in this book, such as the American Civil Liberties Union, the American Bar Association, and the Southern Poverty Law Center. As we noted in the last chapter, attorneys are employed by state and federal bar associations in various capacities, including as ethics panelists. Attorneys who distinguish themselves may become judges or appellate justices, and some serve as state legislators or members of Congress. Some attorneys have even become presidents.[1]

---

1   Twenty-six presidents of the United States were lawyers before their inauguration. They include: John Adams (1797–1801); Thomas Jefferson (1801–1809); James Monroe (1817–1825); John Quincy Adams (1825–1829); Andrew Jackson (1829–1837); Martin Van Buren (1837–1841); John Tyler (1841–1845); James Knox Polk (1845–1849); Millard Fillmore (1850–1853); Franklin Pierce (1853–1857); James Buchanan (1857–1861); Abraham Lincoln (1861–1865); Rutherford B. Hayes (1877–1881); James A. Garfield (1881); Chester A. Arthur (1881–1885); Grover Cleveland (1885–1889 and 1893–1897); Benjamin Harrison (1889–1893); William McKinley (1897–1901); William Howard Taft (1909–1913); Woodrow Wilson (1913–1921); Calvin Coolidge (1923–1929); Franklin Delano Roosevelt (1933–1945); Richard M. Nixon (1969–1974); Gerald R. Ford (1974–1977); William Jefferson Clinton (1993–2001); and Barack Obama (2009–2017).

Although the same law degree is required for all these jobs, they involve different tasks. The attorney who finds it satisfying to assist clients with family law matters would most likely not find it gratifying to prosecute patents. The prosecutor who thrives on fast-paced trial proceedings would likely not enjoy long days of researching and writing appellate briefs. Some areas of law are writing intensive, while others emphasize spoken communication skills. Some legal specializations involve long days of argument and debate, whereas others require lawyers to spend hours preparing documents or giving presentations in boardrooms. Some areas of practice demand deep reviews of complex legal doctrines, while others involve hours of direct personal interaction with clients. Different areas of practice require not only different knowledge but distinct skills and qualities of temperament.

There are also differences in the scope and variety of work. Some attorneys serve a certain cause or business in a particular way with a narrow focus on their daily tasks. Other attorneys provide a broad array of legal services to members of the public. Finally, some law jobs come with fairly standard working hours, while others routinely require night and weekend labor.

In this chapter, you will consider how you might choose an area of law that will suit your preferences and skills. This will be an ongoing endeavor: the process of selecting your practice area should continue as you move into and through your formal legal education. As you become more knowledgeable about the law and about legal careers, you will be able to refine your thinking, and eventually you will comfortably select a reasonable choice.

The Path to the Practice

Thirty years ago, law graduates who started their careers in large law firms could rotate through different practice areas to see what they liked the most. Law firm partners would offer guidance about each practice area, and at the end of a year or two, new lawyers would make their choices. However, the profession is different today. Graduates are expected to enter the profession in a chosen area of law as soon as they have passed their state's bar examination. Law students may feel pressured to select an area of practice as early as their second year of law school.

There are some advantages in making an early selection. Students can immerse in their chosen practice area, focusing their law school coursework on building up relevant knowledge and skills. They can also complete school-sponsored internships that provide valuable connections and hands-on experience. Thus, the student who selects their practice area while still in law school can step more easily into the job market after law school.

Unfortunately, the early choice may not be the correct choice. If a new lawyer receives a great deal of training in a certain practice area, they may need to retool if that area of law does not work out. For this reason, students should think carefully about a range of practice areas and be realistic about what will work for them. Further, if employment opportunities are limited in a student's most desired area of law, a backup choice is essential. Law students should explore internships, as they permit students to sample different areas of law and provide useful information to guide decision-making.

Through the successive chapters of this book, you have had the chance to think about the practice of law in different ways, visiting different areas of law and serving in different roles in the profession.

In the first Law Lab, you served as a lawmaker, a role that does not require a law degree. From there, you were abruptly elevated to a seat on the United States Supreme Court and compelled to address important questions concerning constitutional law. Then, you served as a state court judge in different venues: as an administrative law judge for a state civil rights commission, and then as a state supreme court justice, deciding a civil forfeiture matter. You also served as a state court chancery judge, resolving a complex property dispute.

You subsequently worked as an attorney. You first prepared a contract involving in-home elder care, striving to make it fair to both the caregiver and the elderly patient. You then crafted an argument in a novel area of tort law involving a service animal. Thereafter, you prepared an opening statement in an important personal injury case that arose from a carnival accident. Next, you were asked to draft legislation to protect children who are not receiving adequate medical care. Then, as a prosecuting attorney, you decided upon the types of charges that should be filed against neglectful parents.

You then reprised your role as judges and justices, addressing important criminal law questions about the admissibility of evidence and the scope of proper punishment. To conclude your work, you served as members of a state bar ethics board, supporting an attorney in the midst of a critical decision-making dilemma.

While it is interesting to think about serving as a Supreme Court justice, this job is not offered to many. As of October 2020, only 115 lawyers have served on the nation's highest court. However, many attorneys do work for the state and federal governments as prosecutors, public defenders, inspectors general, administrative law advocates, and judges. Many attorneys also work in the private sphere, serving clients in areas of torts, contracts, intellectual property law, and criminal law. Every venue and area of law can yield a satisfying career for the attorney who is suited to serve there.

Consider which Law Labs you found the most compelling. Did you like a particular Law Lab because of the type of law it featured (the substance) or because of the task involved (the process)? Which areas of doctrinal content (such as torts or family law) were the most interesting? What particular tasks (like making charging decisions, writing laws, or preparing contracts) held your interest the most?

Think about the type of law in each Law Lab, as well as the nature of the task it required. Most areas of doctrinal law can be paired with most types of legal work. For example, lawyers who enjoy advocacy and contract law can litigate contracts. Lawyers who enjoy the process of negotiation and also find property law interesting can work as transactional attorneys, promoting and closing real estate deals. Attorneys who like the concept of agency oversight and working with ethical rules will likely do very well in the offices of federal or state inspectors general. Attorneys who like working with the Fourth Amendment of the United States Constitution and enjoy advocacy can find jobs as prosecutors or public defenders or with legal service agencies.

The Five Components of Legal Jobs

As you reflect on the options available to someone who wishes to pursue a legal career, it is useful to consider the five key components that are part of every job in the law (and many jobs that are not law related). Depending upon individual preferences, different attorneys will naturally reach for different jobs based on which of these components they value the most.

The Compensation and Benefits

In the minds of most people, the first component of any job is the compensation package. How much money does the job pay? Does the job come with benefits such as an insurance plan? Does the job include an employer-sponsored pension or support contributions to a retirement account? How much paid vacation or family leave time is included? Is there a maternity and/or paternity policy? Are you allowed to work from home from time to time?

Your future job must pay enough to support a reasonable quality of life. If you need a particular benefit, such as insurance, you should find a job that offers that benefit. If you plan on having a family, the ideal job will offer some type of paid leave so that you can take time off when a child arrives.

The Nature of the Work and Opportunity for Advancement

The second component concerns the work itself. Does the law job permit you to learn new things, grow in experience, and develop your talents and skills? Can you advance with your talents and become a better lawyer/employee? Will your gifts and talents, as they improve, be recognized and rewarded by your employer?

A dead-end job is one that does not offer a path to increased knowledge or opportunity. Most people like the idea that their job will encourage them to increase their expertise and understanding and that their employer will recognize them for their mastery of new skills.

The Colleagues

Every job comes with a set of colleagues. As a new attorney, you will be working with a particular group of people for many hours each week. Are these people you want to spend time with? Do they have qualities that you admire and respect? Will you be content to work with them?

Most people do not wish to work in an environment that is unfriendly. They like the idea that they can build collegial relationships at work and be comfortable in their work environment. For some people, the idea that some of their colleagues may also become friends is important.

In addition, sometimes people will accept legal jobs because they like the fact that certain people work with a particular employer. They feel that in that job setting, they can learn more, have a better work experience, and form connections that will support them as they do difficult work.

The Legacy Component

The fourth component concerns a job's legacy potential. Does this law job give you the chance to contribute to society in a way that you find personally meaningful or important?

In any legal job, you should feel good about the work you are doing. For some, however, the ability to focus on a particular cause is critically important. They want to serve society in a certain way and feel strongly about finding employment that furthers a cause they value. They may wish to support a particular mission, such as bringing those who harm others to trial, or helping children find families that will care for them, or prosecuting those who pollute the environment. In fact, some people enter the legal profession because they wish to further a particular cause. Most, however, simply hope to serve those who need help with their legal problems in the area of practice that they select. Either choice offers legacy benefits.

The Leisure Time Component

The last component has to do with leisure (or family) time. What are the required working hours for this particular legal job? Will you be comfortable with the pace that the job requires? If it is important for you to be home each night by 5:00 p.m., you will not find it easy to work in many large law firms, where extended hours are the norm. If you wish to pursue a hobby that takes some time each day or engage with friends or family members for hours each day, you will need to select a law job that does not require you to work late frequently.

From these five components, we can conclude that the very best job for any young attorney would:

1. Offer excellent compensation with full health benefits and a nice retirement plan;
2. Give the new lawyer the opportunity to develop skills, learn interesting new things, and be recognized for their increasing talent;
3. Feature a great work environment with interesting and motivating colleagues;
4. Offer the attorney the chance to build a legacy of useful work that furthers an important cause; and
5. End promptly at 5:00 every night.

Sadly, this perfect job does not exist.

Instead, attorneys (young and old) must compromise some of the things on this list they view as less important in order to secure other things that they value more. The usual compromises are an exchange of leisure time for money; a downgrade in salary for the chance to take an important legacy job; or completing work that is not particularly interesting in exchange for a steady and reasonable schedule. Most Legal Aid attorneys are not paid notably high salaries, but they are very satisfied with their work. Most corporate attorneys are paid well, and many are quite satisfied with their jobs. Many attorneys in large firms work long hours at a pace that cannot be sustained without affecting personal time and family life. There are always trade-offs, and they should be recognized.

Conclusion

The practice of law offers the opportunity to work with interesting ideas and serve people in special ways. Many careers in the legal profession are inherently rewarding. As there are so many choices about what kind of law to practice, it is important to think about what matters to you and where your talents rest. Where your skillset and preferences overlap with a particular legal job, you will find the most satisfaction.

Spend some time thinking about the areas of law that interested you the most as you worked through this book. Continue to think about your talents and your options as you progress through law school. Consider the five factors discussed above, and think about which of them matter the most to you. Revisit your priorities from time to time as your thinking about your legal career matures.

FIG. 17.2 Find the right career in the law

If you decide to pursue a law degree, share your preferences with the attorneys who work in your law school's career services office. They can help you match your goals with internships where you can explore the areas of law and types of legal work that may work best for you. Listen to their advice about options in the profession, and step forward toward a reasonable choice. If that choice does not work out, you can retool and change paths, taking the skills you have learned and applying them in a new venue. Many attorneys change jobs and practice areas during their careers. With planning, you can, too.

When you find legal work that pays the bills, permits meaningful growth, connects you with other engaging people, and also allows you to serve the interests of justice in a way that is personally satisfying, you have found your home in the law. As you reach for additional knowledge, skills, and service opportunities, your legacy in the law will naturally follow.

CREDITS

Appendix 1: The Constitution of the United States of America

We the People of the United States, in Order to form a more perfect Union, establish Justice, insure domestic Tranquility, provide for the common defence, promote the general Welfare, and secure the Blessings of Liberty to ourselves and our Posterity, do ordain and establish this Constitution for the United States of America.

Article I.

Section 1.

All legislative Powers herein granted shall be vested in a Congress of the United States, which shall consist of a Senate and House of Representatives.

Section 2.

The House of Representatives shall be composed of Members chosen every second Year by the People of the several States, and the Electors in each State shall have the Qualifications requisite for Electors of the most numerous Branch of the State Legislature.

No Person shall be a Representative who shall not have attained to the Age of twenty five Years, and been seven Years a Citizen of the United States, and who shall not, when elected, be an Inhabitant of that State in which he shall be chosen.

Representatives and direct Taxes shall be apportioned among the several States which may be included within this Union, according to their respective Numbers, which shall be determined by adding to the whole Number of free Persons, including those bound to Service for a Term of Years, and excluding Indians not taxed, three fifths of all other

Persons.[1] The actual Enumeration shall be made within three Years after the first Meeting of the Congress of the United States, and within every subsequent Term of ten Years, in such Manner as they shall by Law direct. The Number of Representatives shall not exceed one for every thirty Thousand, but each State shall have at Least one Representative; and until such enumeration shall be made, the State of New Hampshire shall be entitled to chuse three, Massachusetts eight, Rhode-Island and Providence Plantations one, Connecticut five, New-York six, New Jersey four, Pennsylvania eight, Delaware one, Maryland six, Virginia ten, North Carolina five, South Carolina five, and Georgia three.

When vacancies happen in the Representation from any State, the Executive Authority thereof shall issue Writs of Election to fill such Vacancies.

The House of Representatives shall chuse their Speaker and other Officers; and shall have the sole Power of Impeachment.

Section 3.

The Senate of the United States shall be composed of two Senators from each State, **chosen by the Legislature**[2] thereof, for six Years; and each Senator shall have one Vote.

Immediately after they shall be assembled in Consequence of the first Election, they shall be divided as equally as may be into three Classes. The Seats of the Senators of the first Class shall be vacated at the Expiration of the second Year, of the second Class at the Expiration of the fourth Year, and of the third Class at the Expiration of the sixth Year, so that one third may be chosen every second Year; **and if Vacancies happen by Resignation, or otherwise, during the Recess of the Legislature of any State, the Executive thereof may make temporary Appointments until the next Meeting of the Legislature, which shall then fill such Vacancies**.[3]

No Person shall be a Senator who shall not have attained to the Age of thirty Years, and been nine Years a Citizen of the United States, and who shall not, when elected, be an Inhabitant of that State for which he shall be chosen.

The Vice President of the United States shall be President of the Senate, but shall have no Vote, unless they be equally divided.

---

1   Modified by Section 2 of the Fourteenth Amendment.
2   Modified by the Seventeenth Amendment.
3   Modified by the Seventeenth Amendment.

The Senate shall chuse their other Officers, and also a President pro tempore, in the Absence of the Vice President, or when he shall exercise the Office of President of the United States.

The Senate shall have the sole Power to try all Impeachments. When sitting for that Purpose, they shall be on Oath or Affirmation. When the President of the United States is tried, the Chief Justice shall preside: And no Person shall be convicted without the Concurrence of two thirds of the Members present.

Judgment in Cases of Impeachment shall not extend further than to removal from Office, and disqualification to hold and enjoy any Office of honor, Trust or Profit under the United States: but the Party convicted shall nevertheless be liable and subject to Indictment, Trial, Judgment and Punishment, according to Law.

Section 4.

The Times, Places and Manner of holding Elections for Senators and Representatives, shall be prescribed in each State by the Legislature thereof; but the Congress may at any time by Law make or alter such Regulations, except as to the Places of chusing Senators.

The Congress shall assemble at least once in every Year, and such Meeting shall be on **the first Monday in December**,[4] unless they shall by Law appoint a different Day.

Section 5.

Each House shall be the Judge of the Elections, Returns and Qualifications of its own Members, and a Majority of each shall constitute a Quorum to do Business; but a smaller Number may adjourn from day to day, and may be authorized to compel the Attendance of absent Members, in such Manner, and under such Penalties as each House may provide.

Each House may determine the Rules of its Proceedings, punish its Members for disorderly Behaviour, and, with the Concurrence of two thirds, expel a Member.

Each House shall keep a Journal of its Proceedings, and from time to time publish the same, excepting such Parts as may in their Judgment require Secrecy; and the Yeas and Nays of the Members of either House on any question shall, at the Desire of one fifth of those Present, be entered on the Journal.

Neither House, during the Session of Congress, shall, without the Consent of the other, adjourn for more than three days, nor to any other Place than that in which the two Houses shall be sitting.

---

4   Modified by Section 2 of the Twentieth Amendment.

Section 6.

The Senators and Representatives shall receive a Compensation for their Services, to be ascertained by Law, and paid out of the Treasury of the United States. They shall in all Cases, except Treason, Felony and Breach of the Peace, be privileged from Arrest during their Attendance at the Session of their respective Houses, and in going to and returning from the same; and for any Speech or Debate in either House, they shall not be questioned in any other Place.

No Senator or Representative shall, during the Time for which he was elected, be appointed to any civil Office under the Authority of the United States, which shall have been created, or the Emoluments whereof shall have been encreased during such time; and no Person holding any Office under the United States, shall be a Member of either House during his Continuance in Office.

Section 7.

All Bills for raising Revenue shall originate in the House of Representatives; but the Senate may propose or concur with Amendments as on other Bills.

Every Bill which shall have passed the House of Representatives and the Senate, shall, before it become a Law, be presented to the President of the United States; If he approve he shall sign it, but if not he shall return it, with his Objections to that House in which it shall have originated, who shall enter the Objections at large on their Journal, and proceed to reconsider it. If after such Reconsideration two thirds of that House shall agree to pass the Bill, it shall be sent, together with the Objections, to the other House, by which it shall likewise be reconsidered, and if approved by two thirds of that House, it shall become a Law. But in all such Cases the Votes of both Houses shall be determined by yeas and Nays, and the Names of the Persons voting for and against the Bill shall be entered on the Journal of each House respectively. If any Bill shall not be returned by the President within ten Days (Sundays excepted) after it shall have been presented to him, the Same shall be a Law, in like Manner as if he had signed it, unless the Congress by their Adjournment prevent its Return, in which Case it shall not be a Law.

Every Order, Resolution, or Vote to which the Concurrence of the Senate and House of Representatives may be necessary (except on a question of Adjournment) shall be presented to the President of the United States; and before the Same shall take Effect, shall be approved by him, or being disapproved by him, shall be repassed by two thirds of the Senate and House of Representatives, according to the Rules and Limitations prescribed in the Case of a Bill.

Section 8.

The Congress shall have Power To lay and collect Taxes, Duties, Imposts and Excises, to pay the Debts and provide for the common Defence and general Welfare of the United States; but all Duties, Imposts and Excises shall be uniform throughout the United States;

To borrow Money on the credit of the United States;

To regulate Commerce with foreign Nations, and among the several States, and with the Indian Tribes;

To establish an uniform Rule of Naturalization, and uniform Laws on the subject of Bankruptcies throughout the United States;

To coin Money, regulate the Value thereof, and of foreign Coin, and fix the Standard of Weights and Measures;

To provide for the Punishment of counterfeiting the Securities and current Coin of the United States;

To establish Post Offices and post Roads;

To promote the Progress of Science and useful Arts, by securing for limited Times to Authors and Inventors the exclusive Right to their respective Writings and Discoveries;

To constitute Tribunals inferior to the supreme Court;

To define and punish Piracies and Felonies committed on the high Seas, and Offences against the Law of Nations;

To declare War, grant Letters of Marque and Reprisal, and make Rules concerning Captures on Land and Water;

To raise and support Armies, but no Appropriation of Money to that Use shall be for a longer Term than two Years;

To provide and maintain a Navy;

To make Rules for the Government and Regulation of the land and naval Forces;

To provide for calling forth the Militia to execute the Laws of the Union, suppress Insurrections and repel Invasions;

To provide for organizing, arming, and disciplining, the Militia, and for governing such Part of them as may be employed in the Service of the United States, reserving to the States respectively, the Appointment of the Officers, and the Authority of training the Militia according to the discipline prescribed by Congress;

To exercise exclusive Legislation in all Cases whatsoever, over such District (not exceeding ten Miles square) as may, by Cession of particular States, and the Acceptance of Congress, become the Seat of the Government of the United States, and to exercise like Authority over all Places purchased by the Consent of the Legislature of the State in which the Same shall be, for the Erection of Forts, Magazines, Arsenals, dock-Yards, and other needful Buildings;—And

To make all Laws which shall be necessary and proper for carrying into Execution the foregoing Powers, and all other Powers vested by this Constitution in the Government of the United States, or in any Department or Officer thereof.

Section 9.

The Migration or Importation of such Persons as any of the States now existing shall think proper to admit, shall not be prohibited by the Congress prior to the Year one thousand eight hundred and eight, but a Tax or duty may be imposed on such Importation, not exceeding ten dollars for each Person.

The Privilege of the Writ of Habeas Corpus shall not be suspended, unless when in Cases of Rebellion or Invasion the public Safety may require it.

No Bill of Attainder or ex post facto Law shall be passed.

No Capitation, or other direct, Tax shall be laid, **unless in Proportion to the Census or enumeration herein before directed to be taken**.[5]

No Tax or Duty shall be laid on Articles exported from any State.

---

5   Modified by the Sixteenth Amendment.

No Preference shall be given by any Regulation of Commerce or Revenue to the Ports of one State over those of another: nor shall Vessels bound to, or from, one State, be obliged to enter, clear, or pay Duties in another.

No Money shall be drawn from the Treasury, but in Consequence of Appropriations made by Law; and a regular Statement and Account of the Receipts and Expenditures of all public Money shall be published from time to time.

No Title of Nobility shall be granted by the United States: And no Person holding any Office of Profit or Trust under them, shall, without the Consent of the Congress, accept of any present, Emolument, Office, or Title, of any kind whatever, from any King, Prince, or foreign State.

Section 10.

No State shall enter into any Treaty, Alliance, or Confederation; grant Letters of Marque and Reprisal; coin Money; emit Bills of Credit; make any Thing but gold and silver Coin a Tender in Payment of Debts; pass any Bill of Attainder, ex post facto Law, or Law impairing the Obligation of Contracts, or grant any Title of Nobility.

No State shall, without the Consent of the Congress, lay any Imposts or Duties on Imports or Exports, except what may be absolutely necessary for executing it's inspection Laws: and the net Produce of all Duties and Imposts, laid by any State on Imports or Exports, shall be for the Use of the Treasury of the United States; and all such Laws shall be subject to the Revision and Controul of the Congress.

No State shall, without the Consent of Congress, lay any Duty of Tonnage, keep Troops, or Ships of War in time of Peace, enter into any Agreement or Compact with another State, or with a foreign Power, or engage in War, unless actually invaded, or in such imminent Danger as will not admit of delay.

Article II.
Section 1.

The executive Power shall be vested in a President of the United States of America. He shall hold his Office during the Term of four Years, and, together with the Vice President, chosen for the same Term, be elected, as follows:

Each State shall appoint, in such Manner as the Legislature thereof may direct, a Number of Electors, equal to the whole Number of Senators and Representatives to which the State may be entitled in the

Congress: but no Senator or Representative, or Person holding an Office of Trust or Profit under the United States, shall be appointed an Elector.

The Electors shall meet in their respective States, and vote by Ballot for two Persons, of whom one at least shall not be an Inhabitant of the same State with themselves. And they shall make a List of all the Persons voted for, and of the Number of Votes for each; which List they shall sign and certify, and transmit sealed to the Seat of the Government of the United States, directed to the President of the Senate. The President of the Senate shall, in the Presence of the Senate and House of Representatives, open all the Certificates, and the Votes shall then be counted. The Person having the greatest Number of Votes shall be the President, if such Number be a Majority of the whole Number of Electors appointed; and if there be more than one who have such Majority, and have an equal Number of Votes, then the House of Representatives shall immediately chuse by Ballot one of them for President; and if no Person have a Majority, then from the five highest on the List the said House shall in like Manner chuse the President. But in chusing the President, the Votes shall be taken by States, the Representation from each State having one Vote; A quorum for this Purpose shall consist of a Member or Members from two thirds of the States, and a Majority of all the States shall be necessary to a Choice. In every Case, after the Choice of the President, the Person having the greatest Number of Votes of the Electors shall be the Vice President. But if there should remain two or more who have equal Votes, the Senate shall chuse from them by Ballot the Vice President.[6]

The Congress may determine the Time of chusing the Electors, and the Day on which they shall give their Votes; which Day shall be the same throughout the United States.

No Person except a natural born Citizen, or a Citizen of the United States, at the time of the Adoption of this Constitution, shall be eligible to the Office of President; neither shall any Person be eligible to that Office who shall not have attained to the Age of thirty five Years, and been fourteen Years a Resident within the United States.

In Case of the Removal of the President from Office, or of his Death, Resignation, or Inability to discharge the Powers and Duties of the said Office, the Same shall devolve on the Vice President, and the Congress may by Law provide for the Case of Removal, Death, Resignation or Inability, both of the President and Vice President, declaring what Officer shall then act as President, and such Officer shall act accordingly, until the Disability be removed, or a President shall be elected.[7]

---

6   Affected by the Twenty-Fifth Amendment.
7   Affected by the Twenty-Fifth Amendment.

The President shall, at stated Times, receive for his Services, a Compensation, which shall neither be encreased nor diminished during the Period for which he shall have been elected, and he shall not receive within that Period any other Emolument from the United States, or any of them.

Before he enter on the Execution of his Office, he shall take the following Oath or Affirmation:—"I do solemnly swear (or affirm) that I will faithfully execute the Office of President of the United States, and will to the best of my Ability, preserve, protect and defend the Constitution of the United States."

Section 2.

The President shall be Commander in Chief of the Army and Navy of the United States, and of the Militia of the several States, when called into the actual Service of the United States; he may require the Opinion, in writing, of the principal Officer in each of the executive Departments, upon any Subject relating to the Duties of their respective Offices, and he shall have Power to grant Reprieves and Pardons for Offences against the United States, except in Cases of Impeachment.

He shall have Power, by and with the Advice and Consent of the Senate, to make Treaties, provided two thirds of the Senators present concur; and he shall nominate, and by and with the Advice and Consent of the Senate, shall appoint Ambassadors, other public Ministers and Consuls, Judges of the supreme Court, and all other Officers of the United States, whose Appointments are not herein otherwise provided for, and which shall be established by Law: but the Congress may by Law vest the Appointment of such inferior Officers, as they think proper, in the President alone, in the Courts of Law, or in the Heads of Departments.

The President shall have Power to fill up all Vacancies that may happen during the Recess of the Senate, by granting Commissions which shall expire at the End of their next Session.

Section 3.

He shall from time to time give to the Congress Information of the State of the Union, and recommend to their Consideration such Measures as he shall judge necessary and expedient; he may, on extraordinary Occasions, convene both Houses, or either of them, and in Case of Disagreement between them, with Respect to the Time of Adjournment, he may adjourn them to such Time as he shall think proper; he shall receive Ambassadors and other public Ministers; he shall take Care that the Laws be faithfully executed, and shall Commission all the Officers of the United States.

Section 4.

The President, Vice President and all civil Officers of the United States, shall be removed from Office on Impeachment for, and Conviction of, Treason, Bribery, or other high Crimes and Misdemeanors.

Article III.

Section 1.

The judicial Power of the United States, shall be vested in one supreme Court, and in such inferior Courts as the Congress may from time to time ordain and establish. The Judges, both of the supreme and inferior Courts, shall hold their Offices during good Behaviour, and shall, at stated Times, receive for their Services, a Compensation, which shall not be diminished during their Continuance in Office.

Section 2.

The judicial Power shall extend to all Cases, in Law and Equity, arising under this Constitution, the Laws of the United States, and Treaties made, or which shall be made, under their Authority;—to all Cases affecting Ambassadors, other public Ministers and Consuls;—to all Cases of admiralty and maritime Jurisdiction;—to Controversies to which the United States shall be a Party;—to Controversies between two or more States;— **between a State and Citizens of another State**,[8]—between Citizens of different States,—between Citizens of the same State claiming Lands under Grants of different States, and between a State, or the Citizens thereof, and foreign States, Citizens or Subjects.

In all Cases affecting Ambassadors, other public Ministers and Consuls, and those in which a State shall be Party, the supreme Court shall have original Jurisdiction. In all the other Cases before mentioned, the supreme Court shall have appellate Jurisdiction, both as to Law and Fact, with such Exceptions, and under such Regulations as the Congress shall make.

The Trial of all Crimes, except in Cases of Impeachment, shall be by Jury; and such Trial shall be held in the State where the said Crimes shall have been committed; but when not committed within any State, the Trial shall be at such Place or Places as the Congress may by Law have directed.

---

8   Modified by the Eleventh Amendment.

Section 3.

Treason against the United States, shall consist only in levying War against them, or in adhering to their Enemies, giving them Aid and Comfort. No Person shall be convicted of Treason unless on the Testimony of two Witnesses to the same overt Act, or on Confession in open Court.

The Congress shall have Power to declare the Punishment of Treason, but no Attainder of Treason shall work Corruption of Blood, or Forfeiture except during the Life of the Person attainted.

Article IV.
Section 1.

Full Faith and Credit shall be given in each State to the public Acts, Records, and judicial Proceedings of every other State. And the Congress may by general Laws prescribe the Manner in which such Acts, Records and Proceedings shall be proved, and the Effect thereof.

Section 2.

The Citizens of each State shall be entitled to all Privileges and Immunities of Citizens in the several States.

A Person charged in any State with Treason, Felony, or other Crime, who shall flee from Justice, and be found in another State, shall on Demand of the executive Authority of the State from which he fled, be delivered up, to be removed to the State having Jurisdiction of the Crime.

No Person held to Service or Labour in one State, under the Laws thereof, escaping into another, shall, in Consequence of any Law or Regulation therein, be discharged from such Service or Labour, but shall be delivered up on Claim of the Party to whom such Service or Labour may be due.[9]

Section 3.

New States may be admitted by the Congress into this Union; but no new State shall be formed or erected within the Jurisdiction of any other State; nor any State be formed by the Junction of two or more States, or Parts of States, without the Consent of the Legislatures of the States concerned as well as of the Congress.

---

9   Superseded by the Thirteenth Amendment.

The Congress shall have Power to dispose of and make all needful Rules and Regulations respecting the Territory or other Property belonging to the United States; and nothing in this Constitution shall be so construed as to Prejudice any Claims of the United States, or of any particular State.

Section 4.

The United States shall guarantee to every State in this Union a Republican Form of Government, and shall protect each of them against Invasion; and on Application of the Legislature, or of the Executive (when the Legislature cannot be convened) against domestic Violence.

Article V.

The Congress, whenever two thirds of both Houses shall deem it necessary, shall propose Amendments to this Constitution, or, on the Application of the Legislatures of two thirds of the several States, shall call a Convention for proposing Amendments, which, in either Case, shall be valid to all Intents and Purposes, as Part of this Constitution, when ratified by the Legislatures of three fourths of the several States, or by Conventions in three fourths thereof, as the one or the other Mode of Ratification may be proposed by the Congress; Provided that no Amendment which may be made prior to the Year One thousand eight hundred and eight shall in any Manner affect the first and fourth Clauses in the Ninth Section of the first Article; and that no State, without its Consent, shall be deprived of its equal Suffrage in the Senate.

Article VI.

All Debts contracted and Engagements entered into, before the Adoption of this Constitution, shall be as valid against the United States under this Constitution, as under the Confederation.

This Constitution, and the Laws of the United States which shall be made in Pursuance thereof; and all Treaties made, or which shall be made, under the Authority of the United States, shall be the supreme Law of the Land; and the Judges in every State shall be bound thereby, any Thing in the Constitution or Laws of any State to the Contrary notwithstanding.

The Senators and Representatives before mentioned, and the Members of the several State Legislatures, and all executive and judicial Officers, both of the United States and of the several States, shall be bound by Oath or Affirmation, to support this Constitution; but no religious Test shall ever be required as a Qualification to any Office or public Trust under the United States.

Article VII.

The Ratification of the Conventions of nine States, shall be sufficient for the Establishment of this Constitution between the States so ratifying the Same.

The Bill of Rights

Amendment I

Congress shall make no law respecting an establishment of religion, or prohibiting the free exercise thereof; or abridging the freedom of speech, or of the press; or the right of the people peaceably to assemble, and to petition the Government for a redress of grievances.

Amendment II

A well regulated Militia, being necessary to the security of a free State, the right of the people to keep and bear Arms, shall not be infringed.

Amendment III

No Soldier shall, in time of peace be quartered in any house, without the consent of the Owner, nor in time of war, but in a manner to be prescribed by law.

Amendment IV

The right of the people to be secure in their persons, houses, papers, and effects, against unreasonable searches and seizures, shall not be violated, and no Warrants shall issue, but upon probable cause, supported by Oath or affirmation, and particularly describing the place to be searched, and the persons or things to be seized.

Amendment V

No person shall be held to answer for a capital, or otherwise infamous crime, unless on a presentment or indictment of a Grand Jury, except in cases arising in the land or naval forces, or in the Militia, when in actual service in time of War or public danger; nor shall any person be subject for the same offence to be twice put in jeopardy of life or limb; nor shall be compelled in any criminal case to be a witness against himself, nor be deprived of life, liberty, or property, without due process of law; nor shall private property be taken for public use, without just compensation.

Amendment VI

In all criminal prosecutions, the accused shall enjoy the right to a speedy and public trial, by an impartial jury of the State and district wherein the crime shall have been committed, which district shall have been previously ascertained by law, and to be informed of the nature and cause of the accusation; to be confronted with the witnesses against him; to have compulsory process for obtaining witnesses in his favor, and to have the Assistance of Counsel for his defence.

Amendment VII

In Suits at common law, where the value in controversy shall exceed twenty dollars, the right of trial by jury shall be preserved, and no fact tried by a jury, shall be otherwise re-examined in any Court of the United States, than according to the rules of the common law.

Amendment VIII

Excessive bail shall not be required, nor excessive fines imposed, nor cruel and unusual punishments inflicted.

Amendment IX

The enumeration in the Constitution, of certain rights, shall not be construed to deny or disparage others retained by the people.

Amendment X

The powers not delegated to the United States by the Constitution, nor prohibited by it to the States, are reserved to the States respectively, or to the people.

Remaining Amendments to the Constitution

Amendment XI

Ratified February 7, 1795

Note: Article III, Section 2, of the Constitution was modified by Amendment Eleven.

The Judicial power of the United States shall not be construed to extend to any suit in law or equity, commenced or prosecuted against one of the United States by Citizens of another State, or by Citizens or Subjects of any Foreign State.

Amendment XII

Ratified June 15, 1804

Note: A portion of Article II, Section 1 of the Constitution was superseded by the Twelfth Amendment.

The Electors shall meet in their respective states and vote by ballot for President and Vice-President, one of whom, at least, shall not be an inhabitant of the same state with themselves; they shall name in their ballots the person voted for as President, and in distinct ballots the person voted for as Vice-President, and they shall make distinct lists of all persons voted for as President, and of all persons voted for as Vice-President, and of the number of votes for each, which lists they shall sign and certify, and transmit sealed to the seat of the government of the United States, directed to the President of the Senate;—the President of the Senate shall, in the presence of the Senate and House of Representatives, open all the certificates and the votes shall then be counted;—The person having the greatest number of votes for President, shall be the President, if such number be a majority of the whole number of Electors appointed; and if no person have such majority, then from the persons having the highest numbers not exceeding three on the list of those voted for as President, the House of Representatives shall choose immediately, by ballot, the President. But in choosing the President, the votes shall be taken by states, the representation from each state having one vote; a quorum for this purpose shall consist of a member or members from two-thirds of the states, and a majority of all the states shall be necessary to a choice. [And if the House of Representatives shall not choose a President whenever the right of choice shall devolve upon them, before the fourth day of March next following, then the Vice-President shall act as President, as in case of the death or other constitutional disability of the President.—]* The person having the greatest number of votes as Vice-President, shall be the Vice-President, if such number be a majority of the whole number of Electors appointed, and if no person have a majority, then from the two highest numbers on the list, the Senate shall choose the Vice-President; a quorum for the purpose shall consist of two-thirds of the whole number of Senators, and a majority of the whole number shall be necessary to a choice. But no person constitutionally ineligible to the office of President shall be eligible to that of Vice-President of the United States. *Superseded by Section 3 of the Twentieth amendment.

Amendment XIII

Ratified December 6, 1865

Note: A portion of Article IV, Section 2, of the Constitution was superseded by the Thirteenth Amendment.

Section 1.

Neither slavery nor involuntary servitude, except as a punishment for crime whereof the party shall have been duly convicted, shall exist within the United States, or any place subject to their jurisdiction.

Section 2.

Congress shall have power to enforce this article by appropriate legislation.

Amendment XIV

Ratified July 9, 1868

Note: Article I, Section 2, of the Constitution was modified by Section 2 of the Fourteenth Amendment.

Section 1.

All persons born or naturalized in the United States, and subject to the jurisdiction thereof, are citizens of the United States and of the State wherein they reside. No State shall make or enforce any law which shall abridge the privileges or immunities of citizens of the United States; nor shall any State deprive any person of life, liberty, or property, without due process of law; nor deny to any person within its jurisdiction the equal protection of the laws.

Section 2.

Representatives shall be apportioned among the several States according to their respective numbers, counting the whole number of persons in each State, excluding Indians not taxed. But when the right to vote at any election for the choice of electors for President and Vice-President of the United States, Representatives in Congress, the Executive and Judicial officers of a State, or the members of the Legislature thereof, is denied to any of the male inhabitants of such State, being twenty-one years of age,[10] and citizens of the United States, or in any way abridged, except for participation in rebellion, or other crime, the basis of representation therein shall be reduced in the proportion which the number of such male citizens shall bear to the whole number of male citizens twenty-one years of age in such State.

Section 3.

No person shall be a Senator or Representative in Congress, or elector of President and Vice-President, or hold any office, civil or military, under the United States, or under any State, who, having previously taken an oath, as a member of Congress, or as an officer of the United States, or as a member of any State legislature, or as an executive or judicial officer of any State, to support the Constitution of the United States, shall have engaged in insurrection or rebellion against the same, or given aid or comfort to the enemies thereof. But Congress may by a vote of two-thirds of each House, remove such disability.

Section 4.

The validity of the public debt of the United States, authorized by law, including debts incurred for payment of pensions and bounties for services in suppressing insurrection or rebellion, shall not be questioned. But neither the United States nor any State shall assume or pay any debt or obligation incurred in aid

---

10   Changed by Section 1 of the Twenty-Sixth Amendment.

of insurrection or rebellion against the United States, or any claim for the loss or emancipation of any slave; but all such debts, obligations and claims shall be held illegal and void.

Section 5.

The Congress shall have the power to enforce, by appropriate legislation, the provisions of this article.

Amendment XV

Ratified February 3, 1870

Section 1.

The right of citizens of the United States to vote shall not be denied or abridged by the United States or by any State on account of race, color, or previous condition of servitude—

Section 2.

The Congress shall have the power to enforce this article by appropriate legislation.

Amendment XVI

Ratified February 3, 1913

Note: Article I, Section 9, of the Constitution was modified by Amendment Sixteen.

The Congress shall have power to lay and collect taxes on incomes, from whatever source derived, without apportionment among the several States, and without regard to any census or enumeration.

Amendment XVII

Ratified April 8, 1913

Note: Article I, Section 3, of the Constitution was modified by the Seventeenth Amendment.

The Senate of the United States shall be composed of two Senators from each State, elected by the people thereof, for six years; and each Senator shall have one vote. The electors in each State shall have the qualifications requisite for electors of the most numerous branch of the State legislatures.

When vacancies happen in the representation of any State in the Senate, the executive authority of such State shall issue writs of election to fill such vacancies: Provided, That the legislature of any State may empower the executive thereof to make temporary appointments until the people fill the vacancies by election as the legislature may direct.

This amendment shall not be so construed as to affect the election or term of any Senator chosen before it becomes valid as part of the Constitution.

Amendment XVIII

Ratified January 16, 1919, and repealed by the Twenty-First Amendment

Section 1.

After one year from the ratification of this article the manufacture, sale, or transportation of intoxicating liquors within, the importation thereof into, or the exportation thereof from the United States and all territory subject to the jurisdiction thereof for beverage purposes is hereby prohibited.

Section 2.

The Congress and the several States shall have concurrent power to enforce this article by appropriate legislation.

Section 3.

This article shall be inoperative unless it shall have been ratified as an amendment to the Constitution by the legislatures of the several States, as provided in the Constitution, within seven years from the date of the submission hereof to the States by the Congress.

Amendment XIX

Ratified August 18, 1920

The right of citizens of the United States to vote shall not be denied or abridged by the United States or by any State on account of sex.

Congress shall have power to enforce this article by appropriate legislation.

Amendment XX

Ratified January 23, 1933

Note: Article I, Section 4, of the Constitution was modified by Section 2 of this amendment. In addition, a portion of the Twelfth Amendment was superseded by Section 3.

Section 1.

The terms of the President and the Vice President shall end at noon on the 20th day of January, and the terms of Senators and Representatives at noon on the 3d day of January, of the years in which such terms would have ended if this article had not been ratified; and the terms of their successors shall then begin.

Section 2.

The Congress shall assemble at least once in every year, and such meeting shall begin at noon on the 3d day of January, unless they shall by law appoint a different day.

Section 3.

If, at the time fixed for the beginning of the term of the President, the President elect shall have died, the Vice President elect shall become President. If a President shall not have been chosen before the time fixed for the beginning of his term, or if the President elect shall have failed to qualify, then the Vice President elect shall act as President until a President shall have qualified; and the Congress may by law provide for the case wherein neither a President elect nor a Vice President elect shall have qualified, declaring who shall then act as President, or the manner in which one who is to act shall be selected, and such person shall act accordingly until a President or Vice President shall have qualified.

Section 4.

The Congress may by law provide for the case of the death of any of the persons from whom the House of Representatives may choose a President whenever the right of choice shall have devolved upon them, and for the case of the death of any of the persons from whom the Senate may choose a Vice President whenever the right of choice shall have devolved upon them.

Section 5.

Sections 1 and 2 shall take effect on the 15th day of October following the ratification of this article.

Section 6.

This article shall be inoperative unless it shall have been ratified as an amendment to the Constitution by the legislatures of three-fourths of the several States within seven years from the date of its submission.

Amendment XXI

Ratified December 5, 1933

Section 1.

The eighteenth article of amendment to the Constitution of the United States is hereby repealed.

Section 2.

The transportation or importation into any State, Territory, or possession of the United States for delivery or use therein of intoxicating liquors, in violation of the laws thereof, is hereby prohibited.

Section 3.

This article shall be inoperative unless it shall have been ratified as an amendment to the Constitution by conventions in the several States, as provided in the Constitution, within seven years from the date of the submission hereof to the States by the Congress.

Amendment XXII

Ratified February 27, 1951

Section 1.

No person shall be elected to the office of the President more than twice, and no person who has held the office of President, or acted as President, for more than two years of a term to which some other person was elected President shall be elected to the office of the President more than once. But this Article shall not apply to any person holding the office of President when this Article was proposed by the Congress, and shall not prevent any person who may be holding the office of President, or acting as President, during the term within which this Article becomes operative from holding the office of President or acting as President during the remainder of such term.

Section 2.

This article shall be inoperative unless it shall have been ratified as an amendment to the Constitution by the legislatures of three-fourths of the several States within seven years from the date of its submission to the States by the Congress.

Amendment XXIII

Ratified March 29, 1961

Section 1.

The District constituting the seat of Government of the United States shall appoint in such manner as the Congress may direct:

A number of electors of President and Vice President equal to the whole number of Senators and Representatives in Congress to which the District would be entitled if it were a State, but in no event more than the least populous State; they shall be in addition to those appointed by the States, but they shall be considered, for the purposes of the election of President and Vice President, to be electors appointed by a State; and they shall meet in the District and perform such duties as provided by the twelfth article of amendment.

Section 2.

The Congress shall have power to enforce this article by appropriate legislation.

Amendment XXIV

Ratified January 23, 1964

Section 1.

The right of citizens of the United States to vote in any primary or other election for President or Vice President, for electors for President or Vice President, or for Senator or Representative in Congress, shall not be denied or abridged by the United States or any State by reason of failure to pay any poll tax or other tax.

Section 2.

The Congress shall have power to enforce this article by appropriate legislation.

Amendment XXV

Passed by Congress July 6, 1965. Ratified February 10, 1967.

Note: Article II, Section 1, of the Constitution was affected by the Twenty Fifth Amendment.

Section 1.

In case of the removal of the President from office or of his death or resignation, the Vice President shall become President.

Section 2.

Whenever there is a vacancy in the office of the Vice President, the President shall nominate a Vice President who shall take office upon confirmation by a majority vote of both Houses of Congress.

Section 3.

Whenever the President transmits to the President pro tempore of the Senate and the Speaker of the House of Representatives his written declaration that he is unable to discharge the powers and duties of his office, and until he transmits to them a written declaration to the contrary, such powers and duties shall be discharged by the Vice President as Acting President.

Section 4.

Whenever the Vice President and a majority of either the principal officers of the executive departments or of such other body as Congress may by law provide, transmit to the President pro tempore of the Senate and the Speaker of the House of Representatives their written declaration that the President is unable to discharge the powers and duties of his office, the Vice President shall immediately assume the powers and duties of the office as Acting President.

Thereafter, when the President transmits to the President pro tempore of the Senate and the Speaker of the House of Representatives his written declaration that no inability exists, he shall resume the powers and duties of his office unless the Vice President and a majority of either the principal officers of the executive department or of such other body as Congress may by law provide, transmit within four days to the President pro tempore of the Senate and the Speaker of the House of Representatives their written declaration that the President is unable to discharge the powers and duties of his office. Thereupon Congress shall decide the issue, assembling within forty-eight hours for that purpose if not in session. If the Congress, within twenty-one days after receipt of the latter written declaration, or, if Congress is not in session, within twenty-one days after Congress is required to assemble, determines by two-thirds vote of both Houses that the President is unable to discharge the powers and duties of his office, the Vice President shall continue to discharge the same as Acting President; otherwise, the President shall resume the powers and duties of his office.

Amendment XXVI

Ratified July 1, 1971

Note: Amendment 14, Section 2, of the Constitution was modified by Section 1 of the Twenty-Sixth Amendment.

Section 1.

The right of citizens of the United States, who are eighteen years of age or older, to vote shall not be denied or abridged by the United States or by any State on account of age.

Section 2.

The Congress shall have power to enforce this article by appropriate legislation.

Amendment XXVII

Ratified May 7, 1992

No law, varying the compensation for the services of the Senators and Representatives, shall take effect, until an election of Representatives shall have intervened.

Appendix 2: Summary of Key Court Cases

Batson v. Kentucky, **476 U.S. 79 (1986)** (Criminal Procedure Case) A prosecutor's use of peremptory challenges to exclude Black jurors in a criminal trial involving a Black defendant violates the defendant's rights under the Sixth and Fourteenth Amendments of the United States Constitution. (Burger Court, 7–2 decision.)

Bostock v. Clayton County, **590 U.S. ___ (2020)** (Equal Protection Case) Discrimination based on sexual orientation and gender identity is prohibited by the Civil Rights Act. (Roberts Court, 6–3 decision.)

Brandenburg v. Ohio, **395 U.S. 444 (1969)** (Free Speech Case) An Ohio statute prohibiting the mere advocacy of violence to effect political and economic change is unconstitutional under the "imminent lawless action" test. (Warren Court, per curiam decision.)

Brown v. Board of Education of Topeka, **347 U.S. 483 (1954)** (Equal Protection Case) *Plessy v. Ferguson*'s doctrine of "separate but equal" is expressly overruled. Laws supporting segregation in public schools are unconstitutional. (Warren Court, unanimous decision.)

California v. Greenwood, **486 U.S. 35 (1988)** (Criminal Procedure Case) The Fourth Amendment protection against unreasonable searches and seizures does not extend to garbage that is placed on a public street, as curbside garbage is readily accessible to any member of the public. (Rehnquist Court, 6–2 decision.)

Cohen v. California, **403 U.S. 15, 26 (1971)** (Free Speech Case) Attire bearing the words "Fuck the Draft—Stop the War," which may be offensive but is not directed at a single person, is an expression of a person's political views and is protected speech under the First Amendment. (Burger Court, 5–4 decision.)

***County of Allegheny v. ACLU*, 492 U.S. 573 (1989)** (Religious Freedom Case) The city of Pittsburgh's public display of a nativity endorses Christianity and violates the Establishment Clause. However, its display of a menorah next to a Christmas tree and text declaring "salute to liberty" does not endorse any particular faith and does not violate the Establishment Clause. (Rehnquist Court, 6–3 decision.)

***Davis v. Beason*, 133 U.S. 333 (1890)** (Religious Freedom Case) Statutes prohibiting polygamy do not violate the First Amendment. The First Amendment does not bar the government from prohibiting behavior that would disrupt the "peace, good order and morals of society." (Fuller Court, unanimous.)

***Dillon v. Legg*, 68 Cal.2d 728 (1968)** (Tort Case) A defendant owes a duty of care to a bystander if the defendant's negligence could foreseeably cause that bystander severe emotional distress, and the bystander may recover damages for this harm. (Supreme Court of California, 4–3 decision.)

***District of Columbia v. Heller*, 554 U.S. 70 (2008)** (Right to Bear Arms Case) The Second Amendment's reference to a "militia" is not limited to those in the military, since this term referred to all able-bodied men capable of joining a militia at the time it was written. Citizens are guaranteed the right to bear and keep arms in their home for their protection, and provisions of the District of Columbia's law restricting the licensing and management of handguns is unconstitutional. (Roberts Court, 5–4 decision.)

***Dred Scott v. Sandford*, 60 U.S. 393 (1857)** (Privileges and Immunities Clause Case) Dred Scott, an enslaved man who was taken to a state that had outlawed slavery, could not become a free person. The Constitution did not confer rights and privileges, including citizenship, upon Black persons. (Taney Court, 7–2 decision.)

***Employment Division Department of Human Resources of Oregon v. Smith*, 494 U.S. 872 (1990)** (Religious Freedom Case) An individual's religious beliefs do not entitle them to exemptions from general laws that prohibit conduct that is within the government's power to regulate. (Rehnquist Court, 6–3 decision.)

***Engel v. Vitale*, 370 U.S. 421 (1962)** (Religious Freedom Case) Voluntary prayers in public schools violate the Establishment Clause because they promote religious practices. (Warren Court, 6–1 decision.)

***Everson v. Board of Education*, 330 U.S. 1 (1947)** (Religious Freedom Case) The Establishment Clause applies to states, preventing the states as well as the federal government from establishing or supporting religious practices. (Vinson Court, 5–4 decision.)

Florida v. Riley, 488 U.S. 445 (1989) (Criminal Procedure Case) There is no reasonable expectation of privacy when a person's property is observed by the naked eye from a helicopter flying in navigable airspace. (Rehnquist Court, 5–4 decision.)

Ford v. Wainwright, 477 U.S. 399 (1986) (Cruel and Unusual Punishments Case) The cruel and unusual punishment clause of the Eighth Amendment bars the use of the death penalty upon those who are diagnosed as insane. (Burger Court, 5–4 decision.)

Furman v. Georgia, 408 U.S. 238 (1972) (Cruel and Unusual Punishments Case) The imposition of the death penalty in three specific cases violated the Eighth Amendment's prohibition of cruel and unusual punishment. Following this decision, the death penalty was put on hold, and states could reinstate it only if they revised criminal statutes to ensure that the death penalty was not being applied in an arbitrary or discriminatory manner. (Burger Court, 5–4 decision.)

Gideon v. Wainwright, 372 U.S. 335 (1963) (Criminal Procedure Case) The Sixth Amendment's right to counsel in criminal cases applies to state courts through the Fourteenth Amendment's Due Process Clause. (Warren Court, unanimous decision.)

Gitlow v. New York, 268 U.S. 652 (1925) (Free Speech Case) New York's prohibition against speech advocating for the violent overthrow of the government is constitutional. The First Amendment's protection of free speech applies to the states as well as to the federal government. (Taft Court, 7–2 decision.)

Goldberg v. Kelly, 397 U.S. 254 (1970) (Due Process Case) Due process entitles welfare recipients to a pre-termination hearing before they are deprived of their benefits. (Burger Court, 6–3 decision.)

Gregg v. Georgia, 428 U.S. 153 (1976) (Cruel and Unusual Punishments Case) The death penalty is not prohibited as "cruel and unusual" punishment under the Eighth Amendment. However, capital punishment schemes must 1) have objective criteria to guide and limit death sentencing discretion, including a review of all death sentences to ensure that those objective criteria were appropriately applied; and 2) permit the sentencing agent to consider the record and character of each defendant as part of the sentencing process. (Burger Court, 7–2 decision.)

Hamer v. Sidway, 27 N.E. 256 (N.Y. 1891) (Contract Law Case) Adequate consideration for a contract can take many forms and need not be monetary. Consideration may be provided by promising to perform an action or refraining from taking an action. (New York Court of Appeals, unanimous decision.)

Hazelwood School District v. Kuhlmeier, 484 U.S. 260 (1988) (Free Speech Case) A school need not tolerate speech that is inconsistent with its basic educational mission. It may set high standards for student speech in school-sponsored papers and refuse to sponsor speech that is "inconsistent with the shared values of a civilized social order." (Rehnquist Court, 5–3 decision.)

Katz v. United States, 389 U.S. 347 (1967) (Criminal Procedure Case) The Fourth Amendment protections against unreasonable searches and seizures extend to places where one has a reasonable expectation of privacy. In his concurring opinion, Justice Harlan introduced a two-prong test for determining reasonable expectation of privacy (the *Katz* test). First, an individual must demonstrate that they believed their privacy to have been violated; second, their expectation of privacy must be measured against societal standards and found to be reasonable. (Warren Court, 7–1 decision.)

Korematsu v. United States, 323 U.S. 214 (1944) (Presidential Emergency Powers Case) President Roosevelt did not abuse his emergency powers when he issued an executive order requiring the removal of all Japanese Americans from coastal areas to internment camps during the Second World War. (Stone Court, 6–3 decision.)

Kyllo v. United States, 533 U.S. 27 (2001) (Criminal Procedure Case) The government's use of any device (such as a thermal imaging device which detects heat emanating from a private residence) that is not commonly available to the public and that yields information that otherwise could not be discovered without entering the home is an unconstitutional search in violation of the Fourth Amendment. (Rehnquist Court, 5–4 decision.)

Lawrence v. Texas, 539 U.S. 558 (2003) (Due Process Case) Laws criminalizing sexual relations between members of the same sex violate the Due Process clause of the Fourteenth Amendment. (Rehnquist Court, 6–3 decision.)

Lemon v. Kurtzman, 403 U.S. 602 (1971) (Religious Freedom Case) The Supreme Court created the *Lemon* test, a three-prong test to determine whether governmental action violates the Establishment Clause. Under this test: 1) the governmental action (or statute) must have a secular legislative purpose; 2) its principle or primary effect must be one that neither advances nor inhibits religion; and 3) it must not foster "an excessive governmental entanglement" with religion. (Burger Court, 8–1 decision.)

Lochner v. New York, 198 U.S. 45 (1905) (Contract Law Case) The first in a line of cases where the Court struck down state regulations of employment contracts meant to protect workers from unsafe working conditions on the basis that individuals should be free to contract as they wish. (Fuller Court, 5–4 decision.)

Loving v. Virginia, 388 U.S. 1 (1967) (Equal Protection Case) Anti-miscegenation laws violate the Equal Protection Clause. It is impossible to establish a compelling reason for these laws, which criminalize interracial sex and marriage. (Warren Court, unanimous decision.)

Lucy v. Zehmer, 84 S.E. 2d 516 (1954) (Contract Law Case) Where a party's words or actions indicate agreement, undisclosed intentions do not matter in a contract formation setting. If a party's words or actions have but one reasonable meaning, which indicates that a party intends to complete the agreement, then that party is bound by the agreement. (Supreme Court of Virginia decision.)

Mapp v. Ohio, 367 U.S. 643 (1961) (Criminal Procedure Case) The exclusionary rule, which prevents the use of evidence obtained through unreasonable searches and seizures, applies to the states as well as to the federal government. (Warren Court, 6–3 decision.)

Masterpiece Cakeshop v. Colorado Civil Rights Commission, 584 U.S. __ (2018) (Equal Protection Case) The Colorado Civil Rights Commission did not employ religious neutrality in evaluating a claim against a baker who refused to design a cake for a same-sex couple for religious reasons. Accordingly, the Commission's decision in favor of the couple was reversed. (Roberts Court, 7–2 decision.)

Mathews v. Eldridge, 424 U.S. 319 (1976) (Due Process Case) The Court devised a three-factor test to decide whether to adopt due process procedures requested by a plaintiff in a welfare benefits case: 1) What is the nature of the injury threatened by the governmental action; 2) What is the risk of error using existing procedures, and will any additional procedural safeguards reduce that risk; and 3) What are the government's interests, including the administrative costs and the need for efficiency? (Burger Court, 6–2 decision.)

McCarthy v. Arndstein, 266 U.S. 34 (1924) (Civil Procedure Case) The Fifth Amendment protection against self-incrimination applies to civil proceedings as well as criminal ones. (Taft Court, unanimous decision.)

McCulloch v. Maryland, 17 U.S. 316 (1819) (Necessary and Proper Clause Case) Congress has implied powers under the Necessary and Proper Clause that it may use to further its enumerated constitutional powers. The states cannot interfere with its use of these powers. (Marshall Court, unanimous decision.)

McDonald v. Chicago, 561 U.S. 742 (2010) (Right to Bear Arms Case) The Second Amendment right to keep and bear arms for personal defense is applicable to the states, as it is incorporated by the Fourteenth Amendment. (Roberts Court, 5–4 decision.)

Michael H. v. Gerald D., **491 U.S. 110 (1989)** (Family Law Case) California Evidence Code 261 establishes that a husband is presumed to be the father of any child born into his family, and another man can attempt to obtain parental rights only within two years of the child's birth. This code does not infringe upon the due process rights of the biological father. (Rehnquist Court, 5–4 decision.)

Minersville School District v. Gobitis, **310 U.S. 586 (1940)** (Religious Freedom Case) States are free to enact laws supporting a sense of national unity. As long as these laws are not passed for the purpose of violating religious views, they are not unconstitutional, and personal religious convictions will not permit disobedience to them. (Hughes Court, 8–1 decision.)

Miranda v. Arizona, **384 U.S. 436 (1966)** (Criminal Procedure Case) Law enforcement officials must inform suspects of their rights to remain silent and to obtain an attorney while in police custody. The prosecution may use statements made during police interrogations as evidence only if it is shown that the defendant was made aware of these rights. (Warren Court, 5–4 decision.)

Navarette v. California, **572 U.S. 393 (2014)** (Criminal Procedure Case) The Fourth Amendment does not require an officer who has received an anonymous tip about drunk driving to corroborate this information before stopping the vehicle in question. As long as the officer has reason to believe that the anonymous information is true, the tip satisfies the Fourth Amendment's reasonable suspicion standard, which permits an officer to conduct a stop based on information beyond what he or she has personally observed. (Roberts Court, 5–4 decision.)

Obergefell v. Hodges, **576 U.S. 644 (2015)** (Equal Protection Case) The Equal Protection Clause guarantees same-sex couples the right to marry freely, and no state can deprive them of that right. (Roberts Court, 5–4 decision.)

Palsgraf v. Long Island Railroad Company, **162 N.E. 99 (N.Y. Ct. App. 1928)** (Tort Case) Tort liability in negligence occurs only when the plaintiff's harm was a reasonably foreseeable consequence of the defendant's action. (New York Court of Appeals, 4–3 decision.)

Plessy v. Ferguson, **163 U.S. 537 (1896)** (Equal Protection Case) State segregation laws are constitutional insofar as they provide white and Black people the same benefits under the law. This case created the doctrine of "separate but equal." (Fuller Court, 7–1 decision.)

Prince v. Massachusetts, **321 U.S. 158 (1949)** (Family Law Case) The government has both an interest in and the authority to safeguard children's welfare and may regulate the actions of children as they pertain to this interest. (Stone Court, 5–4 decision.)

***R v. M'Naghten*, 8 E.R. 718 (1843)** (Criminal Law Case) The original English case governing the insanity defense. It provides that a person may be exonerated for their crime if they were laboring under a defect of reason so that they did not understand the nature and quality of their criminal act, or they did not know that it was wrong to do it. (United Kingdom House of Lords decision.)

***Reynolds v. United States*, 98 U.S. 145 (1878)** (Religious Freedom Case) Doctrines of religious belief are not superior to the law of the land, as that would "permit every citizen to become a law unto himself." (Waite Court, unanimous.)

***Roe v. Wade*, 410 U.S. 113 (1973)** (Family Law Case) The "right to privacy" provided in the Due Process Clause of the Fourteenth Amendment ensures that a pregnant woman has a right to terminate her pregnancy by abortion, and state laws that broadly forbid abortion infringe upon this right. State laws may advance their interest in protecting the "potentiality of human life," but they must follow trimester guidelines. While abortions cannot be regulated in the first trimester, they can be subject to regulation in the second semester and prohibited in the third trimester. (Burger Court, 7–2 decision.)

***Roper v. Simmons*, 543 U.S. 551 (2005)** (Cruel and Unusual Punishments Case) It is unconstitutional to execute persons for crimes committed when they were under the age of eighteen. (Rehnquist Court, 5–4 decision.)

***Santosky v. Kramer*, 455 U.S. 745 (1982)** (Family Law Case) States seeking to terminate parental rights must use the evidentiary standard of "clear and convincing evidence" of neglect. The State of New York's "fair preponderance of the evidence" standard violated the Due Process Clause. (Burger Court, 5–4 decision.)

***Schenck v. United States*, 249 U.S. 47 (1919)** (Free Speech Case) A wartime statute prohibiting speech against the draft is constitutional. Congress has greater deference during wartime to decide what is in the nation's interest. The case created the clear and present danger test. (White Court, unanimous decision.)

***School District of Abington Township v. Schempp*, 374 U.S. 203 (1963)** (Religious Freedom Case) The Court devised a test to determine if a statute combining components of the secular regulation rule and religious practices violates the Establishment Clause. The test analyzes the purpose and primary effect of the legislation. If either is to advance (or inhibit) religion, then the statute "exceeds the scope of legislative power" and the enactment is unconstitutional. (Warren Court, 8–1 decision.)

***Sherbert v. Verner*, 374 U.S. 398 (1963)** (Religious Freedom Case) To determine if the Free Exercise Clause had been violated, the court should determine: 1) whether the person has a claim involving a sincere religious belief; and 2) whether the government action is a substantial burden on the person's ability to act on that belief. To defend its actions, the government must prove: 1) it is acting in furtherance of a "compelling state interest"; and 2) it has pursued that interest in the manner least restrictive to religion. This test, the *Sherbert* test, was later replaced by the *Lemon* test. (Warren Court, 7–2 decision.)

***Stambovsky v. Ackley*, 169 A.D.2d 254, 257 (N.Y. App. Div. 1991)** (Contract Law Case) A potential buyer of a home may rescind the purchase contract if the seller failed to disclose a material fact about hidden defects of the property. Those defects can include well-known rumors about the property being haunted. (Decision of Appellate Division of New York Supreme Court.[1])

***Stanford v. Kentucky*, 492 U.S. 361 (1989)** (Cruel and Unusual Punishments Case) The Constitution does not forbid the execution of convicted capital offenders who were sixteen or seventeen when they committed their capital offenses. (Rehnquist Court, 5–4 decision.)

***Stanton v. Stanton*, 421 U.S. 7 (1975)** (Equal Protection Case) A Utah law that defines different ages of adulthood for men and women is a violation of the Equal Protection Clause. (Burger Court, 8–1 decision.)

***Tarasoff v. Regents of the University of California*, 17 Cal. 3d 425 (Cal. 1976)** (Tort Case) Mental health professionals have a duty of care not only to their patients but also to those individuals who are credibly targeted for serious harm by their patients. (Supreme Court of California, 4–3 decision.)

***Terry v. Ohio*, 392 U.S. 1 (1968)** (Criminal Procedure Case) Stop-and-frisk encounters are constitutional if they protect against an immediate danger, the threat of which is determined by an officer's reasonable suspicion that a person has committed, is committing, or is about to commit a crime. An officer's reasonable suspicion must arise from "specific and articulable" facts. (Warren Court, 8–1 decision.)

***Texas v. Johnson*, 491 U.S. 397 (1989)** (Free Speech Case) Flag burning is expressive conduct that is protected by the First Amendment. It does not lose constitutional protection merely because onlookers took offense to it or found it disagreeable. (Rehnquist Court, 5–4 decision.)

***Thompson v. Oklahoma*, 487 U.S. 815 (1988)** (Cruel and Unusual Punishments Case) The execution of a convicted capital offender who is under the age of sixteen violates the Eighth Amendment's prohibition against "cruel and unusual" punishment. (Rehnquist Court, 5–3 decision.)

***Tinker v. Des Moines*, 393 U.S. 503 (1969)** (Free Speech Case) Prohibiting students from wearing armbands as a form of protest in schools is unconstitutional. Pure speech is protected even inside

---

1   The Appellate Division of the Supreme Court of New York is an intermediate appellate court. The highest court in New York is the New York Court of Appeals. Thus, the New York Court of Appeals has the same status as the supreme courts of other states.

schools unless it "materially or substantially interferes" with the operation of the school. (Warren Court, 7–2 decision.)

Trump v. Hawaii, **585 U.S. ___ (2018)** (Presidential Authority and Religious Freedom Case) President Trump's restriction of travel into the United States by people from certain nations and refugees without valid documents does not violate the president's statutory authority or the Establishment Clause. (Roberts Court, 5–4 decision.)

United States v. Jones, **565 U.S. 400 (2012)** (Criminal Procedure Case) The warrantless use of a tracking device on a vehicle is a violation of the Fourth Amendment protection against unreasonable searches and seizures. (Roberts Court, unanimous decision.)

United States v. O'Brien, **391 US 367 (1968)** (Free Speech Case) A federal statute banning the mutilation and destruction of draft cards is constitutional. The Court established a four-part test to determine whether a particular regulation of symbolic speech was permitted under the First Amendment: 1) the regulation must be within the constitutional power of the government to enact; 2) it must further an important or substantial governmental interest; 3) that governmental interest must be unrelated to the suppression of free speech; and 4) the restriction on speech must be no greater than required to further the substantial governmental interest. (Warren Court, 7–1 decision.)

Wal-Mart Stores, Inc. v. Dukes, **564 U.S. 388 (2011)** (Civil Procedure Case) A group of six Walmart employees cannot represent a certified class of 1.5 million women who have been employed by Walmart since 1998. The certification of the plaintiff class is inconsistent with Federal Rule of Civil Procedure 23(a), which requires proof of commonality. (Roberts Court, 5–4 decision.)

Warden v. Hayden, **387 U.S. 294 (1967)** (Criminal Procedure Case) The Fourth Amendment protection against unreasonable searches and seizures does not distinguish between the categories of evidence that are the subject of the search. (Warren Court, 6–3 decision.)

Weems v. United States, **217 U.S. 349 (1910)** (Cruel and Unusual Punishments Case) A prison sentence that includes performing hard labor while chained from wrist to ankle is "cruel and unusual" punishment and violates the Eighth Amendment. (Fuller Court, 4–2 decision.)

West Virginia State Board of Education v. Barnette, **319 U.S. 624 (1943)** (Religious Freedom Case) It is unconstitutional for public schools to compel students to salute the flag even when saluting the flag is an action intended to unite the country. (Stone Court, 6–3 decision.)

Wickard v. Filburn, 317 U.S. 111 (1942) (Interstate Commerce Case) The Commerce Clause should be broadly interpreted so that Congress has the power to regulate all matters that touch upon interstate commerce. (Stone Court, unanimous decision.)

Williams v. Walker-Thomas Furniture Co., 350 F.2d 445 (**D.C. Cir. 1965**) (Contract Law Case) A court may void a contract it finds unconscionable if it overwhelmingly benefits one party at the expense of another party with inferior bargaining power. (D.C. Circuit Court decision.)

Wisconsin v. Yoder, 406 U.S. 205 (1972) (Religious Freedom Case) Applying the *Sherbert test* to a challenge brought from Amish families against a state law which required them to send their children to high school in violation of their religious beliefs, the Court found that the state requirement was unconstitutional. Only governmental "interests of the highest order and not otherwise served can overbalance legitimate claims to the free exercise of religion." (Burger Court, unanimous decision.)

Youngstown Sheet & Tube Company v. Sawyer, 343 U.S. 579 (1952) (Presidential Emergency Powers Case) President Truman's use of emergency powers to take over operations of the nation's privately owned steel mills during the Korean War was an unconstitutional use of his presidential power. Neither the president's powers as commander in chief nor any claimed emergency powers permitted him to seize private property without supporting congressional legislation. (Vinson Court, 5–3 decision.)

Glossary

Abuse of Discretion An erroneous decision made by a trial judge that is arbitrary, unreasonable, or unsupported by the applicable facts or law.

Abuse of Power The misuse of the authority conferred by the law or by the government.

Abuse of Process Filing or pursuing baseless actions or unreasonably using a court process to cause harm or prejudice.

Abused Child A child who has sustained serious physical, psychological, or emotional harm or who has endured sexual abuse or trauma at the hands of parents, caregivers, legal guardians, or others.

Acceptance Assent to the written terms of a contractual offer.

Actus Reus The action or conduct that constitutes the physical, objective element of a crime.

Adhesion Contract A contract between two parties in which one party establishes the terms of a contract and the other party has little or no ability to modify those terms.

Adversarial System A legal system found in common law countries where advocates representing their clients' interests argue against one another at trial to secure judgment for their client.

Adverse Possession The legal process through which a person who does not have legal title to real property can obtain ownership. It usually requires that a person take possession, pay the required taxes, and use the land as if they owned it for a period of years.

Advice and Consent Clause The constitutional provision that requires presidential nominations for executive and judicial posts to be confirmed by two-thirds of the Senate.

Affirmative Defense A defense made by the accused party in a criminal case, or by a defendant in a civil case. If proven true, an affirmative defense eliminates or reduces the defendant's liability.

Age of Criminal Responsibility The age at which a person is deemed responsible for criminal actions and can be legally prosecuted and punished.

Annulment The dissolution of a marriage based on the claim that the marriage was never valid.

Answer A court document filed by a defendant that either accepts or rejects the allegations made by the plaintiff in the plaintiff's complaint.

Appointments Clause The constitutional provision that empowers the president to appoint all members of the federal judiciary and the cabinet officers, subject only to the consent of the Senate.

Arbitration A method of alternative dispute resolution occurring in a private setting that involves one or more arbitrators. An arbitration may be binding on the parties, or it may be nonbinding.

Arraignment A hearing in which a criminal defendant is called before a judge, informed of the charges, and asked to enter a plea.

Arson The act of willfully and deliberately setting fire to or charring property.

Assault The act of intentionally causing another to fear imminent physical harm or unwanted contact.

Attempt The act of exercising a substantial but unsuccessful effort to undertake a criminal action.

Attorney A practitioner who is qualified to represent another in legal or business transactions. In the United States, attorneys must be admitted to the bar of the state in which they wish to practice.

Bad Check Laws Statutes that make it a criminal offense to knowingly issue a check without sufficient funds to cover it.

Bail A sum of money or property that is used to ensure that a defendant released from custody will return to court when required to do so.

Battery The act of intentionally touching another person in a manner that is harmful or offensive.

Bicameral A legislative body that is divided into two branches or chambers.

Bilateral Contracts Agreements between two parties based on an exchange of promises.

Bills of Attainder Legislative acts that punish a person for a crime without the use of a formal trial.

Breach of Duty of Due Care Failing to fulfill a legal duty owed to another. The breach of the duty of due care is one element of the tort of negligence.

Browsewrap Contract A website agreement that permits the user to browse a website or access a downloadable product. The agreement goes into effect when the user visits the website.

Burden of Proof The standard a party must meet to prove claims in a court case. In civil cases, the burden of proof is a *preponderance of the evidence*. In criminal cases, however, the burden of proof is *beyond a reasonable doubt*.

Burglary The unlawful entry of a building for the purpose of committing a crime inside.

Case Law A collection of past legal opinions which provide guidance as to how a court may decide a new case with similar facts.

Case or Controversy Clause The constitutional provision that prohibits the courts from issuing advisory opinions.

Causes of Action The legal claims upon which a party's case is based.

Chain of Custody The detailed documentation of the collection, handling, transferring, and analysis of evidence, designed to protect against evidence tampering or other contamination.

Challenge for Cause The right of an attorney before trial to request removal of a juror who does not appear capable of fairness or impartiality.

Child Abandonment The desertion of a child by a parent, caregiver, or legal guardian without regard for the child's safety or well-being.

Child Abuse and Neglect A caretaker's act or failure to act that results in serious physical, psychological, sexual, or emotional harm to a child.

Child Sexual Abuse A form of child abuse in which an adult engages a child in sexual acts.

Circumstantial Evidence Evidence relying on an inference to connect it with a conclusory fact.

Civil Procedure The set of rules governing the processing of civil cases.

Civil Rights An important and expansive set of rights that protect individuals from discriminatory treatment in a variety of contexts. Civil rights laws ensure equal access to employment, education, public accommodations and housing, no matter a person's race, gender, age, religion, disability, nationality, or other characteristics.

Clickwrap Contract A website agreement in which a user must consent to a company's terms and conditions prior to using a product.

Closing Statement A final statement by an attorney promoting a client's case made at the conclusion of a trial.

Code of Hammurabi A collection of Mesopotamian laws from 1754 BC named for the Babylonian king who enacted them.

Code of Justinian A collection of laws enacted by the Roman emperor Justinian I. Also known as *Corpus Juris Civilis*.

Code of Ur-Nammu An ancient Mesopotamian legal code, dating from about 2100 BC.

Code of Urukagina The earliest known legal code, a Mesopotamian code from about 2400 BC.

Commerce Clause The constitutional provision that bestows upon Congress the right to regulate interstate commerce as well as commerce with foreign countries and Native American tribes.

Common Law A system of judge-made and judicially interpreted rules that are separate from statutory and regulatory rules. The common law historically derived from years of English judicial precedent.

Common Law Marriage A legally recognized marriage based on cohabitation rather than a state-issued marriage license.

Complaint A formal pleading made to a court to request the commencement of a legal action against a defendant.

Concurrent Conditions Conditions that must be performed at the same time, occurring when the parties to a contract have agreed to simultaneously complete performances.

Condition Precedent An event that must take place before parties to a contract are obligated to perform or fulfill any contractual obligations.

Condition Subsequent An event which releases a party from a duty of performance in a contract.

Connecticut Compromise An agreement forged at the Constitutional Convention that divided the national legislature into two chambers: an upper house with equal representation from each state and a lower house with proportional representation based on state population.

Conservation Easement A legal agreement permanently limiting the use of a parcel of land for conservation purposes in order to protect and preserve the parcel and its natural resources.

Consideration A benefit that is bargained for and received by parties who form a contract.

Conspiracy A crime in which two or more people agree to commit an unlawful act and take action to further the agreement.

Contract Law The set of laws governing the creation and termination of contracts and the management of disputes about contracts.

Contractual Conditions The conditions outlined in a contract that determine the parties' obligations to each other.

Copyright The legal right of someone to restrict duplication of their intellectual property.

Corporate Crime Nonviolent crimes committed by individuals within a corporation.

Court of the Star Chamber An English court established in the 15th century. It was comprised of a group of the king's counselors and judges and became famous for its secret meetings, unorthodox procedures, and unfair application of the law.

Covenant of Good Faith and Fair Dealing The assumption that the parties to a contract will act in good faith and deal honestly and fairly. This covenant is implied by law as a term in contracts across the United States.

Credit Card Fraud Fraudulent acts committed with a credit card, such as delivering funds to an account controlled by a criminal or unlawfully taking another's credit card information with the intent to obtain goods or services.

Crime of Fraud The crime of intentionally deceiving another person in order to secure monetary or personal gain or to deprive a person of their legal rights.

Criminal Harassment The crime of targeting another person with unsolicited behavior meant to annoy or disturb them.

Criminal Procedure The set of rules and methods employed by the government to enforce substantive criminal law.

Cross-examination The opportunity given to each party in a lawsuit to question the other party's witnesses after each witness has given their testimony.

Cyberstalking The repeated use of electronic communications to harass an individual, group, or organization.

Declaratory Judgment A determination made by a judge in a case deciding the right or obligation of each party. Declaratory judgments are often used to establish the scope of an insurance company's obligation under an insurance contract or to determine ownership rights in property.

Defeasible Estate An interest in land giving ownership of the land on a conditional basis. If a certain condition or event occurs, the ownership interest is terminated.

Defective in Design When a product is rendered unusable for its intended purpose as a result of its poor design.

Defective in Manufacture When an unintended defect occurs in a product's manufacturing process that renders it more unreasonably dangerous for ordinary use.

Defective in Marketing When a product causes harm that could have been avoided by including a warning or instructions as to its appropriate use.

Defendant The accused party in a civil or criminal case.

Defense of Consent A criminal defense by which a defendant claims that the victim of harm provided legal consent to the harmful action.

Defense of Infancy A criminal defense that excuses an offender from liability due to their young age.

Defense of Intoxication A criminal defense by which a defendant claims diminished responsibility for their actions due to intoxication.

Defense of Others A criminal defense by which a defendant asserts that they are not criminally liable for reasonable force used against another person because they were protecting a third party from harm.

Deliberations Discussions among the jurors to determine the outcome of a court case.

Demand for Inspection A court document that one party files against another party to be able to inspect something that is in the other party's control or custody.

Deposition A pretrial, out-of-court examination of a witness taken under oath by the attorneys in a case.

Deterrence The process of preventing criminal behavior by instilling fear of the consequences.

Direct Examination A series of questions a party asks a witness in a trial to reveal the witness's testimony about facts or opinions in the case.

Discovery A pretrial exchange of relevant documents and information between parties in a lawsuit.

Disorderly Conduct Conduct that disturbs the peace or otherwise disrupts the safety or decorum of a community.

Disparagement of Product A false statement made about a product causing harm to the product's manufacturer.

Dissolution The legal process that terminates a marriage.

Divine Right of Kings The theory that the political and religious authority vested in a monarch is granted by God and therefore may not be constrained or opposed.

Divorce The termination of a marital relationship by a court judgment.

Doctrine of Necessity A criminal defense by which a defendant claims they had to engage in the criminal action to avoid a greater harm.

Doctrine of the Public Trust The principle that the government must preserve certain resources for public use.

Domestic Emoluments Clause The constitutional provision that prevents the president from receiving any remuneration other than his salary from the federal government or any state government.

Domestic Violence Any physical, emotional, economic, or sexual violence within the domestic sphere, typically involving a spouse or partner.

Double Jeopardy The act of being tried twice for the same crime by the same sovereign. The Fifth Amendment protects individuals from double jeopardy.

Draco's Code A seventh-century BC Athenian legal code noteworthy for its extreme punishments.

Drug and Alcohol Offenses The offense of possessing, using, or selling a proscribed substance or paraphernalia relating to its creation or use.

Due Process of Law The legal requirement of fair treatment and the application of constitutional rights to all citizens when the government interferes with their life, liberty, or property. See also *substantive due process*.

Duress A criminal defense by which a defendant claims that they were coerced into engaging in the criminal activity with which they have been charged.

Duty of Due Care The legal obligation one owes another to exercise reasonable care. The duty of due care is an element of the tort of negligence.

Duty of Zealous Advocacy An attorney's commitment to advance the interests of their clients and to advocate with zeal to promote those interests.

Easement A type of equitable estate giving someone the right to enter or use someone else's property in a certain, specified way.

Embezzlement A type of financial fraud in which a person misappropriates funds placed in their trust.

Emergency Search Exception An exception to the Fourth Amendment's warrant requirement. This exception is triggered when a police officer has reason to believe that a search is necessary to protect life or prevent serious injury.

Eminent Domain The right of the government to take private property for public use with just compensation to its owner.

Enumerated Powers Powers granted to the federal government that are explicitly stated in the text of the Constitution.

Equal Protection of the Law The idea that the government must provide all persons access to the same privileges, rights, and protections on the same basis.

Equitable Estate An interest in land that does not include the right of current ownership or possession.

Equitable Remedies A collection of forms of relief available to an injured litigant when money damages will not restore them to their rightful position.

Escheat The right of the state to take ownership of unowned or unclaimed property.

Establishment Clause The First Amendment clause that prohibits the government from making any law "respecting an establishment of religion," through either declaring an official religion or favoring one religion over another.

Estate for Years The leasing of property for a defined period of time.

Estates in Land The many different types of interests an individual can hold in real property.

Evidence Any fact or object, tangible or intangible, introduced in court as a means of proving some legal fact.

***Ex Post Facto* Laws** Laws that retroactively punish conduct from the past which was not criminal at the time.

Exclusionary Rule A law that prevents evidence collected in violation of a defendant's constitutional rights from being used in court proceedings.

Executive Order A directive by the president that affects the operation of the federal government.

Exercise of Discretion When a decision-maker has the scope of authority to make a choice.

Extortion The crime of obtaining money or other benefits through coercive measures, including force or the threat of force.

Extradition   The process by which fugitives are returned to the jurisdictions from which they fled for the purpose of criminal prosecution.

False Imprisonment   The unlawful intentional act of restraining or confining another person against their will.

Fault-based Divorce   The dissolution of a marriage in which one spouse must prove wrongdoing by the other spouse.

Federal System   A governmental system where political authority is divided between state (or provincial) and national governments. In the United States, the federal government is a government of enumerated powers and limited authority. All the remainder of the authority is reserved for the states, and they can broadly manage their affairs within their borders.

Fee Simple Determinable Estate   An interest in land that ends when a stated or determined condition on the land occurs. When the condition occurs, the interest in the land reverts back to the original grantor or the heirs of the grantor.

Fee Simple Estate   The broadest type of freehold estate. In a fee simple estate, an individual owns, possesses, and has the right to convey the real property.

Fee Simple Subject to a Condition Subsequent   An interest in land that ends when a condition occurs or does not occur.

Fee Tail Estate   An estate in land that restricts conveyance to the heirs of the grantor. In the past, grantors used fee tail male estates to ensure that only male heirs of the body could inherit. This type of estate has been abolished in most states.

Felony   A serious crime punishable by more than one year in prison.

Felony Murder   A legal rule that holds a defendant liable for any death that occurs within the course of a felony, whether intentional or not.

Feudal System   A hierarchical governmental system common during the Middle Ages. The king permitted favored nobles to hold lands on his behalf. The nobles, in turn, became landlords for their vassals, requiring their services in exchange for their right of occupancy.

Fiduciary Duty   A relationship that obligates a person to act in the best interests of another. Attorneys owe a fiduciary duty to their clients.

Finite Estate   An interest in land that is limited to the lifetime of a specified individual.

Foreign Emoluments Clause   The constitutional provision declaring that persons holding federal office may not accept remuneration or other benefits from foreign powers.

Forgery   The crime of creating a false document or artifact or altering an existing document or artifact.

Fraud   The intentional act of deceiving another for monetary or other gain.

Fraudulent Contracts   Contracts in which one party intentionally presents misleading or false information during contract formation in order to induce the other party to agree to its terms.

Free Exercise Clause   The First Amendment clause that prevents the government from making laws prohibiting the free exercise of religion.

Freehold Estates   The most expansive types of estates in land. Freehold estates include the rights of ownership and possession of the real property.

Fruit of the Poisonous Tree   A doctrine that makes evidence derived from illegal governmental actions (such as unlawful arrest, search, or seizure) inadmissible in court proceedings.

Fugitive   A person who has fled lawful confinement.

Full Faith and Credit Clause   The constitutional provision that binds states to recognize public acts, records, and court proceedings from other states.

Future Interest   An interest in land that does not include the present right of possession.

General Damages   Damages awarded to a plaintiff for injuries suffered as the result of the defendant's actions for which there is no exact dollar value. These include damages for pain and suffering, for loss of enjoyment of life, for emotional distress, and for permanent or partial disability.

General Welfare Clause   The constitutional provision that grants Congress the right to levy taxes, pay debts, and provide for the "common defense and general Welfare" of the United States.

Grand Jury   A jury empowered to determine whether criminal charges should be brought. Federal cases require grand juries.

Grantee   The individual receiving real property from a grantor.

Grantor   The individual conveying real property to a grantee.

Hearsay   Out-of-court testimony offered to establish the truth of the matter asserted.

High-Wall Theory of Separation   A theoretical paradigm that maintains that the government must not support any religion in any way.

Homicide   The killing of one person by another.

Hot Pursuit Exception   An exception to the Fourth Amendment's warrant requirement that allows police to arrest a criminal suspect on private property if they are in urgent and direct pursuit of the suspect.

Identity Theft   The deliberate use of a person's private identifying information, often in order to derive financial benefits from that person's identity.

Illegal Gambling   Any type of gambling that violates the rules and regulations that govern the industry.

Impeachment   A legislative act that initiates a charge of misconduct in office against a public official.

Implied Powers   Powers that are implied by the language of the Constitution rather than specifically enumerated.

Incapacitation   The removal of an individual from society after they have committed a crime, intended to prevent the offender from committing further crimes.

Inchoate Crime   The offense of preparing for and taking a step toward the commission of a crime.

Incorporation of the Bill of Rights   The process by which the Bill of Rights was made applicable to the states over time.

Indictment   A formal charge or accusation that a person has committed a crime.

Inducing Breach of Contract   Taking action to encourage the breach of an existing legal promise between parties.

Infringement   The violation of an individual's intellectual property rights.

Injunction   A court order requiring someone to do something or to stop doing something.

Insanity Defense   A criminal defense that mental incapacity due to mental illness caused a defendant to commit the criminal act with which they are charged.

Intellectual Property   The original ideas or creations of an individual's own mind that can be copyrighted or trademarked.

Intentional Infliction of Emotional Distress   Outrageous intentional misconduct accomplished to cause another psychological and/or emotional harm.

Intentional Tort   A type of tort that involves purposefully inflicted harm.

Interrogatories   A set of pretrial questions that a party to a lawsuit may ask another party.

Intestate   Dying without a will.

Invasion of Privacy   The act of intruding upon another's personal life without their permission.

Irresistible Impulse Defense   A defense by which a criminal defendant acknowledges their actions were wrong but claims that they are not criminally liable because their mental illness rendered them unable to control their conduct.

Jim Crow Laws   State and local statutes that legalized racial segregation and disenfranchisement and institutionalized racial disparities in the social, educational, and economic sectors.

Joint Custody   The shared responsibility of a child by both parents after divorce.

Joint Tenants with a Right of Survivorship   A type of real property ownership where all tenants have equal, shared rights to real property and automatically inherit in the event of the death of another tenant.

Judgment   A court's final decision in a legal dispute.

Judgment Not Withstanding the Verdict   A trial judge's unilateral decision to overturn a jury's verdict when the judge finds that no reasonable jury would have determined the case the way the jury did.

Judicial Independence The ability of courts and judges to make decisions without improper influence from other branches of government or fear of political or personal consequences.

Justice The remedy for a wrong, achieved by following equitable legal codes implementing fair processes that protect the rights of all parties involved.

Kidnapping The unlawful seizure, transportation, or confinement of a person by force or fraud.

Larceny The unlawful taking of another's personal property without that person's consent.

Law of the Twelve Tables A collection of Roman laws written on tablets and publicly displayed, dating to the fifth century BC.

Laws Binding decrees that say what conduct is proscribed or permitted, establish the penalties for noncompliance, and set forth the processes to be used to accomplish certain civil, commercial, and personal endeavors.

Leasehold Estate An interest in land that includes the right to possess the land leased for a specific period of time, but not an ownership interest in the land.

Legal Cause The direct cause of one's injury; conduct that is a substantial factor in causing harm.

Legal Custody A right awarded to the parents of a child that grants them authority to make decisions about the child's welfare and upbringing.

Legal Guardian An individual with the authority to make decisions regarding the minors for whom they are responsible.

Legal Pragmatism A non-originalist philosophy of interpreting the United States Constitution. Legal pragmatists take a holistic approach to constitutional language. They apply legal precedent and also consider the social and economic consequences that flow from possible interpretations.

Legal Precedent A past legal opinion used to inform the outcomes of cases that follow.

Legal Reasoning Methods that lawyers and judges use to apply the law and facts in order to resolve legal questions. The methods can involve inductive reasoning, the application of legal rules, precedent and public policy concerns, reasoning by analogy and contrast, and economic and social science theory.

Legal Redress Seeking a remedy through the legal system.

Legal Separation An agreement whereby a married couple chooses to live separate and apart from one another while remaining legally married.

***Lemon* Test** A three-pronged test created by the Supreme Court to determine whether a government action violates the Establishment Clause of the First Amendment. To pass constitutional muster under this test, the governmental action (or statute) must 1) have had a secular legislative purpose; 2) its principal or primary effect must have been one that neither advances nor inhibits religion; and 3) it must not have fostered "an excessive governmental entanglement" with religion.

Lex Talionis The Latin name for the concept of "an eye for an eye," where the punishment mirrors the offense.

Liability   An individual's legal responsibility.

Libel   A published false statement defaming another.

Life Estate   An interest in property that allows a person ownership of land for the duration of his or her lifetime.

Living Constitution   A philosophy of interpreting the United States Constitution that requires a more fluid interpretation of the words of the document. This philosophy adheres to the theory that the Framers of the Constitution meant for it to have an "open texture," allowing it to evolve with changing times.

Looting   The act of stealing goods during social crises, such as riots, wars, or in the aftermath of a natural disaster.

Magna Carta   A 13th-century English charter of rights granting certain political liberties to vassals. Among other things, it is famous for the limitations it imposed upon the crown.

Malicious Prosecution   The act of proceeding with criminal charges without legal basis.

Mandatory Reporter   A person who is required by law to report suspected child abuse or neglect.

Manslaughter   The killing of another human being without malicious intent or premeditation, entailing less culpability than murder.

Mediation   A session of formal out-of-court negotiations between parties conducted with a designated mediator in order to reach a settlement.

Mens Rea   The intention to commit a crime or knowledge of moral wrongdoing that constitutes the subjective, mental part of a crime.

Misdemeanor   A criminal offense that is less severely punished than a felony. A misdemeanor carries a jail term of less than one year. Many misdemeanors are punished by a fine or penalty.

M'Naghten Rule   A test for criminal insanity. The M'Naghten Rule states that a defendant is not guilty by reason of insanity if he did not understand the nature of his actions or could not discern right from wrong at the time of his actions.

Monetary Damages   A reward of money to a plaintiff as compensation for injuries.

Mosaic Law (or the Law of Moses)   The term for the collection of laws promulgated by Moses. It primarily refers to the first five books of the Hebrew Bible, or Torah.

Motion   A formal request made to the judge by either party in a lawsuit.

Motion *in Limine*   A formal request to a court to limit the admissibility of certain evidence.

Motion to Compel   A formal request to the court to require someone to do something related to pending litigation. For example, a Motion to Compel Answers to interrogatories asks the court to order a party to respond to interrogatories. A Motion to Compel Attendance at Deposition asks the court to order a party to appear for questioning about the case.

Murder   The act of killing another individual with premeditation.

Mutual Mistake   Occurs when each of the parties to a contract was mistaken about a particular material fact in the formation of the contract. When this occurs, contracts are often rescinded.

Necessary and Proper Clause   The constitutional provision that gives Congress the implied powers to act on the nation's behalf.

Neglected Child   A child whose basic needs are not met by caregivers, legal guardians, or other responsible adults.

Negligence   The failure of a person to act reasonably. The term can also refer to the tort of negligence, which requires a showing of 1) a duty of due care; 2) a breach of that duty; 3) causation; and 4) damages.

No-fault Divorce   The dissolution of a marriage without the necessity of one spouse proving wrongdoing by the other spouse.

Non-preferentialism   A theoretical paradigm connected with the First Amendment Establishment Clause that says the government may take no action that benefits one church group more than another.

Nuisance   Something causing offense or trouble to another. The tort of nuisance involves depriving someone of the enjoyment of their property because of an offensive sound, smell, or other intrusive action.

Objection   An attorney's verbal disagreement with the action or speech of an opposing party that requires the judge to make a legal ruling on whether the action or speech is permitted.

Offer   Speech or conduct by a person constituting a proposal to enter a contract that would lead a reasonable person to expect a binding contract if it is accepted.

Officer of the Court   A person who has an obligation to uphold the law and maintain the effectiveness of the judicial system. Officers of the court include judges, attorneys, and court personnel.

Opening Statement   A statement made by an attorney during trial laying out their client's case, describing what the evidence will show.

Opportunity to Present Evidence   The right of a person in a case to introduce evidence in court supporting their claim or defense. This right is an important component of due process.

Organized Crime   Large-scale illegal activities that are controlled by criminal enterprises.

Originalism   A philosophy of interpreting the United States Constitution that requires that its provisions be given their "original" meaning as the words were written.

Patent   A form of intellectual property that gives an inventor exclusive rights to use or sell their invention for a limited number of years.

Penitentiary   A state or federal facility that detains people convicted of serious crimes.

Peremptory Challenge The right of attorneys before a trial to reject a certain number of potential jurors without stating a reason.

Periodic Estate A lease of real property with no defined end date.

Perjury The act of lying under oath during a legal proceeding.

Permissive Reporter A person who is not required by law to report suspected child abuse but is encouraged to report it voluntarily.

Personal Jurisdiction The authority that a court has to adjudicate a case involving a particular defendant.

Personal Property A person's property other than land and the things attached to the land.

Physical Custody A parent's right to have their child live with him or her.

Plain View Exception An exception to the Fourth Amendment's warrant requirement that permits an officer to seize evidence that is seen in plain view without entry or search.

Plaintiff The person or entity in a lawsuit who files a legal claim.

Plea Bargaining An arrangement between a prosecutor and defendant in which a criminal defendant pleads guilty to some or all of the charges in exchange for concessions. The concessions may include a more lenient sentence or the dismissal of other charges.

Power of Judicial Review The authority of a court to find a legislative, executive, or administrative action to be unconstitutional.

Prayer for Relief The remedy(ies) that the parties to a lawsuit ask the court to give them.

Prenuptial Agreement A written contract that a couple enters into before marriage that settles the ownership of the couple's respective assets in the event of divorce or death.

Prerogative Courts A group of courts established in the 15th century by King Henry VII; the courts exercised discretionary powers reserved to the king.

Presidential Emergency Powers Extraordinary powers that Congress permits the president to invoke in order to resolve national emergencies.

Presidential Veto Power The power of the president to refuse to approve legislation passed by Congress.

Presumption of Innocence The principle that any individual charged with a crime is innocent until proven guilty.

Presumption of Legitimacy A common law rule of evidence that presumes that the biological father of a married woman's child is her husband.

Private Law A classification of law that defines and regulates relationships between individuals and corporations.

Private Nuisance Something that substantially interferes with the use or enjoyment of another's land.

Privilege The right to withhold certain confidential information based on a special relationship. Examples include the attorney-client privilege and the physician-patient privilege.

Privileges and Immunities Clause The constitutional provision that ensures that a state may not favor its own citizens over those of other states.

Privity of Contract A common-law principle establishing that only the parties to a contract are legally bound to the obligations it creates. In addition, they alone are entitled to enforce its terms.

Probable Cause The requirement that police officers, in order to make searches or arrests, must have sufficient reason to believe that a crime has been committed or that property is connected to a crime. Search warrants may only issue upon a showing of probable cause.

Procedural Due Process The constitutional requirement that all proper procedures be followed to ensure that an individual's constitutional rights are protected before the individual is deprived of their life, liberty, or property. Examples of procedural due process include receiving notice of the charges being brought and having the opportunity to bring witnesses to testify during trial.

Procedural Law The body of law establishing rules to be followed by courts to ensure that the interests of justice are supported, and that the legal rights of all parties in litigation are protected.

Promissory Estoppel The legal principle under which a promise made without formal consideration may be legally enforceable if it caused the promisee to take action.

Property Law The law concerning property rights, including how property can be owned and transferred and how disputes regarding property rights are to be resolved.

Prosecutor A lawyer authorized by the government to institute legal proceedings against a criminal defendant.

Prostitution The unlawful exchange of sexual services for money.

Proximate Cause An action that causes an injury in tort law. An action proximately causes an injury if the injury could have reasonably been foreseen at the time of the action.

Public Defender A lawyer appointed to represent criminal defendants who are otherwise unable to afford legal defense.

Public Law A classification of law that deals with the responsibilities of government officials and the relationship between the state and its citizens.

Public Nuisance Something causing a substantial disturbance to the public.

Punitive Damages Damages awarded to a plaintiff that are meant to punish the defendant for their reprehensible conduct.

Real Property Parcels of land and things on those parcels that are permanently attached to the land (such as houses).

Reception Clause The constitutional provision that requires the president to receive all ambassadors from foreign nations. This clause has been interpreted to give the president the power to craft foreign policy and recognize foreign governments.

Recommendations Clause The constitutional provision that describes the president's duty to recommend such measures as are "necessary and expedient" for congressional consideration.

Recompense Compensation provided to those who have been harmed.

Record A written document detailing information relating to a legal case, often created for the purpose of judicial review.

Remedies Types of judicial relief that may be provided to the wronged party in a lawsuit.

Requests for Production A document that asks a party to a lawsuit to produce relevant documents and evidence.

Res Ipsa Loquitur An act that, by itself, demonstrates the existence of a claim for negligence, Latin for "the thing speaks for itself."

Rescind To void or cancel a contract.

Reserved Powers The powers that are neither enumerated nor prohibited in the Constitution but are instead reserved for the states.

Restatement of the Law of Contracts A frequently cited and widely recognized treatise written by legal scholars of the American Law Institute that sets forth the general principles of contract law.

Restitution A legal remedy requiring the defendant to pay the plaintiff money that was wrongfully gained.

Restorative Justice A modern approach to criminal justice that tends to be more victim oriented than other theories of punishment. Often, the offender meets with the victim and community representatives in an attempt to repair the harm done.

Retribution The punishment inflicted on a person as vengeance for their criminal act.

Right of Appeal The legal right of either party in a lawsuit to refer the lower court's decision to a higher court.

Right to a Speedy and Public Trial Guaranteed by the Sixth Amendment, this right requires that a criminal defendant be brought to trial in open court within a reasonable amount of time following their arrest.

Rioting A disturbance of the peace in which a group assembles and engages in violent or unlawful behavior.

Robbery The unlawful taking of another's property through force or threat of force.

Rule of Law Society's adherence to measures that restrict the arbitrary exercise of power, and that support fairness, equality, accountability, legal and procedural transparency, and the supremacy of the law.

Rules of Evidence The state or federal rules governing what evidence is relevant and its admissibility at trial.

Ruling on the Merits The act of deciding a case on the strength of its facts and evidence.

Sanctions Penalties meant to induce an individual to comply with the law.

Search Incident to Arrest A search by police of an arrested individual's person. Such a search does not require a warrant.

Search Warrant A court order authorizing police officials to search a specified person, location, or vehicle for evidence of a crime and seize any evidence that is found.

Secular Regulation Rule A rule used to test compliance with the Free Exercise Clause, which states that laws that do not attempt to alter religious practices are constitutional.

Sedition A type of speech or conduct that incites rebellion against governing authorities.

Self-defense A criminal defense in which a defendant argues that using a reasonable degree of force was necessary to prevent imminent injury or death brought on by an unprovoked attack.

Separate but Equal A nullified legal doctrine that asserts that racial segregation does not violate the Fourteenth Amendment as long as the separate facilities were roughly equivalent.

Separation of Powers The allocation of authority among different branches of government. In the United States, governmental authority is separated into the legislative, the executive, and the judicial branches.

Service of Process The formal delivery of a document or pleading to a party to a lawsuit.

Sex Trafficking Transporting people from one area to another for the purpose of exploiting them sexually.

Sexual Battery The crime of touching another person without their consent for the purpose of sexual gratification.

Shared Parental Responsibility A court-ordered relationship in which both parents maintain parental rights and responsibilities and work together to make major decisions regarding the child.

***Sherbert* Test** A test created by the Supreme Court to determine whether the Free Exercise Clause of the First Amendment has been violated. The test asks whether the governmental regulation substantially restricts a person's religious practices. If so, then the test demands that the government show a compelling interest justifying the restriction and also demonstrate that the regulation is narrowly tailored to achieve that interest.

Slander A spoken false statement defaming another.

Solicitation The criminal offense of urging someone to commit a crime.

Solonian Constitution A sixth-century BC constitution created by the Roman politician Solon to unify a divided Athenian state.

Sovereign Immunity A legal doctrine that maintains that the crown or the government cannot be required to appear in court unless it consents.

Special Damages Damages awarded to a plaintiff for the expenses and costs associated with the occurrence giving rise to the lawsuit. Special damages consist of the defendant's out-of-pocket monetary losses, such as lost wages and medical bills.

Stalking The crime of deliberately and repeatedly surveilling or intimidating another person in a manner that would reasonably cause the victim to fear physical harm.

Stand Your Ground Laws Laws that allow people to use deadly force to defend themselves without first attempting to retreat from threats.

Stare Decisis The doctrine that a case will be decided by legal precedent.

State of the Union Clause The constitutional provision that states that the president must give Congress periodic assessments of the nation's status so that Congress can properly address matters of national importance.

Status Conference A meeting in which the parties update the judge on the status of pretrial legal proceedings in a pending case.

Statute of Frauds A statutory law that requires certain types of contracts to be fixed in writing. These include contracts involving the transfer of real property and contracts that cannot be completed within one year.

Statutory Rape The crime of having sexual contact with a person under the legal age of consent.

Strict Construction A philosophy of interpreting the United States Constitution that requires strict adherence to the text of the document.

Strict Liability A tort claim that requires no proof of a guilty mind or intention to harm.

Subject Matter Jurisdiction The authority of a court to decide a case based upon the type of claim it presents.

Subpoena A court-approved document summoning an individual to a proceeding for the purposes of producing their testimony or documents or items in their possession.

Subrogation The right to pursue another person's legal interests.

Substantial Capacity Test A test used when considering an insanity defense in which a defendant is found not to be criminally responsible if they were unaware of their wrongdoing or acting on an irresistible impulse at the time of the criminal action.

Substantive Due Process The constitutional requirement that no fundamental right of an individual may be infringed upon, even if that right is not mentioned in the Constitution. It has been interpreted to include the right to work and the right to raise one's children.

Substantive Law The law establishing the types of legal rights individuals in a society possess.

Suffrage The right to vote.

Supremacy Clause The constitutional provision that declares that the laws of the United States (including treaties) are the "supreme Law of the Land." The Supremacy Clause confirms that valid federal laws bind the states, no matter what a state law or state constitution says.

Symbolic Speech A type of conduct that expresses a particular message without the use of words.

Take Care Clause The constitutional provision that states that the president has the obligation to "take care that the laws be faithfully executed."

Tenancy at Sufferance When a tenant continues to live on property after their lease expires but before the landlord demands that they vacate.

Tenancy in Common A form of property ownership in which each tenant has an interest in real property. Unlike a joint tenancy or a tenancy by the entirety, the property interest of a tenant in common does not automatically revert to another tenant upon death.

Tenants by the Entirety A form of ownership of property by spouses in which the surviving spouse becomes the owner of the property in the event of the other spouse's death.

Textualism An originalist philosophy of interpreting the United States Constitution, which requires adherents to rely solely on the written language of the document if the original words are clear.

Theft A crime in which a person intentionally takes another's personal property without consent and with the intention of permanently depriving the owner of the property.

Third-party Beneficiary Contracts Contracts which stand to benefit a person who is not an active party to the agreement.

Three-fifths Compromise An agreement reached at the Constitutional Convention of 1787, which determined that, for apportionment purposes in the House of Representatives, three-fifths of a state's enslaved population would be included along with all of its free population.

Tort Law The law governing civil wrongs that are not breaches of contract.

Trademark A word, symbol, emblem, or sound used in connection with a product or service belonging to the company which manufactures it and registered with the United States Patent and Trademark Office.

Treason The act of betraying one's government, either by "levying War" against the government or supporting its enemies.

Trespass The physical, unwanted intrusion upon another's property.

Trial by Ordeal A type of criminal trial during the Medieval Ages in which defendants were subjected to cruel punishments to determine if they were telling the truth.

Trust A three-party legal relationship in which a trustor or settlor transfers title to property or assets to a second party (the trustee) for the benefit of a third party (the beneficiary).

Trustee The legal owner of property who must manage the property according to the terms of a trust document for the benefit of someone else.

Unconscionable Contracts Contracts that are so egregiously one-sided that they may not be legally enforceable.

Unenforceable Contracts Contracts that are valid but that cannot be enforced due to some defect, such as misrepresentation, a party's lack of capacity, or duress or undue influence.

Uniform Commercial Code A standardized set of laws and regulations that govern all commercial transactions.

Unilateral Contracts Contracts in which the offer is accepted only by performance of an act.

Unitary System A system of government where there is only one sovereign or centralized government.

Unlawful Assembly The offense of gathering in a group and engaging in conduct that threatens public peace, order, or safety.

Vandalism The crime of willfully damaging or destroying property.

Vice Crimes Offenses that are deemed immoral by the community, such as pornography, prostitution, or gambling.

Vigilante Justice The act of an individual imposing punishment where they have no legal authority.

Voir Dire The process of questioning jurors as part of jury selection.

Ward of the State A minor or incapacitated adult who is temporarily or permanently placed in the care of a court-appointed guardian.

Warrant Requirement The Fourth Amendment requirement that searches be conducted with warrants, which must be issued by judges, justified by probable cause, supported by oath or affirmation, and describe the specific place to be searched and items to be seized.

White-collar Crime A nonviolent crime in which businesses or employees use deceit, concealment, or violation of trust for financial gain.

Writ A document issued by a court directing an individual or an agency to take or refrain from taking a specific action.

Bibliography

Abrams, David S., Marianne Bertrand, and Sendi Mullainathan. "Do Judges Vary in Their Treatment of Race?" *Journal of Legal Studies* 41, no. 2 (June 2012): 347–383. https://doi.org/10.1086/666006.

Abrams, Kathryn. "Barriers & Boundaries: Exploring Emotion in the Law of the Family." *Virginia Journal of Social Policy & the Law* 16, no. 2 (2009): 301–320. https://www.researchgate.net/publication/254561090_Barriers_and_Boundaries_Exploring_Emotion_in_the_Law_of_the_Family.

Ackermann, Nicole, Melody S. Goodman, Keon Gilbert, Cassandra Arroyo-Johnson, and Marcello Pagano. "Race, Law, and Health: Examination of 'Stand Your Ground' and Defendant Convictions in Florida." *Social Science & Medicine,*" no. 142 (October 2015): 194–201. https://doi.org/10.1016/j.socscimed.2015.08.012.

Amar, Akhil Reed. "Double Jeopardy Law Made Simple." *The Yale Law Journal* 106, no. 6 (April 1997): 1807–1848. https://doi.org/10.2307/797320.

American Bar Association. "Model Rules of Professional Conduct." 2020. https://www.americanbar.org/groups/professional_responsibility/publications/model_rules_of_professional_conduct/model_rules_of_professional_conduct_table_of_contents/.

American Law Institute. Vols. 1–3 of *Restatement (Second) of the Law of Contracts*. St. Paul: American Law Institute, 2013.

American Law Institute. *Restatement (Third) of the Law Governing Lawyers*. St. Paul: American Law Institute, 2021.

American Law Institute, and Ward Farnsworth. *Restatement (Second) of the Law of Torts*. Saint Paul: American Law Institute, 2021.

Ames, R.A., and H.C. Montgomery. "The Influence of Rome on the American Constitution." *The Classical Journal* 30, no. 1 (October 1934): 19–27. https://www.jstor.org/stable/3290141.

Anwar, Shamena, Patrick Bayer, and Randi Hjalmarsson. "The Impact of Jury Race in Criminal Trials." *Quarterly Journal of Economics* 127, no. 2 (May 2012): 1017–1055. https://doi.org/10.1093/qje/qjs014.

Arnold, David, Will Dobbie, and Crystal S. Yang. "Racial Bias in Bail Decisions." *The Quarterly Journal of Economics* 133, no. 4 (May 2018): 1885–1932. https://doi.org/10.1093/qje/qjy012.

Babb, Barbara. "Reevaluating Where We Stand: A Comprehensive Survey of America's Family Justice Systems." *Family Court Review* 46, no. 2 (2008): 230–57. http://scholarworks.law.ubalt.edu/all_fac.

Bagnall, Roger S. and William V. Harris, Eds. *Studies in Roman Law in Memory of A. Arthur Shiller*. Leiden: E. J. Brill, 1986.

Bartlett, Robert. *Trial by Fire and Water: The Medieval Judicial Ordeal*. New York: Clarendon Press, 1986.

Bass, S. Jonathan. *He Calls Me by Lightning: The Life of Caliph Washington and the Forgotten Saga of Jim Crow, Southern Justice, and the Death Penalty*. New York: Liveright Publishing, 2017.

Batheja, Aman. "As Statewide Smoking Ban Burns Out in Capitol, Cities Go it Alone." The *Texas Tribune*, December 19, 2014. https://www.texastribune.org/2014/12/19/smoking-ban-stalls-capitol-cities-go-it-alone/.

Benedek, Elissa P., Peter Ash, M.D., and Charles L Scott, Eds. *Principles and Practice of Child and Adolescent Forensic Mental Health*. Washington: American Psychiatric Publishing, 2010.

Bernard, G.W. "The Making of Religious Policy, 1533–1546: Henry VIII and the Search for the Middle Way." *The Historical Journal* 41, no. 2 (1998): 321–49. http://www.jstor.org/stable/2640109.

Bertman, Stephen. *Handbook to Life in Ancient Mesopotamia*. New York: Facts On File, 2003.

Bessler, John D. "The Anomaly of Executions: The Cruel and Unusual Punishments Clause in the 21st Century." *British Journal of American Legal Studies* 2 (2013): 297–452. http://dx.doi.org/10.2139/ssrn.2341077.

Bingham, Tom. *Lives of the Law*. Oxford: Oxford University Press, 2011.

———. *The Rule of Law*. London: Allen Lane, 2010.

Black, Michelle C., K.C Basile, M.J. Breiding, S.G. Smith, M.L. Walters, M.T. Merrick, J. Chen, and M.R. Stevens. Rep. *The National Intimate Partner and Sexual Violence Survey: 2010 Summary Report*. Atlanta: Centers for Disease Control and Prevention, 2010.

Blackstone, William. *Commentaries on the Laws of England*. Oxford: Clarendon Press, 1765.

Bogus, Carl T. "The Hidden History of the Second Amendment." *UC Davis Law Review* 31, no. 2 (Winter 1998): 311–62. https://ssrn.com/abstract=1465114.

Boorstein, Michelle. "Boy Scouts of America Votes to End Controversial Ban on Openly Gay Scout Leaders." *The Washington Post*, July 27, 2015. https://www.washingtonpost.com/news/acts-of-faith/wp/2015/07/26/the-boy-scouts-are-slated-to-lift-ban-on-openly-gay-adult-leaders/.

Bray, Samuel L. "*The System of Equitable Remedies*." *UCLA Law Review* 63, no. 3 (2016): 530–93. http://dx.doi.org/10.2139/ssrn.2622850.

Brown, Richard Maxwell. *No Duty to Retreat: Violence and Values in American History and Society*. New York: Oxford University Press, 1991.

Bryson, William Hamilton. "English Common Law in Virginia." *Journal of Legal History* 6, no. 3 (1985): 249–56. https://doi.org/10.1080/01440368508530845.

Bulstrode, Whitelocke. *Memorials of the English Affairs*. Oxford: Oxford University Press, 1853.

Burgess, Ann Wolbert, Cheryl Regehr, and Albert R. Roberts. *Victimology: Theories and Applications*. Burlington: Jones & Bartlett Publishers, 2009.

Burns, James Henderson, ed. *The Cambridge History of Medieval Political Thought c.350–c.1450*. Cambridge: Cambridge University Press, 1988.

Cahn, Naomi. "Faithless Wives and Lazy Husbands: Gender Norms in Nineteenth-Century Divorce Law." *University of Illinois Law Review* 2002, no. 3 (2002): 651–98. http://dx.doi.org/10.2139/ssrn.266477.

Carey, Michael W., Larry R. Ellis, and Joseph F. Savage. "Federal Prosecution of State and Local Officials: The Obstacles to Punishing Breaches of the Public Trust and a Proposal for Reform." *West Virginia Law Review* 94, no. 2 (Winter 1991–1992): 302–31. https://heinonline.org/HOL/LandingPage?handle=hein.journals/wvb94&div=20&id=&page=.

Cartwright, Mark, ed. *World History Encyclopedia*. Horsham, 2009. www.worldhistory.org.

Catala, Amélie, Marine Grandgeorge, Jean-Luc Schaff, Hugo Cousillas, Martine Hausberger, and Jennifer Cattet. "Dogs Demonstrate the Existence of an Epileptic Seizure Odour in Humans." *Scientific Reports* 9, no. 4103 (2019). https://doi.org/10.1038/s41598-019-40271-4.

Chen, Danhong, and Li-Tzy Wu. "Association Between Substance Use and Gun-Related Behaviors." *Epidemiologic Reviews* 38, no. 1 (Jan 2016): 46–61. https://doi.org/10.1093/epirev/mxv013.

Cherlin, Andrew J. *The Marriage-Go-Round: The State of Marriage and the Family in America Today*. New York: Vintage Books, 2010.

Cho, Seo-Young, Eric Neumayer, and Axel Dreher. "Does Legalized Prostitution Increase Human Trafficking?" *World Development* 41, no. 1 (2013): 67–82. http://dx.doi.org/10.2139/ssrn.1986065.

Christenson, Ron. *Political Trials in History: From Antiquity to the Present*. Piscataway: Transaction Publishers, 1991.

Cobb, Sanford. *The Rise of Religious Liberty in America*. New York: The Macmillan Co., 1902.

Coleman-Norton, P.R. "Cicero's Contribution to the Text of the Twelve Tables." *The Classical Journal* 46, no. 2 (1950): 51–60. http://www.jstor.org/stable/3292755.

Coogan, Michael D., Pheme Perkins, Marc Z. Brettler, and Carol Newsom, Eds. *The New Oxford Annotated Bible*, 5th ed. New York: Oxford University Press, 2018.

Cooper, Robert Alan. "The English Quakers and Prison Reform 1809–23." *Quaker History* 68, no. 1 (1979): 3–19. http://www.jstor.org/stable/41946871.

Costigan, George P. "The Date and Authorship of the Statute of Frauds." *Harvard Law Review* 26, no. 4 (1913): 329–46. https://doi.org/10.2307/1326318.

Dawson, John P. *A History of Lay Judges*. Cambridge: Harvard University Press, 1960.

Du Plessis, Paul. *Borkowski's Textbook on Roman Law*. Oxford: Oxford University Press, 2015.

Dickens, Arthur Geoffrey. *The English Reformation*. Glasgow: Collins, 1967.

Dingledy, Frederick W. "The Corpus Juris Civilis: A Guide to Its History and Use." *Legal References Quarterly* 35, no. 4 (2016): 231–55. https://doi.org/10.1080/0270319X.2016.1239484.

Doherty, Brian. *Radicals for Capitalism: A Freewheeling History of the Modern American Libertarian Movement*. New York: PublicAffairs, 2007.

Donohue III, John J., and Steven D. Levitt. "The Impact of Race on Policing and Arrests." *The Journal of Law & Economics* 44, no. 2 (2001): 367–94. https://doi.org/10.1086/322810.

Dorsen, David M. *Henry Friendly, Greatest Judge of His Era*. Cambridge: Harvard University Press, 2012.

Douglass, Frederick. *Narrative of the Life of Frederick Douglass, an American Slave*. Boston: Anti-Slavery Office, 1845.

Dudziak, Mary L. "Desegregation as a Cold War Imperative." *Stanford Law Review* 41, no. 1 (1988): 61–120. https://doi.org/10.2307/1228836.

Duthu, N. Bruce. *American Indians and the Law*. Edited by Colin Calloway. New York: Penguin Books, 2008.

Efrati, Amir, and Robert Frank. "Madoff Set to Plead Guilty to 11 Felonies." *The Wall Street Journal*, March 11, 2009. https://www.wsj.com/articles/SB123669568988683829.

Esperian, John H. "The Effect of Prison Education Programs on Recidivism." *Journal of Correctional Education* 61, no. 4 (2010): 316–34. http://www.jstor.org/stable/23282764.

Evans, James Allan Stewart. *The Emperor Justinian and the Byzantine Empire*. Westport: Greenwood Publishing Group, 2005.

Farley, Melissa, Ann Cotton, Jacqueline Lynne, Sybille Zumbeck, Frida Spiwak, Maria E. Reyes, Dinorah Alvarez, and Ufuk Sezgin. "Prostitution and Trafficking in Nine Countries." *Journal of Trauma Practice* 2, no. 3–4 (2004): 33–74. https://doi:10.1300/J189v02n03_03.

Farnsworth, Ward. *The Legal Analyst*. Chicago: University of Chicago Press, 2007.

Finkelman, Paul, Ed. *Encyclopedia of American Civil Liberties*. New York: Routledge, 2006.

Fleming, Robin. *Kings and Lords in Conquest England*. Cambridge: Cambridge University Press, 1991.

Fliter, John A. "Keeping the Faith: Justice David Souter and the First Amendment Religion Clauses." *Journal of Church and State* 40, no. 2 (1998): 387–409. http://www.jstor.org/stable/23919854.

Forsyth, Gary. *A Critical History of Early Rome: From Prehistory to the First Punic War*. Oakland: University of California Press, 2005.

Foster, Benjamin R. "Social Reform in Mesopotamia." In *Social Justice in the Ancient World*, edited by K.D. Irani and Morris Silver. Westport: Greenwood Press, 1995.

Friendly, Henry J. "Some Kind of Hearing." *University of Pennsylvania Law Review* 123, no. 6 (1975): 1267–317. https://doi.org/10.2307/3311426.

Ganong, Lawrence, and Marilyn J. Coleman, eds. *The Social History of the American Family*. Thousand Oaks: SAGE Publications, 2014.

Garner, James W. "Criminal Procedure in France." *The Yale Law Journal* 25, no. 4 (1916): 255–84. https://doi.org/10.2307/786296.

Gates Jr., Henry Louis. "Plessy v. Ferguson: Who Was Plessy?" PBS. https://www.pbs.org/wnet/african-americans-many-rivers-to-cross/history/plessy-v-ferguson-who-was-plessy/.

Georgia Public Broadcasting. "Anatomy of a Land Grab." Accessed August 19, 2021. https://www.gpb.org/georgiastories/stories/thirst_for_new_land.

Goldstein, Joel K., and Charles A. Miller. "Brandeis: The Legacy of a Justice." *Marquette Law Review* 100, no. 2 (Winter 2016): 461–95. http://scholarship.law.marquette.edu/mulr.

Goode, Michael. "Native American-Pennsylvania Relations 1681–1753." *The Encyclopedia of Greater Philadelphia*, 2015. https://philadelphiaencyclopedia.org/archive/native-american-pennsylvania-relations-1681-1753/.

Gray, Sarah. "Here's a Timeline of the Major Gun Control Laws in America." *Time*, April 30, 2019. https://time.com/5169210/us-gun-control-laws-history-timeline/.

Graziano, Manlio. *In Rome We Trust: The Rise of Catholics in American Political Life*. Redwood City: Stanford University Press, 2017.

Hall, Kermit L. *Conscience and Belief: The Supreme Court and Religion*. New York: Routledge, 2000.

———, Ed. *The Oxford Companion to the Supreme Court*, 2nd ed. New York: Oxford University Press, 2005.

Halton, Charles, and Saana Svärd. *Women's Writing of Ancient Mesopotamia: An Anthology of the Earliest Female Authors*. Cambridge: Cambridge University Press, 2017.

Hamil, Frederick Coyne. "Presentment of Englishry and the Murder Fine." *Speculum* 12, no. 3 (1937): 285–98. https://doi.org/10.2307/2848624.

Hardach, Sophie. "The Key to Cracking Long-Dead Languages?" *BBC*, December 9, 2018. https://www.bbc.com/future/article/20181207-how-ai-could-help-us-with-ancient-languages-like-sumerian.

Hardesty, Jennifer. "Separation Assault in the Context of Post-divorce Parenting." *Violence Against Women* 8, no. 5 (2002): 597–625. https://doi.org/10.1177/10778012002008005.

Harrison, Julian, and Claire Breay. "Magna Carta: An Introduction." *British Library*, July 28, 2014. https://www.bl.uk/magna-carta/articles/magna-carta-an-introduction.

Heineman, Jennifer, Rachel T. MacFarlane, and Barbara G. Brents. "Sex Industry and Sex Workers in Nevada." In *Social Health of Nevada: Leading Indicators and Quality of Life in the Silver State*, edited by Dmitri N. Shalin. Las Vegas: Center for Democratic Culture Publications, 2012.

Hiers, Richard H. "The Death Penalty and Due Process in Biblical Law." *University of Detroit Mercy Law Review* 81 (Summer 2004): 751–843. http://scholarship.law.ufl.edu/facultypub/741.

Hill, Matthew W. "*Sir Matthew Hale and Modern Judicial Ethics.*" *Judicature* 11, no. 7 (February 1971): 280–82. http://repository.uchastings.edu/publicity/55.

Holmes, Tara. "Readmission of Jews to Britain in 1656." *BBC*, June 24, 2011. https://www.bbc.co.uk/religion/religions/judaism/history/350.shtml.

Hsieh, Ching-Chi, and M.D. Pugh. "Poverty, Income Inequality and Violent Crime: A Meta-Analysis of Recent Aggregate Data Studies." *Criminal Justice Review* 18, no. 2 (September 1993): 182–202. https://doi.org/10.1177/073401689301800203.

Humfress, Caroline. "Law and Legal Practice in the Age of Justinian." In *The Cambridge Companion to the Age of Justinian*, edited by Michael Maas, 161–84. Cambridge: Cambridge University Press, 2005.

Jardine, David. *A Reading on the Use of Torture in the Criminal Law of England: Previously to the Commonwealth*. London: Baldwin and Cradock Publishing, 1837.

Johnson, Cynthia Mestad. *James DeWolf and the Rhode Island Slave Trade*. Charleston: The History Press, 2014.

Jones-Brown, Delores. *The System in Black and White: Exploring the Connections between Race, Crime, and Justice*. Edited by Michael Markowitz. Westport: Praeger Publishers, 2000.

Jewish Virtual Library. "Judaism: The Written Law—Torah." Accessed June 17, 2020. https://www.jewishvirtuallibrary.org/the-written-law-torah.

Kahneman, Daniel. *Thinking, Fast and Slow*. New York: Farrer, Straus and Giroux, 2013.

Kaminski, John. *A Necessary Evil? Slavery and the Debate Over the Constitution*. Lanham: Rowman & Littlefield Publishers, 1995.

Kaminski, John P., and Richard B. Bernstein. "The Bill of Rights." In *Roots of the Republic: American Founding Documents Interpreted*, edited by Stephen L. Schechter. Lanham: Madison House Books, 1990.

Keating, Jenny. *A Child for Keeps: The History of Adoption in England, 1918–45*. New York: Palgrave Macmillan, 2008.

Kempin Jr., Frederick G. *Historical Introduction to Anglo-American Law in a Nutshell*. Saint Paul: West Publishing Co., 1990.

Klein, Herbert S. *The Atlantic Slave Trade*. New York: Cambridge University Press, 1999.

Knowles, Helen, and Steven Lichtman. *Judging Free Speech: First Amendment Jurisprudence of the US*. New York: Palgrave Macmillan, 2016.

Kommers, Donald P., John E. Finn, and Gary J. Jacobsohn. *American Constitutional Law: Essays, Cases, and Comparative Notes*. Lanham: Rowman & Littlefield Publishers, 2004.

Konig, David Thomas, Paul Finkelman, and Christopher Alan Bracey, Eds. *The Dred Scott Case: Historical and Contemporary Perspectives on Race and Law*. Athens: Ohio University Press, 2010.

Kovera, Margaret Bull. "Racial Disparities in the Criminal Justice System: Prevalence, Causes, and a Search for Solutions." *Journal of Social Issues* 75, no. 4 (2019): 1139–57. https://doi.org/10.1111/josi.12355.

Kramarae, Charis, and Dale Spender, Eds. *Routledge International Encyclopedia of Women*. New York: Routledge, 2004.

Lambert, Frank. *The Founding Fathers and the Place of Religion in America*. Princeton: Princeton University Press, 2003.

Langbein, John, Renee Lettow Lerner, and Bruce P. Smith. *History of the Common Law: The Development of Anglo-American Legal Institutions*. New York: Aspen Publishers, 2009.

Lankford, Andrea. *Ranger Confidential: Living, Working, and Dying in the National Parks*. Guilford: Glove Pequot Press, 2010.

Laycock, Douglas. *Religious Liberty*, New York: Eerdmans, 2018.

Laycock, Douglas, and Richard L. Hasen. *Modern American Remedies*, 5th ed. New York: Wolters Kluwer, 2019.

Library of Congress. "Brown v. Board at Fifty: 'With an Even Hand': The Aftermath." Accessed October 1, 2021. https://www.loc.gov/exhibits/brown/brown-overview.html.

Library of Congress. "Virginia's Early Relations with Native Americans." Accessed August 19, 2021. https://www.loc.gov/classroom-materials/united-states-history-primary-source-timeline/colonial-settlement-1600-1763/virginia-relations-with-native-americans/.

Looney, Adam and Nicholas Turner. "Work and Opportunity Before and After Incarceration." *Brookings Institution*, March 14, 2018. https://www.brookings.edu/research/work-and-opportunity-before-and-after-incarceration/.

Loseke, Donileen R., Richard J. Gelles, and Mary M. Cavanaugh. *Current Controversies on Family Violence*. Thousand Oaks: SAGE Publications, 2005.

Malden, Henry Elliott, M.A. Ed. *Magna Carta Commemoration Essays*. London: Royal Historical Society, 1917.

Maryland Manual Online. "Maryland at a Glance: Native Americans." Last modified June 21, 2021. https://msa.maryland.gov/msa/mdmanual/01glance/native/html/01native.html.

McCarter, P. Kyle. "The River Ordeal in Israelite Literature." *The Harvard Theological Review* 66, no. 4 (1973): 403–12. http://www.jstor.org/stable/1509077.

MacMillan, Catharine. *Contractual Mistakes in Roman Law*. Portland: Hart Publishing, 2010.

McPherson, James M. *Battle Cry of Freedom: The Civil War Era*. New York: Oxford University Press, 1988.

———. *The Struggle for Equality*. Princeton: Princeton University Press, 1964.

Meacham, Jon. *Thomas Jefferson: The Art of Power*. New York: Random House, 2012.

Meekins, Isaac. "The Lawyer as an Officer of the Court—His Duty to the Court in the Administration of Justice." *North Carolina Law Review* 4, no. 3 (1926): 95–103. http://scholarship.law.unc.edu/nclr.

Mejia, Garna. "Tammy Daybell Investigation: Idaho Law Allowed Her Burial Without Autopsy." *East Idaho News*, June 23, 2020. https://www.eastidahonews.com/2020/06/tammy-daybell-investigation-idaho-law-allowed-her-burial-without-an-autopsy/.

Minow, Martha. *When Should the Law Forgive?* New York: W.W. Norton & Company, 2019.

Morgan, Thad. "How an Ex-KKK Member Made His Way onto the U.S. Supreme Court." *History*, October 28, 2018. https://www.history.com/news/kkk-supreme-court-hugo-black-fdr.

Morrin, Brian. "Idaho Laws Protect Faith Healing Even When Children Die." *Idaho News*, November 25, 2013.

Mullen, Lincoln. "These Maps Reveal How Slavery Expanded Across the United States." *Smithsonian Magazine*, May 15, 2014. https://www.smithsonianmag.com/history/maps-reveal-slavery-expanded-across-united-states-180951452/.

Nelson, William E. *The Common Law of Colonial America: The Chesapeake and New England 1607–1660*. New York: Oxford University Press, 2008.

Neubauer, David W., and Henry F. Fradella. *America's Courts and the Criminal Justice System*, 12th ed. Boston: Cengage Learning, 2017.

New Hampshire Folklife. "Native American Heritage." Accessed August 19, 2021. https://www.nh.gov/folklife/learning-center/traditions/native-american.htm.

New Jersey Almanac. "History—Native Americans." Accessed August 19, 2021. https://www.newjerseyalmanac.com/native-americans.html.

Newport, Frank. "Five Key Findings on Religion in the U.S." *Gallup*, Dec. 23, 2016. https://news.gallup.com/poll/200186/five-key-findings-religion.aspx.

New York Public Radio. "The Buried Bodies Case." Accessed August 19, 2021. https://www.wnycstudios.org/podcasts/radiolab/articles/the_buried_bodies_case.

New York Times. "A Solemn Tribute to Henry Friendly, a Quiet Giant of the Appeals Bench." Accessed October 1, 2021. https://www.nytimes.com/1986/06/10/nyregion/a-solemn-tribute-to-henry-friendly-a-quiet-giant-of-the-appeals-bench.html.

North Carolina Museum of History. "North Carolina American Indian History Timeline." Accessed August 19, 2021. https://www.ncmuseumofhistory.org/american-indian/handouts/timeline.

Nowak, John, and Ronald D. Rotunda. *Treatise on Constitutional Law: Substance and Procedure*, 5th ed. Eagan: Thomson Reuters West, 2012.

Orth, John V. *Due Process of Law: A Brief History*. Lawrence: University Press of Kansas, 2003.

O'Toole, Patricia. *The Moralist: Woodrow Wilson and the World He Made*. New York: Simon & Schuster, 2018.

Parker, Karen E., and Matthew V. Pruitt. "Poverty, Poverty Concentration, and Homicide." *Social Science Quarterly* 81, no. 2 (2000): 555–70. http://www.jstor.org/stable/42863975.

Patterson, E. Britt. "*Poverty, Income Inequality, and Community Crime Rate*." *Criminology* 29, no. 4 (Nov. 1991): 755–76. https://doi.org/10.1111/j.1745-9125.1991.tb01087.x.

Pauls, Elizabeth Prine. "Northeast Indians." *Encyclopaedia Britannica*, November 11, 2020. https://www.britannica.com/topic/Northeast-Indian.

Pauly, Madison. "It's 2019, and States Are Still Making Exceptions for Spousal Rape." *Mother Jones*, November 21, 2019. https://www.motherjones.com/crime-justice/2019/11/deval-patrick-spousal-rape-laws/.

Perlman, Harvey S., and Josephine R. Potuto. "The Uniform Law Commissioners' Model Sentencing and Corrections Act: An Overview." *Nebraska Law Review* 58, no. 4 (1979): 925–64. https://digitalcommons.unl.edu.

Peters, Shawn Francis. *Judging Jehovah's Witnesses: Religious Persecution and the Dawn of Rights Revolution*. Lawrence: University Press of Kansas, 2000.

Philpot, R., L.S. Liebst, M. Levine, W. Bernasco, and M.R. Lindegaard. "Would I Be Helped? Cross-national CCTV Footage Shows That Intervention Is the Norm in Public Conflicts." *American Psychologist* 75, no.1 (January 2020): 66–75. https://doi.org/10.1037/amp0000469.

Possley, Maurice. "Archives: Operation Greylord: A Federal Probe of Court Corruption Sets the Standard for Future Investigations." *Chicago Tribune*, January 19, 2017. https://www.chicagotribune.com/nation-world/chi-chicagodays-greylord-story-story.html.

Pryke, Louise M. *Gilgamesh*. New York: Routledge, 2019.

Raboteau, Albert J. *Slave Religion: The Invisible Institution in the Antebellum South*. New York: Oxford University Press, 2004.

Rappleye, Charles. *Sons of Providence: The Brown Brothers, the Slave Trade, and the American Revolution*. New York: Simon & Schuster, 2006.

Rasmussen, Robert K. "The Uneasy Case Against the Uniform Commercial Code." *Louisiana Law Review* 62, no. 4 (2002): 1097–1146. https://digitalcommons.law.lsu.edu/lalrev/vol62/iss4/6.

Rehavi, M. Marit, and Sonja B. Starr. "Racial Disparity in Federal Criminal Sentences." *Journal of Political Economy* 122, no. 6 (2014): 1320–54. https://repository.law.umich.edu/articles/1414.

Rehnquist, William H. "Judicial Compensation." Statement Before the National Commission on the Public Service, Washington, DC, July 15, 2002.

Rein, Lisa. "Mystery of Virginia's First Slaves Is Unlocked 400 Years Later." *African Diaspora Archaeology Newsletter* 9, no. 3 (September 2006): 1–3. https://scholarworks.umass.edu.

Rhode Island Department of State. "Native Americans." Accessed August 19, 2021. https://www.sos.ri.gov/divisions/civics-and-education/for-educators/themed-collections/native-americans.

Robinson, Paul, and Michael T. Cahill. "Can a Model Penal Code Second Save the States from Themselves?" *Ohio State Journal of Criminal Law* 1, no. 1 (2003): 169–77. http://hdl.handle.net/1811/72583.

Robinson, Paul H., and Tyler Scott Williams. *Mapping American Criminal Law: Variations Across the 50 States*. Santa Barbara: Praeger, 2018.

Roosevelt, Eleanor, P.C. Chang, C.H. Malik, H. Santa Cruz, R. Cassin, A.E. Bogomolov, C. Dukes, and J.P. Humphrey. *Universal Declaration of Human Rights*. Paris: United Nations General Assembly, 1948.

Roosevelt, Theodore. "Municipal Administration: The New York Police Force." *The Atlantic*, September 1896. https://www.theatlantic.com/magazine/archive/1897/09/municipal-administration-the-new-york-police-force/519849/.

Rosenfeld, Esther, Michelle Oberman, Jordan Bernard, and Erika Lee. "Confronting the Challenge of the High-Conflict Personality in Family Court." *Family Law Quarterly* 53, no. 2 (May 2020): 79–113. https://www.npdandlaw.com/wp-content/uploads/2020/10/Confronting-the-Challenge-of-the-High-Conflict-Personality-in-Family-Court.pdf.

Rosser, John Hutchins. *Historical Dictionary of Byzantium*. Plymouth: Scarecrow Press, 2012.

Rothman, Emily F., Jeanne Hathaway, Andrea Stidsen, and Heather F. de Vries. "How Employment Helps Female Victims of Intimate Partner Violence: A Qualitative Study." *Journal of Occupational Health Psychology* 12, no. 2 (2007): 136–43. https://doi:10.1037/1076-8998.12.2.136.

Ruggiero, Angela, and Aaron Davis. "Outbursts from Family Disrupt Court Appearance of Livermore Stabbing Suspects." *East Bay Times* (February 14, 2018). https://www.eastbaytimes.com/2018/02/14/stabbing-suspects-in-tracy-womans-death-to-appear-in-court/

Saikowski, Charlotte. "The Power of Judicial Review." *The Christian Science Monitor*, Feb. 11, 1987. https://www.csmonitor.com/1987/0211/zcon4.html.

Scheb, John M., and Hemant Sharma. *An Introduction to the American Legal System*, 4th ed. New York: Wolters Kluwer, 2015.

Schmidt, Benno C. "Principle and Prejudice: The Supreme Court and Race in the Progressive Era. Part 3: Black Disfranchisement from the KKK to the Grandfather Clause." *Columbia Law Review* 82, no. 5 (1982): 835–905. https://doi.org/10.2307/1122210.

Schultz, Fritz. *History of Roman Legal Science*. Oxford: Clarendon Press, 1967.

Scott, Shelby B., Galena K. Rhoades, Stanley M. Scott, Elizabeth S. Allen, and Howard J. Markman. "Reasons for Divorce and Recollections of Premarital Intervention: Implications for Improving Relationship Education." *Couple and Family Psychology: Research and Practice* 2, no. 2, (2013): 131-145. https://psycnet.apa.org/doi/10.1037/a0032025.

Seager, George. "Domestic Faction in a Republic." *National Association of Scholars Blog*, June 23, 2010. https://www.nas.org/blogs/article/domestic_faction_in_a_republic_part_i.

Shaffer, Jennifer, and R. Barry Ruback. *Violent Victimization as a Risk Factor for Violent Offending Among Juveniles*. Washington, DC: Office of Juvenile Justice and Delinquency Prevention, 2002.

Shaw, Brent D. "Raising and Killing Children: Two Roman Myths." *Mnemosyne*, Fourth Series, 54, no. 1 (2001): 31–77. http://www.jstor.org/stable/4433183.

Sherman, Lawrence W., and Heather Strang. *Restorative Justice: The Evidence*. London: Smith Institute, 2009.

Shively, Michael, Kristina Kliorys, Kristin Wheeler, and Dana Hunt. *A National Overview of Prostitution and Sex Trafficking Demand Reduction Efforts*. Washington, DC: U.S. Department of Justice, 2012.

Simon, James F. *Lincoln and Chief Justice Taney: Slavery, Secession, and the President's War Powers*. New York: Simon & Schuster, 2006.

Smith, Ronald P. "Criminal Law—Criminal Responsibility of Epileptic Driver Who Causes Death When Stricken with Sudden Epileptic 'Blackout.'" *Notre Dame Law Review* 32, no. 4 (1957): 688–707. http://scholarship.law.nd.edu/.

Smithsonian Magazine. "New York's Native American History." Accessed August 19, 2021. https://www.smithsonianmag.com/videos/category/history/new-yorks-native-american-history/.

Sofroniou, Andreas. *Pericles, Golden Age of Athens*. Self-published, 2015.

South, Stanley. "The Unabridged Version of Tribes of the Carolina Lowland: Pedee—Sewee—Winyaw—Waccamaw—Cape Fear—Wateree—Santee." *Research Manuscript Series* 16, no. 4 (April 1972): 1–54. https://scholarcommons.sc.edu/archanth_books/16.

Stern, Seth, and Wermiel, Stephen. *Justice Brennan: Liberal Champion*. New York: Houghton Mifflin Harcourt, 2010.

Storgaard, Anette. "Juvenile Justice in Scandinavia." *J. of Scandinavian Studies in Criminology and Crime Prevention* 5, no. 2 (2005): 188-204.

Strum, Philippa. *Louis Brandeis: Justice for the People*. Cambridge: Harvard University Press, 1984.

Summers, Anthony. *Official and Confidential: The Secret Life of J. Edgar Hoover*. New York: Putnam, 1993.

Tetlow, Elizabeth Meier. *Women, Crime and Punishment in Ancient Law and Society*. New York: Bloomsbury Publishing, 2004.

Traflet, Janice, and Robert E. Wright. "America Doesn't Just Have a Gender Pay Gap. It Has a Gender Wealth Gap." *The Washington Post*, April 2, 2019. https://www.washingtonpost.com/outlook/2019/04/02/america-doesnt-just-have-gender-pay-gap-it-has-gender-wealth-gap/.

Tribe, Laurence H. *American Constitutional Law*. New York: Foundation Press, 1988.

Twersky, Isadore. *Introduction to the Code of Maimonides (Mishneh Torah)*. New Haven: Yale University Press, 1980.

Ulmer, Jeffrey T., and Darrell J. Steffensmeier. "The Age and Crime Relationship: Social Variation, Social Explanations." In *The Nurture Versus Biosocial Debate in Criminology: On the Origins of Criminal Behavior and Criminality*. Thousand Oaks: SAGE Publications, 2014.

Urofsky, Melvin I. *Louis D. Brandeis: A Life*. New York: Schocken Books, 2009.

Viel, H. Dieter. *The New Complete Code of Hammurabi*. Lanham: University Press of America, 2012.

Walliss, John. *The Bloody Code in England and Wales, 1760–1830*. New York: Palgrave Macmillan, 2018.

Watson, Alan. "The Importance of 'Nutshells.'" *The American Journal of Comparative Law* 42, no. 1 (1994): 1–23. https://doi.org/10.2307/840726.

Weninger, Robert. "The Abolition of Plea Bargaining: A Case Study of El Paso County, Texas." *UCLA Law Review* 35 (1987): 265–313. https://ssrn.com/abstract=2264459.

West, Ellis M. *The Religion Clauses of the First Amendment: Guarantees of States' Rights?* Lanham: Lexington Books, 2011.

Wilson, James. *The Works of the Honourable James Wilson, L.L.D., Late One of the Associate Judges of the Supreme Court of the United States, and Professor of Law in the College of Philadelphia*. Philadelphia: Lorenzo Press, Printed for Bronson and Chauncey, 1804.

Winterer, Caroline. *The Culture of Classism: Ancient Greece and Rome in American Intellectual Life, 1780–1910*. Baltimore: Johns Hopkins University Press, 2002.

Wise, Edward. "Criminal Law." In *Introduction to the Law of the United States*, edited by David S. Clark and Tugrul Ansay. New York: Kluwer Law International, 2002.

Wharton, Claudene. "College of Education Researchers Conduct Study on Impacts of School Uniforms." UNR.edu, April 23, 2013. https://www.unr.edu/nevada-today/news/2013/school-uniform-study.

Wolfe, Patrick. *Traces of History: Elemental Structures of Race*. New York: Verso, 2016.

Woodham, Chai. "*Eastern State Penitentiary: A Prison with a Past.*" *Smithsonian Magazine*, September 30, 2008. https://www.smithsonianmag.com/history/eastern-state-penitentiary-a-prison-with-a-past-14274660/.

Yale Law School. "The Twelve Tables." Accessed August 17, 2021. https://avalon.law.yale.edu/ancient/twelve_tables.asp.

Young, William. "Civic Virtue and Western Civilization." *National Association of Scholars Blog*, December 1, 2011. https://www.nas.org/blogs/article/civic_virtue_and_western_civilization.

Yudell, Michael. "A Short History of the Race Concept." In *Race and the Genetic Revolution: Science, Myth and Culture*. New York: Columbia University Press, 1971.

Zengerle, Patricia, Jonathan Landay, and David Morgan. "Under Heavy Guard, Congress Back to Work After Trump Supporters Storm U.S. Capitol." *Reuters*, January 6, 2021. https://www.reuters.com/article/usa-election-int/under-heavy-guard-congress-back-to-work-after-trump-supporters-storm-u-s-capitol-idUSKBN29B2RJ.

Printed in the USA
CPSIA information can be obtained
at www.ICGtesting.com
LVHW070834260124
769994LV00024B/94